A GUIDE TO

COMPOSITION
PEDAGOGIES

A GUIDE TO
COMPOSITION
PEDAGOGIES

Gary Tate

Amy Rupiper

Kurt Schick

New York   Oxford
Oxford University Press
2001

Oxford University Press

Oxford   New York
Athens   Auckland   Bangkok   Bogotá   Buenos Aires   Calcutta
Cape Town   Chennai   Dar es Salaam   Delhi   Florence   Hong Kong   Istanbul
Karachi   Kuala Lumpur   Madrid   Melbourne   Mexico City   Mumbai
Nairobi   Paris   São Paulo   Singapore   Taipei   Tokyo   Toronto   Warsaw

and associated companies in
Berlin   Ibadan

Copyright © 2001 by Oxford University Press, Inc.

Published by Oxford University Press, Inc.,
198 Madison Avenue, New York,New York, 10016
http://www.oup-usa.org

Oxford is a registered trademark of Oxford University Press

Library of Congress Cataloging-in-Publication Data
A guide to composition pedagogies / [edited by] Gary Tate, Amy
Rupiper, Kurt Schick.
    p. cm.
  Includes bibliographical references and indexes.
  ISBN 0-19-512536-3 (acid-free paper)
  1. English language—Rhetoric—Study and teaching.   2. Report
writing—Study and teaching (Higher)   I. Tate, Gary.   II. Rupiper,
Amy, 1973-III. Schick, Kurt, 1964–
  PE1404 .G85 2000
  808'.0071'1—dc21   99-35473
                                                       CIP

Printing (last digit): 9 8 7 6 5 4 3 2

Printed in the United States of America
on acid-free paper

Contents

Preface

Pedagogy is among the most commonly used, yet least defined, terms in composition studies. In our professional discussions, the term variously refers to the practices of teaching, the theories underlying those practices, and perhaps most often, as some combination of the two—as praxis. This book reflects this varied usage by surveying pedagogy in its many forms. Practical applications can be found interspersed among relatively theoretical discussions of teaching, while the theories underlying classroom strategies are often emphasized. The theory/practice nexus undergirds these essays as it does the discipline. As a result of these complexities and our belief that pedagogical variety is a hallmark of our discipline, we have chosen to use the plural "pedagogies" in our title.

The variety of approaches to the teaching of writing that have developed in recent years hints at the richness of composition studies. Multivocality is not a sign of confusion or uncertainty, but a clear signal that the teaching of writing is grounded in something beyond what colleagues, administrators, and the public often say they want: "good" grammar and correct spelling. The teaching of writing concerns not only technical skills, but the minds and lives of students and teachers and the environments in which writing can exist. Diverse voices invigorate our disciplinary conversations, but can also present a formidable challenge to those just entering the field, those who form the primary audience addressed in these essays.

This guide was conceived specifically to help graduate students and new writing teachers orient themselves within our ongoing discussions. Since the publication of *Teaching Freshman Composition* by Gary Tate and Edward P.J. Corbett (Oxford, 1967), the collection of either reprinted or original essays has become a major genre in the field. Collections of essays about evaluating student writing; issues of class, race, and gender; the politics of teaching writing; the training of graduate students; and so on have appeared over the past thirty years in increasing numbers. But there remains a real need, we think, for a current map of composition pedagogies for the uninitiated. No other book provides such a map. This book is unique in its combining of personal experience and bibliographic information. We encouraged contributors to do two things: (1) mention the titles of books and journal articles that the reader interested in a certain pedagogy should read in order to begin to understand that way of teaching and (2) explain their own relationship to and experiences with the pedagogy. The response of contributors has been varied. Some essays in this book are extremely personal; others are much less so. In their variety of tone and stance, the essays hint at the range of styles that one encounters in the discipline today.

The breadth of these essays should provide ample material and opportunity to explore the rich complexity of our field. Each of the twelve pedagogies chosen for inclusion in this book was selected because of its importance in the discipline today. Although we would not argue that these are the only major approaches to the teaching of writing at the end of the century in American colleges and universities, we would contend that these are twelve of the most important. The student who begins to understand these approaches to the teaching of writing is well on the way to understanding an important segment of a discipline that continues to grow and change. As perceptions and paradigms are continuously challenged, critical but open and well-informed minds are vital to this sustained growth and change. Our hope is that this book will provide the young teacher/scholar with an introduction to our field that will begin a lifelong process of open-minded, critical, passionate inquiry.

The organization of the book is not strictly historical. Any such attempt would have met with failure because of the ways in which these approaches to the teaching of writing overlap. We chose to begin with process pedagogy because the turn to process represented for many teachers a defining moment in the discipline—and in their lives as teachers. And because process and expressive pedagogies are so closely linked, we decided to pair them before introducing rhetorical pedagogy, which, in a very real sense, underlies all the others. The close ties between critical and cultural studies pedagogies led us to place them together. Finally, the very important role that many writing centers play in writing across the curriculum programs encouraged us to pair these two essays. Of course, many other organizational schemes are possible, and we are confident that teachers and other readers will reorganize the book to suit their needs and will use it as a textbook in a variety of ways.

One of the book's editors has used the manuscript of this book in a graduate seminar in which students were asked to read two essays a week, plus two or three articles mentioned in each essay. The seminar thus worked its way quickly through the book in six weeks. During the remaining eight or nine weeks, each student chose a particular pedagogy to research in more depth and to write about in an extended paper. The possibilities here are almost endless: create a syllabus for a writing course based on one of the pedagogies and then, in an attached essay, defend the syllabus; compare and contrast two closely related pedagogies; write a report to a departmental composition committee, arguing that a particular pedagogy should be the foundation of the department's writing sequence; discuss how rhetorical pedagogy underlies all (or many) of the others, and so on. Shorter papers might be written along the way. One important issue that students might explore in a short essay is this: why do you react positively to some pedagogies and negatively to others? In other words, what is there about your upbringing, your beliefs, your education, and so on that inclines you toward some ways of teaching and away from others? Such a paper might well lead toward that self-understanding that is so essential to the effective writing teacher.

However this book is used, the editors hope that it will provide many new (and some old) students of composition studies with the kind of information and insights that will help them better understand the discipline and the enormous range of pedagogical opportunities that it provides today.

Fort Worth   *G.T.*
                                                                          A.R.
                                                                          K.S.

A GUIDE TO

COMPOSITION
PEDAGOGIES

Process Pedagogy

LAD TOBIN

✣ O BRAVE NEW WORLD . . .

I took my first composition course in 1971. During that semester we wrote a dozen papers—an argument, a compare and contrast essay, a description, a research paper, and eight *explications de textes* (which were "close readings" of stories, novels, poems, and plays). Almost all of the papers were five-paragraph essays (an introduction with a thesis statement, three supporting paragraphs which each had to contain three supporting points which each had to be supported by three details or examples, and a conclusion); the exceptions were the compare and contrast paper (in which we could choose between what my teacher called an AAABBB form or an ABABAB form) and the research paper (which had its own rules and restrictions governing everything right down to the size, color, and number of notecards you had to use).

We almost always wrote our essays the night before they were due, usually getting going after midnight, and swore to—and at—ourselves the whole time that we would never again put off a paper till the last minute. We didn't get our essays back for a week or so because, I am convinced, my teacher carried them around in his briefcase until the night before he returned them, at which time he reluctantly took them out, graded them, corrected them, meticulously marked them up in the margins, wrote a long end comment explaining or justifying the grade, and swore to—and at—himself that he'd never again put off grading till the last minute. We did no revision, except for the one paper we could choose to rewrite each quarter for a revised grade.

Class time was divided between animated, thought-provoking discussions of the assigned literary texts and our teacher's listless lectures on composition topics, including thesis writing; kinds of evidence; outlining; introductions, transitions, and conclusions; sentence structure; grammar and usage; and proper citation form. We never wrote during class; never read our own essays aloud; never peer reviewed, workshopped, or even read each other's essays; never were asked to write before we outlined; and never talked about how writers found their ideas, got unstuck when they were blocked, or used revision to discover new meaning, focus, or form.

As odd and as counterintuitive as it seems to me now to teach writing without ever talking about writing, I need to confess several things. First, though I found that approach to writing instruction exceptionally uninspiring, I learned certain stylistic conventions, organizational strategies, and forms of argument that turned out to be useful to me throughout my college career. Second, the explications that I wrote made me a more perceptive and enthusiastic reader and critic. And third, when I taught my first composition course sometime in the mid-1970s it looked almost exactly like the course I just described. Even though I had not much enjoyed my own experience as a composition student, I could not think of any alternative to organizing the course around the identification and appreciation of the rhetorical features of good writing.

And so when I think back to the time in the late 1970s when I first discovered process pedagogy in the form of books and articles by Donald Murray and Peter Elbow, I am moved to the language of a conversion narrative (or at least to the "O Brave New World" speech from *The Tempest*). In his 1972 manifesto, "Teach Writing as a Process Not a Product," Murray sounds like the visionary I immediately recognized him to be:

> What is the process we should teach? It is the process of discovery through language. It is the process of exploration of what we know and what we feel about what we know through language. . . . Instead of teaching finished writing, we should teach unfinished writing, and glory in its unfinishedness. . . . This is not a question of correct or incorrect, of etiquette or custom. This is a matter of far higher importance. The writer, as he writes, is making ethical decisions. He doesn't test his words by a rule book, but by life. He uses language to reveal the truth to himself so that he can tell it to others. It is an exciting, eventful, evolving process. (*Learning by Teaching* 15)

This was the sort of stuff I expected to find in Whitman or Emerson, not in a book on writing instruction. And Murray's *A Writer Teaches Writing* (first published in 1968), with its talk about cultivating surprise, writing for discovery, encouraging risky failures, and teaching writing as if your students were not students but *real writers*, did nothing to dampen my enthusiasm.

Elbow's book *Writing Without Teachers*, first published in 1973, was no less eye-opening for me: "Most books on writing try to describe the characteristics of good writing so as to help you produce it, and the characteristics of bad writing to help you avoid it. But not this book," Elbow writes on the first page, and then continues:

> Instead I try for two things: (1) to help you actually generate words better—more freely, lucidly, and powerfully: not make judgments about words but generate them better; (2) to help you improve your ability to make your *own* judgment about which parts of your own writing to keep and which parts to throw away. (vii–viii)

To accomplish these goals, Elbow suggests that writers "freewrite" (write nonstop without worrying about correctness, form, logic, etc.); play with words and ideas; form writing groups; and rely less at first on doubting and more on believing, less on criticism, more on imagination.

All this caught me off guard. I was only teaching writing because that was the price I had to pay to be in the field and occasionally get a chance to do what I really wanted to do—study and teach literature. I had left the graduate program in English Language and Literature at the University of Chicago because at that time the job market for lit Ph.D.s was terrible ("The more things change, the more . . .") and taken a job teaching high school English on Chicago's southwest side. From there, I had moved to a small New England college where, based on my Master's degree from Chicago, high school teaching experience, and limited success as a freelance writer, I was hired as an adjunct instructor and founding director of the college writing center. During those first years, I taught writing conscientiously, diligently, even passionately, but I never imagined it had much or anything to do with imagination, play, surprise, or experimentation. I had never thought of my students as *real writers*. I had talked a great deal about what writing ought to look like when it was read but I had never thought to demystify the process by talking about the craft, mechanics, rituals, logistics, atmospherics of the process.

I had never once asked my students the kinds of questions that I now discovered process practitioners were asking: "What time of day do you write? Where? Do you write your first drafts in long hand or directly on the computer? Do you take breaks for snacks? Do you rely on caffeine and other stimulants for energy and inspiration? Do you show your work-in-progress to other writers? Do you read your work aloud? Have you identified which of your composing strategies work for you and which ones don't?" To be honest, I had never thought much about any of this for my own composing process. I was still working on the think, outline, write, revise model. And so when I came across Murray's and Elbow's elegantly logical, nuts and bolts advice about the conditions that foster good writing and the ones that seem to inhibit it, I was intrigued—and hooked.

From those first two books, I went on to the journal articles in which Murray explained and extended the process approach, most notably "Write Before Writing," "Writing as Process: How Writing Finds Its Own Meaning," "Teaching the Other Self: The Writer's First Reader," and "The Maker's Eye: Revising Your Own Manuscripts" (now all collected in *Learning by Teaching*); to Elbow's *Writing with Power*, which clarifies his argument that creating and criticizing are very different skills that usually conflict with each other; to Ken Macrorie's books, *Telling Writing* and *Writing to Be Read*, in which he argues for writing freely, for telling truths, and for finding your authentic voice; to Ann Berthoff's explanation of the dialectic relationship between writing and thinking and the uses of chaos in meaning-making; to Janet Emig's learned essays from the 1960s and 1970s (now collected in *The Web of Meaning*), in which she identifies an intellectual tradition and philosophical basis for a process pedagogy; and to Natalie Goldberg's Zen-inspired writing exercises and prompts.

Scholars and teachers new to composition studies may be a bit baffled when told that when I discovered these ideas in the late seventies (which was already fifteen years after Emig's breakthrough essay, "The Uses of the Unconscious in

Composing," *The Web of Meaning*) and began implementing them in the early eighties (which, again, was years after teachers like Murray, Elbow, Macrorie, Emig, Berthoff, and William Coles had been practicing process for years), they still represented something of a pedagogical revolution. After all, it hardly seems daring any longer to suggest that in a writing course we ought to talk about the practice of writing or that we ought to devote at least as much time and attention to the production of texts as to their consumption. And yet, as many composition scholars (including Maxine Hairston in "Winds of Change: Thomas Kuhn and the Revolution in the Teaching of Writing") have pointed out, the argument that writing should be viewed and taught as an activity represented a true paradigm shift for the field.

It also represented an approach so controversial as to serve as a kind of disciplinary shibboleth: in the late 1970s and early 1980s you were either one of the process-oriented teachers arguing for student choice of topics and forms; the necessity of authentic voice; writing as a messy, organic, recursive form of discovery, growth, and personal expression; or you were a teacher who believed that we needed to resist process' attack on rules, conventions, standards, quality, and rigor. Or if you listened to what each side said about the other, you were either a soft-headed, mush-minded mystic clinging to 1960s nostalgia or an old fuddy-duddy schoolmarm or master clinging to canned assignments, dying forms, and outdated autocratic methods. By the mid-1980s, process pedagogy was so prominent that you were, as Ken Kesey used to say about the acid tests of the 1960s, either on the bus or off it.

In fact, the binary camps organized around attitudes about standards and authority may seem reminiscent of 1960s political battles because in many ways it was the result of 1960s political battles, a point persuasively argued by James Marshall in "Of What Does Skill in Writing Really Consist?: The Political Life of the Writing Process Movement" and in Thomas Newkirk's "The Writing Process—Visions and Revisions" in *To Compose: Teaching Writing in High School and College:*

> The writing process movement reflects the political era in which it was born, the turbulent years between 1966 and 1975. True to those times, much of the process pedagogy has an anti-institutional bias. The student was portrayed not as someone entering the academy, learning the practices of academic writing; it was more common to view academic writing as the enemy because it seemed to suppress the individual voice of the writer. The movement was clearly a challenge to literature specialists who controlled English departments; the attempt was to ask students to read their life experiences as text rather than to restrict their attention to the literary canon. And it was a challenge to the authority structure of the classroom and the "transmission" model symbolized by the podium placed before rows of immovable seats. (xvi)

What process theorists were reacting against was as important to the movement as what they were arguing for. Process pedagogy was decidedly anti-establishment, antiauthoritarian, anti-inauthenticity. Process teachers did not hate all written products; they only hated the kind of written products they claimed the traditional process inevitably produced—the canned, dull, lifeless student essay that seemed the logical outcome of a rules-driven, teacher-centered curriculum that ignored student interests, needs, and talents. For Emig, process was the fight against the "fifty-star theme"; for Macrorie, the enemy was the pretentious, inauthentic school prose he dubbed "Engfish." Elbow talked about how premature editing and the "two-step method" (think, then write) lead to "dead" writing. And, perhaps as a takeoff on Linda Flower's notion of writer-based and reader-based prose, process advocates began to talk about school writing as "author-vacated" prose. Bad, boring, uninspired student writing was not inevitable; it was only a symptom of a bad, boring, uninspired writing process that, in turn, was a symptom of bad, boring, uninspired pedagogy.

Process practitioners claimed that their emphasis on craft, voice, and technique could lead to something we had rarely thought to ask or hope for—lively, engaging, dynamic, strongly voiced student essays. Murray, who championed the weekly, one-to-one teacher-student writing conference, wrote with a Zen-like appeal of teaching by not teaching and, amazingly, about the thrill of reading dozens, hundreds, even thousands of student essays in which he learned more than he taught:

> It was dark when I arrived this winter morning, and it is dark as I wait for my last writing student to step out of the shadows in the corridor for my last conference. I am tired, but it is a good tired, for my students have generated energy as well as absorbed it. I've learned something of what it is to be a childhood diabetic, to raise oxen, to work across from your father at 115 degrees in a steel-drum factory, to be a welfare mother with three children, to build a bluebird trail, to cruise the disco scene, to be a teen-age alcoholic, to salvage World War II wreckage under the Atlantic, to teach invented spelling to first graders, to bring your father home to die of cancer. I have been instructed in other lives, heard the voices of my students they had not heard before, shared their satisfaction in solving problems of writing with clarity and grace. I sit quietly in the late afternoon waiting to hear what Andrea, my next student, will say about what she has accomplished on her last draft and what she intends on her next draft. (*Learning by Teaching* 157)

These ideas—that students actually have something important and original to say and will find ways to say it if we can just get out of their way, give them the freedom to choose their own material, and show them that we are interested—run throughout early process pedagogy. It is not so much a matter of teaching students new rules or strategies but of helping them gain access to their "real" or "authentic" voice and perspective that traditional school has taught them to distrust and suppress. Macrorie, who railed against "phony and pretentious" writing, argues that we had more access to vigorous, honest, engaging writing before we were ever schooled and socialized (*Telling Writing* 14), while Elbow suggests that his theory is based on the "assumption that virtually everyone has available great skill with words. That is everyone can, under certain conditions, speak with clarity and power" (*Writing with Power* 7).

At the time I first came across these arguments, I was still assigning topics and dictating forms. When I talked to colleagues about writing instruction, it was usually to commiserate about the drudgery of grading or to complain that only a few students in my classes seemed to be very good writers. "It's not that Johnny can't write," process pedagogues were suddenly saying to the rest of us, "it's just that you, Professor Stuffed Shirt, can't teach. *My* students write wonderful essays." I was somewhat skeptical but mostly I was envious. And so I started the next semester by telling my students they could write their first essay on any subject, in any form, and that I would read and respond to their first drafts but that I would not grade them.

It is not as if all of my students suddenly leapt up in applause and hoisted me upon their shoulders, cheering (they didn't); it's not even as if those first drafts were all that good. But the energy and balance in the classroom, as well as my role as a teacher, were clearly changed, and I felt there was no going back. Instead of choosing topics, teaching conventions, correcting, and grading, I now had the responsibility (and, hokey as it might sound, the opportunity and even pleasure) to read and respond to each evolving student essay as perceptively and creatively as possible. My primary job was not to tell the writer where she had gone wrong or right but to help her see what she had accomplished and what the essay might become in its next incarnation. I was now reading not for error and assessment but for nuance, possibility, gaps, potential. For the first time, I realized that student essays were texts to be interpreted, discussed, marveled at, and that writing students were, amazingly enough, writers.

What made the process movement all the more remarkable was that it was not just occurring in college English departments; it was happening everywhere writing was taught and practiced, from preschool through the work place. What Murray, Elbow, Coles, Emig, Macrorie, and others were suggesting for college composition, educators like Donald Graves (*Writing: Teachers and Children at Work*); Lucy Calkins (*The Art of Teaching Writing*); Nancie Atwell (*In the Middle: New Understanding About Writing, Reading, and Learning*); James Britton (*The Development of Writing Abilities 11–18*); and Tom Romano (*Clearing the Way: Working with Teenage Writers*) were advocating for children in schools K–12. In elementary schools where process pedagogy came to be known as the "whole language" movement, the key issues were whether students should be given basal readers, spelling tests, drill-and-skill lessons, and instruction in phonics and vocabulary or whether they should learn to read and write in the process and context of *real* reading and writing. Again the assumption was that students could write if, Graves explained, we designed a pedagogy that built on the skills, strengths, and interests they already possessed:

> Children want to write. They want to write the first day they attend school. This is no accident. Before they went to school they marked up walls, pavements, newspapers with crayons, chalk, pens or pencils ... anything that makes a mark. The child mark says, "I am." "No, you aren't," say most school ap-

proaches to the teaching of writing. We underestimate the urge because of a lack of understanding of the writing process and what children do in order to control it. Instead, we take the control away from children and place unnecessary road blocks in the way of their intentions. Then we say, "They don't want to write. How can we motivate them?" (*Writing* 3)

Again, the key assumptions were that students are writers when they come to the classroom (even in kindergarten) and that the writing classroom should be a workshop in which they are encouraged through the supportive response of teachers and peers to use writing as a way to figure out what they think and feel and eventually to "publish" their work to be read and celebrated by the community of writers they have become.

There are critics who have suggested that this wasn't such a big deal, that we always recognized writing as a process (Faigley), that process pedagogy never displaced "current-traditional" instruction (Crowley, "Around 1971: The Emergence of Process Pedagogy"), or that all that changed in the 1970s was the emphasis and the terminology. It is probably true that some of us in our nearly evangelical zeal exaggerated the contributions of Murray, Elbow, Macrorie, and Graves, but it is also true that, having long ago adopted the assumptions, attitudes, and methods of process pedagogy, many of its critics too easily forget the revolutionary nature of the movement. Just like critics of psychoanalysis who tell you how far we have moved beyond Freud's quaint practices and beliefs but who still talk comfortably about the unconscious, slips of the tongue, dream interpretation, or repression, there are those who claim that process has had its day and then acknowledge that in their teaching they still employ freewriting and journals and peer response groups and the idea that writing generates as well as reflects meaning.

Of course, these critics are right in suggesting that "process versus product" is in some ways a misleading slogan: even the most process-oriented teachers acknowledge that a meaningful process ought to lead eventually to some sort of written product, and even the most product-oriented teacher accepts the fact that writing occurs in series of steps and stages. In fact, we can find all sorts of acknowledgment going back at least to Aristotle that writers need to proceed in stages and steps. The way I taught writing in 1975, when I paid no attention to invention, freewriting, peer review, or revision, was still based on the assumption that successful writing was the result of some sort of process: think, outline, gather evidence, write, proofread. It is a mistake, as I will try to point out in the next section, to idealize the process movement and to pretend that process teachers invented invention or rhetoric or writing instruction, but I bristle at the suggestion that the process approach was just a slightly different version of what came before. You might as well say that walking into a course in art history or art appreciation and handing each student a paintbrush, palette, and smock and telling them to get started is just a slightly different version of what art historians or critics usually do, for the elegantly radical changes these practitioners were suggesting in our field's attitudes and practices were no less dramatic or far-reaching.

⮑ PROCESS GOES TO SCHOOL

Determined to gain a scholarly footing in the field and determined to change my adjunct status for a tenure track position, I returned to grad school in the early 1980s, this time in composition studies. I chose the University of New Hampshire since it was close to my job and one of the bastions of process pedagogy: UNH was the home not only of Don Murray but also of Don Graves, whose work on the writing process of seven-year-olds had done for elementary school teachers and students what Murray's work had done on the college level, and of Tom Newkirk, whose books, articles, and edited collections had sketched out the boundaries of process pedagogy for the elementary, secondary, and college classroom.

When I arrived in grad school, I had an experiential, empirical belief in process but no real scholarly basis for my approach. I soon found that I was not alone. Process pedagogies were popular because they critiqued old, traditional forms; because they seemed open, new and daring; and because they seemed to work better than the system they replaced. But they hardly represented a theoretically consistent or unified approach. Now scholars scrambled to identify and establish the theoretical and scholarly raison d'être for process pedagogy by arguing that this approach was actually (or merely) the modern culmination or manifestation of the ideas of Plato or Coleridge or Virginia Woolf or John Dewey or the Russian psychologist Lev Vygotsky. And of course in some sense all of these scholars were right, as were those who pointed out how freewriting grows directly from Freud's definition of free association or how the notion that writing does not merely reflect what the writer knows but actually generates meaning through the identification of the writer's own unconscious thoughts is the very cornerstone of psychoanalytic practice.

However, it was not these philosophical or historical studies that were at the center of process scholarship: that center was the quickly proliferating body of scholarly articles and dissertations on the nature of the writing process and of writers at work. Throughout the 1970s and early 1980s, hundreds of scholars in the field began to publish studies of writers writing. The scope and breadth of this scholarship were stunning: researchers began to focus on writers at all stages of their education, at all stages of the process, at all levels of ability, and in all sorts of environments.

Though the relationship was not always logical or direct, process research and process pedagogy clearly informed each other. As Stephen North points out in *The Making of Knowledge in Composition*, practitioners were apt to pick and choose research findings to cite in a somewhat arbitrary or even self-serving way, while much experimental research on process was flawed because its findings had little to do with what happens in actual classrooms. Still there can be little doubt that the research grew out of and into the changes we were witnessing in the classroom. Studies such as Gordon Wells' *The Meaning Makers: Children Learning Language and Using Language to Learn*, Graves' "An Examination of the Writing Processes of Seven Year Old Children," and Atwell's *In the Middle* reinforced whole language pedagogy at the preschool, elementary, and middle-school level, respectively. Two highly influential books—James Britton's *The Development of Writing Abilities (11–18)* and Janet Emig's *The Composing Process of Twelfth Graders*—pointed the way toward new ways of assigning and responding to the writing of secondary school students; and studies of the works of professional writers, such as Carol Berkenkotter and Murray's "Decisions and Revisions: The Planning Strategies of a Publishing Writer, and Response of a Laboratory Rat—or, Being Protocoled," and Lee Odell and Dixie Goswami's *Writing in Nonacademic Settings*, helped us to reimagine the writing that goes on outside of school.

Most significantly for college composition, though, were the thousands of case studies, experimental projects, and ethnographies of college composition students. Of particular significance were (1) the studies of the least accomplished writers, including Mina Shaughnessy's *Errors and Expectations: A Guide for the Teacher of Basic Writing*, David Bartholomae's "The Study of Error," and Sondra Perl's "The Composing Processes of Unskilled College Writers"; (2) the important scholarship that compared and contrasted the composing processes of novice and skilled writers (such as the work of Nancy Sommers and Linda Flower); (3) the research that viewed writing as a cognitive act and that focused on what was going on in a writer's mind when, for instance, she framed a problem (Flower and Hayes), was on the verge or point of utterance (Britton, "Writing to Learn and Learning to Write"), was translating inner speech to written discourse (Moffett), or was blocked or stuck (Rose); and (4) the persuasive body of scholarship (including works such as Kenneth Bruffee's "Collaborative Learning and the Conversation of Mankind," Karen Burke LeFevre's *Invention as a Social Act*, Anne Ruggles Gere's *Writing Groups: History, Theory, and Implications*, and John Trimbur's "Consensus and Difference in Collaborative Learning") that examined the social nature of composing and the ways in which language, meaning, and texts are always and inevitably socially constructed.

In spite of this very wide range of scholarly approaches, it was the version of process that emphasized freewriting, voice, personal narrative, and writing as a form of discovery—that is, the version articulated by Murray, Elbow, Macrorie, Graves, and other so-called "expressivists"—that had the greatest influence on classroom practice and drew the most impassioned support and criticism. For that reason, it was not unusual to hear "process" and "expressivism" used almost interchangeably, as if expressivism were the only kind of process and process teachers were only expressivists. In fact, a teacher could emphasize the organic nature of the composing process but not assign or even allow personal writing, just as a teacher could insist on personal expression while still clinging to a traditional two-step (think first, then write) notion of the process.

To some historians of composition, especially those historians critical of expressivism, the different approaches that emerged in the 1970s mark significant and competing divisions within the process movement. James Berlin, for example, faults the "Neo-Platonists or Expressivists" for identifying truth within the individual "attainable only through an internal apprehension" ("Contemporary Composition: The Major Pedagogical Theories" 773–774) and for fostering naive notions of self, truth, and authenticity. In Berlin's narrative of progress, "the New Rhetoricians," a group that includes scholars such as Anne Berthoff, Andrea Lunsford, Linda Flower, and apparently Berlin himself, have displaced expressivist pedagogy by recognizing the social construction of knowledge and by developing a theory of composing that "treats all the offices of classical rhetoric that apply to written language—invention, arrangement, and style—and does so by calling upon the best that has been thought and said about them by contemporary observers" (776).

Similarly, Lester Faigley argues that there are four clearly defined, competing theories of process: expressive, cognitive, social, and Marxist. In order to fit various theorists into the various categories, however, Faigley overlooks areas of agreement or overlap, such as cognitive aspects of expressivism or social aspects of cognitivism. Murray and Elbow, for example, while emphasizing an expressivist sense of the agency of the individual writer or the power of voice, also pay careful attention to audience and to the ways in which response shapes revision as well as invention. I am not suggesting that there are no significant differences in the underlying assumptions of scholars in these different camps; however, the differences in theory are less clear and less significant in the classroom, where most process practitioners borrow liberally from research of various kinds at various times in the course for various purposes. As a teacher in the early 1980s whose pedagogical approach had been completely transformed by expressivist pedagogy, for example, I found the reading I was doing as a grad student about social and cognitive approaches to be immediately relevant and useful.

My point is that the bitter debates that were raging in the professional journals between advocates of various theoretical camps caused much less conflict in the classroom, where practitioners usually found something to borrow from each approach. In my own case, I remained committed to an expressivist approach with, I will admit, something of the convert's zeal, but I still found many classroom strategies to borrow from cognitive scholars (such as Flower's explanation of how students move from writer-based to reader-based prose), from social constructivists (such as the collaborative writing assignments recommended by Gere or Bruffee), and from cultural critics (such as the use of advertisements and popular culture as a way to alert students to the ways in which language manipulates and sustains power).

I should also confess that I was open to new approaches because expressivist pedagogy, while it represented an immeasurable improvement over what I had been doing, was not a panacea for the frustration and failure that inevitably crop up for writing teachers and students. This frustration, combined with the backlash to the evangelical rhetoric and claims of process teachers that developed during the late 1980s, led to some powerful critiques:

- *Process pedagogy has become so regimented that it has turned into the kind of rules-driven product that it originally critiqued.*

As process pedagogy became more widely practiced and more widely disseminated in textbooks and in-service workshops, it is undeniably true that it became much more domesticated and much less daring. Early process peda-gogy offered a view of composing that was not fixed or static. Murray, fol-lowing the lead of creative writers, celebrated surprise, discovery, even failure. Elbow talked about writing as growth. And Perl, in "Understanding Compos-ing," pointed out that composing was not linear but "recursive"; that is, writ-ers did not think and then neatly transmit that complete thought; instead the writing helped them clarify their thinking, just as in a messy, back-and-forth way, the thinking led to more writing. However, much of that perspective was lost in the translation of process pedagogy into a regimented sequence that di-vided *the writing process* into neat stages of prewriting, writing, and revising.

I still remember the day in the mid-1980s when my office mate, a very tra-ditional teacher who had always required each student to go through a series of prescribed steps that she would check off before moving to the next (i.e., an approved thesis was required before the student could move on to the outline; an outline was required before the student could write the five-paragraph es-say, etc.) came back from summer break to announce that she had finally been won over. I remember being surprised and pleased that Evelyn had come over to the process side of the force, but not so surprised or pleased when the next week, from the other side of the partition, I heard her explaining her version of the method to one of her students: "You have not done any freewriting here. You can't just jump from brainstorming straight to composing. You can't skip steps."

So while I would not dispute the fact that process pedagogy has in many cases become a regimented product, I would point out that this regimentation has more to do with the quirks of some individual teachers and the nature of the textbook business than with some inherent flaw in the process approach.

- *Process pedagogies are irresponsible because they fail to teach basic and nec-essary skills and conventions.*

This has been a concern from the very beginning—that process was too soft, too touchy-feely, too student directed to do its job: teach students how to write. By discarding phonics and spelling tests and basal readers and grammar lessons in first-grade classrooms, whole language teachers were accused of shirking their responsibility and failing their students who needed skills, content, and direct instruction if they were to succeed in second grade and beyond; simi-larly, by allowing students to choose their own topics and forms and by not emphasizing the teaching of grammar, usage, audience analysis, and proof-reading, college composition teachers were accused of failing students who needed to learn the conventions of academic discourse.

Some critics, such as George Hillocks, argue further that the "natural process" approach is flawed because the teacher, playing too much of a pas-sive role, fails to provide enough structure, guidance, and direct instruction about particular conventions and strategies. Where, Hillocks asks, is the proof that process works? An important question, of course, but hardly an innocent one. Given the wide range of differing and necessarily subjective opinions about what constitutes good writing, it is unclear what could possibly constitute proof in this case. In addition, since process practitioners aim not simply to help a student write several successful essays but to change fundamental attitudes and practices ("focus more on the writer than on the writing" is a common process slogan), the success of the approach needs to be measured by something other than standardized pretests and posttests of writing ability. If process pedagogy works, its proponents argue, students will adopt more productive attitudes and practices (e.g., starting earlier, employing freewriting and other invention strategies, seeking feedback, relying on revision, etc.) that may take time to integrate but that will remain long after the course has ended.

But beyond that, defenders of process explain that many of the critiques of irresponsibility are founded on distortions and exaggerations of actual process approaches. The whole language movement has never ignored standards or skills, Regie Routman explains in *Literacy at the Crossroads: Critical Talk About Reading, Writing, and Other Teaching Dilemmas,* a compelling critique of whole language critiquers. Similarly, in *The Performance of Self in Student Writing,* Newkirk responds persuasively to critics who believe that the process pedagogies that allow personal writing are without sufficient rigor or content by demonstrating the enormously complex rhetorical task this kind of writing requires.

- *Process pedagogy is outmoded because it posits a view of "the writer" that fails to take into account differences of race, gender, and class.*

To some extent, this criticism is also based on a distortion of what early process theorists actually said about the process. Murray and Elbow, for example, go out of their way to make the point that different writers work in different ways, that no one model will work for every student and every teacher. However, it is true that early process texts refer often to "the writer" or "the writing process." But the critique that process pedagogy offers an essentialist view of the writer has merit not because of what process theorists said but because of what they didn't say. That is, early process manifestos said very little about differences in race, gender, and class and therefore may be faulted (as they have been by, for example, Lisa Delpit and bell hooks) for implying that those differences were not relevant or significant.

- *By focusing on the individual writer, process pedagogy fails to recognize the role and significance of context.*

This is an extension of the critiques of Faigley, Berlin, and LeFevre about the ways in which expressivist pedagogy overlooked the social nature of composing. By focusing so much on individual writers, expressivists are faulted for not focusing on the factors that shape composing. To some critics (Bartholomae, for instance, in "Study"), this meant that a writing class should focus more on the immediate context of the university and that the process should be the introduction to and eventual mastery of academic discourse. To others, this meant that the class should focus on the multiple systems, codes, and cultures that form a writer's environment and shape her discourse (e.g., Cooper); and to still others (e.g., Berlin), this meant that writing teachers should focus more on the larger context of late Western twentieth-century capitalism and that the process should teach students to resist the ways in which they are being controlled and manipulated by the dominant languages in the culture.

As I moved through graduate school, my reading of composition journals, and attendance at national conferences, I found these critiques all had roughly the same effect on me. They made me say "Yes, but. . . . " I could see the logic of the criticism; in fact, I ended up writing a dissertation and a book (*Writing Relationships: What Really Happens in the Composition Class*) that in many ways criticize process theorists for idealizing their results. I had run into enough disappointments as a process teacher to know that it was never as easy as putting the desks in a circle, announcing that we had decentered our authority, telling students to write what they wanted, and watching as they worked together harmoniously in peer groups to push themselves toward better and better revisions.

Still, even as I criticized process theorists for not talking enough about failure, conflict, competition, resistance, and the various contexts that inevitably shape texts, even as I found much of the social aspects of composing to be useful and compelling, I still found nothing that displaced or disproved the fundamental vision offered by the first process practitioners.

❧ POSTPROCESS, ANYONE?

A few years ago I was invited to a regional conference of rhetoricians and composition experts. The invitation stated that now that we had entered an age of "postprocess" it was important for us to come together and figure out what to do next. Since I thought reports of the death of process pedagogy were premature and presumptuous, I was more than a little irritated and defensive. It turned out, I learned once I got to the conference, that we all were in agreement that process had been fine in its day—after all it had displaced the old hulking, decaying materials and methods of the preprocess days—but its time had come and gone and we were now left with a terrible void. Process, according the postprocess theorists, had left us with no content.

Students can't write about nothing, the argument goes, which apparently is what they were writing about when the course was organized around their choice of topics and issues. However, what would count as content in a postprocess stage is not quite what counted as content in a preprocess stage: there was no one at the conference arguing for a return to a course organized around canonical works of literature; the postprocess courses that were proposed at the conference were about cultural critiques and "contact zones"; there were courses about the semiotics of the cosmetics industry, the rhetoric of Japanese-American trade agreements, the politics of medical research on AIDS.

During the morning, I sulked; by lunch, I simmered; and at the afternoon session (at which we were supposed to divide into groups and come up with new postprocess courses), I threw a tantrum. "I refuse to develop a postprocess course," I told my group mates, "because I refuse to accept the whole premise of this conference—that process is dead. These courses are fine as electives or as units within a writing course, but how can anyone seriously argue that they can replace process pedagogy as our core?"

I could have gone on. I could have said that organizing a course around a huge collection of readings that are chosen and controlled by the teacher and that reflect the teacher's interests and agendas sets back composition pedagogy thirty years—no matter how hip or leftist or progressive the readings are meant to be. And I could have said, if we learned anything from Murray, Emig, and Elbow, we know that you don't teach students to write by telling them that their views on issues that concern them or their narratives about events that shaped them—their experience caring for a grandparent with Alzheimer's, their solutions for the problems of homelessness, even their stories about winning the big game or pulling a great Halloween prank—don't count as content or count only as naive opinions to be corrected during the course.

Fortunately, I didn't say all of that because the people in my group who first looked only irritated by my harangue now were looking seriously worried about my mental health and their own well being. "I just wish that we had the nerve to do what some of the first process teachers did in the early seventies," I concluded. "I wish we had the nerve to throw everything overboard—paper assignments, the modes of discourse, a course reading list, grading, lectures on grammar and usage—and just leave the student's writing at the center of what we do every day and every class."

This elicited a few patronizing smiles, as if I had just said I wished that we could go back to a time when life was simpler, when we didn't have electricity and telephones and automobiles. "Yes, well, that might be interesting," one of my group mates said dismissively, "but our task today is to develop a post-process course that has some *real content*, OK?"

Like all binary oppositions, the distinction between content and noncontent can be easily deconstructed. But it is not the only topic on which process' proponents and its critics are each guilty of exaggeration. Actually I don't want to go back to the time when I first discovered process and when I did, in fact, throw everything out of my course except student writing. It was exhilarating at first, but after a while I found the course a little thin and a little insulated; slowly, over the years, I rediscovered the value of a well-placed writing prompt, an instructive or inspirational reading assignment, a cogent minilesson on some aspect of rhetoric, a unit on collaborative writing or cultural studies, and I introduced or reintroduced some of those materials and methods into the course.

My refusal to admit all this to my group mates grew out of my desire to counteract what I took to be their too-easy dismissal of process' contributions. But, of course, in some sense, process had it coming. After all, those of us who supported process pedagogies often misrepresented preprocess approaches as retrograde and ineffectual when, in fact, much of what we know about the teaching of writing long preceded the process movement. Further, much of the most interesting contemporary scholarship, such as Lunsford and Ede's landmark research on audience analysis or the perceptive observations of Wayne Booth, Gary Tate, and Daniel Reagan on the use of literature in a writing course, applies a process sensibility to questions that go back long before the process movement to classical rhetoric.

Dividing the history of our field into preprocess, process, and postprocess is as reductive and misleading as dividing the composing process into prewriting, writing, and revising. In fact, many of the postprocess critiques of the '90s rely heavily on process methods, just as process pedagogy continues to make use of traditional ideas about invention, development, thesis definition, notions of authorship, and so on (an argument that Crowley persuasively develops in "Around 1971"). However, while the original resistance to process had come primarily from traditional teachers trying to hold on to the past and from process teachers suggesting friendly amendments, the postprocess critiques were more likely to come from scholars on the left trying to move composition toward cultural studies (e.g., Harris), poststructuralism (e.g., Schilb), and, in some cases, the replacement of required composition courses with elective offerings in rhetoric (e.g., Crowley, "A Personal Essay on Freshman English").

It is not hard to see the postprocess movement of the late 1990s as an extension of the critiques in the mid-1980s. The criticism of process for promoting a view of writing that was too rigid and that ignored differences of race, class, and gender became an outright rejection of process for its naively positivist notions of language, truth, self, authorship, and individual agency. Similarly, the criticism of process for not providing students with sufficiently significant and challenging content and context became a rejection of process as ahistorical or arhetorical. As a product of contemporary critical theory, these critiques make some sense to me. As a classroom teacher, though, I have my doubts, for while positivist notions of agency, authorship, voice, and self may be philosophically naive, they can still be pedagogically powerful. In other words, it may be enormously useful for a student writer (or any writer for that matter) to believe at certain moments and stages of the process that she actually has agency, authority, an authentic voice, and a unified self.

As the administrator of a university writing program that employs seventy instructors each year (after finishing my Ph.D., I took a job developing and directing the writing program at Boston College), I have had to develop an appreciation for differing approaches to these issues. In the end, however, the underlying philosophical assumptions still seem less significant to me than the way in which a writing teacher answers this question: should a writing course be organized around production or consumption? It is around this very basic question that (at least) two paths diverge, and how a teacher chooses usually makes all the difference.

Process pedagogues are still apt to devote most class time to responses to student works-in-progress; to discussions of "the process" (that is, to the methods that successful writers use to find and focus topics, to discover their meaning and voice, to productively give and take peer review); and to writing exercises. They are likely to emphasize invention strategies, the necessity of revision after feedback, and reading assignments designed to support the students as writers. On the other hand, preprocess and postprocess teachers are apt to assign more reading and to devote more class time to discussions, interpretations, and assessments of the works of professional writers, to the identification of the characteristics of effective writing, to the teaching of rhetorical conventions and strategies, and to writing assignments designed to support the students as readers.

There is of course value in both (or all three) approaches, and my own current classroom approach shows a high degree of pedagogical diversity (or dilettantism). In most respects, I still remain clearly committed to a process design: I allow students to choose most of their own topics and forms and to work on essays for long periods of time punctuated by frequent feedback and revision. And I devote most class time to workshops, group work, writing activities, and discussions of invention and revision strategies. But I am no longer as rigid or as pure about teaching by not teaching. I have gone back to my earliest days by reinserting some of my old minilessons on how to identify your audience, how to establish a credible ethos, how to cite sources, and even how to write a five-paragraph essay (I figure it comes in handy on essay exams). At the same time, I find myself borrowing postprocess language and methods to help students see how texts and writers and readers are always and inevitably embedded in multiple contexts and cultures.

In my current incarnation, I am likely to ask my students to read a Nike ad alongside an essay by Orwell or Woolf and to introduce Bakhtin's notion of heteroglossia alongside Strunk and White's advice about word choice. But no matter how much I draw on current-traditional rhetoric or postprocess theory, I still strive to keep my students' evolving drafts and their sense of themselves as evolving writers at the very center of the course. For that reason, the model offered by early process practitioners remains, in spite of the important critiques, amendments, and clarifications offered by the theorists who preceded and followed them, as elegant, daring, and compelling as any pedagogical design I've yet come across.

Bibliography

Atwell, Nancie. *In the Middle: New Understanding About Writing, Reading, and Learning.* 2nd ed. Portsmouth, NH: Heinemann, 1998.

Bartholomae, David. "The Study of Error." *College Composition and Communication* 31 (1980): 253–69.

———. "Writing with Teachers: A Conversation with Peter Elbow." *College Composition and Communication* 46 (1995): 62–71.

Berkenkotter, Carol, and Donald Murray. "Decisions and Revisions: The Planning Strategies of a Publishing Writer, and Response of a Laboratory Rat—or, Being Protocoled." *College Composition and Communication* 34 (1983): 156–72.

Berlin, James, "Contemporary Composition: The Major Pedagogical Theories." *College English* 44 (1982): 765–77.

Berthoff, Ann E. *The Making of Meaning: Metaphors, Models, and Maxims for Writing Teachers*. Montclair, NJ: Boynton/Cook, 1981.

Booth, Wayne. "LITCOMP: Some Rhetoric Addressed to Cryptorhetoricians about a Rhetorical Solution to a Rhetorical Problem." *Composition and Literature: Bridging the Gap*. Ed. Winifred Byran Horner. Chicago: U of Chicago P, 57–80.

Britton, James. *The Development of Writing Abilities (11–18)*. London: Macmillan, 1975.

———. "Writing to Learn and Learning to Write." *Prospect and Retrospect: Selected Essays of James Britton*. Ed. Gordon Pradl. Montclair, NJ: Boynton/Cook, 1982. 94–111.

Bruffee, Kenneth. "Collaborative Learning and the Conversation of Mankind." *College English* 46 (1984): 65–52.

Calkins, Lucy McCormick. *The Art of Teaching Writing*. Portsmouth, NH: Heinemann, 1994.

Coles, William E., Jr. *The Plural I—and After*. Portsmouth, NH: Boynton/Cook, 1988.

Cooper, Marilyn. "The Ecology of Writing." *College English* 48 (1986): 364–75.

Crowley, Sharon. "Around 1971: The Emergence of Process Pedagogy." *Composition in the University: Historical and Polemical Essays*. Pittsburgh: U of Pittsburgh P, 1988. 187–214.

———. "A Personal Essay on Freshman English." *Composition in the University: Historical and Polemical Essays*. Pittsburgh: U of Pittsburgh P, 1988. 228–49.

Delpit. Lisa. *Other People's Children: Cultural Conflict in the Classroom*. New York: New Press, 1995.

Elbow, Peter. "Closing My Eyes as I Speak: An Argument for Ignoring Audience." *College English* 49 (1987): 50–69.

———. *Writing with Power*. New York: Oxford UP, 1981.

———. *Writing Without Teachers*. New York: Oxford UP, 1973.

Emig, Janet. *The Composing Process of Twelfth Graders*. Urbana, IL: NCTE, 1971.

———. *The Web of Meaning: Essays on Writing, Teaching, Learning, and Thinking*. Ed. Dixie Goswami and Maureen Butler. Upper Montclair, NJ: Boynton/Cook, 1983.

Faigley, Lester. "Competing Theories of Process: A Critique and a Proposal." *College English*. 48 (1986): 527–42.

Flower, Linda. "Writer-based Prose: A Cognitive Basis for Problems in Writing." *To Compose: Teaching Writing in High School and College*. Ed. Thomas Newkirk. Portsmouth, NH: Heinemann, 1990, 125–52.

Flower, Linda S. and John R. Hayes. "Problem Solving Strategies and the Writing Process." *College English* 39 (1977): 449–61.

Gere, Anne Ruggles. *Writing Groups: History, Theory, and Implications*. Carbondale, IL: Southern Illinois UP, 1987.

Goldberg, Natalie. *Writing Down the Bones: Freeing the Writer Within*. Boston: Shambhala, 1986.

Graves, Donald. "An Examination of the Writing Processes of Seven Year Old Children." *Research in the Teaching of English* 9 (1975): 138–43.

———. *Writing: Teachers and Children at Work*. Portsmouth, NH: Heinemann, 1983.

Hairston, Maxine. "Winds of Change: Thomas Kuhn and the Revolution in the Teaching of Writing." *College Composition and Communication* 33 (1982): 78–86.

Harris, Joseph. *A Teaching Subject: Composition Since 1966*. Upper Saddle River, NJ: Prentice-Hall, 1996.

Hillocks, George. *Research on Written Composition*. Urbana, IL: NCTE, 1986.

hooks, bell. *Teaching to Transgress: Education as the Practice of Freedom*. New York: Routledge, 1994.

LeFevre, Karen Burke. *Invention as a Social Act*. Carbondale, IL: Southern Illinois UP, 1987.

Lunsford, Andrea and Lisa Ede. "Audience Addressed/Audience Invoked: The Role of Audience in Composition Theory and Pedagogy." *College Composition and Communication* 35 (1984): 155–71.

Macrorie, Ken. *Telling Writing*. Rochelle Park, NJ: Hayden, 1970.

———. *Writing to Be Read*. New York: Hayden, 1968.

Marshall, James. "Of What Does Skill in Writing Really Consist?: The Political Life of the Writing Process Movement." Tobin and Newkirk, 45–55.

Moffett, James. *Teaching the Universe of Discourse*. Boston: Houghton Mifflin, 1968.

Murray, Donald. *Learning by Teaching: Selected Articles on Learning and Teaching*. Portsmouth, NH: Boynton/Cook, 1982.

———. *A Writer Teaches Writing*. 2nd ed. Boston: Houghton Mifflin, 1985.

Newkirk, Thomas. *The Performance of Self in Student Writing*. Portsmouth, NH: Boynton/Cook, 1997.

Newkirk, Thomas, ed. *To Compose: Teaching Writing in High School and College*. 2nd ed. Portsmouth, NH: Heinemann, 1990.

Newkirk, Thomas and Nancie Atwell, eds. *Understanding Writing*. 2nd ed. Portsmouth, NH: Heinemann. 1986.

North, Stephen. *The Making of Knowledge in Composition: Portrait of an Emerging Field*. Upper Montclair, NJ: Boynton/Cook, 1987.

Odell, Lee and Dixie Goswami, eds. *Writing in Nonacademic Settings*. New York: Guilford Press, 1988.

Perl, Sondra. "The Composing Processes of Unskilled College Writers." *Research in the Teaching of English* 13 (1978): 317–36.

———. "Understanding Composing." Tobin and Newkirk, 43–52.

Reagan, Daniel. "The Process of Poetry: Rethinking Literature in the Composition Course." Tobin and Newkirk, 83–96.

Romano, Tom. *Clearing the Way: Working with Teenage Writers*. Portsmouth, NH: Heinemann. 1987.

Rose, Mike. *Writer's Block: The Cognitive Dimension*. Carbondale, IL: Southern Illinois UP, 1984.

Routman, Regie. *Literacy at the Crossroads: Crucial Talk About Reading, Writing, and Other Teaching Dilemmas*. Portsmouth, NH: Heinemann, 1996.

Schilb, John. *Between the Lines: Relating Composition Theory and Literary Theory*. Portsmouth, NH: Boynton/Cook, 1996.

Shaughnessy, Mina. *Errors and Expectations: A Guide for the Teacher of Basic Writing*. New York: Oxford UP, 1977.

Sommers, Nancy. "Revision Strategies of Student Writers and Experienced Adult Writers." *College Composition and Communication* 31 (1980): 378–88.

Tate, Gary. "A Place for Literature in Freshman Composition." *College English* 57 (1995): 303–9.

Tobin, Lad. *Writing Relationships: What Really Happens in the Composition Class*. Portsmouth, NH: Boynton/Cook, 1991.

Tobin, Lad and Thomas Newkirk. *Taking Stock: The Writing Process Movement in the '90s*. Portsmouth, NH: Boynton/Cook, 1994.

Trimbur, John. "Consensus and Difference in Collaborative Learning." *College English* 51 (1989): 602–16.

Wells, Gordon. *The Meaning Makers: Children Learning Language and Using Language to Learn*. Portsmouth, NH: Heinemann, 1986.

Expressive Pedagogy: Practice/Theory, Theory/Practice

CHRISTOPHER BURNHAM

✦ INTRODUCTION

In "Contemporary Composition: The Major Pedagogical Theories," James Berlin reminds us that all pedagogy is ideological; any single approach supports an underlying set of values while questioning others. He analyzes the teaching of writing according to a set of interactions among the four separate elements that constitute a rhetorical act: writer, audience, message, and language. These are often represented as a triangle. The element placed within the triangle assumes greatest prominence, mediating the others. [Expressivism places the writer in the center,)articulates its theory, and develops its pedagogical system by assigning highest value to the writer and her imaginative, psychological, social, and spiritual development and how that development influences individual consciousness and social behavior. Expressivist pedagogy employs freewriting, journal keeping, reflective writing, and small-group dialogic collaborative response to foster a writer's aesthetic, cognitive, and moral development. Expressivist pedagogy encourages, even insists upon, a sense of writer presence even in research-based writing. This presence—"voice" or *ethos*—whether explicit, implicit, or absent, functions as a key evaluation criterion when expressivists examine writing.

Invoking expressivist values in conversations about teaching writing generally arouses controversy. Allies come from various, sometimes conflicting, ideological backgrounds. bell hooks, the African-American feminist and liberatory teacher, presents an arguably expressivist pedagogy in *Sisters of the Yam: Black Women and Self-Recovery* (1993) and *Teaching to Transgress: Education as the Practice of Freedom* (1994). She assigns great value and responsibility to the teacher as well as to the writer or person, insisting that education at every level and in every context attends to ethical formation. She argues that community morality depends on the ethical discrimination and consequent individual action of each of its members and implicates dominant institutions for failures in education. She invokes Thomas Merton, Trappist monk and peace and justice activist, to challenge teachers to accept the ethical responsibility of professing. Confronted with students "desperately yearning to be touched by knowledge," many professors fail to rekindle the passion they once felt and reject the challenge and the opportunity their students offer. Her answer destabilizes the contemporary, academic sense of the term *profess*, recalling its original sense of passionate commitment in professing a vow. She raises the stakes for university teachers to a level that would surely frighten many:

> If, as Thomas Merton suggests in his essay on pedagogy "Learning to Live," the purpose of education is to show students how to define themselves "authentically and spontaneously in relation" to the world, then professors can best teach if we are self-actualized. Merton reminds us that the "original and authentic 'paradise' idea, both in the monastery and in the university, implied not simply a celestial source of theoretic ideas to which Magistri and Doctores held the key, but the inner self of the student" who would discover the ground of their being in relation to themselves, to higher powers, to community. That the "fruit of education . . . was in the activation of that utmost center." (*Teaching to Transgress* 199)

In "Learning to Live," Merton emphasizes student self-discovery and the responsibility to make informed life choices:

> The purpose of education is to show a person how to define himself authentically and spontaneously in relation to the world—not to impose a prefabricated definition of the world, still less an arbitrary definition of the individual himself. . . . The world is, therefore, more real in proportion as the people in it are able to be more fully and more humanly alive: that is to say, better able to make a lucid and conscious use of their freedom. Basically, this freedom must consist first of all in the capacity to choose their own lives, to find themselves on the deepest possible level. . . .
>
> The function of the university is, then, first of all to help the student discover himself: to recognize himself, and to identify who it is that chooses. (358)

Though hooks would reject Merton's masculine gender references, she endorses his aim. In her own work she accepts the responsibility to be passionate and to develop socially and morally aware citizens whose actions begin in mutual respect. Education, she asserts, is the responsibility of individual teachers and small communities connected by cultural identity or a shared experience of marginalization or alienation. *Sisters of the Yam* offers a specific program to accomplish this reclaiming of the person. She and, as I argue later, Peter Elbow offer paradigmatic examples of expressivist teachers.

Critics of expressivism range broadly across the ideological spectrum from Marxists to cultural conservatives. Depending on political orientation, opponents deride expressivism as arhetorical, atheoretical, anti-intellectual and elitist, or, conversely, standardless, antitraditional, and relativistic. Either perspective blames expressivism for everything that is wrong in contemporary culture and education. Demonized and dismissed from both sides of the political spectrum, expressivism, however, as it has in hooks, transforms and reasserts itself.

From its inception, rhetoric has been concerned with the relationship between the writer/speaker and all the other elements of the rhetorical triangle. From a philosophical perspective, Merton, invoked in hooks, reasserts Socrates' assertion in the *Gorgias* that rhetorical training, central to all education, is a moral undertaking concerned with justice, self-control, and virtue. Even Aristotle, an arch empiricist, postpones his concern with technical rhetoric long enough to concede the centrality of *ethos* as an appeal in the *Rhetoric*. And recently, Linda Flower discusses the significant but problematic influence of the expressive in *The Construction of Negotiated Meaning: A Social-Cognitive Theory of Writing*. Present at the beginning and still present, expressivist concerns cut across subdisciplinary boundaries and methodologies. They are in us and of us as humans.

The education of the writer is a central problem. We resist the implications that grow from hooks and Merton and others, however, by placing writing, and not the writer, at our disciplinary center. I previously argued that we must teach reflection, and we must use journals in various contexts to help students develop intellectually, cognitively, and ethically. Now the best I can do is provide a context and encourage your persistence through the argument and sources that will follow. Remember, however, that bibliographic entries begin with names of persons. These are the people who have shaped my thinking about expressivist issues.

↔ BACKGROUND

For our purposes, any reference to expressivism will invoke both the theory and the pedagogy developed from that theory, as well as the contributing writers, teachers, and thinkers. The relationship between theory and practice, especially in expressivism, is complex. Practice is often based in intuition or convention and precedes theorizing. Theory can attack and thus neutralize counterarguments. Theory can defend against attack from opposing perspectives. Theory can result from synthesis; the creative act resides in bringing together ideas from various sources. Theory and practice can self-consciously merge as is the case with liberatory praxis. The strange theory/practice relationship in expressivism explains my title.

Expressivism weaves together several sources: nontraditional textbooks offering innovative practices for teaching writing, commentaries by first-generation expressivists that began to articulate theory, theorizing in reaction to scholarly and ideological attacks, and, recently, syntheses that integrate expressivism with social and liberatory rhetorics. The movement originated in the 1960s and 1970s as a set of values and practices opposing current-traditional rhetoric.

Current-traditional teaching emphasized academic writing in standard forms and "correct" grammar. It reinforced middle-class values, such as social stability and cultural homogeneity, and supported the meritocracy associated with the military-industrial complex. Male students attending universities on the GI bill were its primary audience. Current-traditional rhetoric assumed the gate-keeping role class and economics had previously played, making sure that these veterans, whether supply sergeants, tank mechanics, sailors, flyers, or infantrymen, could write easily enough to pass their courses and subsequently meet the engineering, production, and managerial needs of the prosperous postwar American society. In "Contemporary Composition: The Major Pedagogical Theories," Berlin critiques current-traditional rhetoric for its static, empirically based epistemology that holds that all knowledge can be found in concrete reality through close observation, that language is an uncomplicated medium for communicating already existing knowledge, and that the work of teaching writing is limited to getting students to use grammar correctly, to conform to formal and stylistic conventions, and to argue exclusively from existing authority available in books. Sharon Crowley in *The Methodical Memory* (1990) completes a close analysis of current-traditional rhetoric, tracing its origin back to Ramus' splitting of logic from rhetoric. She demonstrates that current-traditional approaches to teaching writing undervalue the role of the writer and language in shaping knowledge and reflect an indefensibly reductive view of reality. Current-traditionalism, she argues, is not really a rhetoric because it does not consider the interactions between all the elements of the rhetorical triangle. These critiques are significant to expressivists because the relation among the individual, language and epistemology, and the nature of rhetoric, not accounted for in current-traditional thinking, became the unarticulated originating force for the original expressivists, as well as the central focus for the more recent syntheses of expressivism and social rhetoric.

Current-traditional pedagogy clearly dominated the teaching of writing in universities between the ends of World War II and the Vietnam War. During that same time, graduate studies in English concentrated on professionalizing literary criticism, in the process ignoring or devaluing pedagogy. Several nontraditional textbooks and commentaries date to this period and mark the emergence of expressivism as defined in this essay. Donald Murray, Ken Macrorie, Peter Elbow, and William Coles all offered counter approaches to current traditional pedagogy in anti-textbooks. They wrote for an audience of teachers as much as for students. Though radical departures for the time, many of these methods now constitute mainstream writing instruction.

✧ ANTITEXTBOOKS

Originating in and committed to classroom practice, expressivism's first coherent statements of value and methodology occur in alternative textbooks. These were antitextbooks offered as critiques of standard institutional practice. Murray's *A Writer Teaches Writing* (1968) organizes the writing course as a workshop and exemplifies the process approach. Murray's use of nondirective feedback from both teacher and students turns the responsibility for writing back to the student. In *Telling Writing* (1970) and elsewhere, Macrorie insists that individual writers recreate their original experience in "telling" details. He protests against the academic language of the schools, which he calls "Engfish." He instructs students to keep a journal as a reflective exercise for documenting individual experience and personal development.

Elbow's *Writing Without Teachers* (1973) values the act of writing as a means for both making meaning and creating identity. The "teacherless" classroom returns the responsibility for and control over learning to students. The book attends mostly to invention. Freewriting helps students discover ideas and their significance, center of gravity exercises develop and focus these ideas, and peer response groups allow writers to test their writing on an actual audience and revise on the basis of that response. In an appendix, "The Doubting Game and the Believing Game—An Analysis of the Intellectual Enterprise," Elbow critiques conventional Western skepticism, encouraging writers to engage a dialectic of perspectives—self and others, the familiar and the strange—to make themselves better writers, thinkers, and citizens.

In *Writing with Power* (1981), Elbow shows how objective as well as subjective evaluation criteria can help writers revise for specific audiences to accomplish specific purposes. His approach becomes more rhetorical. The emphasis on process continues. The context is social and active; the writer is concerned with having an impact on an actual audience. Elbow instructs writers to maintain a productive paradoxical tension between individual and group. Equipped with well-developed personal identities, individuals can function effectively in groups or culture. Interdependence is both the source and locus of power. Voice is a central concern in *Writing with Power*. It symbolizes the expressivist value system. Elbow and the expressivists, anticipating feminist pedagogy, work to subvert teaching practices and institutional structures that oppress, appropriate, or silence an individual's voice.

In collaboration with Pat Belanoff, Elbow further elaborates the role of groups in *A Community of Writers* (1989) and a companion pamphlet developed for teachers, *Sharing and Responding*. The expressivist use of groups anticipates John Trimbur's critique of collaborative writing in "Consensus and Difference in Collaborative Learning." Trimbur champions dissensus. Dissensus recognizes, celebrates, and explores difference to reestablish social autonomy. Dissensus concedes the power of groups and culture to shape individuals, but maintains the possibility of individual agency. Expressivism shares this belief and purpose. The proof of dissensus, for Elbow and the expressivists, is voice, the individual identity of the writer working in a community.

❧ EXPRESSIVIST COMMENTARIES AND BACKGROUND THEORY

In 1968, Elbow offers a pedagogical commentary, "A Method for Teaching Writing," that reflects the flavor and intensity of the early expressivists. He argues that voice empowers individuals to act in the world. He recounts his experience counseling applicants for conscientious objector (CO) draft status during the Vietnam conflict. Elbow, a CO himself, sees writing as a means of political action. He teaches those he counsels that they must do more than just make sense when writing applications for CO status; they must communicate intense belief through voice. Writing thus becomes a form of political or social activism. The essay establishes voice as a central concern for expressivists.

However, most first-generation expressivists were not inclined to theorize. They considered themselves teachers. When necessary they provided anecdotal narrative, metadiscourse rather than theory, to rationalize their practices. Macrorie's *Uptaught* (1970) and *A Vulnerable Teacher* (1974) serve as good examples. Expressivist metadiscourse shows the influence of various disciplines, especially linguistics, cognitive and developmental psychology, phenomenology, and existential philosophy.

The theoretical background includes two major sources: Britton's expressive function in language and Kinneavy's expressive discourse. The combination creates something of an ambiguity. Expressivists do not distinguish between the expressive function of language and expressive discourse, a type of text. This eventually causes a problem for some critics, especially Jeanette Harris. She condemns the indiscriminate use of the term *expressive*, suggesting rather four separate labels for textual phenomena that describe more precisely the various forms of discourse considered expressive. However, expressivists reject dualistic thinking, viewing ambiguity as a source of productive dialectic. In "Expressive Rhetoric: A Source Study," I examine Britton, Kinneavy, and commentary by Murray, Coles, and Elbow to construct an expressivist theory of language and epistemology.

Murray attends to epistemology in "Writing as Process: How Writing Finds Its Own Meaning" in Timothy Donovan and Ben McClelland's *Eight Approaches to Teaching Composition* (1980), an anthology with a strong expressivist bent. In this "speculation upon the composing process" (3), Murray proposes an instrumental relation between composing and meaning-making. He examines three related activities: rehearsing, drafting, and revising. These involve complex interactions between contrary impulses: exploring and clarifying; collecting and combining; and writing and reading. Through these interactions, meaning evolves. Murray's commentary resembles James Britton's analysis of the function of expressive language in *Language and Learning* (1970): writing is a process of discovering meaning through shifting back and forth from participant to spectator modes, and writing involves interaction between self and subject. Through several iterations, writers use language to generate, connect, shape, and then evaluate for a purpose. According to Murray, "The writer is constantly learning from the writing what it intends to say. The writer listens for evolving meaning. . . . The writing itself helps the writer see the subject" (7). Murray includes a social element in the process, insisting that his students work within a writing community. Meaning results from the interaction of teacher and students, writers and readers, process and product—all accomplished through language.

Expressivist pedagogy is systematic and purposeful, based on a theory of relations between language, meaning making, and self-development. Elbow's freewriting, based originally on his own journal writing, requires self-conscious language processing. In "Toward a Phenomenology of Freewriting," Elbow notes that the initial "experimental form of freewriting" occurred in his own personal journal (190). He describes a process similar to the generating/structuring/evaluating movement in Murray's model of the writing process. Elbow posits an analytic urge based in writing that results in understanding leading to action. Through the process the writer gains control of his subject, either himself or an intellectual concept. He mentions Progoff, a student of Jung, whose work in depth psychology culminated in the "Journal Workshop" method, a formal journal program.

Expressive writing exercises require students, in a sense, to write a phenomenology of self. In *A Theory of Discourse*, James Kinneavy argues that the expressive aim is psychologically prior to all others. Using Sartre and the phenomenologists, Kinneavy argues that through expressive discourse the self moves from private meaning to shared meaning that results ultimately in some action. Rather than a "primal whine," expressive discourse traces a path away from solipsism toward accommodation with the world and thus accomplishes purposeful action. As a consequence, Kinneavy elevates expressive discourse to the same order as referential, persuasive, and literary discourse.

But expressive discourse is not the exclusive province of the individual; it also has a social function. Kinneavy's analysis of the *Declaration of Independence* makes this clear. Contesting the claim that the purpose of the declaration is persuasive, Kinneavy traces its evolution through several drafts to prove that its primary aim is expressive: to establish an American group identity (410). Kinneavy's analysis suggests that rather than being individualistic and otherworldly, or naive and narcissistic, expressive discourse can be ideologically empowering.

✧ BRITTON'S EXPRESSIVE FUNCTION

Though expressivism borrows freely, some would say shamelessly, from a wide variety of sources, Britton's expressive function contains its theoretical center and so requires treatment in some detail. Britton offered a developmental taxonomy of writing derived from close observation of the process through which children learn language. With origins in linguistics and cognitive and developmental psychology, the taxonomy emphasizes the expressive function of language, providing a wealth of linguistic and pedagogical insights that can be developed for a variety of purposes, from theorizing expressivist rhetoric to justifying the study of literature to providing a write-to-learn methodology for writing across the curriculum. Britton's is the only discourse theory that attends to the regulative function of language and includes a developmental matrix that considers both mature and immature uses of language. Britton's expressivism has, in a sense, become part of the tacit tradition in contemporary teaching of writing; it is at the center of the National Writing Project and Whole Language movements.

Language and Learning presents Britton in the role of theorist. He blends narrative based on his experiences as teacher, writer, and parent with then cutting-edge literary criticism, linguistics, philosophy, and psychology. He invokes Edward Sapir's distinction between the referential and expressive functions of language. Britton emphasizes the expressive function. It opposes the referential, whose purpose is to represent and transcribe material reality. For Britton, the expressive function makes language personal and idiosyncratic. It provides a means for individuals to connect abstract concepts with personal experience and to negotiate the boundaries between public and private significance. The result is concrete understanding and learning. Additional sources for Britton's theory include L. S. Vygotsky's "inner speech"; Bruner's cognitive psychology, with its emphasis on the instrumental relationship between language and learning; and Noam Chomsky's generative transformational theory of language.

The Development of Writing Abilities (11–18) (1975) presents Britton as a researcher validating the theoretical insights offered in the earlier book. It offers an observational and empirical analysis of the writing students do in school. Britton and his colleagues focus on the two primary roles writers can play when producing language: the participant role in which writers use language to get things done and the spectator role in which writers use language to relive the past. As participants, writers shape reality to an end. As spectators, writers recreate reality.

Locating participant and spectator roles at either end of a continuum, he introduces a third mediating role, the expressive, in which the writer functions as both participant and spectator. From each role he derives a category of writing. In the participant role, writers produce *transactional* writing, in which language is used to accomplish the business of the world. Transactional writing is divided further into *informative* and *conative* writing, roughly corresponding to the traditional classifications of exposition and persuasion. In material added to the second edition of *Language and Learning* (1993), Britton adjusts these categories slightly to include *informative, regulative,* and *persuasive* writing. Informative writing makes information available, regulative writing impels or commands action, and persuasive writing moves readers from inaction or ambivalence to specific action. In each instance the writing involves a transaction between writer and reader, hence its name.

On the other end of the continuum, writers acting in the spectator role produce *poetic* writing. Poetic writing is language used as an art medium, as a verbal icon, whose purpose is to be an object that pleases or satisfies the writer. The reader's response is to share that satisfaction. In traditional terms poetic writing is literary discourse, language that "exists for *its own sake* and not as a means of achieving something else" (Britton et al., 91).

With transactional and poetic writing constituting boundaries of the participant/spectator continuum, Britton establishes a third category, *expressive* writing, that mediates the two. As a functional category, expressive writing represents a mode rather than a form. More important than its existence as a text, expressive writing achieves its purpose through allowing the text to come to existence. Examples include "thinking out loud on paper" (89); notes and drafts intended for the personal and private use of writers and their collaborators;

journal writing documenting or exploring immediate thoughts, feelings, and moods; and personal letters.

In the expressive mode, writers shuttle back and forth between participant and spectator roles, generating ideas, then shaping them into language that can stand on its own. With its generative function, expressive writing plays an obvious role in learning to write: "Thus, in developmental terms, the expressive is a kind of matrix from which differentiated forms of mature writing are developed" (83). In addition, as a link between the private and personal and the public and social, as the language of association and connection, expressive language is the language of learning.

From its inception, Britton's taxonomy has influenced process-based approaches to teaching writing. The approaches developed by Murray and Elbow, for example, implicitly or explicitly use Britton's developmental taxonomy to help students and teachers navigate the journey through which personal and private insights and sensations become coherent, publicly accessible writing. In "Expressive Rhetoric," I argue that Britton's taxonomy creates common space that contains the seeming oppositions among expressive, cognitive, and social approaches to rhetoric, providing a coherent model for understanding writing as the result of interactions among individually and culturally defined forces.

Returning to alternative textbooks for a moment, William Coles uses the realization that expressive discourse has both individual and social functions to great advantage. *The Plural I: The Teaching of Writing* (1978) presents a semester-long sequence of writing assignments that engages students in writing self-critical phenomenology. Through the sequence, the class, as individuals and as a group, come to agree on a set of meanings and values concerning the purpose of education, in the process achieving Coles' goal of forming his students into practicing humanists. The sequence culminates in a formal review and evaluation of the work of the course. Anticipating the reflective self-assessments that have become important in current portfolio evaluation practice, Coles' final assignment asks for formal reflection: "Where did you start this term? Where did you seem to come out? . . . who were you? Who are you now?" (258). Those interested in more work connecting expressivism and reflective thinking should consult Jean MacGregor's *Student Self-Evaluation: Fostering Reflective Learning* (1993), especially Richard Haswell's "Student Self-Evaluations and Developmental Change" that argues a causal relationship between expressive work in reflective contexts and progression through schemes of both cognitive and moral development. In Kinneavy's terms, Coles is asking his students to write *apologia*, a high level of expressive discourse.

✧ RECEPTION, IDEOLOGICAL CRITIQUES, AND THEORETICAL DEFENSES

Expressivism originated in opposition to mainstream practice, offering an alternative to current-traditional teaching. The mainstream reacted in a variety of ways. Chief among these was simple dismissal. Expressivism was labeled a fringe movement. More substantial opposition came in the form of the back-to-basics movement which, with its emphasis on grammar and standard formats, was really current-traditional teaching dressed in new clothes.

Several other rhetorical schools grew up along with expressivism, all part of the renaissance in rhetoric in the 1960s and 1970s. These other schools, especially neoclassicism and cognitive rhetoric, were not averse to theory. Expressivists distrusted theory because it often distracted attention from students and teaching. Given the early expressivist aversion to theory, it is no surprise that formal theoretical considerations of expressivism are generally critical. William Covino notes the antipathy of both classicists and cognitivists, both of whom label expressivism's sense of the self and its importance irrational (4). Lately, however, cognitivists have reaffirmed the important but problematic role of the self. The arch-cognitivist Jerome Bruner, though "acutely uncomfortable" with considerations of the self, concedes that merely labeling the self a cultural construct does not negate its power. In *Actual Minds, Possible Worlds* (1986), he theorizes a "transactional self" (57–69) that through metacognition and reflection "penetrates knowledge," allowing us to own that knowledge and ultimately become "a member of the culture-creating community" (132). Membership in such a community is the goal of much expressivist work. In *The Construction of Negotiated Meaning*, cognitivist Linda Flower includes expressive practices along with rhetorical practices among the "basics" that are the beginning point of all literacy education. She references John Willinsky's *The New Literacy* (1990) to confirm the centrality of Britton's expressive writing as both the originating point and the "heart of meaning making" (25).

The most aggressive critiques originate in social rhetoric, specifically from Berlin and Lester Faigley. Berlin offers an extended ideological critique in "Contemporary Composition: The Major Pedagogical Theories," where he portrays "expressionism" as an untheorized and ideologically debased form of neo-Platonism. Elsewhere he links expressivism to "Emersonian romantic" rhetoric and subsequently to the "rhetoric of liberal culture" and to Dewey and the progressive education movement. He locates expressivist rhetoric among "subjective" theories of rhetoric. His critique is rich, attending in considerable detail to expressivist practices to construct a theory despite his own claim that expressivism has none. His self-admitted allegiance to social epistemic rhetoric, however, results in readings that are not verified by close analysis of expressivist work. Berlin and the other social rhetoricians view expressivism's primary flaw as a false and otherworldly epistemology of the self that privileges individualism and rejects the material world. Faigley argues that expressivism's romantic view of the self is philosophically and politically retrograde, making it ineffectual in postmodern times. Further, expressivism's concern with the individual and authentic voice directs students away from social and political problems in the material world.

❧ SYNTHESES

Attacks by expressivism's critics have resulted in several syntheses that challenge the presumption that expressivism is atheoretical. Responding to attacks, however, places expressivism's defenders in a position of alienation, not a position of power. Such alienation has resulted in a new and powerful strand of expressivist work that articulates the theoretical base that has always been present though latent in expressivist work. Elbow, after he gets his work with students and teachers done in *Writing Without Teachers*, turns to the theoretical with an appendix essay criticizing Western epistemology and the institutional control it exerts in education.

Merging theory and practice is the aim of much current expressivist work, work informed by feminism and critical pedagogy. Sherrie Gradin, working from a feminist perspective, has attempted to synthesize the expressivist potential for reflective consciousness raising with liberatory and critical pedagogy to articulate more clearly the practice of left and radical epistemicism. The two constituent urges, the expressive concern to potentiate self-aware individuals as agents and the epistemic concern with social context and ideology, create social expressivism.

Gradin's purpose in *Romancing Rhetorics: Social Expressivist Perspectives on the Teaching of Writing* (1995) is to politicize expressivism and "establish a pedagogy of equity" in which all can contribute and be heard (121). She explores a commonly overlooked connection between romanticism and expressivism. Pointing to German romanticism's concern for social justice and political action, she counters the claim that expressivism values individualism to the exclusion of social concerns. Rather, expressivists value autonomy as signaled in the concern to empower people through voice, and they believe that individuals can use personal awareness to act against oppressive material and psychological conditions. She also connects expressivism with feminism, noting that Elbow and his pedagogy are referenced in Mary Belenky and colleagues' *Women's Ways of Knowing: The Development of Self, Voice, and Mind* (1986). Similarly, in *Writing from the Margins: Power and Pedagogy for Teachers of Composition* (1990), Carolyn Erikson Hill considers Elbow and other expressivists as models for building a new pedagogy of awareness and equity. Another book connecting expressivist theory, feminism, and the teaching of writing is Cynthia Gannett's *Gender and the Journal: Diaries and Academic Discourse* (1992), a work of teacher-research that offers historical as well as ideological analyses of journal use in personal and pedagogical contexts.

Responding to the complaint that expressivists are antitheoretical, Elbow reconsiders his own practice. He elaborates a theoretical frame, examines his application, and provides an extended defense of voice in *Landmark Essays: On Voice and Writing* (1994), a collection of sixteen essays by various theorists, including Bakhtin, Walker Gibson, and Walter Ong, as well as allies and critics of expressivism such as bell hooks and Faigley. In an introductory essay, "About Voice and Writing," Elbow traces the voice controversy as far back as Aristotle and Plato. He equates voice and ethos. He argues that because Aristotle includes techniques to, in Aristotle's words, "make ourselves *thought to be* sensible and morally good . . ." (Elbow's emphasis), Aristotle affirms Plato's earlier declaration that ethos—good character—is the central concern in all rhetoric. Aristotle "is affirming both positions in what is in fact a common sense view: 'It's nice to *be* trustworthy; but if you're skilled you can fake it'" (xli).

"Resonant" voice, one of five empirically verifiable instances of voice, is Elbow's primary concern. Sensitive to critiques of the expressivist view of self, Elbow walks a careful theoretical line. Resonant voice manages to get a great deal of the self *"behind* the words." Discourse can never "articulate a whole person," but at times we can "find words that seem to capture the rich complexity of the unconscious . . . that somehow seem to *resonate with* or *have behind them* the unconscious as well as the conscious [his italics]. . . . [W]ords of this sort . . . we experience as resonant—and through them we have a sense of presence with the writer" (xxxiv). As with voice, Elbow relates "presence" to ethos in classical rhetoric. A significant article illuminating the issue of ethos in classical rhetoric, especially as it is applied, correctly or incorrectly, in contemporary work on the teaching of writing is Roger Cherry's "Ethos Versus Persona: Self-Representation in Written Discourse."

Later in "Introduction: About Voice and Writing," Elbow connects resonant voice with self-identity and argues that voice in writing is a locus for power. From a pragmatic perspective, he argues against a binary view that opposes sentimental (expressivist) and sophisticated (postmodern) views of self; writers need to use both. The sentimental self (the believer) functions best in exploratory writing. The sophisticated self (the doubter) works well when revising with a pragmatic end in mind.

In the same volume, Randall Freisinger's "Voicing the Self: Toward a Pedagogy of Resistance in a Postmodern Age" counters the claim that expressivism devalues social and political engagement, arguing instead that the expressivist concept of self is a starting point for resistance as defined by Henry Giroux. Freisinger undertakes a serious examination of postmodern theory and its relation to expressivism. Examining the critiques of Berlin and Faigley in the light of Ira Shor's liberatory practice and current postmodern theories of agency and self-construction, Freisinger notes with appropriate irony that liberatory pedagogy makes extensive use of expressivist strategies to accomplish the goal of creating a consciousness of social and cultural formation in students that empowers them to resist that formation. More about that at the end.

✧ OTHER RECENT WORK

The best index of any movement's significance is its persistence in the professional literature. By that measure, expressivism thrives. The ideological critiques inspired the several volumes of expressivist theory and application noted above. In addition, two small books implicitly critique expressivism but offer expressivist applications. Both address issues of self and identity in the writing classroom. Both steer clear of the expressivist/social rhetoric anomalies addressed above to avoid tarring or being tarred in the process. Robert Brooke uses learning and identity negotiation theory in *Writing and the Sense of Self* (1991) to explore the social and intellectual dynamics of the writing workshop. In *The Performance of Self in Student Writing* (1997), Thomas Newkirk uses narrative theory to repair what he views as an unproductive disciplinary split between the social science-dominated professional compositionists, whom I would place in the long tradition of rhetorical inquiry, and the "writers," among whom he positions the expressivists Donald Murray and Ken Macrorie. Both books offer contributions but limit their value by not engaging the controversies as thoroughly as Elbow and hooks do.

In addition, expressivism continues to receive attention in *College English, College Composition and Communication, Rhetoric Review,* and the *Journal of Advanced Composition.* Expressivism's kinship with philosophy, evident in Kinneavy, explains a recent defense against the ideological critiques. In "Politics and Ordinary Language: A Defense of Expressivist Rhetorics," Thomas O'Donnell questions the motivation of some ideological critics, accusing them of being more interested in teaching a particular ideology than in providing students with the tools of social and political critique. Expressivism's strength is its insistence that all concerns, whether individual, social, or political, must originate in personal experience and be documented in the student's own language. What O'Donnell calls expressivism's "unguardedness" makes it attractive to teachers concerned with raising political consciousness. He offers a defense based on ordinary language philosophy, showing how expressivist practices "facilitate investigations of political issues in unique, sometimes necessary ways" (424).

Another strong contribution comes in the work of Steven Fishman, a philosophy professor who teaches from a writing across the curriculum perspective, and Lucille McCarthy, who introduced Fishman to writing across the curriculum theory and practice. They constitute an effective collaborative team using Fishman's teaching in general education philosophy courses as a pedagogical laboratory. In addition, McCarthy serves as research methodologist and evaluator for their pedagogical experiments.

In a series of articles, Fishman and McCarthy examine attacks on expressivism based in discourse community theory. Led by Bartholomae, critics argue that emphasizing personal writing, as expressivism does, wastes students' time. Rather, students need training in the conventions of academic discourse, so they can succeed in the institutions that will provide them access to economic and social power. Fishman and McCarthy begin their counterargument by asking "Is Expressivism Dead?" Answering no, they argue that expressivism does not endorse the concept of the isolated individual. Arguing from the same socially concerned German romanticism as Gradin, they contend that expressivist techniques can be used to achieve social-constructivist goals in a writing across the curriculum context. In "Community in the Expressivist Classroom," they explore the tension between conventional authoritarian and expressivist liberal and communitarian classroom values. Fishman claims some success in promoting student voice while teaching disciplinary conventions. However, his experience underscores the complexity of the expressivist classroom where students function as experts and teachers as learners. They conclude that this complexity, rather than the reductive either/or positions generally presented in the scholarly literature, offers significant opportunities for progress.

The last essay, "Teaching for Student Change: A Deweyan Alternative to

Radical Pedagogy," defends the safe and cooperative classroom championed by the expressivists against recent charges by feminists and critical teachers that expressivist pedagogy protects the status quo by encouraging politeness that camouflages inherent conflicts in the classroom and society at large. Fishman and McCarthy offer an alternative that privileges diversity and encourages transformation for teachers who "find certain types of conflict unattractive but who seek student critique and change" (344). In *John Dewey and the Challenge of Classroom Practice* (1998), Fishman and McCarthy propose an approach that integrates the curricular interests and needs of teachers and the needs and experiences of students. The approach is writing intensive, employing dialogical written commentaries where students pose and answer each others' questions, with Fishman providing additional written commentary as a mentor and co-inquirer. Very much in the spirit of Shor's approach in *Critical Teaching and Everyday Life*, but without ideological and political agenda, Fishman's question and answer approach merges class topics with student experience and exigencies, allowing Fishman to accomplish his goal of having students learn substantive intellectual content through personalizing and applying philosophical concepts in their own lives. McCarthy analyzes the students' written work to demonstrate that they do engage and apply the course topics and learn in the process. Their approach offers a paradigmatic example that applies expressive values to integrate the individual with the social and to serve the ultimate educational goal of fostering individual moral and ethical development to influence civic and cultural life.

↪ CODA: PRACTICE/THEORY, THEORY/PRACTICE

Freisinger's analysis of voice and agency noted above makes extensive use of Paul Smith's *Discerning the Subject* (1988). Smith critiques postmodern theory for being a victim of its own world view, invoking the common failure of "disciplinary self-reflexivity" as the origin of the problem. He argues that postmodern theory relies so intensely on the view that humans are created entirely by their social/cultural experience—that culture and history determine identity—that postmodernism is unable to conceptualize a subject that can recognize and move beyond its determined nature. A socially constructed, totally determined self, even if it could achieve self-consciousness, is not capable of seeing anything other than social construction and determinism. This world view can only perpetuate itself, circling more and more in upon itself in its constraining views of determinism. In Smith's terms:

> Approaching disciplines in this way puts the accent not on the "nature" of the object as such, but on the aspects of agency inscribed within it. What blocks disciplinary self-reflection then is the untheorizability of the activation of its own objects—their *fabrication* as determinations of experience—and this is precisely why, contrary to certain hysterically defensive views, interdisciplinary research has always been immanent to the disciplines. Every discipline is obliged to turn to its "others" to resolve its self doubt. (xviii)

That is to say, I think, either that cultural theory in rhetoric establishes its identity only by devaluing its other—in this case the presumed naive and ideologically retrograde vision of self and resistance in expressivism—or that cultural theory in rhetoric will have to look beyond itself for an answer to its own self-contradiction: the problem is agency, but agency is impossible in a determined system. Specifically, Freisinger argues, resistance becomes possible only through expressivist strategies. The problem is disciplinary definition, and an imperative to violate those boundaries. Postmodern theory depends on resistance to alter the determined system it describes and decries, and expressivism depends on a social constructive view to discover and activate the self it theorizes.

Back to bell hooks. *Teaching to Transgress* centers itself squarely on the problem of dichotomizing theory and practice. A student of Paulo Freire, she views praxis, the convergence of theory and practice, as the primary concern of liberatory pedagogy. She recalls her childhood, a time of alienation in which she felt the oppressive power of her family shaping her into a proper black girl-child. It was then that she developed a habit of theorizing. She calls that experience her introduction to critical thinking:

> Living a childhood without a sense of home, I found a place of sanctuary in "theorizing," in making sense out of what was happening. I found a place where I could imagine possible futures, a place where life could be lived differently. This "lived" experience of critical thinking, of reflection and analysis, because [sic] a place where I worked at explaining the hurt and making it go away. Fundamentally, I learned from this experience that theory could be a healing place. (61)

Praxis is the means and locus for building critical consciousness. With Elbow she shares a goal; the aim of her pedagogy is to create a place for voices. The voices in the classroom include the voice of the teacher as well as those of the students. Her expectations of the teacher are extremely high: to bring students to voice, teachers must have and understand voice. And voice is related to self-actualization. She calls this kind of teaching, "engaged pedagogy": "Progressive, holistic education, 'engaged pedagogy,' is more demanding than conventional critical or feminist pedagogy. For unlike these two teaching practices, it emphasizes well-being. That means that teachers must be actively committed to a process of self-actualization that promotes their own well-being if they are to teach in a manner that empowers students" (15).

Engaged pedagogy involves a holism that repairs the habitual dichotomizing of conventional thinking, repairing splits between body and mind, intellect and spirit, teaching and learning, and theory and practice. hooks describes a set of dialectical relationships that echoes Elbow's theme in "A Method for Teaching Writing": "Any classroom that employs a holistic model of learning will also be a place where teachers grow, and are empowered by the process. That empowerment cannot happen if we refuse to be vulnerable while encouraging students to take risks" (21). Engaged pedagogy, holistic teaching, these are the expressivist project.

Bibliography

Belenky, Mary, Blythe Clinchy, Nancy Goldberger, and Jill Tarule. *Women's Ways of Knowing: The Development of Self, Voice, and Mind*. New York: Basic Books, 1986.

Berlin, James A. "Contemporary Composition: The Major Pedagogical Theories." *College English* 44 (1982): 765–77.

———. *Rhetoric and Reality: Writing Instruction in American Colleges, 1900–1985*. Carbondale: Southern Illinois UP, 1987.

———. *Writing Instruction in Nineteenth-Century American Colleges*. Carbondale: Southern Illinois UP, 1984.

Britton, James. *Language and Learning*. New York: Penguin, 1970.

———. *Language and Learning*. 2nd ed. Portsmouth, NH: Boynton/Cook, 1993.

Britton, James, et al. *The Development of Writing Abilities 11–18*. London: Macmillan, 1975.

Brooke, Robert. *Writing and the Sense of Self: Identity Negotiation in Writing Workshops*. Urbana, IL: NCTE, 1991.

Bruner, Jerome. *Actual Minds, Possible Worlds*. Cambridge, MA: Harvard UP, 1986.

———. *A Theory of Instruction*. Cambridge, MA: Belknap Press, 1963.

Burnham, Christopher C. "Expressive Rhetoric: A Source Study." *Defining the New Rhetorics*. Ed. Theresa Enos and Stuart C. Brown. Newbury Park, CA: Sage, 1993. 154–70.

Cherry, Roger. "Ethos Versus Persona: Self-Representation in Written Discourse." *Written Communication* 5 (1988): 251–76.

Coles, William E., Jr. *The Plural I: The Teaching of Writing*. New York: Holt, 1978.

Covino, William. *Magic, Rhetoric, and Literacy*. Albany: SUNY P, 1994.

Crowley, Sharon. *The Methodical Memory: Invention in Current-traditional Rhetoric*. Carbondale: Southern Illinois UP, 1990.

Elbow, Peter. "Being an Academic vs. Being a Writer." *College English* 46 (1995): 72–83.

———. "Introduction: About Voice in Writing." *Landmark Essays on Voice and Writing*. Ed. Peter Elbow. Davis, CA: Hermagoras Press, 1994. xi–xlvii.

———. "A Method for Teaching Writing." *College English* 30 (1968): 115–25.

———. "Toward a Phenomenology of Freewriting." *Nothing Begins with N: New Investigations of Freewriting*. Ed. Pat Belanoff, Peter Elbow, and Sheryl I. Fontaine. Carbondale: Southern Illinois UP, 1991. 189–213.

———. *Writing Without Teachers*. New York: Oxford UP, 1973.

———. *Writing with Power*. New York: Oxford UP, 1981.

Elbow, Peter, and Pat Belanoff. *A Community of Writers: A Workshop Course in Writing*. New York: Random House, 1989.

———. *Sharing and Responding*. New York: Random House, 1989.

Faigley, Lester. *Fragments of Rationality: Postmodernity and the Subject of Composition*. Pittsburgh: U of Pittsburgh P, 1992.

Fishman, Stephen M., and Lucille P. McCarthy. "Is Expressivism Dead? Reconsidering Its Romantic Roots and Its Relation to Social Constructionism." *College English* 54 (1992): 647–61.

———. "Community in the Expressivist Classroom: Juggling Liberal and Communitarian Visions." *College English* 57 (1995): 62–81.

———. *John Dewey and the Challenge of Classroom Practice*. New York: Teachers College, 1998.

———. "Teaching for Student Change: A Deweyan Alternative to Radical Pedagogy." *College Composition and Communication* 47 (1996): 342–66.

Flower, Linda. *The Construction of Negotiated Meaning: A Social-Cognitive Theory of Writing*. Carbondale: Southern Illinois UP, 1994.

Freisinger, Randall R. "Voicing the Self: Toward a Pedagogy of Resistance in a Post-modern Age." *Landmark Essays on Voice and Writing.* Ed. Peter Elbow. Davis, CA: Hermagoras, 1994. 187–211.

Gannett, Cinthia. *Gender and the Journal: Diaries and Academic Discourse.* Albany: SUNY P, 1992.

Gradin, Sherrie L. *Romancing Rhetorics: Social Expressivist Perspectives on the Teaching of Writing.* Portsmouth, NH: Boynton/Cook, 1995.

Harris, Jeanette. *Expressive Discourse.* Dallas: Southern Methodist UP, 1990.

Haswell, Richard. "Student Self-Evaluation and Developmental Change." *Student Self-Evaluation: Fostering Reflective Learning.* Ed. Jean MacGregor. New Directions in Teaching and Learning. No. 56. San Francisco: Jossey-Bass, 1993.

Hill, Carolyn Erikson. *Writing from the Margins: Power and Pedagogy for Teachers of Composition.* New York: Oxford UP, 1990.

hooks, bell. *Sisters of the Yam: Black Women and Self-Recovery.* Boston: South End, 1993.

———. *Teaching to Transgress: Education as the Practice of Freedom.* New York: Routledge, 1994.

Kinneavy, James. *A Theory of Discourse.* Englewood Cliffs, NJ: Prentice-Hall, 1971.

Macrorie, Ken. *A Vulnerable Teacher.* Rochelle Park, NJ: Hayden, 1974.

———. *Telling Writing.* Rochelle Park, NJ: Hayden, 1970.

———. *Uptaught.* New York: Hayden, 1970.

Merton, Thomas. "Learning to Live." *Thomas Merton: Spiritual Master.* Ed. Lawrence Cunningham. New York: Paulist, 1992.

Murray, Donald. "Writing as Process: How Writing Finds Its Own Meaning." *Eight Approaches to Teaching Composition.* Ed. Timothy R. Donovan and Ben McClelland. Urbana, IL: NCTE, 1980. 3–20.

———. *A Writer Teaches Writing.* New York: Holt, 1968.

Newkirk, Thomas. *The Performance of Self in Student Writing.* Portsmouth, NH: Boynton/Cook, 1997.

O'Donnell, Thomas. "Politics and Ordinary Language: A Defense of Expressivist Rhetorics." *College English* 58 (1996): 423–39.

Progoff, Ira. *At a Journal Workshop.* New York: Dialogue House, 1975.

Shor, Ira. *Critical Teaching and Everyday Life.* Chicago: U of Chicago P, 1980.

Smith, Paul. *Discerning the Subject.* Minneapolis: U of Minnesota P, 1988.

Trimbur, John. "Consensus and Difference in Collaborative Learning." *College English* 51 (1989): 602–16.

Vygotsky, L. S. *Thought in Language.* Trans. Hoffman and Vahn. Cambridge, MA: MIT, 1962.

Willinsky, John. *The New Literacy: Redefining Reading and Writing in the Schools.* New York: Routledge, 1990.

Rhetorical Pedagogy

WILLIAM A. COVINO

Rules for Successful Paragraphs:

1. Before writing your paragraph, make an outline. List the details you intend to include.
2. Start with a topic sentence.
3. Have an orderly plan.
4. Use transitional words to help your reader follow your plan.
5. Develop your paragraph by means of examples, facts, statistics, reasons, or incidents supporting the topic sentence.
6. Think up a strong clincher sentence. (McKowen 240)

This set of "rules" appears in Clark McKowen's *Image: Reflections on Language*, a popular 1973 composition textbook that was part of the expressivist movement of the 1960s and 1970s. The rules are published in the midst of a continuous montage of language games, koans, epigrams, and psychedelic pictures that stress students' capacities for imagination and self-expression. Thus situated, they seem awfully stiff and spare, and are intended to suggest that rules for writing are antiexpressivist, that they pale in comparison with the varieties of language play that can develop the imagination, and that a prescriptive approach to writing is dull and unnatural (and, to boot, the source of impossible advice). The expressivist movement produced influential textbooks such as Ken Macrorie's *Telling Writing* (1970) and Peter Elbow's *Writing Without Teachers* (1973), along with a number of well-received approaches like *Image*. Emphasis on self-expression complemented approaches to composition derived from Chomskyan linguistics, such as John Mellon's *Transformational Sentence Combining* (1969) and Frank O'Hare's *Sentence Combining: Improving Student Writing Without Formal Grammar Instruction* (1973), which recognized an inherent ability in students to develop syntactic fluency in the absence of extrinsic rules.

The emergence of antirules pedagogies also coincided with—and to some extent provoked—a "return" to *rhetoric*, specifically, the history of rhetoric. This return to rhetoric had begun in the 1930s, when proponents of New Criticism (in particular, I. A. Richards, discussed below) began to connect the importance of ambiguity as a characteristic of language to a reconsideration of rhetoric as the explanation of ambiguity. The "return" developed in other directions during the postwar era, when considerations of rhetoric as a mode of making ethical and moral judgments provoked discussions of its philosophical character (see, for instance, Weaver, discussed below). The relevance of rhetoric and the history of rhetoric to the teaching of writing emerged most forcibly in the 1960s, for two reasons: (1) In general, increased professional attention to the teaching of writing prompted the legitimation of composition as a field, and reestablishing its history was part of that legitimation. (2) Some saw the increased attention to self-expressive writing as an unfortunate constraint upon the range of discourses available to student writers. Reestablishing that range of discourses meant reviewing a rich rhetorical tradition, as James Kinneavy proposes in *A Theory of Discourse* (1971): "It is the thesis of this work that the field of composition—or discourse as it will presently be termed—is a rich and fertile discipline with a worthy past which should be consulted before being consigned to oblivion" (2). Kinneavy presents what has become an often-adapted "communication triangle," which stands for the relationship that he argues attends all language use, among an encoder (writer), decoder (audience), and a reality (context). In this connection, we might say that a rhetorical pedagogy consists in encouraging writing that is not restricted to self-expression or the acontextual generation of syntactic structures or the formulaic obedience to rules, but instead keeps in view the skills and contingencies that attend a variety of situations and circumstances. We learn about this sort of writing, Kinneavy argues (along with contemporaries who include Edward P. J. Corbett, W. Ross Winterowd, James J. Murphy, and Winifred Bryan Horner) both by studying the history of rhetoric and by maintaining a working sense of rhetoric that allows for varied applications.

Significantly, calls for renewed attention to self-expression found support in the stress on rhetorical invention voiced in a number of historicized approaches to pedagogy, especially those that inveighed against "current-traditional" rhetoric that prescribed "plain style" (Covino, *The Art of Wondering*; Crowley, *The Methodical Memory*; Freedman and Pringle, *Reinventing the Rhetorical Tradition*; Knoblauch and Brannon, *Rhetorical Traditions and the Teaching of Writing*; Lauer, "Issues in Rhetorical Invention"; Winterowd, *Rhetoric: A Synthesis*; Young, "Concepts of Art and the Teaching of Writing"). The renewed interest in rhetoric has outlasted interest in unfettered (and by some lights, unlettered) self-expression: from the 1970s forward, increasing interest in the history of rhetoric has focused in large part on how to adapt the best of the past to present classroom situations and challenges. Most recently, scholarship aimed at recognizing greater historical and cultural diversity has affected the scope of rhetorical pedagogy. To overgeneralize a bit, we might say that the 1970s and 1980s defined rhetorical pedagogy with reference to a classroom that was self-consciously Aristotelian or Ciceronian or otherwise reverent to a canonical history, while the 1990s further complicated historical rhetoric and rhetorical pedagogy by pointing up the mismatch between a Western pedagogical tradition aimed at educating privileged males, and the promise and challenges of the multicultural classroom. This later movement is evident in the explicit connection of rhetoric to cultural studies at the 1994 conference of the Rhetoric Society of America (with selected proceedings published in Reynolds, ed., *Rhetoric, Cultural Studies, and Literacy*), and in books that include Andrea Lunsford, ed., *Reclaiming Rhetorica* (1995); Jasper Neel, *Aristotle's Voice* (1994); Cheryl Glenn, *Rhetoric Retold* (1997); and George Kennedy, *Comparative Rhetoric* (1998).

A number of collections, textbooks, and monographs argue for the relevance of traditional practice to twentieth-century pedagogical issues, and are usefully read alongside comprehensive introductions to the history of rhetoric. James J. Murphy's *The Rhetorical Tradition and Modern Writing* (1982) begins with an essay by Murphy that establishes considerable urgency; in "Rhetorical History as a Guide to the Salvation of American Reading and Writing: A Plea for Curricular Change," Murphy proposes that "those who do not study the history of rhetoric will be the victims of it" (11). The collection continues with essays on rhetorical theory and practice in classical Greece and Rome and in eighteenth- and nineteenth-century England and America, all with a view to culling advice that will benefit current teachers of writing. Murphy's 1990 collection, *A Short History of Writing Instruction from Ancient Greece to Twentieth-Century America*, is especially valuable for its brief introductions to the nature of writing instruction in specific historical periods, and is complemented by the 1995 *Festschrift* in honor of Murphy, *Rhetoric and Pedagogy: Its History, Philosophy, and Practice*, edited by Winifred Bryan Horner and Michael Leff. Robert Connors, Lisa Ede, and Lunsford, in *Essays on Classical Rhetoric and Modern Discourse* (1984), collect reexaminations of classical theory and practice that help explicate "the revival of rhetoric in America." Gary Tate and Edward P. J. Corbett's *The Writing Teacher's Sourcebook* (1988) offers a section on "Our History" that includes three important and illuminating essays on the recent history of composition in English departments, by William Riley Parker, Donald Stewart, and Robert J. Connors; the history of English teaching—understood as a movement from rhetorical study to literary study—is also surveyed by Robert Scholes in *The Rise and Fall of English* (1998).

Textbooks that survey the history of rhetoric and its relevance to the teaching of writing include Corbett's *Classical Rhetoric for the Modern Student* (1965; revised with Connors, 1998), Horner's *Rhetoric in the Classical Tradition* (1988), and Crowley's *Ancient Rhetorics for Contemporary Students* (1994). Monographs that offer an overarching construction of the history of rhetorical pedagogy include my *Art of Wondering*; Knoblauch and Brannon, *Rhetorical Traditions*; Susan Miller, *Rescuing the Subject: A Critical Introduction to Rhetoric and the Writer* (1989); and Winterowd, *A Teacher's Introduction to Composition in the Rhetorical Tradition* (1994).

Kennedy's *Classical Rhetoric in Its Christian and Secular Traditions* (1980) remains a standard introduction to classical rhetoric, and is accompanied by Kennedy's *Comparative Rhetoric* (1998), which discusses non-Western and Native American contributions to rhetoric. Patricia Bizzell and Bruce Herzberg's

The Rhetorical Tradition: Readings from Classical Times to the Present (1990) includes substantial excerpts from a full range of canonical primary texts, each reading accompanied by a well-documented introduction. James L. Golden and colleagues, in *The Rhetoric of Western Thought* (1976), present a comprehensive undergraduate survey of classical and contemporary rhetorical theory. My coauthored book with David A. Jolliffe, *Rhetoric: Concepts, Definitions, Boundaries* (1995), includes a "Glossary of Major Concepts, Historical Periods, and Rhetors," and a collection of readings that represent "Perspectives on the History of Rhetoric."

Rhetorical pedagogy, as I will survey it here, consists in both more deliberate attention to the history of rhetoric and the acknowledgment that "rhetoric" names a complex set of factors that affect the production and interpretation of texts. Attention to the history of rhetoric reveals that rhetoric is a concept that expands and contracts, sometimes defined as a global art, other times defined as formulaic attention to correctness and style. Developing a full sense of rhetorical pedagogy must include a historical survey of rhetorical theory and practice, for this is the foundation for the adaptations and divergences that might define rhetorical pedagogy today. The development of historically based rhetorical pedagogies has focused primarily on classical Greece and Rome, and on the establishment of "current-traditional" rhetoric in the eighteenth and nineteenth centuries. Interest in these periods reflects a prevailing construction of the history of rhetoric that (1) privileges invention and contingency, locating their appreciation in classical philosophical rhetoric, and (2) disapproves the formulary inculcation of "plain style" associated with Enlightenment rhetorics, so that the investigation and explication of these rhetorics becomes a way of verifying their shortcomings.

↭ CLASSICAL RHETORIC

The role of the fourth- and fifth-century-BCE sophists in the history of rhetoric, and the value of the pedagogy they enfranchise, has been an emergent concern over the last ten years. As Edward Schiappa explains in Teresa Enos' *Encyclopedia of Rhetoric and Composition: Communication from Ancient Times to the Information Age* (1996),

> A scholar interested in contemporary appropriation for the purposes of describing neosophistic theory, criticism, or pedagogy might try to answer questions such as these: Who are today's "sophists"? Can we devise a postmodern neosophistic theory of rhetoric? Which aspects of Gorgias' composition style can inform contemporary composition studies? Can Protagoras' vision of education serve as a useful model today? (685–86)

Crowley's *Ancient Rhetorics for Contemporary Students*, Susan Jarratt's *Rereading the Sophists: Classical Rhetoric Refigured* (1991), and Neel's *Plato, Derrida, and Writing* (1988) have been particularly concerned with what sorts of "sophistry" should best inform pedagogy, and all have stressed—in very different ways—the sophistic view that human knowledge is both limited and plastic, and have insisted that writing should always approach "truth" as a contingent phenomenon. Crowley's is an undergraduate composition textbook, notable as a substantial and successful attempt to adapt classical rhetoric—including sophistic precepts and practices—to contemporary pedagogy. Current studies of the sophists all have recourse to standard texts: Rosamond Kent Sprague's *The Older Sophists* (1972), which collects many of the extant primary texts by sophists who include Protagoras, Gorgias, Prodicus, Thrasymachus, Hippias, and Antiphon; W. K. C. Guthrie's *The Sophists* (1971); and G. B. Kerferd's *The Sophistic Movement* (1981).

In "The *Phaedrus* Idyll as Ethical Play" (1982), Virginia Steinhoff writes a clever summary of the sort of pedagogy that Plato's Socrates might recommend:

1. Don't profess what you know (or remember) too readily. Make the students ask for it, and then surprise them by appearing not to comply.
2. Profess less knowledge and sophistication than your students. Go barefoot whenever possible and try to get them to make fun of you. Enjoy all this.
3. Use a lot of questionable pseudo-historical anecdotes to assert important points. When pressed for interpretation, assume a pious and literal persona.
4. Bewilder your students with metaphors and images so that you can avoid lengthy explications of crucial propositions, but be sure to tune these complicated and unstable discourses to the complicated and unstable souls of your students. One student at a time is enough.
5. Once you have achieved a rapport with a student, keep the student with you until the play of ideas and language satisfies you with its formal and ideological consonances and then break off instruction.
6. Make fun of yourself, and go ahead, be ironic: students should go away with so many questions about you, as well as about your discourse, that you risk scandal and oblivion in the long run. But know you were right to anticipate this and incorporate it into your teaching. Some students will long remember you.
7. Put nothing in writing, but talk so well that one of your students is driven to the forcing-area, impelled to memorialize or utilize you for purposes beyond your own prophetic vision. And certainly don't write textbooks. (40)

The Socrates in Plato's *Gorgias* and *Phaedrus* has most often been the source of Platonic approaches to rhetoric and pedagogy. Steinhoff here provides some irreverence in the face of traditional applications of Plato to rhetorical pedagogy, such as the classic 1925 essay by Everett Lee Hunt that focuses on this famous definition of ideal rhetoric, by Plato's Socrates:

Socrates: A man must first know the truth about every single subject on which he speaks or writes. He must be able to define each in terms of a universal class that stands by itself. When he has successively defined his subjects according to their specific classes, he must know how to continue the division until he reaches the point of indivisibility. He must make the same sort of distinction with reference to the nature of the soul. He must then discover the kind of speech that matches each type of nature. When that is accomplished, he must arrange and adorn each speech in such a way as to present complicated and unstable souls with complex speeches, speeches exactly attuned to every changing mood of the complicated soul—while the simple soul must be presented with simple speech. Not until a man acquires this capacity will it be possible to produce a speech in a scientific way, in so far as its nature permits such treatment, either for the purposes of instruction or of persuasion. (*Phaedrus* 277)

Hunt draws formulary advice from this passage, noting that the speaker must know the truth, clearly define the terms of his argument, impose strict and precise order, fit the language of the speech to the audience, and maintain a moral purpose.

It is generally supposed that Plato's Socrates suspects rhetoric—especially as it is practiced by the sophists—as a dangerous deferral of the pursuit of ideal truth. In line with this view, Platonic rhetoric has been identified with ethical idealism, especially in Richard Weaver's *The Ethics of Rhetoric* (1953), in which Weaver discusses the *Phaedrus* as an illustration of the differences between "base rhetoric" and "noble rhetoric," associating the former with writing that values persuasion over the search for truth, and the latter with moral reason. Donald Stewart's 1984 "The Continuing Relevance of Plato's *Phaedrus*" revisits the importance of the pursuit of truth in the writing classroom. More recent work on Platonic pedagogy stresses the irony and indeterminacy of the dialogues, and the ambiguity of Plato as author: Discussions of Plato in my *Art of Wondering*; in Neel's *Plato*; and in C. Jan Swearingen, *Rhetoric and Irony: Western Literacy and Western Lies*, suggest that Platonic and Sophistic pedagogies are not inimical. I argue that the *Phaedrus* defines writing as play with ambiguity, Neel forms an uneasy alliance between Platonic philosophy and Derridean deconstruction, and Swearingen proposes that Platonic irony "undermines alternate criteria of truth, knowledge, and meaning" (93).

Aristotle's *On Rhetoric* has provoked numerous pedagogical applications in this century; as Crowley points out,

Aristotle's text on rhetoric has received more scholarly attention during the twentieth century than it did during all the rest of its long history (some 2300 years). Probably for this reason, the Aristotelian theory of rhetoric is usually what is meant when a modern scholar or teacher refers to classical rhetoric. (*Ancient Rhetorics* 24)

We might speculate that *On Rhetoric* appeals to teachers of writing both because Aristotle posits rhetorical truth as contingent, thereby appealing to the relativistic bent of our time, and because his ostensible division of the rhetorical "triangle" into *ethos* (the character of the speaker/writer), *pathos* (the character of the audience), and *logos* (the logical reasoning of the speech) allows for a conveniently schematic approach. Further, *On Rhetoric* is mainly devoted to rhetorical invention, the ability to "see the available means of persuasion," and thus suits the turn away from product-oriented pedagogy to process-oriented pedagogy. George Kennedy's translation of *On Rhetoric* provides substantial explication and clarification of Aristotle's work, and may be consulted alongside William M. A. Grimaldi's *Studies in the Philosophy of Aristotle's Rhetoric*. Neel's *Aristotle's Voice* addresses Aristotle's influence on twentieth-century pedagogy, and the relationship of an Aristotelian model of rhetoric and writing to critical thinking and political change. Janet Atwill's *Rhetoric Reclaimed: Aristotle and the Liberal Arts Tradition* investigates the ways in which Aristotle's taxonomy of knowledge has been adapted over two millennia.

There has been considerable effort to define Aristotle's enthymeme, which names a kind of "format" for rhetorical proof. Among textbooks, Corbett's *Classical Rhetoric* defines the enthymeme as "an abbreviated syllogism—that is, an argumentative statement that contains a conclusion and one of the premises, the other premise being implied" (73). Crowley's *Ancient Rhetorics* stresses that "enthymematic premises represent common-sense beliefs about the way people behave" (156), and my *Elements of Persuasion* calls the enthymeme "a claim that invites the audience to supply missing premises" (160). Lloyd Bitzer, Carol Poster, James C. Raymond, and Lawrence D. Green provide modern revaluations of the enthymeme, all seeking to complicate a traditional tendency to worry about how many premises an enthymeme may contain, and to study the enthymeme as a complex philosophical concept rather than a ready practical structure. As Green concludes,

> The process starts not with premises but with conclusions, and we work backwards; first, we seize upon what we want another person to think or do, and then we seek reasons sufficient for that goal. There may be a syllogism inherent in some enthymemes, but this is hardly the entire story. ("Aristotle's Enthymeme" 41)

To the extent that Roman rhetorical pedagogy is defined by *Rhetorica Ad Herennium*, a highly schematized codification of precepts and principles that was the basis for textbooks and classroom practice through the Renaissance, it has come to represent both the elaboration of a full rhetorical system and the ossification of structures, rules, and principles. As Murphy tells us in *A Short History*, Roman teaching methods, initially indicated in the first-century-BCE *Ad Herennium* and ratified in Quintilian's first-century-CE *Institutio Oratoria*, fall into five categories:

1. Precept: "a set of rules that provide a definite method and system of speaking." Grammar as precept deals with "the art of speaking correctly, and the interpretation of the poets. . . ."
2. Imitation: the use of models to learn how others have used language. . . .

3. Composition exercises (*progymnasmata* or *praeexercitamenta*): a graded series of exercises in writing and speaking themes. . . .
   a. Retelling a fable.
   b. Retelling an episode from a poet or historian.
   c. *Chreia*, or amplification of a moral theme.
   d. Amplification of an aphorism (*sententia*) or proverb.
   e. Refutation or confirmation of an allegation.
   f. Commonplace, or confirmation of a thing admitted.
   g. Encomium, or eulogy (or dispraise) of a person or thing.
   h. Comparison of things or persons.
   i. Impersonation (*prosopopeia*), or speaking or writing in the character of a given person.
   j. Description (*ecphrasis*), or vivid presentation of details.
   k. Thesis, or argument for/against an answer to a general question (*quaestio infinita*) not involving individuals.
   l. Laws, or arguments for or against a law.
4. Declamation (*declamatio*), or fictitious speeches, in two types:
   a. *Suasoria*, or deliberative (political) speech arguing that an action be taken or not taken.
   b. *Controversia*, or forensic (legal) speech prosecuting or defending a fictitious or historical person in a law case.
5. Sequencing, or the systematic ordering or classroom activities. . . . (75–76)

Descriptions such as Murphy's suggest that Roman rhetorical pedagogy, though it may seem all too schematized from our postmodern perspective, presents a rich, complex, and comprehensive system of discourse that should not be adapted or dismissed ignorantly. Marjorie Woods makes a similar case for medieval rhetorical pedagogy, when she argues that passing on a textual heritage was and should be a central pedagogical goal, one in which medieval teachers were invested (Murphy, *Short History* 77–94).

✎ CURRENT-TRADITIONAL RHETORIC

My own view of the fortunes of rhetorical pedagogy informs, and by some lights, corrupts this essay. Committed to a model of the composing imagination that includes rhetorical invention as a potentially radical associative process, I have, along with others, seized upon the rise of science as correspondent to the disappearance of rhetorical pedagogy, arguing for "the failure of objectivity, Cartesian rationality, and detachment to account for our complicated perception of a world in flux where matters are never settled" (*Art* 121). That fluctuant world is acknowledged in one way or another through the Renaissance, in theories of rhetoric that—even at their most formulary—associate eloquence with broad knowledge and comprehensive practice in surveying and structuring the "available means of persuasion." The beginning of a decisive shift to a more "objective" rhetoric and to conceptions of rhetoric and composition that eliminated invention, has been traced to the sixteenth-century works of Peter Ramus. As Walter Ong establishes in *Ramus, Method, and the Decay of Dialogue* (1958), and as Murphy summarizes with particular reference to pedagogy in his introduction to Ramus' *Arguments in Rhetoric Against Quintilian* (1–76), Ramus successfully challenged the longstanding identification of rhetoric with five canons—invention, arrangement, style, memory, and delivery—leaving only style and delivery as proper to rhetoric, and thus enfranchising a pedagogy focused on clarity and correctness judged apart from intention, audience, and purpose. The idea that language is transparent and capable of expressing truth, and the insistence that its use should be governed by rules of logic, were advanced further in Descartes' 1650 *Discourse on Method*, and began to exert decided Anglo-American influence on the teaching of rhetoric with the chartering in 1662 of the Royal Society of London, and the publication in 1667 of Thomas Sprat's *History of the Royal Society*, which called for a return to plain expression: "a close, naked, natural way of speaking; positive expressions; clear senses; a native easiness; bringing all things as near the Mathematical plainness as they can."

What happened to rhetorical pedagogy in the eighteenth and nineteenth centuries especially concerns the development of "current-traditional rhetoric," which is traced by Albert Kitzhaber (*Rhetoric in American Colleges, 1850–1900*), Crowley (*Methodical Memory*), and James Berlin (*Writing Instruction in Nineteenth-Century American Colleges*) to the influence of Lockean empiricism, the British rhetorics of Hugh Blair, George Campbell, and Richard Whately, and the American rhetorics of Adams Sherman Hill, Barrett Wendell, and John Franklin Genung. Given the identification of rhetoric with formal rather than contextual properties, current-traditional rhetoric maintains unity, coherence, and correctness as primary virtues, and generates textbooks that emphasize four modes of discourse—narration, description, exposition, and argumentation—as the standard venues for writers (Connors, "The Rise and Fall of the Modes of Discourse"). Nan Johnson counters the position that rhetoric suffered in the nineteenth century by explaining that "throughout the century, rhetoricians promoted the notion that rhetorical skill enables the individual to participate in and contribute to society and to engage in that communication which ensures an informed populace" (*Nineteenth-Century Rhetoric in North America* 252); for Johnson, then, characterizations of current-traditional rhetoric as reductive should be corrected by full attention to the complex aims and purposes of rhetorical education.

❧ TWENTIETH-CENTURY RHETORIC

In this century, the beginnings of a reaction against current-traditional rhetoric might be traced to I. A. Richards' *The Philosophy of Rhetoric*, which associates representative works such as Lord Kames' 1762 *Elements of Criticism* with the undue regulation of language and meaning, and proposes that rhetoric should be "the study of misunderstanding and its remedies," which includes the interpretation of meaning in context. One of the most ardent translators of Richards' views to composition pedagogy has been Ann E. Berthoff, who stresses the nature of the composing intellect as a "speculative instrument," especially in her edition of *Richards on Rhetoric: Selected Essays of I. A. Richards* (1991). Winterowd discusses Richards as one of "Two Modern Masters" in *Teacher's Introduction to Composition.*

Winterowd's other modern master is Kenneth Burke. I would agree with Winterowd that "this disturbing, different, perhaps dangerous thinker has come to be regarded not only as important, but as essential to literary and rhetorical theory" (70). Burke's most influential and important contributions to rhetorical pedagogy are his *Lexicon Rhetoricae* from the *Counter-Statement* (1931); *A Grammar of Motives* (1945); and *A Rhetoric of Motives* (1950). He defines rhetoric as "the use of language as a symbolic means of inducing cooperation in beings that by nature respond to symbols" (43), thus revealing his essential and ongoing interest in the *associational* uses of language, for bringing together disparate or incongruous ideas, and for promoting the *identification* of different individuals and groups with one another. In the *Lexicon Rhetoricae* he addresses the formalism that characterized literary and rhetorical theory by offering a psychological rather than logical definition of form: form is "the arousal and fulfillment of desires," and must therefore vary with reference to the audience and context to which it appeals. Any form of writing is only "correct" with reference to the effect of its appeal, and that effect cannot be calculated determinately. To account for the ambiguity of any formal appeal, that is, for the range of meanings that it might entail, Burke develops his pentad of Act, Agent, Scene, Agency, and Purpose; as I explain to undergraduates in *Elements of Persuasion*:

> Kenneth Burke [in *A Grammar of Motives*] proposes that the ways in which different audiences categorize, or label, a given statement can vary widely. This depends on how the audience understands:
>
> 1. the Act being performed
> 2. the Scene in which it is taking place
> 3. the Agent, or originator of the Act
> 4. the Agency, or medium, through which the Act is delivered
> 5. the Purpose of the Act
>
> . . . The Act of a seven-year-old Agent yelling (Agency) "Yabba Dabba Do" in his second-grade classroom (Scene) might be labeled "disobedience" by the teacher and understood to have disruption as its Purpose. But the same statement, yelled in the playground during recess, might be labeled "happy exuberance." (27)

Burke's pentad defines the set of relationships he identifies with *dramatism*, which names the sets of relationships that inform all symbolic action. Enthusiasm for the adaptability of the pentad to the composition classroom has resulted in its use in a number of textbooks as a five-fold invention system akin to the journalistic Who-What-When-Where-How; this is often a severe simplification of Burke's rhetoric. A fuller pedagogical appreciation for his rhetoric involves locating what Burke calls "the strategic spots at which ambiguities arise" in our naming of things, and efforts to create "perspectives by incongruity" that promote new kinds of identification. Rhetorical invention, then, becomes the process of exploiting the *dialogical* relationship among ideas, attitudes, and beliefs. One textbook that illustrates dialogical invention extensively is my *Forms of Wondering* (1988); Irene Ward offers a comprehensive scholarly study of the pedagogical uses of dialogue in *Literacy, Ideology, and Dialogue: Towards a Dialogic Pedagogy* (1994).

Burke's pentad anticipates more recent attempts to construct broadly articulate models of rhetoric, which include the communication triangle I cited above, and the more elaborate model that Roman Jakobson advanced in 1970, summarized usefully by Winterowd in *Contemporary Rhetoric*:

> There is first an *addresser* (speaker/writer, discourser) and second an *addressee:*
> Third, the discourse has a *context*, or something referred to. The context is virtually synonymous with the term *referent*, as used by other theorists. Fourth, there is the *message* itself, and fifth, a *contact*, or "a physical channel and psychological connection between the addresser and the addressee, enabling both of them to enter and stay in communication." Sixth, there must be a *code* that is at least partially comprehensible to both addresser and addressee. (2–3)

Terry Eagleton, in *Literary Theory: An Introduction*, emphasizes the sociocultural dimensions of rhetoric, proposing that classical rhetoric, because it provided a model for the critical analysis and discussion of public issues, should be recalled today as we attempt to move beyond formalist and deconstructive models of critical writing: "[Rhetoric] saw speaking and writing not merely as textual objects, to be aesthetically contemplated or endlessly deconstructed, but as forms of *activity* inseparable from the wider social relations between writers and readers, orators and audiences, and as largely unintelligible outside the social purposes and conditions in which they were embedded" (206). This view activates a rhetorical pedagogy that gives social change a central role, maintaining an understanding of rhetoric that is implied in political approaches to teaching such as Paulo Freire's *Education for Critical Consciousness* and Ira Shor's *Critical Teaching and Everyday Life*.

Worry about both the radical politics and the moral relativism that began to attend conceptions of rhetoric and writing in the 1960s and 1970s informed what we now call the "good reasons" approach, whose most influential advocates were Wayne Booth, Chaim Perelman and Lucia Olbrechts-Tyteca, and Robert Pirsig. Booth's 1974 *Modern Dogma and the Rhetoric of Assent* defines rhetoric as "the whole art of discovering and sharing warrantable assertions." This definition puts shared values at the center of a rhetorical pedagogy, and confronts postmodern theory that calls into question the possibility of stabilizing a set of values without enacting cultural oppression. The relevance of postmodern critical theory to rhetorical theory and pedagogy is apparent in

Gary Olson and Irene Gale, eds., *(Inter)views: Cross-Disciplinary Perspectives on Rhetoric and Literacy,* and Olson, ed., *Philosophy, Rhetoric, Literary Criticism: (Inter)views,* collections of interviews in which theorists such as Jacques Derrida, Noam Chomsky, Paulo Freire, Mary Field Belenky, Stanley Fish, and Richard Rorty discuss both their experience as writers and the relevance of their work to rhetoric and composition.

The assertion by many of these theorists that reality is constructed by language has raised the question whether material reality is indeed subject to and changed by the ways in which we describe it. This has become an especially important issue in the rhetoric of science, in which Thomas Kuhn's conception of the "paradigm shift" and Paul Feyerabend's radical relativism initiated the 1970s debates about the materiality of facts and truth that continue in Alan Gross's *The Rhetoric of Science* (1990). Michael Bernard-Donals, through a reading of the twentieth-century philosophers that inform Mikhail Bakhtin's dialogical materialism, argues for a rhetorical pedagogy that (1) recognizes that material reality is ideologically and linguistically constructed and (2) asks questions about the relation of that construction to lived experience. Rhetoric, then, becomes a study of the mismatch between constructed and actual experience. The nature of material rhetoric was the theme of the 1997 Penn State Conference on Rhetoric and Composition, with proceedings edited by Jack Selzer and Crowley, and published as *Rhetorical Bodies.*

The idea that reality is "rhetorical" has brought into focus the problem of defining rhetoric itself. When we teach "rhetoric," what is it that we are teaching? One answer is, "everything." This global quality is implied by Aristotle's famous definition of rhetoric as the generation of "available means of persuasion," if we realize that, as I have said elsewhere, "persuasion can involve the complex interaction of premises, intentions, beliefs, assumptions, and experiences" (*Elements* 3). Further, if we agree that, as Burke proposes, *all* symbolic action has some suasive quality, rhetoric-as-persuasion extends to the whole "universe of discourse," and definitions such as Paolo Valesio's emerge: "I specify now that rhetoric is the functional organization of discourse, within its social and cultural context, in all its aspects. . . . In other words: rhetoric is *all* of language, in its realization as discourse" (7). Such encompassing views are mediated by more constrained propositions, such as in Bitzer's famous and influential "The Rhetorical Situation":

> Rhetoric is a mode of altering reality, not by the direct application of energy to objects, but by the creation of discourse which changes reality through the mediation of thought and action. The rhetor alters reality by bringing into existence a discourse of such a character that the audience, in thought and action, is so engaged that it becomes mediator of change. In this sense rhetoric is always persuasive. (4)

And then there is Kennedy's most recent definition of rhetoric as—contra Bitzer—the *energy* that attends communication (which is part of a larger argument that rhetoric is inherent in the natural world, and can be studied in crows as well as in orators):

> Rhetoric in the most general sense may perhaps be identified with the energy inherent in communication: the emotional energy that impels the speaker to speak, the physical energy expended in the utterance, the energy level coded in the message, and the energy experienced by the recipient in decoding the message. ("A Hoot in the Dark" 2)

Obviously, the definition of rhetoric is not going to be settled. Through its canonical history, rhetoric has been identified with persuasion, ornate style, empty and manipulative language, and plain speaking. As an alternative to limiting definitions, the argument that rhetoric is "everything" does not help us much in the development of a pedagogy, except to the extent that it helps to broaden the repertory of content and methods from which teachers of writing might draw. It is more helpful for us to take contentions over the nature of rhetoric, along with recognitions that meaning is interpretive rather than determinate, in order to posit rhetoric as (1) dynamic and (2) interested.

The dynamism of rhetoric is apparent in models that take into account the effect of context on meaning, and acknowledge that the interaction of author and reader always occurs in specific circumstances, and that those circumstances are constantly undergoing change. Such models include Kinneavy's communication triangle, Jakobson's transactional scheme, and Burke's pentad, which have their sources in classical conceptions that include Aristotelian interaction of *ethos, pathos,* and *logos.* To say that rhetoric is *interested* stresses the ways in which discourse indicates the motives and desires—the interests—of writers, audiences, and the institutions they represent.

Arguably, conceptions of rhetoric have excluded the interests of significant cultures and groups, while the mainstream tradition was developed through the modern period as a largely Anglocentric, male domain. Recent feminist challenges to this tradition include Lunsford, ed., *Reclaiming Rhetorica,* Krista Ratcliffe, *Anglo-American Feminist Challenges to the Rhetorical Traditions* (1996); and Cheryl Glenn, *Rhetoric Retold: Regendering the Tradition from Antiquity Through the Renaissance* (1997). New interest in women students and teachers is represented by Catherine Hobbs, ed., *Nineteenth-Century Women Learn To Write* (1995), and by Louise Phelps and Janet Emig, eds., *Feminine Principles and Women's Experience in American Composition and Rhetoric* (1995). Such scholarship presents alternative models of rhetoric that may diverge radically from convention, as with, for instance, Ratcliffe's presentation of Mary Daly's *Wickedary.* Belenky and colleagues', *Women's Ways of Knowing* (1986) complements historical approaches to masculinist strictures on effective rhetoric, and has significantly influenced pedagogical approaches to the teaching of writing.

Feminist revisions of the history and definitions of rhetoric are part of the larger cultural studies movement that began to influence rhetoric and the teaching of writing most decisively over the last ten years. As Berlin notes, "Cultural studies argues that the division between the cultivated poetic and the mundane rhetorical or popular is based on class, race, and gender bias and is the result of particular groups forwarding their own interests as universal values" (Enos, *Encyclopedia* 155; see also Berlin, *Rhetorics, Poetics, and Cultures: Refiguring English Studies* and Berlin and Vivion's *Cultural Studies in the English Classroom*). The conjunction of rhetoric, composition, and cultural studies is addressed in several essays in Patricia Harkin and John Schilb, eds., *Contending With Words: Composition and Rhetoric in a Postmodern Age* (1991), notably Bizzell's "Marxist Ideas in Composition Studies" (52–68), Harkin's "Postdisciplinary Politics of Lore" (124–37), and Schilb's "Cultural Studies, Postmodernism, and Composition" (173–88). The ways in which prevailing conceptions of rhetoric can enfranchise or disenfranchise different cultural groups gets attention from all of those interviewed in Olson and Lynn Worsham, eds., *Race, Rhetoric, and the Postcolonial* (1998); interviewees include Homi Bhaba, Gloria Anzaldua, Michael Eric Dyson, Ernesto Laclau, Chantal Mouffe, and Stuart Hall.

The relationship of rhetoric to literacy has become more fully addressed in recent years; as Covino and Jolliffe note in *Rhetoric,*

> *Literacy* is a term that, like *rhetoric,* has been defined in a number of ways. Apart from any particular definition, literacy refers to ways in which people use language to communicate and to understanding their world, and in this respect the kinship of literacy and rhetoric is apparent. William Covino has recently called rhetoric "the performance of literacy," stressing that any prevailing definition of literacy determines what sorts of rhetorical performances are deemed appropriate and allowable. In other words, literacy implies rhetoric. (664)

Attention to cultural literacies and the rhetorics they imply is especially evident in the work of Shirley Brice Heath, whose 1983 *Ways with Words: Language, Life, and Work in Communities and Classrooms* has become a classic ethnographic study; Beverly Moss, whose 1994 *Literacy Across Communities* presents a collection of essays that represent a range of literacies and rhetorics of color that inform American cities; and Jacqueline Jones Royster, whose 1997 edition of *Southern Horrors and Other Writings: The Anti-Lynching Campaign of Ida B. Wells* offers an important addition to the history of rhetoric and the history of cultural literacy.

Rhetorical pedagogy has perhaps arrived at a point when the era of "Rules for Successful Paragraphs" seems a curiosity, or more accurately, an interruption in a history that has often associated rhetorical skill with a shifting complex of aims, audiences, and versions of truth. As the century turns, we have returned from the current-traditional compression of rhetoric to an expansive sense of its scope and a more fully inclusive and international appreciation for the range of backgrounds, needs, and desires that inform the teaching of reading and writing. The question, now as always it seems, is whether a rich conception of rhetorical pedagogy can be sustained in academic and institutional contexts that continue to value formulaic models of writing and learning.

Bibliography

Aristotle. *On Rhetoric*. Trans. George A. Kennedy. New York: Oxford UP, 1991.

Atwill, Janet. *Rhetoric Reclaimed: Aristotle and the Liberal Arts Tradition*. Ithaca, NY: Cornell UP, 1998.

Belenky, Mary Field, Blythe McVicker Clinchy, Nancy Rule Goldberger, and Jill Mattuck Tarule. *Women's Ways of Knowing: The Development of Self, Voice, and Mind*. New York: Basic, 1986.

Berlin, James A. *Rhetorics, Poetics, and Cultures: Refiguring College English Studies*. Urbana, IL: NCTE, 1996.

———. *Writing Instruction in Nineteenth-Century American Colleges*. Carbondale: Southern Illinois UP, 1984.

Berlin, James A., and Michael J. Vivion. *Cultural Studies in the English Classroom*. Portsmouth, NH: Boynton/Cook, 1992.

Bernard-Donals, Michael. *Mikhail Bakhtin: Between Phenomenology and Marxism*. Cambridge, MA: Cambridge UP, 1994.

Berthoff, Ann E. *Richards on Rhetoric: Selected Essays of I. A. Richards, 1929–1974*. New York: Oxford UP, 1991.

Bitzer, Lloyd. "Aristotle's Enthymeme Revisited." *Quarterly Journal of Speech* 45 (1959): 399–408.

———. "The Rhetorical Situation." *Philosophy and Rhetoric* 1.1 (1968): 1–14.

Bizzell, Patricia, and Bruce Herzberg. *The Rhetorical Tradition: Readings from Classical Times to the Present*. Boston: Bedford Books, 1990.

Booth, Wayne C. *Modern Dogma and the Rhetoric of Assent*. Chicago: U of Chicago P, 1974.

Burke, Kenneth. *Counter-Statement*. 1931. 2nd ed. 1953. Berkeley: U of California P, 1968.

———. *A Grammar of Motives*. 1945. Berkeley: U of California P, 1969.

———. *A Rhetoric of Motives*. 1950. Berkeley: U of California P, 1969.

Connors, Robert J. "The Rise and Fall of the Modes of Discourse." *College Composition and Communication* 32 (1981): 444–55.

Connors, Robert J., Lisa Ede, and Andrea Lunsford. *Essays on Classical Rhetoric and Modern Discourse*. Carbondale: Southern Illinois UP, 1984.

Corbett, Edward P. J. *Classical Rhetoric for the Modern Student*. New York: Oxford UP, 1965.

Covino, William A. *The Art of Wondering: A Revisionist Return to the History of Rhetoric*. Portsmouth, NH: Boynton/Cook, 1988.

———. *The Elements of Persuasion*. Boston: Allyn & Bacon, 1997.

———. *Forms of Wondering: A Dialogue on Writing, for Writers*. Portsmouth, NH: Boynton/Cook, 1988.

Covino, William A., and David A. Jolliffe. *Rhetoric: Concepts, Definitions, Boundaries*. Boston: Allyn & Bacon, 1995.

Crowley, Sharon. *Ancient Rhetorics for Contemporary Students*. New York: Macmillan, 1994.

———. *The Methodical Memory*. Carbondale: Southern Illinois UP, 1990.

Eagleton, Terry. *Literary Theory: An Introduction*. Minneapolis: U of Minnesota P, 1983.

Elbow, Peter. *Writing Without Teachers*. New York: Oxford UP, 1973.

Enos, Teresa. *Encyclopedia of Rhetoric and Composition: Communication from Ancient Times to the Information Age*. New York: Garland, 1996.

Feyerabend, Paul. *Against Method: Outline of an Anarchistic Theory of Knowledge*. London: NLB, 1975.

Freire, Paulo. *Education for Critical Consciousness.* Trans. Myra Bergman Ramos. New York: Continuum, 1973.

Freedman, Aviva, and Ian Pringle, eds. *Reinventing the Rhetorical Tradition.* Conway, AK: L&S Books, 1980.

Glenn, Cheryl. *Rhetoric Retold: Regendering the Tradition from Antiquity Through the Renaissance.* Carbondale: Southern Illinois UP, 1997.

Golden, James L., Goodwin F. Berquist, and William E. Coleman. *The Rhetoric of Western Thought.* 4th ed. Dubuque, IA: Kendall/Hunt, 1976.

Green, Lawrence D. "Aristotle's Enthymeme and the Imperfect Syllogism." *Rhetoric and Pedagogy: Its History, Philosophy, and Practice.* Ed. Winifred Bryan Horner and Michael Leff. Mahwah, NJ: Erlbaum, 1995: 19–41.

Grimaldi, William M. A. *Studies in the Philosophy of Aristotle's Rhetoric.* Wiesbaden: Franz Steiner Verlag GMBH, 1972.

Gross, Alan G. *The Rhetoric of Science.* Cambridge, MA: Harvard UP, 1990.

Guthrie, W. K. C. *The Sophists.* Cambridge: Cambridge UP, 1971.

Harkin, Patricia, and John Schilb, eds. *Contending with Words: Composition and Rhetoric in a Postmodern Age.* New York: MLA, 1991.

Heath, Shirley Brice. *Ways with Words: Language, Life, and Work in Communities and Classrooms.* Cambridge: Cambridge UP, 1983.

Hobbs, Catherine, ed. *Nineteenth-Century Women Learn to Write.* Charlottesville: UP of Virginia, 1995.

Horner, Winifred Bryan. *Rhetoric in the Classical Tradition.* New York: St. Martin's, 1988.

Horner, Winifred Bryan, and Michael Leff, eds. *Rhetoric and Pedagogy: Its History, Philosophy, and Practice.* Manwah, NJ: Erlbaum, 1995.

Hunt, Everett Lee. "Plato and Aristotle on Rhetoric and Rhetoricians." *Studies in Rhetoric and Public Speaking in Honor of James A. Winans.* New York: Century, 1925. 19–70.

Jarratt, Susan C. *Rereading the Sophists: Classical Rhetoric Refigured.* Carbondale: Southern Illinois UP, 1991.

Johnson, Nan. *Nineteenth-Century Rhetoric in North America.* Carbondale: Southern Illinois UP, 1991.

Kennedy, George. *Classical Rhetoric in Its Christian and Secular Traditions.* Chapel Hill: U of North Carolina P, 1980.

———. *Comparative Rhetoric.* New York: Oxford UP, 1998.

———. "A Hoot in the Dark: The Evolution of General Rhetoric." *Philosophy and Rhetoric* 25.1 (1992): 1–21.

Kerferd, G. B. *The Sophistic Movement.* Cambridge: Cambridge UP, 1981.

Kinneavy, James L. *A Theory of Discourse.* Englewood Cliffs, NJ: Prentice-Hall, 1971.

Kitzhaber, Albert R. *Rhetoric in American Colleges, 1850–1900.* Dallas: Southern Methodist UP, 1990.

Knoblauch, C. H., and Lil Brannon. *Rhetorical Traditions and the Teaching of Writing.* Montclair, NJ: Boynton/Cook, 1984.

Kuhn, Thomas S. *The Structure of Scientific Revolutions.* 2nd ed. Chicago: U of Chicago P, 1970.

Lauer, Janice. "Issues in Rhetorical Invention." *Essays on Classical Rhetoric and Modern Discourse.* Ed. Robert Connors, Lisa Ede, and Andrea Lunsford. Carbondale: Southern Illinois UP, 1984. 127–40.

Lunsford, Andrea A., ed. *Reclaiming Rhetorica: Women in the Rhetorical Tradition.* Pittsburgh: U of Pittsburgh P, 1995.

Macrorie, Ken. *Telling Writing.* Rochelle Park, NJ: Hayden, 1970.

McKowen, Clark. *Image: Reflections on Language.* New York: Macmillan, 1973.

Mellon, John. *Transformational Sentence Combining.* Urbana, IL: NCTE, 1969.

Miller, Susan. *Rescuing the Subject: A Critical Introduction to Rhetoric and the Writer.* Carbondale: Southern Illinois UP, 1989.

Moss, Beverly J., ed. *Literacy Across Communities.* Cresskill, NJ: Hampton P, 1994.

Murphy, James J. "Introduction." *Arguments in Rhetoric Against Quintilian.* Trans. Carole Newlands. DeKalb: Northern Illinois UP, 1986. 1–76.

Murphy, James J., ed. *A Short History of Writing Instruction from Ancient Greece to Twentieth-Century America.* Davis, CA: Hermagoras, 1990.

———. *The Rhetorical Tradition and Modern Writing.* New York: MLA, 1982.

Neel, Jasper. *Aristotle's Voice: Rhetoric, Theory, and Writing in America.* Carbondale: Southern Illinois UP, 1994.

———. *Plato, Derrida, and Writing.* Carbondale: Southern Illinois UP, 1988.

O'Hare, Frank. *Sentence Combining: Improving Student Writing Without Formal Grammar Instruction.* Urbana, IL: NCTE, 1973.

Olson, Gary, ed. *Philosophy, Rhetoric, Literary Criticism: (Inter)views.* Carbondale: Southern Illinois UP, 1994.

Olson, Gary, and Irene Gale, eds. *(Inter)views: Cross-Disciplinary Perspectives on Rhetoric and Literacy.* Carbondale: Southern Illinois UP, 1991.

Olson, Gary, and Lynn Worsham, eds. *Race, Rhetoric, and the Postcolonial.* New York: SUNY P, 1998.

Ong, Walter J. *Ramus, Method, and the Decay of Dialogue.* Cambridge, MA: Harvard UP, 1958.

Perelman, Chaim, and Lucia Olbrechts-Tyteca. *The New Rhetoric: A Treatise on Argumentation.* Trans. John Wilkinson and Purcell Weaver. Notre Dame, IN: U of Notre Dame P, 1969.

Phelps, Louise Wetherbee, and Janet Emig, eds. *Feminine Principles and Women's Experience in American Composition and Rhetoric.* Pittsburgh: U of Pittsburgh P, 1995.

Pirsig, Robert. *Zen and the Art of Motorcycle Maintenance.* New York: Bantam, 1974.

Plato. *Phaedrus.* Trans. W. C. Helmbold and W. G. Rabinowitz. Indianapolis: Bobbs-Merrill, 1956.

Poster, Carol. "A Historicist Reconceptualization of the Enthymeme." *Rhetoric Society Quarterly* 22 (1992): 1–24.

Ratcliffe, Krista. *Anglo-American Feminist Challenges to the Rhetorical Traditions.* Carbondale: Southern Illinois UP, 1996.

Raymond, James C. "Enthymeme, Examples, and Rhetorical Mood." *Essays on Classical Rhetoric and Modern Discourse.* Ed. Robert J. Connors, et al. Carbondale: Southern Illinois UP, 1984.

Reynolds, John Frederick, ed. *Rhetoric, Cultural Studies, and Literacy: Selected Papers from the 1994 Conference of the Rhetoric Society of America.* Hillsdale, NJ: Erlbaum, 1995.

Rhetorica Ad Herennium. Trans. Harry Caplan. Cambridge, MA: Harvard UP, 1954.

Richards, I. A. *The Philosophy of Rhetoric.* London: Oxford UP, 1936.

Royster, Jacqueline Jones, ed. *Southern Horrors and Other Writings: The Anti-Lynching Campaign of Ida B. Wells, 1892–1900.* Boston: Bedford Books, 1997.

Scholes, Robert. *The Rise and Fall of English: Reconstructing English as a Discipline.* New Haven, CT: Yale UP, 1998.

Selzer, Jack, and Sharon Crowley, eds. *Rhetorical Bodies.* Madison: U of Wisconsin P, 1999.

Shor, Ira. *Critical Teaching and Everyday Life.* Boston: South End, 1980.

Sprague, Rosamond Kent, ed. *The Older Sophists.* Columbia: U of South Carolina P, 1972.

Sprat, Thomas. *History of the Royal Society.* Ed. Jackson Cope and Harold Jones. St. Louis: Washington UP, 1958.

Steinhoff, Virginia. "The *Phaedrus* Idyll as Ethical Play." *The Rhetorical Tradition and Modern Writing.* Ed. James J. Murphy. New York: MLA, 1982. 31–46.

Stewart, Donald C. "The Continuing Relevance of Plato's *Phaedrus.*" *Essays on Classical Rhetoric and Modern Discourse.* Ed. Robert J. Connors, et al. Carbondale: Southern Illinois UP, 1984.

Swearingen, C. Jan. *Rhetoric and Irony: Western Literacy and Western Lies.* New York: Oxford, 1991.

Tate, Gary, and Edward P. J. Corbett. *The Writing Teacher's Sourcebook.* 2nd ed. New York: Oxford UP, 1988.

Valesio, Paolo. *Novantiqua: Rhetorics as a Contemporary Theory.* Bloomington: Indiana UP, 1980.

Ward, Irene. *Literacy, Ideology, and Dialogue: Towards a Dialogic Pedagogy.* Albany: SUNY P, 1994.

Weaver, Richard M. *The Ethics of Rhetoric.* Chicago: Regnery, 1953.

Winterowd, W. Ross. *Rhetoric: A Synthesis.* New York: Holt, 1968.

Winterowd, W. Ross, ed. *Contemporary Rhetoric: A Conceptual Background with Readings.* New York: Harcourt, 1975.

———. *A Teacher's Introduction to Composition in the Rhetorical Tradition.* Urbana, IL: NCTE, 1994.

Young, Richard. "Concepts of Art and the Teaching of Writing." *The Rhetorical Tradition and Modern Writing.* Ed. James J. Murphy. New York: MLA, 1982.

Collaborative Pedagogy

R E B E C C A   M O O R E   H O W A R D

The term *collaborative pedagogy* covers a wide range of practices. In its broadest sense, collaborative pedagogy has no necessary link to the teaching of composition; scholars throughout the disciplines recognize collaboration as an aid to learning. Students who work together learn more and retain more.

Kenneth A. Bruffee, whose scholarship brought collaboration to the conversation of composition studies, dates modern interest in collaborative learning to universities' open-admission policies of the 1970s. Individualistic teaching methods proved ineffective for the new population of nontraditional university students, whereas collaborative pedagogies such as peer tutoring answered their needs. Bruffee, in "Collaborative Learning and the 'Conversation of Mankind,'" articulates three principles of collaborative learning that have now become canonical in composition studies:

1. [B]ecause thought is internalized conversation, thought and conversation tend to work largely in the same way. (639)
2. If thought is internalized public and social talk, then writing of all kinds is internalized social talk made public and social again. If thought is internalized conversation, then writing is internalized conversation re-externalized. (641)
3. To learn is to work collaboratively to establish and maintain knowledge among a community of knowledgeable peers through the process that Richard Rorty calls "socially justifying belief." (646)

Because composition studies includes pedagogy as a central concern, collaboration holds a particular fascination for the discipline. As in other disciplines, small-group discussion has become a staple of composition pedagogy. Even more common to composition classrooms is the practice of peer response to writing: students each draft an assigned paper, and then classmates respond to and make suggestions for improving the draft. Less common yet valued in composition studies is the collaborative writing assignment, in which students work together from start to finish, producing a single paper from the group.

Each of these collaborative pedagogies—small-group discussion, peer response, and collaborative writing—can enhance students' experience of writing classes, but the perils are also well documented: many teachers count among their worst disasters the collaborative assignment gone wrong. Among the published descriptions of collaborative composition pedagogy, many focus as much on how to avoid problems as on what can be accomplished in collaborative pedagogy.

Composition studies' embrace of collaboration involves more than exploring pedagogical methods, for the very notion of collaboration contradicts a long cultural tradition that privileges the individual agent and especially the solitary author. Kurt Spellmeyer traces this tradition to the work of John Locke. Elizabeth Ervin and Dana L. Fox trace it to Descartes. More commonly, the figure of the solitary, autonomous genius who produces original works is associated with the Romantic literary theory of Wordsworth and Emerson, and it also figures into copyright legislation today: the solitary author is heroic and deserves sole ownership of the words that he or she produces. Though associated with Romantic theory, these precepts continue to exert a strong hold on our culture's perceptions of writing, and they exert a significant counterforce to collaborative pedagogy. John Clifford writes, "Academics have never existed as autonomous agents outside disciplinary or institutional discourse." To Clifford, the tenacity with which "traditional humanism" clings to the "sanctity of literary ownership" poses a barrier to collaborative pedagogy (174). For that reason, proponents of collaboration—in fields such as computers and composition (Handa); law (Jaszi); cross-cultural rhetoric (Miller & Vander Lei); and literary studies (Stillinger)—contest the notion of the solitary, autonomous author.

Many go so far as to assert that all writing is collaborative. Jeanette Harris offers an authoritative overview of the assumptions and consequences of this assertion. Charlotte Thralls specifies several dimensions in which all writing is collaborative: active readers function as collaborative partners; the writer's sense of anticipated audience constitutes a form of collaboration; the community in which the act of writing takes place or toward which it is aimed contributes constraining (and enabling) conventions such as word choice, tone, organization; and sources that the writer has read exert their influence (67–69). For scholars such as Thralls and Patricia Sullivan, collaborative pedagogy is not so much an alternative pedagogy as it is an accurate mirroring of the true nature of writing.

Yet so firm a grip does the solitary author have on modern representations of writing that collaboration is sometimes perceived as plagiarism—as cheating (see Ervin and Fox; McCabe and Cole). Although this extreme resistance to collaboration is today less frequent than it was when scholars such as Bruffee began their work, it continues as a palpable counterforce to collaborative pedagogy. Rhetorician Susan Miller remarks,

> In my teaching and research, "collaboration" has focused a series of semantic fields. At first, if I recognized the term at all, it was as a kind of cheating. It

would have involved plagiarizing other people's ideas instead of relying on my own work, and would have meant abandoning my emerging teacherly responsibility to be an "expert," universalized reader. (283)

Then Miller developed a second definition, in which she "imagined collaboration at its best as a 'workshop' where students could get all the help possible by tinkering with one another's writing" (283). The intellectual movement that Miller describes is mirrored in the discipline of composition in general, but that movement—away from a normative solitary writer and toward an appreciation for collaboration—must continue if collaboration is to establish an enduring place in composition pedagogy.

✧ BENEFITS OF COLLABORATIVE PEDAGOGY

Bruffee offers a broad view of the benefits of collaboration: collaborative learning, he says, is "a way of engaging students more deeply with the text" ("Collaborative Learning" 635); collaborative pedagogy provides a social context in which students can experience and practice the kinds of conversation valued by college teachers" (642). Collaborative pedagogy traces its philosophical roots to the social constructivist philosophy of Richard Rorty. Knowledge for Rorty and his followers is not something "out there" that can be discovered by the persistent, gifted learner; rather, it is socially justified belief, constructed in the community and acquired in interaction with that community. Andrea Lunsford describes composition's embrace of collaboration as an epistemological shift in the field:

> The shift involves a move from viewing knowledge and reality as things exterior to or outside of us, as immediately accessible, individually knowable, measurable, and shareable—to viewing knowledge and reality as mediated by or constructed through language in social use, as socially constructed, contextualized, as, in short, the product of *collaboration*. (4)

Anne Ruggles Gere specifies the implications of this theory for composition pedagogy:

> Knowledge conceived as socially constructed or generated validates the "learning" part of collaborative learning because it assumes that the interactions of collaboration can lead to new knowledge or learning. A fixed and hierarchical view of knowledge, in contrast, assumes that learning can occur only when a designated "knower" imparts wisdom to those less well informed. (72–73)

Among those who further explore the epistemological foundations of collaborative learning are Kris Bosworth and Sharon Hamilton; Bruffee, *Collaborative Learning;* Marilyn Cooper, Diana George, and Susan Sanders; Chet Meyers and Thomas Jones; and Donna Qualley and Elizabeth Chiseri-Strater. Their arguments are not, however, universally accepted. Invoking other critics' objections, Bruce Horner says that the collaborative pedagogies described in the theories of Bruffee equate collaboration with democracy and assume that if peer work is taking place in the classroom, so is democracy and social change. Collaborative pedagogy, Horner charges, does not necessarily offer students anything of use outside the classroom, notwithstanding that it claims to model how knowledge is really made (514–16).

The social constructionist premises on which early work in collaboration was based have been criticized for an inattention to the unequal distribution of power in any given community. Too often social constructionist theory assumes a community of like-minded peers, a community in which every member is free to contribute to and participate in the making of knowledge. A Foucaudian approach to education, on the other hand, focuses on how power and difference are defined and distributed in community activities. For composition pedagogy, this can mean an attention to the relation between collaboration and hierarchy. Ann Hill Duin notes that collaborative pedagogy reduces competition between students. Much more frequently, scholars note ways in which collaborative pedagogy levels the teacher-student hierarchy. When teachers are no longer dispensing knowledge in lectures but are guiding students in the collaborative process of discovering and constructing knowledge, students are empowered. Social constructionist approaches to collaboration recognize this dynamic; see, for example, Bruffee ("Collaborative Learning") and Gere. Later scholarship, informed by New Historicist principles, advocates a collaborative pedagogy in which students' empowerment becomes explicit. Clifford, for example, recommends that students become reflexive learners, "learn[ing] firsthand how domination and resistance work" (173). Other scholars (e.g., Lunsford and Ede, "Rhetoric") draw on feminist theory to describe the counterhierarchical possibilities of collaboration.

Scholars recommend the pedagogy of collaborative learning and writing not only because of its epistemological felicities but also because it offers students practice in common forms of work-place writing. Geoffrey Cross, Kitty Locker, and Lunsford and Ede *(Singular Texts)* describe collaborative writing in the world of business. For scientists, too, collaborative writing is a familiar method; see, for example, Ronald Schliefer and John Trimbur and Lundy Braun. Even preachers engage in collaborative writing. Rex Veeder explains, "The authorship of a sermon is indeed thought to be an act of collaboration between the writer/speaker and the spirit" (306). Miller and Vander Lei, moreover, describe ways in which African American folk preachers collaborate, unattributed, with each other's sermons and with sacred texts.

When collaborative pedagogy aims to prepare students for work-place tasks, it should be designed not just on general precepts but also with a well-developed conception of work-place writing. Lunsford offers a taxonomy of work-place tasks "that seem to call consistently for collaboration: high-order problem defining and solving; division of labor tasks, in which the job is simply too big for any one person; and division of expertise tasks" (6).

✧ METHODS OF COLLABORATIVE PEDAGOGY

Collaborative Learning

As attested by Bruffee's "Peer Tutoring and the 'Conversation of Mankind,'" writing centers are a primary site for implementing collaborative learning. In fact, the distinction between collaborative learning and collaborative writing has been crucial to legitimating the work of writing centers. Teachers throughout the university, while wanting their students to become better writers, are also concerned that their students not have others "do" their writing for them; they may regard collaboration as plagiarism. Hence writing center staff suffer perennial criticism from colleagues in the university. Hence, too, some of the scholarship of writing centers develops theories and procedures for collaborative learning. (See, for example, Muriel Harris.)

Irene Clark and Dave Healy charge the writing center itself with some of the blame for the conflation of collaboration with plagiarism:

> The writing center's response to such suspicions has been to embrace a pedagogy of noninterventionism that precludes both the appropriation of student texts and any challenge to teachers' authority occasioned by questioning their judgment of a writer's work. (32)

The policy of noninterventionism is, however, "ethically suspect," for it constrains the potential learning experience. Clark and Healy would have the writing center involved not only in collaborative learning but also in collaborative writing.

Advocating a writing center that would "place control, power, and authority not in the tutor or staff, not in the individual student, but in the negotiating group" (8), Lunsford, too, challenges the boundaries that have traditionally constrained the nature of writing center collaboration. Such a writing center (although Lunsford does not explicitly say so) would not only forestall the common charge that tutors are writing students' papers for them, but it would also (and about this Lunsford is specific) enable a community meaning-making that far exceeds what any single individual could accomplish.

Often overlooked as a vehicle of collaborative pedagogy is whole-class discussion (Howard and Jamieson 166–68). When the teacher asks questions to which he or she already knows the "right" answers, class discussion is hardly collaborative; instead, students are performers. But when the teacher gets conversation started and then acts as secretary and synthesizer (see Wiener 59), class discussion can be very collaborative, indeed. The teacher asks a question that can have a variety of "correct" interpretive answers: the question can be as general as, "How did this text make you feel?" ("Why?" is an essential follow-up question, if the teacher wants to move conversation beyond affective response and toward analysis and synthesis.) A crucial technique for collaborative class discussion is to ask students to listen to each other. When one student makes a statement, the teacher turns to another and asks to what extent he or she agrees or disagrees. (Again, "Why?" is a necessary follow-up

AFFIRM
w/o judging,
r.sit wing?

question.) If the student was not listening to the classmate, the teacher can cheerfully ask the classmate to repeat. This time, of course, the whole class is listening to the statement, and waiting for the response. Another useful technique is to call upon students rather than to ask for raised hands, a situation in which a few students will reliably respond and others will reliably sit silent. If a student is stumped for a response, the teacher can look for raised hands or turn to another and invite "rescue." But once a student has been called upon, the teacher should ask that student's permission before giving the floor to another: "Miles has his hand up. Do you want to give the floor to him, or do you want to talk first?" Once Miles has spoken, the teacher may want to turn again to the stumped student and ask if he or she now has something to say. Often students' reluctance to answer a question signals not actually being stumped but rather needing to think before responding. Avoiding summative remarks like "good answer" constitutes yet another important technique for facilitating whole-class collaborative discussion by casting the teacher's role as that of facilitator rather than judge. When students make errors or introduce potentially fruitful avenues of thought, the teacher should point these out to the class. At the same time, though, the teacher must avoid remarks that suggest the too-familiar performance model of class discussion.

To employ small-group pedagogy is to decenter the classroom, opening it up to difference and dissent, and teachers must welcome rather than squelch such responses (Roskelly). One of the guiding principles of small-group pedagogy is the effort to relinquish teacher control. Students can teach each other; more important, together they can discover things that individually they might not. And in small groups, students are necessarily more involved than they are in the potentially passive whole-class context.

Dividing large classes into smaller groups offers all students the opportunity to talk. These groups can be formulated for discussion, problem-solving, or accomplishment of certain tasks. In any case, though, the teacher should make sure that each group knows its charge. The teacher may want to tell the groups how to accomplish that charge or may want to have the groups figure out their own methods.

The teacher's role in small-group pedagogy is again that of facilitator. Part of this facilitation may involve teaching students effective pragmatics: if they sit close to each other and make eye contact, they will talk more freely and sincerely (Bell-Metereau). Monitoring pragmatics, the teacher may want to encourage students who push their chairs out of the circle or who sprawl out, preventing proximity, to join the group. The teacher's lighthearted remarks about the need to violate American notions of personal space can alleviate students' anxieties about an unfamiliar classroom activity, one very different from the lecture method in which the teacher dispenses knowledge.

Collaborative Contributions to Solo-authored Texts

Although small-group pedagogy lends itself well to collaborative learning, it is most often used in writing classes for collaborative response to individually drafted texts. Many scholars using the term *collaborative writing* are actually talking about collaborative response to individually drafted texts. Others call the pedagogy *response groups;* Gere prefers *writing groups* (56) and describes their benefits: "[T]hey bring writers and readers closer together, thereby providing writers a direct experience with audiences" (66). Muriel Harris, though, cautions that the peer respondents are minimally trained, if at all: writers gain a greater sense of audience but are not tutored in peer response groups. Peer response, she says, works differently from tutoring, in part because tutors "are trained to use methods that lead to results very different from the outcome of response groups" (369). Peer response focuses on general skills; tutoring, on the skills of one individual (373). Writing groups usually focus on revision; tutoring can address any stage of the writing process (375). Tutorials strive for the tutee's discovery, whereas peer response groups, Harris says, often provide information in a directive way (376–77).

Yet in the expressivist rhetoric on which much of peer response theory is based, pedagogy is more facilitative than directive in its effort to elicit a student's best work. Peter Elbow's *Writing Without Teachers*, a flagship document for this approach, describes techniques for a pedagogy in which writers not only work in small groups without teachers but also do not themselves model traditional teacherly methods. Instead of talking about whether a paper is "good" or "bad," and instead of playing what Elbow calls the "doubting game," group members respond to a paper by describing how it makes them feel. Playing the "believing game," they point to the features of the paper that elicited positive responses (Elbow 147–91). One of the values of expressivist peer-response pedagogy is that it not only removes the teacher from directive in-struction, but it also prevents students from assuming that role in their responses. Instead of offering each other untrained and often incorrect instruction, peer respondents assume the role of reader and give the writer a heightened sense of audience.

Connie Hale and Susan Wyche-Smith's 1988 video, intended to be shown to composition classes, models small-group composition pedagogy in which the writer reads aloud and then the group members offer their responses. Because the students in the video were advanced writers, in 1991 Hale, Tim Mallon, and Wyche-Smith offered a second video, one that depicted beginning composition students. An underlying principle of both videos is crucial to the pedagogy: if group members silently read the paper themselves, marking on it, they inevitably assume teacherly roles, becoming doubters and critics. If, however, they listen while the writer reads aloud, they more readily assume audience roles and can better focus on their responses rather than their judgments.

As Duin notes in her list of teachers' responsibilities in small-group pedagogy (317), students may benefit from the teacher's specifying objectives and tasks. Many teachers go so far as to pose questions or tasks for the group, questions such as, "How did you *feel* about this paper? Where were you excited? Confused? Bored? Angry? Happy? Intrigued? And why?" (See, for example, Booher.) As a result of questions such as these, writers learn how their work affects readers—and that is one of the main benefits of small-group pedagog. To allow students to assume teacherly roles is to offer writers inexpert teaching, but to encourage students to articulate their readerly responses is to offer writers an understanding of the effects of their work. Equipped with this understanding, the writer can then better anticipate and provide for readers' needs and expectations. For additional advice on facilitating peer-response groups, see Jeffrey Copeland and Earl Lomax, Marie Foley, and Edgar Thompson.

"[W]riting groups highlight the social dimension of writing. They provide tangible evidence that writing involves human interaction as well as solitary inscription" (Gere 3). Supporting this statement is the assumption that solitary writing is possible; that assumption, in turn, supports the pedagogy of peer-*response* groups and gives it the name *collaborative writing*. David Bleich's model of collaboration, for example, is one in which "the work of each student change[s] in response to the analytical commentaries of the other students" (*Double Perspective* 295). The initial work, in other words, is not collaborative. Lunsford and Ede point out that scholars like Elbow who are most associated with collaborative learning "hold implicitly to traditional concepts of autonomous individualism, authorship, and authority for texts" ("Collaborative Authorship" 426). The early scholarship of Bruffee, the foremost proponent of collaborative learning, posits the solitary, autonomous author. In fact, say Lunsford and Ede, "collaborative learning theory has from its inception failed to challenge traditional concepts of radical individualism and ownership of ideas and has operated primarily in a traditional and largely hierarchical way" (431).

Karen Burke LeFevre offers a corrective to this limitation. In a book whose challenge has yet to be fully explored in composition scholarship, she describes not just revision but also invention as a collaborative act. LeFevre offers four models of invention: Platonic, internal dialogic, collaborative, and collective. The Platonic model (in which invention is an individual act) and the internal dialogic (in which invention is accomplished by an individual who is in mental conversation with the anticipated audience) have dominated composition studies, including the work of Elbow (51–61). In their place LeFevre offers collaborative invention (in which people work together to generate ideas) and collective invention ("invention is influenced by a social collective, a supra-individual entity whose rules and conventions may enable or inhibit the invention of certain ideas") (62, 80).

Subsequent scholarship has not taken up LeFevre's proposals with the enthusiasm that heralded peer-response pedagogy. The most likely explanation for the difference is that peer-response pedagogy does not challenge the long-accepted model of the individual author, whereas collective or collaborative invention does. No potpourri of pedagogical suggestions is therefore available to the interested teacher. Viewed another way: an entire strand of collaborative pedagogy awaits further scholarship. Those wishing to employ collaborative invention in their writing classes might start with collaborative invention on writing assignments. Instead of (or in preparation for) peer-response groups for drafts in progress, the teacher can distribute a writing assignment and then immediately convene small groups to brainstorm ideas for how the assignment

ached. At the end of the class period, the groups share their
ass, and everyone discusses the potentials and pitfalls of the
…ities.

Collaborative Writing

Of all the collaborative pedagogies, the one that has proven most difficult is collaborative writing. When students are assigned to *write together,* a variety of problems can arise, most of them deriving from the dominant cultural model of individual authorship. Because not only students but also teachers are accustomed to thinking of authorship in terms of the individual—and because the entire educational institution predicates its judgments on individual performance—collaborative writing pedagogies seem foreign and fraught with peril. Yet collaborative writing dominates the corporate work place and many academic disciplines, and critical theory increasingly insists that all writing is collaborative. Thus, despite the perils, some teachers persevere in assigning and teaching collaborative writing.

And when the perils can be averted or overcome, the benefits are impressive. In spring 1998, I assigned five papers in my sophomore composition class. The first four were individually authored, with collaborative invention and revision. The fifth paper was collaboratively written, with random constitution of groups. I assigned tasks and suggested methods, and the groups decided on topic, thesis, and method. For the last month of the term, they conducted collaborative research; divided up the work; met regularly; reported to me regularly; consulted me about questions and problems (the most prominent problem being one group member who did not do her share); argued energetically about style, structure, and content; handed in astonishingly good papers; and expressed pride in and enthusiasm for the process and its product. Fresh from that gratifyingly successful collaborative writing pedagogy, I offer the following suggestions for assigning collaborative writing:

1. Although the collaborative writing assignment may be announced and distributed on the very first day of class, it should not be begun until a substantial portion of the term has elapsed. In the interim, pedagogy should be sufficiently collaborative (e.g., collaborative class discussion, small-group work, collaborative invention, collaborative revision) that the students get to know each other, resolve some of the small interpersonal tensions that inevitably arise, and anticipate each other's collaborative assets and shortcomings.

2. The collaborative writing assignment should be one that is best accomplished by a group rather than an individual; otherwise, the task is artificial, leading to students' frustration and irritation. Lunsford and Ede describe

    . . . three types of tasks which invite . . . collaboration: "labor-intensive" tasks that need to be divided into smaller subtasks in order to be accomplished effectively and efficiently; "specialization" tasks that call for multi-

ple areas of expertise; and "synthesis" tasks that demand that divergent perspectives be brought together into a solution acceptable to the whole group
or an outside group. (*Singular Texts* 123)

In my sophomore composition class, the collaborative groups were assigned to write a new chapter for a style textbook used in the course. Because the students had criticized its shortcomings, I directed each group
to write a new chapter for the book. One group wrote on wired style; another, on the ways style varies in different discourse communities. These
were not topics that solitary sophomores could have treated authorita-
tively, for they demanded intensive labor and high-level synthesis.

3. Provide for student-initiated collaboration. While planning the course,
   consider whether any of the assignments designated for individual authorship might lend themselves to collaborative authorship. Alert the class
   to these possibilities and introduce them to methods and rationales for
   collaboration. If some of the students opt to write collaboratively, work
   with the groups to ensure that they are accomplishing something other
   than dividing up an individual paper among several writers.

4. Discuss methods and problems of collaborative writing before the project
   begins. If online collaboration is a possibility, explore available methods
   (see Forbes; Selfe). Alert students to the ways in which stereotyped role
   expectations (based on factors such as gender and race) can affect the distribution of power within the group; encourage students to use the collaborative experience as an opportunity for greater attention to each other's
   ideas and for delegating responsibility according to the actual characteristics of the individuals in the group, rather than their stereotyped role expectations (see Fox; Morgan; Villanueva). Two additional observations are
   especially important to share:
   a. Collaborative writing can take many forms. Lunsford and Ede describe
      dialogic and *hierarchical* collaboration: in dialogic collaboration, the
      group works together on all aspects of the project, whereas in hierarchi-
      cal collaboration, the group divides the task into component parts and
      assigns certain components to each group member. Lunsford and Ede
      point out that these are not mutually exclusive categories; many collab-
      orative writing projects involve both dialogic and hierarchical collabo-
      ration (*Singular Texts* 133–34). Dialogic collaboration offers the benefit of
      discovery: students learn more by working together. In my class, the
      group working on wired style collaborated dialogically to define and
      expand the unfamiliar topic. Hierarchical collaboration offers the bene-
      fit of efficiency: that same group worked dialogically to develop a pre-
      liminary bibliography and then worked hierarchically to read the
      sources. Each member reported his or her findings to the group, and
      then they again worked dialogically to construct an argument and hier-
      archically to draft sections of that argument.
   b. Certain problems regularly arise in collaborative writing. One is that
      some students are better prepared to accomplish their tasks than are

others—hence a variation in quality. Writing groups need to be prepared for each person's contributions to be revised and even deleted. The group must be ready to exert critical judgment, and the members must be braced for the sobering prospect of having their work changed or eliminated. The group must dedicate itself to the best possible written product, and its members must be ready to help each other through potentially ego-deflating moments.

c. Another common problem in collaborative writing is the student who does not carry his or her load. The group should deliberate this possibility at the beginning of the project and report to the teacher its decision for how such a phenomenon should be handled if it arises. Generally, this involves the group's deciding whether one grade will be assigned to the paper regardless of the balance of effort; whether a shirking member will receive a lesser grade than the others; or whether a shirking member will be ejected from the group and either given a zero or required to write his or her own paper.

5. Anticipate and prepare for student resistance to collaboration. In part because Western literary theory has, for the past century and more, so firmly endorsed a model of solitary authorship, some students have difficulty accepting collaborative writing assignments. They may be uncertain as to whether their classmates will accept them as coauthors, or they may have a much higher opinion of their own writing "ability" than their classmates have. Whatever the cause of their resistance, most of these students will nevertheless benefit from the collaborative assignment, if they are given to understand how prevalent collaboration is in work-place writing, how much their "individual" writing will benefit from having worked in a group and having seen firsthand how others articulate and solve writing problems, and how much more they can accomplish than if they were working alone—what Linda Hughes and Michael Lund call "a union that is greater than the . . . parts that composed it" (49). (Priscilla Rogers and Marjorie Horton detail the benefits of collaborative writing, especially in the dialogic mode.) But some students are implacably opposed to collaboration, and the teacher must decide whether to require them to participate or to offer the option of individual writing. The decision rests on the pedagogical motivation for assigning collaboration. If it is to improve the students' skill in writing collaboratively, they must all participate. If, however, the class is designed to enhance individual writing skills (as is the case in most required introductory composition classes) and a student persists in objecting to collaboration, the teacher may want to allow solitary composition, reasoning that the student's writing skills will not benefit from an activity that he or she so firmly resists.

6. Let the class decide how the groups will be constituted, and discuss the pros and cons of each possibility. I told my class that choosing their own groups would allow them maximum comfort but would leave some students feeling unloved, and I also told them that the comfort of self-chosen groups could sometimes result in poor decision-making, with too much

consideration for established relations and not enough for the collaborative project. Our alternatives were my designating the groups, trying to fix each group with a range of writing skills—e.g., a good researcher, a good editor, etc., in each group. The class decided on random selection, and they also chose the size of groups. I recommended against too-small groups (in which one person's absence might be devastating) or too-large groups (in which leadership issues could too easily arise and in which one person could too easily disappear). They decided on six-person writing groups.

7. Give the groups autonomy in deciding their methods and timetables (my class even decided how often, when, and why class would meet during the month of the project), but also require that they commit their timetable to writing. Give students maximum guidance to help them make sound decisions. The sophomores were sobered, for example, when they realized that once the paper was constructed, they would have to allow not a few hours but a week for editing, since they were all required to read and sign off on the final product. And indeed, for one group, editing was the most lively and protracted passage of the project. One student was determined that the paper be well edited and was certain he knew what good editing was. The other members were less enthusiastic but more knowledgeable about editing. The result was fights, dictionaries, handbooks, delegations to my office for grammar arbitration, a great deal of learning, and a beautifully edited paper.

8. Prepare for dissent within the groups, and prepare to manage it in two dimensions: the teacher and the students. Neither should attempt to suppress dissent or enforce consensus (see Clark and Ede; Flower; Janangelo; Spellmeyer; Trimbur; Villanueva; and Wolf). Successful collaboration, say Lunsford and Ede, allows not only for "group cohesion" but also for "creative conflict" and the protection of "minority views" (*Singular Texts* 123). Linda Flower recommends that the teacher welcome rather than dread dissent: "Conflict, embedded in a spirit of stubborn generosity, is not only generative but necessary because it acknowledges the undeniable—the social and economic substructures of power, of racism, of identity that will not be erased by goodwill" (51). From such conflict can emerge "a joint inquiry into thorny problems, opening up live options that let us construct a language of possibility and a more complicated ground for action" (50–52). It is important for students to anticipate in advance that dissent and conflict will arise and to be ready to respond to it productively rather than wasting time trying to suppress, reform, or eject dissenters. Two textual presentations of dissent that my students have found useful are counterevidence and minority opinions. The presentation of counterevidence draws on established models of academic persuasion, in which a thesis (the opinion of the majority) is advanced but in which counterevidence as well as evidence is presented. In employing this option, students must avoid the approach to counterevidence that traditional argument offers. Counterevidence must not be discounted or "refuted";

rather, it should serve to enrich the thesis, showing its complexities and ambiguities. The presentation of minority opinions draws on Supreme Court practice. Collaborative writing groups employing this tactic present a final paper, to which is attached one or more statements of dissenting opinion. Nor are these statements individually authored; the entire group works dialogically not only on the majority paper but also on the minority opinion(s).

9. Explain in advance how the project will be graded, preferably involving the students in the decision. I told my sophomore composition class that each collaborative group would receive a single grade but that the groups would decide in advance how a shirker would be graded. I provided my criteria for grading, telling them that I expected a better product than I would of a single individual but that I expected sophomore- and not professional-level work. Some teachers try to assign individual grades for a collaborative project—a method that I cannot recommend, since it undermines the purposes of collaboration. Such quandaries can arise from the gatekeeping responsibility for judging and ranking individuals that is endemic to many writing programs (see Holdstein). Before assigning collaborative writing projects, the teacher should ascertain that the institutional purposes for the course and the teacher's own purposes in assigning collaboration are sufficiently harmonious that the institutional agenda will not undermine the collaborative pedagogy—or vice versa.

Writer/Text Collaboration

Of all collaborative pedagogies, the one least acknowledged in writing classes is writer/text collaboration, in which a writer overtly collaborates with a written text. The received models of collaboration acknowledge that which takes place between writer and anticipated audience (LeFevre's internal dialogic model); between writers and readers, face to face (peer response pedagogy); or between several writers (collaborative authorship). In contrast, writers' work with texts has traditionally been characterized not as collaboration but as quotation, paraphrase, summary, synthesis, research—or plagiarism. Increasingly, however, composition scholars describe writers' work with texts as a form of collaboration, as Lunsford and Ede demonstrate when referring to their own conversation with texts (*Singular Texts* 138). And Thralls uses the category of collaboration to describe sources that the writer has read and that influenced him or her (69).

When I say, "writers' work with texts has traditionally been characterized," I use the term *traditionally* to refer to mainstream representations of authorship, those that do not typically tend to acknowledge difference. In American culture, though, many other representations of the solitary-collaborative continuum can be found. Gere's research reveals that in nineteenth-century women's literary groups, collaborative reading and writing were the norm. And Keith Miller's research asserts collaborative writing and shared language as the norm in American preaching, especially African American preaching.

Asserting that all writing is collaborative, I have used the term *(re)formative composition* to describe a pedagogy of writer/text collaboration that would facilitate "the *jouissance* of unfettered authorship, of exercises in which [students] play freely with language, without regard for ownership"[1] Such pedagogy is first described by Glynda Hull and Mike Rose and then developed by Mary Minock. It is not, however, widely employed in composition studies. Not only does it inescapably violate the notion of the solitary author, but it also brings collaborative pedagogy back into contact with plagiarism, an association that scholars of collaboration have for years striven to undo. The teacher employing such pedagogy has the task of making sure it does not lead students into textual activities that would be interpreted as academic dishonesty. Perhaps equally important, the teacher also has to ensure that colleagues do not conclude from the pedagogy of writer/text collaboration that the teacher is indifferent to textual ethics. Despite these perils, the pedagogy of writer/text collaboration has the potential for expanding students' linguistic repertoires and increasing the authority of their academic prose voices. And because Hull and Rose, Minock, and I are almost alone in publishing descriptions of such pedagogy, writer/text collaboration is a topic ripe for further research.

Note

1. The term originates in as-yet-unpublished work by a scholarly collaborative, the (In)Citers.

Bibliography

Bell-Metereau, Rebecca. "Breaking Boundaries, Solving Problems, Giving Gifts: Student Empowerment in Small Group Work." Reagan, Fox, and Bleich. 247–64.

Bleich, David. "Collaboration and the Pedagogy of Disclosure." *College English* 57.1 (January 1995): 43–61.

———. *The Double Perspective: Language, Literacy, and Social Relations.* New York: Oxford UP, 1988.

Booher, E. Kathleen. "A Writing Teacher's Guide to Processing Small-Group Work." *Focus on Collaborative Learning: Classroom Practices in Teaching English, 1988.* Ed. Jeff Golub et al. Urbana, IL: NCTE, 1988. 43–46.

Bosworth, Kris, and Sharon J. Hamilton, eds. *Collaborative Learning: Underlying Processes and Effective Techniques.* San Francisco: Jossey-Bass, 1994.

Bruffee, Kenneth A. "Collaborative Learning and the 'Conversation of Mankind.'" *College English* 46.7 (November 1984): 635–52.

———. *Collaborative Learning: Higher Education, Interdependence, and the Authority of Knowledge.* Baltimore: Johns Hopkins UP, 1993.

———. "Peer Tutoring and the 'Conversation of Mankind.'" *Writing Centers: Theory and Administration.* Ed. Gary A. Olson. Urbana, IL: NCTE, 1984. 3–15.

Clark, Irene L., and Dave Healy. "Are Writing Centers Ethical?" *WPA: Writing Program Administration* 20.1–2 (Fall/Winter 1996): 32–48.

Clark, Suzanne, and Lisa Ede. "Collaboration, Resistance, and the Teaching of Writing." *The Right to Literacy.* Ed. Andrea A. Lunsford, Helene Moglen, and James Slevin. New York: MLA, 1990. 276–85.

Clifford, John. "Responses to the Essays: Toward an Ethical Community of Writers." *New Visions of Collaborative Writing.* Ed. Janis Forman. Portsmouth, NH: Boynton/Cook, 1992. 170–76.

Cooper, Marilyn M., Diana George, and Susan Sanders. "Collaboration for a Change: Collaborative Learning and Social Action." Reagan, Fox, and Bleich. 31–46.

Copeland, Jeffrey S., and Earl D. Lomax. "Building Effective Student Writing Groups." *Focus on Collaborative Learning: Classroom Practices in Teaching English, 1988.* Ed. Jeff Golub et al. Urbana, IL: NCTE, 1988. 99–104.

Cross, Geoffrey A. "A Bakhtinian Exploration of Factors Affecting the Collaborative Writing of an Executive Letter of an Annual Report." *Research in the Teaching of English* 24 (May 1990): 173–204.

Duin, Ann Hill. "Implementing Cooperative Learning Groups in the Writing Curriculum." *Journal of Teaching Writing* 5 (1986): 315–24.

Elbow, Peter. *Writing Without Teachers.* New York: Oxford UP, 1973.

Ervin, Elizabeth, and Dana L. Fox. "Collaboration as Political Action." *Journal of Advanced Composition* 14.1 (Winter 1994): 53–72.

Flower, Linda. "Negotiating the Meaning of Difference." *Written Communication* 13.1 (January 1996): 44–92.

Foley, Marie. "Revising Response Groups." *Focus on Collaborative Learning: Classroom Practices in Teaching English, 1988.* Ed. Jeff Golub et al. Urbana, IL: NCTE, 1988. 117–22.

Forbes, Cheryl. "Cowriting, Overwriting, and Overriding in Portfolio Land Online." *Computers and Composition* 13.2 (1996): 195–206.

Foucault, Michel. *Discipline and Punish: The Birth of the Prison.* Trans. Alan Sheridan. New York: Vintage, 1979.

Fox, Thomas. "Race and Gender in Collaborative Learning." Reagan, Fox, and Bleich. 111–22.

Gere, Anne Ruggles. *Writing Groups: History, Theory, and Implications.* Carbondale: Southern Illinois UP, 1987.

Hale, Connie, and Susan Wyche-Smith. *Student Writing Groups: Demonstrating the Process.* Tacoma, WA: Wordshop Productions, 1988.

Hale, Connie, Tim Mallon, and Susan Wyche-Smith. *Beginning Writing Groups.* Tacoma, WA: Wordshop Productions, 1991.

Handa, Carolyn. "Politics, Ideology, and the Strange, Slow Death of the Isolated Composer or Why We Need Community in the Writing Classroom." *Computers and Community: Teaching Composition in the Twenty-first Century.* Portsmouth, NH: Boynton/Cook, 1990. 160–84.

Harris, Jeanette. "Toward a Working Definition of Collaborative Writing." *Author-ity and Textuality: Current Views of Collaborative Writing.* Ed. James S. Leonard, Christine E. Wharton, Robert Murray Davis, and Jeanette Harris. West Cornwall, CT: Locust Hill P, 1994. 77–84.

Harris, Muriel. "Collaboration Is Not Collaboration Is Not Collaboration: Writing Center Tutorials vs. Peer-Response Groups." *College Composition and Communication* 43.3 (October 1992): 369–83.

Holdstein, Deborah H. "The Institutional Agenda, Collaboration, and Writing Assessment." Reagan, Fox, and Bleich. 77–88.

Horner, Bruce. "Students, Authorship, and the Work of Composition." *College English* 59.5 (Sept. 1997): 505–29.

Howard, Rebecca Moore. *Standing in the Shadow of Giants: Plagiarists, Authors, Collaborators.* Norwood, NJ: Ablex. Forthcoming.

Howard, Rebecca Moore, and Sandra Jamieson. *The Bedford Guide to Teaching Writing in the Disciplines: An Instructor's Desk Reference.* Boston: Bedford, 1995.

Hughes, Linda K., and Michael Lund. "Union and Reunion: Collaborative Authorship." *Author-ity and Textuality: Current Views of Collaborative Writing.* Ed. James S. Leonard, Christine E. Wharton, Robert Murray Davis, and Jeanette Harris. West Cornwall, CT: Locust Hill P, 1994. 241–60.

Hull, Glynda, and Mike Rose. "Rethinking Remediation: Toward a Social-Cognitive Understanding of Problematic Reading and Writing." *Written Communication* 6.2 (1989): 139–54.

Janangelo, Joseph. "Intricate Inscriptions: Negotiating Conflict Between Collaborative Writers." *Journal of Teaching Writing* 15.1 (1996): 91–106.

Jaszi, Peter. "On the Author Effect: Contemporary Copyright and Collective Creativity." *The Construction of Authorship: Textual Appropriation in Law and Literature.* Ed. Martha Woodmansee and Peter Jaszi. Durham, NC: Duke UP, 1994. 29–56.

LeFevre, Karen Burke. *Invention as a Social Act.* Carbondale: Southern Illinois UP, 1987.

Locker, Kitty O. "What Makes a Collaborative Writing Team Successful? A Case Study of Lawyers and Social Service Workers in a State Agency." *New Visions of Collaborative Writing.* Ed. Janis Forman. Portsmouth, NH: Boynton/Cook, 1992. 37–62.

Lunsford, Andrea. "Collaboration, Control, and the Idea of a Writing Center." *The Writing Center Journal* 12.1 (Fall 1991): 3–10.

Lunsford, Andrea, and Lisa Ede. "Collaborative Authorship and the Teaching of Writing." *The Construction of Authorship: Textual Appropriation in Law and Literature.* Ed. Martha Woodmansee and Peter Jaszi. Durham, NC: Duke UP, 1994. 417–38.

———. Rhetoric in a New Key: Women and Collaboration." *Rhetoric Review* 8 (1990): 234–41.

———. *Singular Texts/Plural Authors: Perspectives on Collaborative Writing.* Carbondale: Southern Illinois UP, 1990.

McCabe, Donald L., and Sally Cole. "Student Collaboration: Not Always What the Instructor Wants." *AAHE Bulletin* (Nov. 1995): 3–6.

Meyers, Chet, and Thomas B. Jones. *Promoting Active Learning: Strategies for the College Classroom.* San Francisco: Jossey-Bass, 1993.

Miller, Keith D. *Voice of Deliverance: The Language of Martin Luther King, Jr. and Its Sources.* New York: Free P, 1992.

Miller, Keith D., and Elizabeth A. Vander Lei. "Collaboration, Collaborative Communities, and Black Folk Culture." *The Right to Literacy.* Ed. Andrea A. Lunsford, Helene Moglen, and James Slevin. New York: MLA, 1990. 50–60.

Miller, Susan. "New Discourse City: An Alternative Model for Collaboration." Reagan, Fox, and Bleich. 283–300.

Minock, Mary. "Toward a Postmodern Pedagogy of Imitation." *JAC: A Journal of Composition Theory* 15.3 (Fall 1995): 489–510.

Morgan, Meg. "Women as Emergent Leaders in Student Collaborative Writing Groups." *Journal of Advanced Composition* 14.1 (Winter 1994): 203–20.

Qualley, Donna J., and Elizabeth Chiseri-Strater. "Collaboration as Reflexive Dialogue: A Knowing 'Deeper Than Reason.'" *Journal of Advanced Composition* 14.1 (Winter 1994): 111–30.

Reagan, Sally Barr, Thomas Fox, and David Bleich, eds. *Writing With: New Directions in Collaborative Teaching, Learning, and Research.* Albany, NY: SUNY, 1994.

Rogers, Priscilla S., and Marjorie S. Horton. "Exploring the Value of Face-to-Face Collaborative Writing." *New Visions of Collaborative Writing*. Ed. Janis Forman. Portsmouth, NH: Boynton/Cook, 1992. 120–46.

Rorty, Richard. *Philosophy and the Mirror of Nature*. Princeton, NJ: Princeton UP, 1979.

Roskelly, Hephzibah. "The Risky Business of Group Work." *ATAC Forum* 4 (Spring 1992). Rpt. *The Writing Teacher's Sourcebook*. Ed. Gary Tate, Edward P. J. Corbett, and Nancy Myers. 3rd ed. New York: Oxford UP, 1994. 141–48.

Schliefer, Ronald. "Disciplinarity and Collaboration in the Sciences and Humanities." *College English* 59.4 (Apr. 1997): 438–52.

Selfe, Cynthia L. "Computer-based Conversations and the Changing Nature of Collaboration." *New Visions of Collaborative Writing*. Ed. Janis Forman. Portsmouth, NH: Boynton/Cook, 1992. 147–69.

Spellmeyer, Kurt. "On Conventions and Collaboration: The Open Road and the Iron Cage." *Writing Theory and Critical Theory*. Ed. John Clifford and John Schilb. New York: MLA, 1994. 73–95.

Stillinger, Jack. *Multiple Authorship and the Myth of Solitary Genius*. New York: Oxford UP, 1991.

Sullivan, Patricia A. "Revising the Myth of the Independent Scholar." Reagan, Fox, and Bleich. 11–30.

Thompson, Edgar H. "Ensuring the Success of Peer Revision Groups." *Focus on Collaborative Learning: Classroom Practices in Teaching English, 1988*. Ed. Jeff Golub et al. Urbana, IL: NCTE, 1988. 109–16.

Thralls, Charlotte. "Bakhtin, Collaborative Partners, and Published Discourse: A Collaborative View of Composing." *New Visions of Collaborative Writing*. Ed. Janis Forman. Portsmouth, NH: Boynton/Cook, 1992. 63–81.

Trimbur, John. "Consensus and Difference in Collaborative Learning." *College English* 51.6 (Oct. 1989): 602–16.

Trimbur, John, and Lundy A. Braun. "Laboratory Life and the Determination of Authorship." *New Visions of Collaborative Writing*. Ed. Janis Forman. Portsmouth, NH: Boynton/Cook, 1992. 19–36.

Veeder, Rex L. "Romantic Rhetoric and the Rhetorical Tradition." *Rhetoric Review* 15.2 (Spring 1997): 300–21.

Villanueva, Victor, Jr. "On Writing Groups, Class, and Culture: Studying Oral and Literate Language Features in Writing." Reagan, Fox, and Bleich. 123–40.

Wiener, Harvey S. "Collaborative Learning in the Classroom: A Guide to Evaluation." *College English* 48 (1986): 52–61.

Wolf, Thia. "Conflict as Opportunity in Collaborative Praxis." Reagan, Fox, and Bleich. 91–110.

Cultural Studies and Composition

DIANA GEORGE
JOHN TRIMBUR

The idea that cultural studies was about to become the "next thing" in composition theory and practice appeared in the late 1980s and early 1990s, in the depths of the Reagan-Bush era of conservative restoration and American triumphalism. In the intervening decade, cultural studies has insinuated itself into the mainstream of composition—as a category to check on CCCC (Conference on College Composition and Communication) proposals, a type of textbook, a curricular organizing principle, a set of questions about literacy practices, the thematic focus of essay collections and monographs, in its most general sense an orientation toward the study and teaching of writing and a milieu of loosely affiliated theorists and practitioners. To say that cultural studies has arrived, however, only poses a series of questions we will be concerned with in this bibliographical essay: namely, (to borrow the title of Richard Johnson's seminal essay) what is cultural studies anyway, where does it come from, what does it want, what does it do, and why has it become, virtually overnight, a distinct current in composition studies—and a source of anxiety and contention?

A simple answer to the latter question, and one that possesses a certain though sharply limited truth, is that cultural studies is the latest import of theory into composition: a moment in the global circulation of intellectual commodities marked by the transmission of British cultural studies from the Birmingham Centre for Contemporary Cultural Studies (CCCS) to replace the depleted exchange value of continental high theory in its various guises (structuralism, poststructuralism, hermeneutics, deconstruction, and so on) with the more worldly goods of Raymond Williams and Stuart Hall.

At any rate, this is the view one often finds in the establishment press, whether the *New York Times* or the *Chronicle of Higher Education*, in reporting that typically styles figures such as Stanley Aronowitz, Lawrence Grossberg, Andrew Ross, and Janice Radway as hip purveyors of the latest academic fad. Such a view turns up as well in Richard Rorty's and others' majoritarian critique of the "cultural left" as an academic coterie and in commentaries from

Barbara Ehrenreich and Katha Pollit on the left to George Will on the right that can scarcely disguise their delight at Alan Sokal's audacious bearding of *Social Text* with his mean-spirited send-up of postmodern science studies.

Embedded in these sensationalistic accounts of cultural studies as irrelevant vanguardism and academic spectacle are a number of important issues about the dissemination of cultural studies, the pressures and limits of its domestication in the American academy, the coverage of academic work in the popular press, and the recent shift in attacks on "political correctness" from the humanities to science studies. But what these accounts often leave out is the recognition that the arrival of cultural studies marks a wider resurfacing of political desire in academic work—an awakening, as it were, from the psychic Thermidor following the decline of the popular movements of the 1960s, the failure of the French worker-student alliance to overthrow Gaullism in May 1968, and the breakup of the New Left by the mid-1970s.

The Reagan-Bush years prompted a sense of urgency about the rightward direction of the country, with its "back to basics" attacks on the "permissive" 1960s, backlash against feminism, and revanchist yearnings to purge memories of Vietnam through military adventures in Grenada, Panama, Libya, and the Persian Gulf. If anything, the Clinton era of NAFTA (North American Free Trade Agreement), welfare "reform," and corporate restructuring intensified the felt need on the part of American leftist academics to articulate a role for themselves in public forums and to cope (at least rhetorically if not actually) with the globalization of capital and its relentless war against working people and the poor.

Such a political turn in rhetoric and composition can be seen by the late 1980s in a new emphasis on multiculturalism, the politics of literacy, and the implications of race, class, and gender for the study and teaching of writing. It is evident, for example, in the political struggle over E306 "Writing About Difference," the first-year course at the University of Texas that Linda Brodkey designed but then was canceled under pressure from the right (Brodkey, "Federal Case"), as well as in increasingly heated debates in the journals about the ethics of politically engaged teaching. More recently, this political turn appears in calls for civic rhetoric, public writing, and community service learning (Cushman; Herzberg; Wells).

From one perspective, the turn to the politics of writing instruction figures as a logical outgrowth of "postprocess" composition theory and practice (Trimbur, "Social Turn"), bringing a heightened emphasis on the dynamics of power and a call for social justice to an already well-established social orientation in the study and teaching of writing. But there are discontinuities as well—new themes and new issues that cannot be assimilated to a linear history of progressive traditions in composition studies. And besides, what we are loosely calling the political turn in composition is itself hardly a homogeneous or unified phenomenon. Indeed, the political turn amounts to a set of sometimes discrete and sometimes overlapping responses to the present historical conjuncture.

Our purpose is to chart one of these responses—what has become known as the "cultural-studies-approach-to-teaching-writing"—to explain how cultural studies has infiltrated composition studies, its relation to other theories and practices, and its results. We go about this task first by mapping some conceptual terrain—the various histories, definitions, and traditions that have characterized cultural studies as a distinct political and intellectual tendency. The main part of this bibliographical essay will then review how cultural studies enters composition and, in roughly chronological order, will present some of the central themes and issues that cultural studies has raised for the study and teaching of writing.

Our remarks, as many readers will recognize right away, are not from afar. Together and separately, we have been caught up in the emergence of cultural studies in composition theory and pedagogy—writing articles, coauthoring a textbook, giving talks, and leading workshops. We mention this to alert readers to the fact that the account we offer is one of involved participants and to note that, in the absence of a serviceable alternative, we will be referring to ourselves and our work in the awkward construction of the third person.

↬ CULTURAL STUDIES: HISTORIES, DEFINITIONS, TRADITIONS

There are many possible histories and definitions of cultural studies, but surely the most influential one is how a cluster of works published within a few years of each other in the late 1950s and early 1960s—Richard Hoggart's *The Uses of Literacy* (1957), Raymond Williams' *Culture and Society* (1958) and *The Long Revolution* (1961), and E. P. Thompson's *The Making of the English Working Class* (1963)—marked a decisive break with established ways of thinking about culture, literature, and history, thereby constituting what Stuart Hall calls "the *caesura* out of which . . . 'Cultural Studies' emerged" ("Two Paradigms" 34). In this account of the heroic founding of cultural studies, Hoggart, Williams, and Thompson are joined in a common project of articulating a notion of culture to replace the cultivation of sensibility implied in the high/low binaries of literary studies and mass culture critiques, on the one hand, and the reductionist sense of culture as an epiphenomenal superstructure of the economic base in mechanical Marxism, on the other. All three figures wanted to think of culture as a way of life, a set of ordinary, everyday practices linked in creative and consequential fashion to the social order and the formation of class consciousness. Most of all (as themselves the founding culture heroes in this account) they wanted to recover the culture of the common people as a Promethean political act, to reclaim culture from its monopoly by antidemocratic and elitist forces both inside and outside the academy.

This noble history establishes a cultural studies tradition of politically engaged and theoretically eclectic critique and intervention into the "history of the contemporary." It also points to the historical and political moment the CCCS was established at the University of Birmingham in 1963 with Hoggart (later Stuart Hall, then Richard Johnson) as director. Beginning (at least symbolically) in 1956, with the Suez crisis, the Soviet invasion of Hungary, and the Khruschev revelations about Stalinist terror, as well as the formation the following year of the Campaign for Nuclear Disarmament, a New Left was forming in the UK, activated by the crisis in traditional Marxism and the growing sense that the Old Left was unable to engage the realities of postwar capitalism, the persistence of racism and imperialism, the role of ideology in maintaining class society, and the growing influence of consumer culture and "Americanization" among the British working classes. Against this historical backdrop and with the upheavals of the 1960s about to take place, the CCCS sought to develop an open Marxism and socialist humanism distinct from the doctrinaire Marxism of the Stalinized Communist parties of the Third International and the postwar welfare-state settlement engineered by the reformist British Labor Party.

From these New Left origins in the late 1950s and early 1960s, cultural studies in the UK has taken up the leading political and intellectual questions of its time. Unlike the traditional established disciplines, however, the version of cultural studies that spread from Birmingham has relied not so much on systematic research programs and questions that define the field as on what Johnson has called "a kind of alchemy for producing useful knowledge" (38). This alchemy has typically involved collaborative and interdisciplinary—in some cases nondisciplinary and even antidisciplinary—work, such as the multiauthored studies *Resistance Through Rituals: Youth Subcultures in Post War Britain* (Hall and Jefferson, 1976), *Policing the Crisis: Mugging, the State, and Law and Order* (Hall et al., 1979), and *Working Class Culture: Studies in History and Theory* (Clarke et al., 1979), as well as the collections issued directly under the name of CCCS, *Making Histories: History-Writing and Politics* (1982) and *The Empire Strikes Back: Race and Racism in 70s Britain* (1982), and the CCCS Education Group, *Unpopular Education: Schooling and Social Democracy in England Since 1944* (1981) and *Education Limited: Schooling and Training and the New Right Since 1979* (1991). Linked to moments of engagement and analysis—whether of Thatcherism, the Falklands crisis, the New Times initiative, or the Sony Walkman— British cultural studies has insisted on seeing itself as an unfinished practice inserted into the conjunctures of contemporary history, an open project that is politically committed but nondoctrinaire, that resists reductive and absolutist conceptions of culture, and that refuses to police its own disciplinary borders.

Because the work of the Centre is mobile and resistant to codification, any characterization of cultural studies must remain provisional. The tendency in overviews of cultural studies, as we will see in accounts offered by Stuart Hall, Lawrence Grossberg, and Richard Johnson, is not to stipulate the field and its methods but to chart its ongoing development, crises, and contradictions. In what is perhaps the best known map of the field, "Cultural Studies: Two Paradigms," Hall presents cultural studies as an encounter between the "culturalism" of Hoggart, Williams, and Thompson (with its socialist humanism, its emphasis on class formation as a shared way of life, and its deep appreciation of the authenticity of working-class experience) and the "structuralism" of Althusser (with its antihumanism, its emphasis on the formation of subjectivity through signifying practices, and its sense of how relatively autonomous institutions and practices form an overdetermined unity of differences). Hall's strategy is to read Williams and Althusser against each other, thereby setting limits to the essentialism of class identity in the culturalist paradigm, while at the same time expanding the historical agency available to the interpolated subject in the structuralist paradigm. For Hall, the problem is to find a way of representing culture and the formation of consciousness that avoids, on the one hand, the Old Left view of a dominant ideology (or "false consciousness") imposed from above by the ruling classes and, on the other, the populist view of the masses as always and necessarily resistant to the ideas and political authority of the established order. To this end, Hall turned to the Italian Marxist Antonio Gramsci (or, perhaps better put, invented a version of Gramsci that proved useful to him).

From Gramsci, Hall took the notion that political rule is only rarely, as in times of deep social crisis, the result of physical coercion by the state. Rather political domination is more typically negotiated between rulers and the ruled in the arena of civil society, where social groups and class fractions struggle for political and moral leadership in education, religion, the mass media, and so on. The hegemony of the ruling elites, in Gramsci's view, is therefore based not so much on brute force as on the popular consent of the masses to the extent that they identify their own interests with those of the dominant class. From this perspective, moreover, cultural struggle becomes as important as economic struggle at the point of production or direct confrontation with the state. For if the masses at times cooperate in their own domination by accepting the "common sense" of ruling interests, they can also change the terms of popular belief and the relation of forces between the people and the ruling bloc through what Gramsci called a "war of positions" on the cultural front—a notion that became particularly attractive to Hall and others as a way to counteract the popularity of Thatcherism and the New Right in the UK.

As Hall developed his neo-Gramscian synthesis more fully in what has become known as "articulation theory" (see "On Postmodernism and Articulation"), he argues that the outcome of the struggle for hegemony and popular consent is crucial to contemporary political practice but cannot be predicted in advance. Neither cultural dupes nor incipient revolutionists by a priori definition, the popular forces, as Hall represents them, are not propelled forward automatically by "laws of history" or "relations of production." According to Hall, there is no necessary belongingness between the political connotation of ideological elements and class or social location. Rather, political consciousness is a link between ideas and agents that must be formed (or, as Hall puts it, "articulated" in the double sense of connecting and putting into words) concretely and conjuncturally within determinate conditions by specific human interventions. Thus, Hall's rendition of Gramsci results in a "Marxism without guarantees," where people make their own history but not in a way that can be determined ahead of time on the basis of their socioeconomic or class position, and the key political issue therefore is to understand "how ideological elements come, under certain conditions, to cohere together within a discourse . . . and how they do or do not become articulated, at specific conjunctures, to certain political subjects" ("On Postmodernism and Articulation" 53).

Hall's mediation of culturalist and structuralist positions points out a characteristic habit of British cultural studies: namely, its tendency (and apparent desire) to occupy a middle ground—to use the tools of poststructuralism to understand the discursive formation of identity and cultural codes but to keep in sight consciousness as a lived experience that cannot be reduced to an ideological effect. This rhetoric of the middle ground, moreover, establishes a topos by which cultural studies distinguishes itself from the extremes ascribed to other intellectual tendencies, whether *Screen's* avantgardist emphasis on the media production of viewers' subject positions, *Media, Culture, and Society's* backward-looking reliance on political economy, or the political irresponsibility of ludic postmodernism. Hall's characteristic move is not to polemicize against these tendencies so much as to place himself between the extreme versions of, say, Lacan, Foucault, or Baudrillard, on the one side, and their foes, on the other—in order to rehabilitate and use what he can of their work by rereading it from his own developing neo-Gramscian perspective.

Like Hall, in "The Formation(s) of Cultural Studies: An American in Birmingham," Lawrence Grossberg wants to map the development of cultural studies but without writing a linear narrative that insists on the progressive evolution of the field. To do this, Grossberg identifies five "temporarily stable moments" in the uneven development of the Centre. For Grossberg, the history of cultural studies resembles a "war of positions" more than a rational unfolding of increasingly sophisticated insights, where theorizing proceeds erratically, with false starts and retraced steps as well as discontinuous leaps, and theoretical terrain is seized, abandoned, reshaped, and reoccupied as cultural studies constantly struggles with both the larger arena of cultural theory and its own internal differences.

The first moment Grossberg points to is characterized by the "literary humanism" of Hoggart, with its emphasis on the use of literary tools ("close readings") to discover a Leavisite "felt quality of life" as an alternative to existing research on mass culture and mass communication. The second, "dialectical sociology," is a moment in the late sixties and early seventies when the terrain of cultural studies was reorganized by adding a "sociological pull" and a focus on intersubjectivity to the "literary-humanistic pull" of Hoggart. The third moment occurs in the mid-seventies, when a distinctly "Centre position" emerges with studies of youth subcultures and of encoding/decoding in mass communication. The fourth or "structural-conjuncturalist" moment in the early to mid-eighties registers the assimilation of Gramsci, the emergence of articulation theory, and a "marxism without guarantees." Finally, the fifth or "postmodern-conjuncturalist" moment of the late eighties and early nineties emphasizes links in a Gramscian perspective to feminism, transnationalism, and the affective work of the popular. In many respects, Grossberg suggests that cultural studies keeps learning what it has always known: namely, that the key questions, however they are framed, have to do with social communication, the production of common sense, and the determination of popular discourses and practices in ordinary life—questions, in other words, that link the "literary-humanistic pull" of Hoggart to the latest appropriation of Gramsci's notion of the "national popular."

In "What Is Cultural Studies, Anyway?," Johnson acknowledges the importance of histories of cultural studies, discussions of its relation to the academic disciplines, and analyses of its theoretical problematics as possible "definitional strategies." His "preferred" strategy, however, is to ask what the objects or topics of cultural studies are. Johnson begins by describing the circulation of cultural products as a series of distinct but interrelated moments or passages of form, from production to texts to readings to lived cultures. According to Johnson, work in cultural studies has fallen largely under three main models: production-based studies (which focus on the standpoint of the producer, the political organization of the conditions of production, and knowledge of its performative codes), text-based studies (which examine from a literary/critical standpoint the formal features of cultural products and the subject positions they make available), and studies of lived culture (for Johnson, the "privileged form of analysis" [71] which use ethnographic, historical, and semiotic methods to look at how people appropriate elements of mass culture for their own ends according to the needs and cultural logics of their social location). Notably, Johnson does not call for a synthesis of the three models into a comprehensive research program. Instead, typical of cultural studies' open-ended engagement with tensions and differences, he wants to "rethink each moment in light of the others, importing objects and methods usually developed in one moment into the next" (73).

The accounts of cultural studies presented here are as much mythologies as definitive histories. In one sense, cultural studies is not just a New Left formation in the UK but a more generalized response to the rise of mass society and the forms of cultural experience characteristic of modernity, the metropolis, and the emergence of the "people" (or the popular masses) as a force in history. From this perspective, cultural studies cannot be a simple genealogy from Williams, Hoggart, and Thompson to Hall, Grossberg, and Johnson but needs to include cultural commentary that can be traced back to Baudelaire's observations of street life in *Paris Spleen*, Engel's *Condition of the Working Classes in 1844*, and Henry Mayhew's *London Labour and the London Poor* and followed forward through the work of Walter Benjamin, Berthold Brecht, the Frankfurt School, C. Wright Mill, John Berger, Pierre Bourdieu, Roland Barthes, Michel de Certeau, and Jurgen Habermas, among others.

And from another angle, it should be noted that these accounts do not fully represent the struggles within cultural studies. Of these, perhaps the most telling are the interventions of feminism and antiracism. The appearance in 1978 of *Women Take Issue: Aspects of Women's Subordination* from the Women's Studies Group at CCCS challenged the masculinist tradition in cultural studies and its focus on class cultures to the exclusion of race and gender, and Angela McRobbie's "Settling Accounts with Subcultures: A Feminist Critique" pointed out that the category "youth" in Paul Willis' *Learning to Labor: How Working-Class Kids Get Working-Class Jobs* and Dick Hebdige's *Subculture: The*

Meaning of Style is coded as male. Paul Gilroy has noted the ethnocentric biases in British cultural studies' fixation on "Englishness" and the nation as the natural unit of class struggle (*There Ain't No Black in the Union Jack*), proposing instead a "transnational" perspective to take into account the African diaspora and the circulation of hybrid identities throughout the "black Atlantic" (*Black Atlantic: Modernity and Double Consciousness*).

✧ CONNECTIONS TO COMPOSITION

The brief overview of British cultural studies we have offered may have already suggested some connections to composition theory and practice: a view of communication that replaces the linear model of sender/message/ receiver with relatively autonomous and variably negotiated moments of production and reception; a shift from inferring the meaning of a cultural text from the expert readings of specialist critics to the ordinary experience of readers; a decentering of literary texts from their privileged cultural position and a reconceptualization of literature as an institution and a form of writing continuous with other forms of writing; a notion of subjectivity that is nonessentialist, nomadic, and self-productive; the study of representation not as more or less accurate depictions but as ideologically contested constructions of the real.

It is easy enough to see how these ideas could be stitched rather readily into the study and teaching of writing, and in fact, by the late 1980s, a number of trends in composition had already established an intellectual context that proved remarkably conducive to cultural studies. These include the shift from composing research and a narrowly cognitivist model of writing to poststructuralist textual rhetorics (Bartholomae, "Inventing the University"; Miller, *Rescuing the Subject*), social epistemic rhetoric (Berlin), and postcognitivist approaches drawing on figures such as Richard Rorty, Lev Vygotsky, and Mikhail Bakhtin (Bizzell, "Cognition"; Bruffee; Trimbur, "Beyond Cognition"); the impact of revisionist literacy studies (Heath; Scribner and Cole; Street), the influence of sociolinguistics (Bernstein; Halliday and Hasan; Hodge and Kress; Smitherman), and a turn to ethnographic methods (Brodkey, "Literacy Letters"; Fox) to understand the relations among culture, intellectual development, and language; and finally political and cultural histories (instead of intellectual taxonomies) of rhetoric and composition as a social formation and academic institution (Susan Miller, *Textual Carnivals*; Ohmann, *English in America*).

From a somewhat different perspective, Raymond Williams offers another point of convergence in "The Future of Cultural Studies" when he argues that the sources of cultural studies reside not only in texts but in traditions of popular education that can be traced back to the self-educating organizations of working people of the late eighteenth and nineteenth centuries and the adult extension and women's continuing education courses that arose around the turn of the century when ordinary readers pressed for opportunities to discuss literature in relation to their own lives. For Williams, Hoggart, Thompson, and others of their generation, teaching in the postwar adult education movement was a conscious choice that enabled them to develop courses in response to popular interests that could not at the time be taught in the university—courses in visual arts, popular music, town planning, film, radio, the press, and so on that helped shape an emerging sense of what cultural studies could be and how its intellectual work could articulate to popular aspirations.

The issues Williams looks at in the development of cultural studies—the tradition of an open-access democratic education and culture, the popular desire of ordinary people to understand intellectual questions in relation to their own lives, the limits and pressures of professionalizing intellectual projects as academic disciplines, the need to link critical education and work experience—are familiar ones in composition. As Williams notes, while the effort "to define a clearer subject, to establish a discipline, to bring order into the work" are "laudable ambitions," there is the danger of forgetting or losing touch with the original point of the project, namely that "people's questions are not answered by the existing distribution of the educational curriculum" (160). For composition studies, this conflict between finding a sanctioned place in the academy and determining whose questions should be addressed is taken up by, among others, Anne Ruggles Gere ("Long Revolution") Richard Ohmann ("Graduate Students"), and Trimbur ("Writing Instruction").

While there are certainly major points of convergence between cultural studies and composition, we do not want to give the impression that cultural studies has flowed effortlessly into the mainstream of composition theory and practice. Cultural studies has also raised issues that seem periodically to trouble the teaching of writing—in particular the relation of composition to mass communication and popular culture. Given its own institutional history as Freshman English, with its ties to liberal culture and belletristic rhetoric, composition teaching has had a rather ambivalent relationship to modernity and mass culture. As Charles Paine notes, part of the raison d'être for the first-year course, from the days of Adam Sherman Hill to the present, has been a kind of "cultural inoculation" against the threat posed to literacy by the mass media, whether the tabloid journalism and pulp fiction of Hill's era or MTV, talk radio, and Web surfing today.

[This deep-seated suspicion of mass communication and popular culture on the part of writing teachers and English studies has been exacerbated by the institutional separation of rhetoric and speech communication from English in the early part of the century and the subsequent development of mass communication research and media studies in communication departments.] While the founding of the Conference on College Composition and Communication in the late 1940s was an important initiative to repair this separation, the attempted alliance between composition and communication was an unstable one that ultimately fell apart (George and Trimbur, "The 'Communication Battle' "). Moreover, although communication studies (along with Michael Apple's work in education) provided the earliest entry points for British cultural studies into the American academy, mass communication—from Harold Innis, Marshall McLuhan, and the pioneering collections *Mass Culture* (Rosenberg and White, 1957) and *Culture for the Millions?* (Jacobs, 1961) to James Carey's call for a distinctly American cultural studies tradition based on Dewey and the Chicago School of Sociology—remains largely unassimilated.

✎ ARGUING FOR THE PLACE OF CULTURAL STUDIES AND COMPOSITION

As cultural studies entered composition, the first task was to explain what it was doing there, and early discussions typically presented arguments for the place of cultural studies in the writing classroom. The most prominent voices in those introductions to cultural studies and composition—Trimbur, James A. Berlin, John Schilb, and Lester Faigley—offered somewhat different accounts of how cultural studies fit into composition.

Trimbur's 1988 article "Cultural Studies and the Teaching of Writing" was the first to make explicit connections between cultural studies and composition pedagogy. In this and later discussions ("Articulation Theory"; "Radical Pedagogy"), Trimbur drew upon cultural studies to emphasize the concerns of popular education, especially the ties of writing instruction to the democratization of higher education through the land grant universities, the GI bill, and open admissions. For Trimbur, contemporary composition emerges in the late 1960s and early 1970s as part of a larger struggle to rerepresent students and adult learners stigmatized as uneducable because of cognitive deficiencies, the culture of poverty, or the restricted codes of oral culture. Much of what the field now takes for granted in composition pedagogy resulted from this historical moment, when writing teachers responded to the extension of higher learning by articulating their expertise as close readers to popular aspirations for advanced literacy, especially in basic writing programs.

James A. Berlin, the figure most readily associated with cultural studies and composition, on the other hand, focused on the role of cultural studies in the English department, especially as it brings to the surface what Berlin called "the invidious distinction between poetics and rhetoric . . . that has valorized poetics while considering rhetorical texts and their production as not worth serious study" ("Composition," 48). For Berlin, cultural studies offered a way to address such privileging of poetics by restoring rhetoric to the center of the curriculum, as an integrative method that emphasized both textual interpretation and production. In a series of articles and chapters ("Poststructuralism, Cultural Studies"; "Composition Studies"; "Rhetoric, Poetic"), and culminating in the posthumous *Rhetorics, Poetics, and Cultures,* Berlin elaborated the goal of rhetoric as enabling students to "master the operations of signification in the distribution of power" and thus "to become better writers and readers as citizens, workers, and critics of their cultures" (*Rhetorics* 145).

For John Schilb and Lester Faigley, cultural studies must be understood in its problematic relations to postmodernism. As Schilb notes in "Cultural Studies, Postmodernism, and Composition," the term *postmodernism* contains a range of meanings: "a critique of traditional epistemology, a set of artistic practices, and an ensemble of larger social conditions" (174). Given debates about the usefulness of the term, especially as it is developed by Frederic Jameson to designate the "cultural logic of late capitalism," the question, for Schilb, is whether "we should link or oppose cultural studies and postmodernism" (174). Schilb's answer is to "delay firm conclusions" while using the encounter between cultural studies and postmodernism as the basis of classroom work, involving students as "coinquirers" into the "influence of the media, the lure of commodities, the pressures of schooling, the limits of a certain social status, the virtues and illusions of theories themselves," as well as producers of play and pastiche (187). (For a more critical look at Jameson's notion of postmodernism, see Trimbur, "Composition Studies").

Like Schilb, Faigley sees postmodernism not just as a theoretical problem but as a sensibility that increasingly pervades contemporary social life. In *Fragments of Rationality: Postmodernity and the Subject of Composition*, Faigley links postmodernism to the transition from a Fordist world of mass production and consumption to a post-Fordist order of flexible and mobile production and the fragmentation of national markets into specialized niches. The result, Faigley says, is the "breakup of mass culture as it was constituted in the United States throughout much of this century into a pluralization of tastes, styles, and practices," with a consuming subject whose unstable and unfulfillable desires are shaped by "not so much objects but images of objects" (12). Composition studies, however, in Faigley's view, has been tied to a unitary and ahistorical subject, and, among other things, *Fragments* offers ways for students to use microethnographies to explore their shifting cultural locations and networked classrooms to experiment with different personae and "forbidden" discourses.

In a recent challenge to the standard accounts of the advent of cultural studies in composition, Nedra Reynolds charges Trimbur, Berlin, and Faigley with having written a male narrative of cultural studies and composition, missing "radical changes wrought by feminism's intervention into cultural studies" following, she argues, "the rhetorical pattern of so many cultural studies narratives, which walk neatly through the 'seminal' texts of the all-male trinity of Hoggart, Williams, and Thompson" ("Interrupting" 68). Reynolds likens this omission in composition studies to the omissions of gender in Birmingham noted above. Much the same could be said about the ways race and ethnicity have been omitted in composition studies, subsumed, as Catherine Prendergast points out, "into the powerful tropes of 'basic writer,' 'stranger' in the academy, or the trope of the generalized, marginalized 'other'" (36).

✧ CULTURAL STUDIES, COMPOSITION, AND CLASSROOM PRACTICE

In matters of classroom practice, cultural studies is no doubt most closely associated with bringing a more deliberate use of popular culture and media studies into the composition course. One can get an overview of the range of classroom practices indebted to cultural studies by consulting two collections—*Cultural Studies in the English Classroom* (Berlin and Vivion, 1992), which includes chapters on cultural studies as a means of curriculum reform in English studies (Farris; Kennedy; Zebroski), and *Left Margins: Cultural Studies and Composition Pedagogy* (Fitts and France, 1995). In addition, textbooks associated with cultural studies have appeared, offering a variety of approaches. *Rereading America* (Colombo et al., 1989), for example, focuses on a series of distinctly American myths. *Signs of Life in the USA: Readings on Popular Culture for Writers* (Maasik and Solomon, 1994) relies on semiotics to teach close readings of popular culture texts. *Reading Culture: Contexts for Critical Reading and Writing* (George and Trimbur, 1999) draws attention to culture both as lived experience and as a problem of representation. *Media Journal: Reading and Writing about Popular Culture* (Harris and Rosen, 1994) focuses on popular media and media criticism.

The persistent use of materials from popular culture and media studies one finds in these volumes requires some explanation, especially considering the longstanding suspicion of mass communication among writing teachers that we have already noted. The popularity of the popular in writing classrooms may be attributed in part to the fact that such topics enabled writing teachers to retain two commonplace practices: (1) to begin student writing with a topic "close to the self," close to students' experiences, and (2) to teach close reading and interpretation of texts, in this case, substituting popular culture or media for literary texts. In a sense, the cultural studies approach to the writing classroom addressed the question of what constitutes the content of a composition course with the idea that content is right under our noses, in the culture of everyday life, while shifting the emphasis from the personal experience of the individual to the lived experience of participants in the larger culture. In retaining the second commonplace—close reading—the cultural studies-based writing class distinguished itself from traditional classroom practice by resisting hierarchies that privileged certain kinds of texts (literary) over others (e.g., television sitcoms) and by imagining a wide range of social phenomena—not only the media and advertising but also malls, city streets, classrooms, work places, the rituals of everyday life, and so on—as cultural texts that can be read and analyzed.

Berlin offers a particularly rich discussion of what such reading of cultural texts might amount to in his description of "Codes and Critiques," a lower-division course that made fruitful use of Hall's encoding/decoding model and the neo-Gramscian synthesis that underwrites it (*Rhetorics* 116–31). Berlin designed assignments to help students understand the performative rules that code the production of messages (such as privileged dichotomies, denotation and connotation, underlying narrative, and preferred meanings) as well as the variable positions (dominant, negotiated, and oppositional) available in decoding at the point of consumption. For Berlin, such analysis could examine not only media representations but also narrative codings of social relationships and cultural settings such as boss and employee in the work place. (For a critique of the implicit "progressivism" in Berlin's version of cultural studies and its ties to a service ethic for the first-year course, see Michael Murphy's

"After Progressivism: Modern Composition, Institutional Service, and Cultural Studies").

The complexities of the cultural analysis and critique that Berlin argued for so forcefully and so influentially have subsequently been taken up by a number of commentators. Bruce McComiskey, for example, draws on Johnson's cycle of production, distribution, and consumption to amplify what he sees as the "production criticism" in Berlin's work by following the circulation of cultural texts. From another perspective, Alan France points out potential problems in asking students to imitate the methods of cultural critique. After charging the practice and politics of expressivist pedagogy with reinforcing "students' social alienation and insularity by encouraging them to identify good writing with the ideal of the autonomous self" (600) and thereby ignoring the role culture plays in forming subjectivities—a point that has become a familiar criticism from the left—France goes on to criticize Bartholomae and Petroskey's practice in *Ways of Reading* of calling on students to emulate the expert readings of such cultural critics as Mark Crispin Miller and Simon Frith included in the anthology as an "acquiescence in the extant distribution of power" equivalent to "expressivism's autonomous subject" (602). Instead, France calls for materialist readings that link text and world in a radical pedagogy that goes beyond both expressivism and poststructuralist textualism.

Drawing on popular culture in the classroom, as Richard Miller notes in an extended analysis of the Open University's course on popular culture designed by Tony Bennett, Stuart Hall, and others (*As If Learning*, 121–55), risks appropriating the lived experience of participants in that culture and subordinating it to the critical debates and methodological issues of academics. Joseph Harris likewise worries that the cultural studies classroom, though committed ostensibly to the way "forms of culture are taken up and revised by the people living in it" ("Other Reader," 228), subsumes the experience of ordinary readers in the ideological analysis of the teacher. For Harris, the student as the "other reader" is too often represented as seduced and injured by the pop text and in need of the training and correction available through the professional critic. To deal with this dilemma, Harris suggests looking at students as "at once rock fans and intellectuals, who watch old sitcoms and read criticism, who wear Levis and look skeptically at advertising" (233). He recommends such assignments as asking students to look at the way they use popular texts in forming their own identities and, instead of simply applying an interpretive method, to think about how that method works and what its uses and limits might be.

Along similar lines, Frank Farmer says that students sometimes consider cultural critique to be a "privileged, elitist mode of inquiry, one that is indifferent to, if not contemptuous of those it presumably seeks to enlighten or liberate" (204). Drawing on Bakhtin, Farmer notes the need for both dialogue and critique—and the difficulties of negotiating between the two. To this end, Farmer suggests a number of strategies: calling on students to consider "the figure of the consumer" and "the figure of the critic" inscribed in cultural critique, going beyond unmasking the contradictions and dominant interests in popular texts to identify what Terry Eagleton calls the "utopian kernel," and finally exploring the constraints on dialogue and the possibilities of forming more reciprocal relations in the writing classroom.

On the other hand, some cultural studies theorists have noted that the representation of ordinary readers, viewers, spectators, and fans can go too far in validating the authority and authenticity of the "active audience." The notion that people are not the "cultural dupes" of the dominant ideology but in fact make their own meanings and uses from the cultural products of late capitalism has been one of the central insights of encoding/decoding theory and ethnographic studies of readers such as Radway's *Reading the Romance* and McRobbie's "Jackie: An Ideology of Adolescent Femininity." Nonetheless, there is the danger that the emphasis on the active audience in cultural studies can lead to an uncritical populist celebration of popular culture, in which the audience is "never wrong" and the practice of everyday life is persistently (if in John Fiske's view "pre-politically") resistant to the dominant culture. Moreover, as Trimbur notes about Henry Giroux's *Border Crossings*, such "figures of resistance" are too often represented as "the postmodern subjects of a deindustrialized landscape—textual selves, bricoleurs, and semiotic guerrillas whose identities are shaped by popular culture, acts of consumption, and the absence of any connection to productive labor" ("Radical Pedagogy" 199).

The impact of cultural studies on the composition classroom has also raised a number of issues about the relation between cultural studies and writing instruction. Gary Tate, for example, notes that a cultural studies approach begins with the assumption shared by many teachers that composition is "an empty pedagogical space that needs to be filled with 'content'" (269). The problem, as Tate sees it, is that the desire to find a "content" for composition can all too easily lead to the neglect of writing. He worries that the absence of examples of student writing in the collection *Left Margins* indicates that the contributors to the collection represent students as either victims of the dominant culture or potential political allies—but not as writers. This concern for the place of writing in the cultural studies classroom also appears, from another perspective, when Susan Miller suggests that a cultural studies approach to teaching writing is too often limited to a "hermeneutics of suspicion" by teaching "texts rather than their making, by teaching awareness rather than rhetoric, and by teaching the power of meanings rather than the making of statements"—a pedagogy she sees as resulting in "political stasis" ("Technologies" 499).

No doubt the most widely publicized objection to cultural studies in the writing classroom came in 1992 from Maxine Hairston, who charged various composition scholars and teachers (Hairston lists Charles Paine, Patricia Bizzell, C. H. Knoblauch, Berlin, Ohmann, Trimbur, Faigley, and Brodkey) with forcing leftist ideology on vulnerable young people instead of teaching writing. This has come about, Hairston believes, in part because of the emergence of a theory-happy (and implicitly authoritarian) cultural left within composition and in part because of the increasing cultural diversity in college classrooms. In Hairston's view, however, the way for writing courses to become responsibly multicultural is not through the course content the teacher assigns but through the diversity of life experiences reflected in the students' writing. The job of writing teachers, Hairston asserts, is to set up the classroom as a "nurturant writing community" so that students can "understand the rich tapestry of cultures that their individual stories make up" (191).

Responses to Hairston's attack were swift and multiple. In their introduction to *Pedagogy in the Age of Politics*, Patricia Sullivan and Donna Qualley note how Hairston attempts to pose terms such as *dogma, ideology,* and *politics* against terms like *diversity, craft,* and *critical thinking,* implying the latter are "ideologically pure, devoid of the political commitments of anyone in particular" (x). Others (Strickland; Trimbur, "Response") point out that what Hairston really rejects is the reintroduction of rhetoric into the writing classroom, the insistence that language use is always rhetorical and that negotiation of cultural differences is a proper practice in any writing classroom.

Hairston's critique and the ensuing debate reveal some telling fissures in the current practices of teaching writing. For example, it is important to note that when Hairston says that politics are inappropriate in writing instruction, she is not arguing that the composition classroom can or should be a neutral setting. Rather she is speaking on behalf of the politics of the process movement and its investment in making the classroom a collaborative "low-risk environment" where the "students' own writing must be the center of the course" (185). This familiar vision of a community of writers has, of course, been challenged repeatedly in the past decade (c.f. Harris, "Idea of Community"; Trimbur, "Consensus and Difference") as nostalgia for the face-to-face communication of the preindustrial village and a serious underestimation of the cultural differences students bring with them. Instead of assuming a common ground that unites students in the classroom community, composition theorists and practitioners have increasingly drawn on other metaphors, such as Iris Marion Young's notion of the postmodern "city of strangers" in which identities and meanings are not given ahead of time but must be negotiated through communicative exchange.

Perhaps the most influential metaphor to replace the process movement's notion of community (what Trimbur calls Hairston's vision of the multicultural classroom as "sharing time in the metropolis" ["Response" 24]) is Mary Louise Pratt's idea of the "Arts of the Contact Zone," the social space "where cultures meet, clash, and grapple with each other, often in contexts of highly asymmetrical relations of power" (34). Pratt's "contact zone" has led Bartholomae, for example, to imagine the basic writing classroom as a place for "experiments in transculturation . . . and in the arts of critique, parody, and comparison, . . . the redemption of the oral, . . . [and] ways to move into and out of rhetorics of authenticity" ("Tidy House" 13). For Patricia Bizzell, Pratt's "contact zone" offers a means of curriculum design, to organize courses around points in American history when various groups struggled for the right to represent themselves to each other and to shape the direction of events ("Contact Zones"; Bizzell and Herzberg, *Negotiating Differences*). Richard Miller's "Fault Lines in the Contact Zone" offers a detailed analysis of the "place of unsolicited oppositional discourse, parody, resistance, critique in the imagined classroom community" (Pratt 39)—in particular how teachers might respond "when the kind of racist, sexist, and homophobic sentiments now signified by the term 'hate speech' surface in our classrooms" (Miller, "Fault Lines" 391).

↫ THE FUTURE OF CULTURAL STUDIES IN COMPOSITION

Despite the objections to cultural studies we have noted, it is probably safe to say that its place in composition teaching is now well established. A cultural studies approach to writing instruction has over the past decade elaborated a range of pedagogical practices and allied itself with others—encoding/decoding studies, ideological critiques, microethnographies, literacy narratives, networked classrooms, contact zone pedagogy. Its interests, moreover, overlap with other significant currents in composition studies, especially feminism, race and ethnic studies, and queer theory. Some of the work facing cultural studies proponents in composition, we believe, is to explore these connections more fully, to probe cultural studies' historical commitments to a masculinist view of class culture as the privileged object of inquiry and to devise approaches that go beyond the English-only First Worldism that often pervades composition teaching. Moreover, as we see it, the affinities between cultural studies and the recent emphasis on civic rhetoric and public writing are particularly promising, in part because they may well help to correct the tendency in some versions of cultural studies to picture students as culture consumers instead of culture producers and thereby provide an impetus to imagine writing assignments that take students beyond the critical essay of culture analysis and critique into the rhetoric of public discourse.

We expect, furthermore, that the study of writing will continue to benefit from the appearance of cultural studies. Anne Ruggles Gere's 1993 CCCC Chair's address ("Kitchen Tables") pointed out the importance of research on the self-sponsored writing of ordinary people—what she calls the "extracurriculum" of composition—and there have already been notable examples of such work, including Gere's study of the literacy and cultural practices of women's clubs between 1880 and 1920 (*Intimate Practices*) and Susan Miller's study of "commonplace writing" before the advent of mass schooling, *Assuming the Positions*. Based on in-depth interviews with over one hundred "ordinary Americans," Deborah Brandt has written a sequence of articles that look at how individuals develop cultural attitudes toward reading and writing ("Remembering"), how individuals cope with the "ideological congestion" of accumulating literacies in the late twentieth century ("Accumulating"), and the role of "sponsors" in literacy development ("Sponsors"). In a work that in part recalls McRobbie's study of British female teen readers ("Jackie"), Margaret Finders investigated in *Just Girls* such "hidden literacies" as note passing and magazine reading among junior high girls in the United States.

Such historical and ethnographic work on ordinary readers and writers, of course, is not the only direction suggested by cultural studies. Carl Herndl has brought a cultural studies approach to the study of writing in the work place and in science ("Tactics"; "Cultural Studies"). Others, such as Trimbur ("Literacy") and Janet Carey Eldred and Peter Mortensen ("Reading"; "Figuring Illiteracy") have looked at representations of literacy that circulate across a range of discourses. Geoffrey Sirc's "Never Mind Tagmemics, Where's the Sex Pistols?" is perhaps the first and only exploration of punk subculture and its relation to shifts in composition teaching. Nedra Reynolds' analysis of the metaphors of space in composition studies ("Imagined Geographies") draws suggestively on postmodern cultural geography. All of these (and other works we lack the space to discuss) provide directions for future research projects.

We are less sanguine, however, about the role of cultural studies in promoting the reconfiguration of English studies envisioned by Berlin and others. It is not that the theoretical grounds are lacking to realign rhetoric and poetic. Rather we point to the lack of political will, as composition and literature remain largely polarized and increasingly at odds in the scramble for scarce resources. If anything, we expect compositionists to call into question the messianic role the field often assumes to "save English studies from itself" and to raise again the issue of separating institutionally from literary studies.

Finally, as we close, we must note a sense of misgiving that seems to pervade cultural studies in the United States at this moment. As Janice Radway notes, "You'd think that some of us who have long been associated with cultural studies would be happy. But we're concerned by how easily it has been taken up and by the kind of research and writing that it increasingly seems to generate" (quoted in Grossberg, "Genealogy" 272). The sense of foreboding we hear in Radway's voice cuts in a number of directions. Is the problem cultural studies pretenders and a field that needs policing? bell hooks' experience at the 1990 Conference on Cultural Studies at the University of Illinois, what she describes as her "sense of terror" at the silencing discourse and academic hierarchies, sounds a warning about this line of thought. Perhaps the problem, as Grossberg suggests, is that cultural studies has been produced and circulated in the United States primarily through individual publication instead of the ongoing work of a collective, as in Birmingham. This is no doubt part of it. But our sense is that cultural studies here is experiencing the unavoidable anxieties of professional work and the contradictions inherent in the production of scholarly commodities—the clash, namely, between their exchange value (and the need to accumulate individual credentials) and their use value (and the desire to articulate intellectual work to popular aspirations). Our belief is that the future of cultural studies in composition depends on how we keep that contradiction in sight.

Bibliography

Bartholomae, David. "Inventing the University." *When a Writer Can't Write: Studies in Writer's Block and Other Composing-Process Problems.* Ed. Mike Rose. New York: Guilford, 1985. 134–65.

———. "The Tidy House: Basic Writing in the American Curriculum." *Journal of Basic Writing* 12 (1993): 4–21.

Bartholomae, David, and Anthony Petrosky, eds. *Ways of Reading: An Anthology for Writers*. 4th ed. Boston: Bedford, 1996.

Berlin, James A. "Composition and Cultural Studies." *Composition and Resistance*. Ed. C. Mark Hurlbert and Michael Blitz. Portsmouth, NH: Boynton/Cook, 1991. 47–55.

———. "Composition Studies and Cultural Studies: Collapsing Boundaries." *Into the Field: Sites of Composition Studies*. Ed. Anne Ruggles Gere. New York: MLA, 1993. 99–116.

———. "Poststructuralism, Cultural Studies, and the Composition Classroom: Postmodern Theory in Practice." *Rhetoric Review* 11.1 (1992): 16–33.

———. "Rhetoric, Poetic, and Culture: Contested Boundaries in English Studies." Bullock, Trimbur, and Schuster 23–38.

———. *Rhetorics, Poetics, and Cultures: Refiguring English Studies*. Urbana IL: NCTE, 1996.

Berlin, James A., and Michael J. Vivion. *Cultural Studies in the English Classroom*. Portsmouth, NH: Heinemann, Boynton/Cook, 1992.

Bernstein, Basil. *Class, Codes, and Control*. New York: Schocken, 1975.

Bizzell, Patricia. "Cognition, Convention, and Certainty: What We Need to Know About Writing." *Pre/Text* 3.3 (1982): 213–43.

———. " 'Contact Zones' and English Studies." *College English* 56.2 (1994): 163–69.

Bizzell, Patricia, and Bruce Herzberg. *Negotiating Differences: Cultural Case Studies for Composition*. Boston: Bedford, 1996.

Bloom, Lynn Z., Donald A. Daiker, and Edward M. White, eds. *Composition in the Twenty-first Century: Crisis and Change*. Carbondale: Southern Illinois UP, 1996.

Brandt, Deborah. "Accumulating Literacy: Writing and Learning to Write in the 20th Century." *College English* 57.6 (1995): 649–68.

———. "Remembering Reading, Remembering Writing." *College Composition and Communication* 45.4 (1994): 459–79.

———. "Sponsors of Literacy." *College Composition and Communication* 49.2 (1998): 165–85.

Brodkey, Linda. "Making a Federal Case Out of Difference: The Politics of Pedagogy, Publicity, and Postponement." *Writing Theory and Critical Theory*. Ed. John Clifford and John Schilb. New York: MLA, 1994. 236–61.

———. "On the Subjects of Class and Gender in 'The Literacy Letters.' " *College English* 51.2 (1989): 125–41.

Bruffee, Kenneth A. "Social Construction, Language, and the Authority of Knowledge: A Bibliographical Essay." *College English* 48.8 (1986): 773–90.

Bullock, Richard, John Trimbur, and Charles Schuster, eds. *The Politics of Writing Instruction: Postsecondary*. Portsmouth, NH: Heinemann, Boynton/Cook, 1991.

Centre for Contemporary Cultural Studies. *The Empire Strikes Back: Race and Racism in 70s Britain*. London: Hutchinson, 1982.

———. *Making Histories: History-Writing and Politics*. London: Hutchinson, 1982.

Centre for Contemporary Cultural Studies Education Group. *Education Limited: Schooling and Training and the New Right Since 1979*. London: Unwin Hyman, 1991.

———. *Unpopular Education: Schooling and Social Democracy in England Since 1944*. London: Hutchinson, 1981.

Clarke, John, Chas. Cricher, and Richard Johnson, eds. *Working Class Culture: Studies in History and Theory*. New York: St. Martin's, 1979.

Colombo, Gary, et al. *Rereading America: Cultural Contexts for Critical Thinking and Writing*. New York: Bedford, St. Martin's, 1989.

Cushman, Ellen. "The Rhetorician as an Agent of Social Change." *College Composition and Communication* 47.1 (1996): 7–28.

Eldred, Janet Carey, and Peter Mortensen. "Reading Literacy Narratives." *College English* 54.5 (1992): 512–39.

Faigley, Lester. *Fragments of Rationality: Postmodernity and the Subject of Composition*. Pittsburgh: Pittsburgh UP, 1992.

Farmer, Frank. "Dialogue and Critique: Bakhtin and the Cultural Studies Writing Classroom." *College Composition and Communication* 49.2 (1998): 186–207.

Finders, Margaret J. *Just Girls: Hidden Literacies and Life in Junior High*. New York: Teachers College, 1997.

Fiske, John. *Understanding Popular Culture*. Boston: Unwin Hyman, 1989.

Fitts, Karen, and Alan W. France, eds. *Left Margins: Cultural Studies and Composition Pedagogy*. Albany: SUNY P, 1995.

Fox, Tom. *The Social Uses of Literacy: Politics and Pedagogy*. Norwood, NJ: Ablex, 1990.

France, Alan W. "Assigning Places: The Function of Introductory Composition as Cultural Discourse." *College English* 55.6 (1993): 593–609.

George, Diana, and John Trimbur. "The Communication Battle, or, Whatever Happened to the Fourth C?" *College Composition and Communication* 50.4 (1999): 681–98.

———. *Reading Culture: Contexts for Critical Reading and Writing*. 3rd ed. New York: Longman, 1999.

Gere, Anne Ruggles. "Kitchen Tables and Rented Rooms: The Extracurriculum of Composition." *College Composition and Communication* 45.1 (1994): 75–92.

———. *Intimate Practices: Literacy and Cultural Work in US Women's Clubs, 1880–1920*. Urbana: U of Illinois P, 1997.

———. "The Long Revolution in Composition." Bloom, Daiker, and White 119–32.

Gilroy, Paul. *There Ain't No Black in the Union Jack*. London: Hutchinson, 1987.

———. *Black Atlantic: Modernity and Double Consciousness*. Cambridge, MA: Harvard UP, 1993.

Grossberg, Lawrence. "The Formation(s) of Cultural Studies: An American in Birmingham." *Bringing It All Back Home: Essays on Cultural Studies*. Durham, NC: Duke UP, 1997. 195–233.

———. "Toward a Genealogy of the State of Cultural Studies." *Bringing It All Back Home: Essays on Cultural Studies*. Durham, NC: Duke UP, 1997. 272–86.

Hairston, Maxine. "Diversity, Ideology, and Teaching Writing." *College Composition and Communication* 43.2 (1992): 179–93.

Hall, Stuart. "Cultural Studies: Two Paradigms." *Media, Culture, and Society: A Critical Reader*. Ed. Richard Collins et al. London: Sage, 1986. 33–48.

———. "On Postmodernism and Articulation: An Interview with Stuart Hall." Ed. Lawrence Grossberg. *Journal of Communication Inquiry* 10.2 (1986): 45–60.

Hall, Stuart, Chas. Cricher, Tony Jefferson, John Clarke, and Brian Roberts, eds. *Policing the Crisis: Mugging, the State, and Law and Order*. London: Macmillan, 1979.

Hall, Stuart, and Tony Jefferson, eds. *Resistance Through Rituals: Youth Subcultures in Post War Britain*. London: Hutchinson, 1976.

Halliday, M. A. K., and Ruquiya Hasan. *Language, Context, and Text: Aspects of Language in Social-Semiotic Perspective*. Oxford: Oxford UP, 1989.

Harris, Joseph. "The Idea of Community in the Teaching of Writing." *College Composition and Communication* 40.1 (1989): 11–22.

———. "The Other Reader." *JAC* 12.1 (1992): 27–37.

Harris, Joseph, and Jay Rosen. *Media Journal: Reading and Writing About Popular Culture*. Needham Heights, MA: Allyn & Bacon, 1994.

Heath, Shirley Brice. *Ways with Words: Language, Life, and Work in Communities and Classrooms*. New York: Cambridge UP, 1983.

Hebdige, Dick. *Subculture: The Meaning of Style*. New York: Routledge, 1979.

Herndl, Carl G. "Cultural Studies and Critical Science." *Understanding Scientific Prose*. Ed. Jack Selzer. Madison: U of Wisconsin P, 1993. 61–81.

———. "Tactics and the Quotidian: Resistance and Professional Discourse." *JAC* 16.3 (1996): 455–70.

Herzberg, Bruce. "Community Service and Critical Teaching." *College Composition and Communication* 45.3 (1994): 307–19.

Hodge, Robert and Gunther Kress. *Social Semiotics*. Ithaca, NY: Cornell UP, 1988.

Hoggart, Richard. *The Uses of Literacy*. London: Essential Books, 1957.

hooks, bell. "Discussion: John Fiske." *Cultural Studies*. Ed. Lawrence Grossberg, Cary Nelson, and Paula Treichler. New York: Routledge, 1992. 171.

Jacobs, Norman, ed. *Culture for the Millions?* Princeton, NJ: Van Nostrand, 1961.

Johnson, Richard. "What Is Cultural Studies, Anyway?" *Social Text* 16.1 (1986–87): 38–80.

Maasik, Sonia, and Jack Solomon. *Signs of Life in the USA: Readings on Popular Culture for Writers*. Boston: St. Martin's, 1994.

McComiskey, Bruce. "Social-Process Rhetorical Inquiry: Cultural Studies Methodologies for Critical Writing About Advertisements." *JAC* 17.3 (1997): 381–400.

McRobbie, Angela. "Jackie: An Ideology of Adolescent Femininity." *Popular Culture: Past and Present*. Ed. Bernard Waites et al. London: Croom Helm. 263–83.

———. "Settling Accounts with Subcultures: A Feminist Critique." *Screen Education* 34.1 (1980): 37–49.

Miller, Richard E. *As If Learning Mattered: Reforming Higher Education*. Ithaca, NY: Cornell UP, 1998.

———. "Fault Lines in the Contact Zone." *College English* 56.4 (1994): 389–408.

Miller, Susan. *Assuming the Positions: Cultural Pedagogy and the Politics of Commonplace Writing*. Pittsburgh: U of Pittsburgh P, 1998.

———. *Rescuing the Subject: A Critical Introduction to Rhetoric and the Writer*. Carbondale: Southern Illinois UP, 1989.

———. "Technologies of Self?-Formation." *JAC* 17.3 (1997): 497–500.

———. *Textual Carnivals: The Politics of Composition*. Carbondale: Southern Illinois UP, 1991.

Mortensen, Peter. "Figuring Illiteracy: Rustic Bodies and Unlettered Minds in Rural America." *Rhetorical Bodies*. Ed. Sharon Crowley and Jack Selzer. Madison: U of Wisconsin P, 1999.

Murphy, Michael. "After Progressivism: Modern Composition, Institutional Service, and Cultural Studies." *Composition Theory for the Postmodern Classroom*. Ed. Gary A. Olson and Sidney I. Dobrin. Albany: SUNY P, 1994. 205–24.

Ohmann, Richard. "Graduate Students, Professionals, Intellectuals." *College English* 52.3 (1990): 247–57.

———. *English in America: A Radical View of the Profession*. New York: Oxford UP, 1976.

Paine, Charles. "The Composition Course and Public Discourse." *Rhetoric Review* 15.2 (1997): 282–98.

Pratt, Mary Louise. "Arts of the Contact Zone." *Profession* 91 (1991): 33–40.

Prendergast, Catherine. "Race: The Absent Presence in Composition Studies." *College Composition and Communication* 50.1 (1998): 36–53.

Radway, Janice. *Reading the Romance: Women, Patriarchy, and Popular Literature*. Chapel Hill: U of North Carolina P, 1984.

Reynolds, Nedra. "Composition's Imagined Geographies: The Politics of Space in the Frontier, City, and Cyberspace." *College Composition and Communication* 50.1 (1998): 12–35.

Rosenberg, Bernard, and David White, eds. *Mass Culture*. Glencoe, IL: Free Press, 1957.

———. "Interrupting Our Way to Agency: Feminist Cultural Studies and Composition." *Feminism and Composition Studies: In Other Words*. Ed. Susan C. Jarratt and Lynn Worsham. New York: MLA, 1998. 58–73.

Schilb, John. "Cultural Studies, Postmodernism, and Composition." *Contending with Words: Composition and Rhetoric in a Postmodern Age*. Ed. Patricia Harkin and John Schilb. New York: MLA, 1991. 173–88.

Scribner, Sylvia, and Michael Cole. *The Psychology of Literacy*. Cambridge, MA: Harvard UP, 1981.

Sirc, Geoffrey. "Never Mind Tagmemics, Where's the Sex Pistols?" *College Composition and Communication* 48.1 (1997): 9–29.

Smitherman, Geneva. *Talkin' and Testifyin'*. Boston: Houghton Mifflin, 1977.

Street, Brian V. *Literacy in Theory and Practice*. Cambridge: Cambridge UP, 1984.

Strickland, Ron. "Response to Maxine Hairston." *College Composition and Communication* 44.2 (1993): 250–52.

Sullivan, Patricia A., and Donna J. Qualley, eds. *Pedagogy in the Age of Politics: Writing and Reading (in) the Academy*. Urbana, IL: NCTE, 1994.

Tate, Gary. "Empty Pedagogical Space and Silent Students." Fitts and France 269–73.

Thompson, E. P. *The Making of the English Working Class*. New York: Vintage, 1963.

Trimbur, John. "Articulation Theory and the Problem of Determination: A Reading of Lives on the Boundary." *JAC* 13.1 (1993): 31–49.

———. "Beyond Cognition: The Voices in Inner Speech." *Rhetoric Review* 5.2 (1987): 211–21.

———. "Composition Studies: Postmodern or Popular." *Into the Field: Sites of Composition Studies*. Ed. Anne Ruggles Gere. New York: MLA, 1993. 117–32.

———. "Consensus and Difference in Collaborative Learning." *College English* 51.6 (1989): 602–16.

———. "Cultural Studies and the Teaching of Writing." *Focuses* 1.2 (1988): 5–18.

———. "Literacy and the Discourse of Crisis." *The Politics of Writing Instruction: Postsecondary*. Ed. Richard Bullock et al. Portsmouth, NH: Heinemann, Boynton/Cook, 1991. 277–96.

———. "The Politics of Radical Pedagogy: A Plea for 'A Dose of Vulgar Marxism.'" *College English* 56.2 (1994): 194–206.

———. "Response to Maxine Hairston." *College Composition and Communication* 44.2 (1993): 248–49.

———. "Taking the Social Turn: Teaching Writing Post-Process." *College Composition and Communication* 45.1 (1994): 108–18.

———. "Writing Instruction and the Politics of Professionalization." Bloom, et al. 133–45.

Wells, Susan. "Rogue Cops and Health Care: What Do We Want from Public Writing?" *College Composition and Communication* 47.3 (1996): 325–41.

Williams, Raymond. *Culture and Society, 1780–1950*. London: Chatto and Windus, 1958.

———. *The Long Revolution*. London: Chatto and Windus, 1961.

———. "The Future of Cultural Studies." *The Politics of Modernism: Against the New Conformists*. London: Verso, 1989. 151–62.

Willis, Paul. *Learning to Labor: How Working-Class Kids Get Working-Class Jobs*. New York: Columbia UP, 1977.

Women's Study Group, Centre for Contemporary Cultural Studies. *Women Take Issue: Aspects of Women's Subordination*. London: Hutchinson, 1978.

Young, Iris Marion. *Justice and the Politics of Difference*. Princeton, NJ: Princeton UP, 1990.

Critical Pedagogy: Dreaming of Democracy

ANN GEORGE

In two weeks, classes will begin at the small, private Texas university where I now teach. The tapes of vigorous, radical class discussions that I've played in my head all summer mysteriously begin to fade as I struggle with the syllabus for my first-year composition course. Like many writing teachers, I am attracted to the student-centered pedagogies and themes of social justice it has become fashionable to espouse; I want to empower students, to engage them in cultural critique, to make a change. But as Ira Shor remarks in *Empowering Education*, the start of a new semester is both "rich in possibilities and cluttered with disabling routines" (200), and as I plan my fall class, I am reminded that, despite my subversive intentions and the liberatory rhetoric of my course descriptions, my teaching often retreats to the level of sporadic creativity or, worse, to rather predictable English-teacher experimentation and circling of chairs. I fear that I am, in Peter Elbow's phrase, "bamboozled"—that is, I "call things by the wrong name. . . . [I] preach freedom, but [I] don't really practice it" (*Embracing Contraries* 92, 98). I write this essay, then, in hopes of reducing the bamboozlement of compositionists everywhere (including myself)—if that is, indeed, what we suffer from—by examining the goals, the realities, and the controversies of critical pedagogy.

"To propose a pedagogy," says Roger Simon, "is to propose a political vision," a "[dream] for ourselves, our children, and our communities" (371). Critical pedagogy (a.k.a. liberatory pedagogy, empowering pedagogy, radical pedagogy, engaged pedagogy, or pedagogy of possibility) envisions a society not simply pledged to but successfully enacting the principles of equality, of liberty and justice for all.[1] "Dedicated to the emancipatory imperatives of *self-empowerment* and *social transformation*," critical pedagogy engages students in analyses of the unequal power relations that produce and are produced by cultural practices and institutions (including schools), and it aims to help students develop the tools that will enable them to challenge this inequality (McLaren 163). In this, as in the controversy it has generated, critical pedagogy closely resembles and often overlaps with cultural studies and feminist pedagogies (see essays by Diana George and John Trimbur and by Susan Jarratt in this vol-

ume). However, critical pedagogy can be distinguished from these two pedagogies by its usually explicit commitment to education for citizenship. Henry
Giroux, arguably the foremost American theorist of radical education, claims
that the task of critical pedagogy is nothing short of "reconstructing democratic public life" ("Liberal Arts Education" 120). McLaren, Giroux's former colleague, asserts that the commitment of critical pedagogy stems from

> the moral choice put before us as teachers and citizens, a choice that Ameri-
> can philosopher John Dewey suggested is the distinction between education
> as a function of society and society as a function of education. We need to ex-
> amine that choice: do we want our schools to create a passive, risk-free citi-
> zenry, or a politicized citizenry capable of fighting for various forms of public
> life and informed by a concern for equality and social justice? (158)

To create this "politicized citizenry," critical pedagogy reinvents the roles
of teachers and students in the classroom and the kind of activities they engage in.

At the center of critical pedagogy scholarship, ironically—though, perhaps,
given current gender configurations within the academy, not too surprisingly—
is a group of mostly white, middle-class men: Paulo Freire, Henry Giroux, Ira
Shor, Stanley Aronowitz, Donaldo Macedo, Peter McLaren, and Roger Simon,
with Freire, Giroux, and Shor constituting a kind of "Big Three" in the field.
The "ur text" for critical pedagogy is Paulo Freire's *Pedagogy of the Oppressed*.
A Brazilian educator, Freire was exiled after a military coup in 1964 for his work
in the national literacy campaign, teaching peasants to read both the word and
the world of oppressive economic and political domination in which they lived.
During a nearly twenty-year exile, Freire became well known for his work developing literacy programs in Latin America and Africa.[2]

Pedagogy of the Oppressed (1970) lays out many of the terms, assumptions,
and basic methods that still define the project of critical pedagogy today. Freire's
educational philosophy is grounded in his conviction that oppression "inter-
feres with man's [sic] ontological and historical vocation to be more fully
human"—that is, to know oneself as a subject in history capable of understanding and transforming the world (40–41).[3] In *Pedagogy of the Oppressed*,
Freire presents his well-known critique (often excerpted in first-year readers)
of the "banking" concept of education, in which students are seen as "receptacles" waiting to be filled with the teacher's official knowledge; education thus
becomes little more than information transfer, "an act of depositing" (58). Instead, Freire practices what he calls problem-posing or dialogic education, in
which teachers work with students to develop *conscientização* or critical consciousness—the ability to define, to analyze, to problematize the economic, political, and cultural forces that shape but, according to Freire, do not completely
determine their lives. Hence, the content of problem-posing education is material from students' experience; dialogue among students and teacher revolves
around "generative themes"—domination, marriage, or work—that represent
students' perceptions of the world.[4] "This pedagogy," Freire writes, "makes op-

pression and its causes objects of reflection by the oppressed, and from that reflection will come their necessary engagement in the struggle for their liberation" (33).[This relationship between reflection and action is what Freire refers
to as "praxis," and it is essential for Freire: neither critical consciousness nor
unreflective action alone will enable people to transform the world.]

Critical theorists and teachers have found Freire attractive for a number of
reasons, not least of which are his radical analysis of schooling as an instrument of domination and his understanding of the situatedness of all theory
and practice. Shor's volumes *Freire for the Classroom* (1987) and *Empowering Education* (1992) illustrate the interdisciplinary appeal and applicability of Freirean
pedagogy; teachers from disciplines such as history, media studies, and
women's studies as well as some from departments we might not expect like
architecture, the life sciences, and mathematics are implementing critical pedagogy in their classrooms. However, as James Berlin suggests, Freire has become especially interesting to scholars and teachers in English studies and
particularly in composition because of his insistence that thought and knowledge are socially constructed, linguistic products: "language—in its mediation
between the world and the individual, the object and the subject—contains
within its shaping force the power of creating humans as agents of action"
("Freirean Pedagogy in the U.S." 170). Because language and thought are in-
extricably linked, language instruction becomes a key site where dominant ideology is reproduced—or disrupted. Finally, Freire's belief in the possibility of
resistance to oppression has been vital to radical theorists like Aronowitz and
Giroux, among others, who seek to move beyond the overly pessimistic assessments of domination typical of much leftist critical and cultural theory.

✦ THE ROLE OF SCHOOLS:
RADICAL DREAMS OF DEMOCRACY

In *Illiterate America*, Jonathan Kozol quotes Sir William Berkeley, governor of
Virginia in the seventeenth century, on the dangers of mass literacy: "I thank
God there are no free schools nor printing [in this land]. For learning has
brought disobedience, and heresy, and sects into the world, and printing
hath divulged them . . . God save us from both!" (93). Kozol's study of literacy in the United States—he estimates that one-third of adult Americans are
illiterate—leads him to conclude that Berkeley needn't have worried: public
education has not produced unrest or disobedience among the masses; it has,
Kozol argues, been designed to ensure that students, particularly working-class
students, are thoroughly schooled in passive compliance, if little else. That is,
these children receive substandard educations not because their teachers are
unqualified or too permissive nor because of cafeteria-style curricula that ig-
nore the basics (as repeatedly asserted in conservative studies) but because
schools function as "sorting mechanisms" (McLaren 160) to maintain inequality:

If all of this is not political in purpose and result, if it is all a matter of "defective methods," of "inadequate technique," it is remarkable with what sustained coincidence we have assigned the worst techniques, the least efficient methods, to the poorest people in our nation. But we know well that none of this is true. It isn't coincidence. It isn't technique. It isn't the wrong method. It is, in William Berkeley's terms, precisely the *right* method. It is a method that assures perpetuation of disparities in power and of inequities in every form of day-to-day existence. (Kozol 93)

Kozol's by now familiar claim that cultural institutions function to reproduce the ideology and power of dominant groups was seconded by many radical educators during the 1980s when conservative administrations in both England and the United States prompted increased response from the left.

Indeed, although American critical pedagogy has roots in the turn-of-the-century progressive educational reform movement, the 1980s marks the contemporary rebirth of the project. One look at this essay's bibliography reveals the boom in critical pedagogy scholarship during the Reagan-Bush years, as radical educators responded to a host of conservative reports on education released beginning in 1983, the two most influential of which were *A Nation at Risk* (produced by Secretary of Education T. H. Bell's National Commission on Excellence in Education) and *Action for Excellence* (written by the Education Commission of the States). These reports announced a crisis in American education, a system wallowing in mediocrity that crippled America's ability to compete in the world economic market; they proposed an authoritarian, back-to-basics, teacher-proof curriculum to restore excellence to the schools. Giroux argues that the 1980s signaled a "major ideological shift" (*Schooling* 16) in public education as conservatives worked to undo reforms of the 1960s and to redefine schools not as sites for civic education and social justice but as "company stores" in which good citizenship is equated with economic productivity and "cultural uniformity" (*Schooling* 18).[5] The popularity and success of conservative educational reform suggested to radical educators that the country was experiencing not just a crisis in education but, as Giroux and McLaren argue, "a crisis in American democracy itself" (216).

Hence, in *Critical Teaching and Everyday Life* (1980), Shor presents a blistering Marxist critique of the community college system, developed during the late 1950s and bulging by the late 1970s, as a warehouse for surplus workers. Community colleges, Shor argues, simultaneously feed off the American Dream and shortcircuit it by building a large pool of skilled workers for a shrinking number of increasingly deskilled jobs. Unlike elite liberal arts colleges, which prepare students for roles as future problem-solvers and decision-makers, community colleges with their vocational curricula train students to follow orders and accept subordinate roles in society: "mass colleges were not to be Ivory Towers or 'the best years of your life' or homecoming parades on crisp autumn afternoons. They were from the start shaped outside the elite traditions of the academy, by the state for the masses, in the genre of public housing and the welfare bureaucracy" (13). Given American mass culture and mass education,

Shor suggests, it is hardly surprising that ours is a country in which " 'freedom' is not the practice of democracy but rather the practice of shopping, casual complaining, and individualism, in a society which offers wide license for individualism" (xi).

Three important studies by Giroux—*Theory and Resistance in Education* (1983), *Education Under Siege* (coauthored with Aronowitz) (1985), and *Schooling and the Struggle for Public Life* (1988)—further advance the radical critique of public education. Like Shor, Giroux explores the "hidden curriculum," the subtle but powerful ways schools construct students' and teachers' knowledge and behavior, validating positivism and competitiveness over other forms of knowing or behaving. For Giroux, then, it is crucial that radical educators contest conservative definitions of education and citizenship in the interests of "naming and transforming those ideological and social conditions that undermine the possibility for forms of community and public life organized around the imperatives of a critical democracy" ("Literacy" 5). This project is important, he argues, not only to give voice to the poor and minorities but also to reach countless middle-class Americans who have "withdrawn from public life into a world of sweeping privatization, pessimism, and greed" ("Literacy" 5).

This utopian move toward social transformation signals a clear break that Giroux, Aronowitz, and other liberatory educators have made with more orthodox Marxist theory that, by focusing entirely on schools as mechanisms that reproduce dominant culture, gives radicals a language of critique but not one of intervention. At the risk of oversimplifying, if schools simply reproduce dominant ideology, and if they are as good at it as leftist critics insist, then there's no escape and no hope: students and teachers alike become victims of false consciousness, trapped in or by an oppressive ideology they will not even recognize because it seems as natural, as unquestionable, as air ("that's just the way things are"). Aronowitz and Giroux reject this "profound pessimism," insisting that although schools *are* reproductive, they are not *merely* reproductive—that is, insisting that schools are arenas characterized by struggle between competing ideologies, discourses, and behaviors and which, thus, include spaces for resistance and agency. Hence, Giroux writes of "cultural production" rather than cultural *re*production, acknowledging that cultural institutions produce varying degrees of accommodation and resistance (*Schooling* 136).

Similarly, Shor argues that community colleges, like the one he teaches in, complete with diverse or nontraditional student populations, cramped classrooms, and functional architecture, can open up spaces for critique and resistance by focusing students' attention on their all-too-obvious place in the socioeconomic hierarchy. Like Giroux, Shor describes students not as dupes of dominant ideology but as people fighting for their humanity without quite realizing how they might reclaim it:

> Beneath the hesitancy, the doubt, and the rigidity of my students, there remain stores of intellect, emotion, comedy, and Utopian needs, waiting to happen. They have fought the robotizing of their characters to a kind of stand-off. In class or on the job, they know how to sabotage any process which alienates them. They have ways to set limits on their own dehumanization. . . . Still, they

have been invaded and distorted by machine culture. . . . While they limit their cooperation with the corporate order, they don't have a vision of alternatives. . . . They learn how to break the rules and get away with it, but they don't yet assume the responsibility of being the makers of the rules, together. (*Critical Teaching* 53)

This, then, is the aim of critical pedagogy—to enable students to envision alternatives, to inspire them to assume the responsibility for collectively recreating society. To do this, Giroux and McLaren argue in "Teacher Education and the Politics of Engagement," critical teachers need to conceive of schools as democratic public spheres: "schools can be public places where students learn the knowledge and skills necessary to live in a critical democracy." In these schools-as-public-spheres, "students are given the opportunity to learn the discourse of public association and civic responsibility" by doing—that is, by participating in democratic dialogue about lived experience, including the content and conduct of their own education (224).

In calling for schools constituted as public spheres, Aronowitz and Giroux seek to recover the nearly forgotten American tradition of radical education found in the work of John Dewey and his fellow progressives such as George Counts, John Childs, and William Kilpatrick. Dewey, whom Shor dubs "the patron saint of American education" (*When Students Have Power* x), pioneered experiential, student-centered learning that aims to integrate education with home and public life as well as develop the "free and equitable intercourse" and hence the shared interests essential for communal life (*Democracy and Education* 98). Dismissed by many radical theorists as merely liberal, Dewey is making a long-overdue comeback. Readers today may find his texts surprisingly in tune with current understandings of the relationships among knowledge, ideology, cultural practice, and language. Indeed, Aronowitz and Giroux stress the parallels between Dewey's work and that of Freire and Antonio Gramsci (10).[6] All three sought to create a theory of critical literacy that would empower citizens to disrupt dominant ideology and to revitalize democratic practice.

It's this vision of a democratic public discourse that attracts me to critical pedagogy. It's why I teach or, rather, why I teach writing—an occupation that has always been for me a high-stakes enterprise with implications not only for students' academic and professional success—important as those are—but also for the health of participatory democracy. I admire critical educators who struggle to enact a pedagogy devoted not just to dreams or texts or talk about democracy, but a pedagogy that would itself be the practice of democracy, that would use democratic means to reach democratic ends. But that, alas, is where the trouble begins.

✎ MEANS AND ENDS

Shor says that "it's a tricky business to organize an untraditional class in a traditional school" (*Freire for the Classroom* 106). Just how tricky critical pedagogy can be is not always readily apparent, however, in stories by critical teachers which, as Knoblauch and Brannon point out, tend to represent the teacher as classroom superhero (67–68). (Brannon rightly singles out Shor as the most heroic—it's no accident that in those imaginary tapes of successful classes I've played all summer in my head, I resemble some sort of Ira Shor in drag.) Shor's two most recent accounts of his teaching experiences, *Empowering Education* (1992) and *When Students Have Power* (1996), are frankly inspirational—funny and provocative and so full of handy tips and interesting assignments that even the most bamboozled among us will be reassured that we, too, can be effective critical teachers. *Empowering Education* is quite simply the most compelling book on education I've read since Mike Rose's *Lives on the Boundary*. From the first day of class, Shor foregrounds student writing and student voices as he poses questions that ask students to critically examine course material and institutional power: "What is good writing?" "How do you become a good writer?" "What questions do you have about good writing?" Why are you taking this course? Why is it required? (37). Shor encourages students to talk to each other by backloading his comments and breaking eye contact when students speak only to him. Students in Shor's classes negotiate grading contracts, write classroom bylaws, choose reading materials and paper topics. *When Students Have Power* is, in part, a cautionary tale: Shor tells the story of one group of students who very nearly used their authority to negotiate the class out of existence. Despite Shor's encountering such difficulties, however, everything comes right in the end.

Similarly, Alex McLeod's "Critical Literacy: Taking Control of Our Own Lives" recounts the work he and John Hardcastle did with teens from one of London's most impoverished districts. Hardcastle's class of disruptive students, many of whom spoke nonstandard dialects or had serious difficulties writing, reportedly produced remarkably improved writing on topics such as the Falklands War, Nigerian history and culture, and the myth of objective media coverage. The article's title, taken from a student-produced documentary on education, highlights the transformative power of critical pedagogy: "if the type of English work which we have been discussing continues, then the possibility of taking control of our own lives, our own education, and becoming our own experts, is extremely exciting" (49). I do not mean to be flip or to devalue the efforts of these talented teachers; writing instructors, especially those teaching against the grain, need the reassurance these success stories provide. But we need stories of failure, too—stories that keep expectations realistic, stories that enable the ongoing self-critique essential for sound pedagogy. And those are hard to come by.

Of all the examples of liberatory pedagogy I've read, *Composition and Resistance* (1991), edited by Mark Hurlbert and Michael Blitz, is one of the few that clearly illustrates the difficulties of implementing—or even defining—critical pedagogy. This collection contains some interesting pieces by Berlin, Knoblauch (who tells a failure story), Stephen North, Kurt Spellmeyer, and James Sledd and a wonderful essay by Marian Yee on resisting, reevaluating, and recovering cultural narratives. But the real bonus in this volume is transcripts from round-table discussions at three CCCC and NCTE conventions that contributors attended as part of the process of writing their essays. In these transcripts, participants interrupt each other with claims and counterclaims and generally disagree on everything from the meaning of resistance to the viability of the whole project of critical pedagogy. So, Donna Singleton challenges students to write complaints about campus problems to university officials, but Joe Harris calls the urge to validate discourse only when it moves beyond the classroom a "trap"; he argues that academic work can be resistant in and of itself, regardless of its "real-world application" (*Composition and Resistance* 152–53). So, Knoblauch argues that the classroom can be a site for social change—that human agency does exist. Nancy Mack agrees, claiming that students already have the power to "intentionally [author] their lives," but they don't realize it, don't use it; according to Mack, the job of writing teachers is to make students aware of their power. But Jeff Golub suggests that not realizing one's power might be the same as not having any and, further, that Mack's reasoning makes social change too easy: all we do is show students their power, and, poof, the revolution will begin. Singleton says that her inner-city students, who may truly be powerless, often see education as their only hope. Mack warns that "we have to be really careful that we aren't selling that—'a college education gives you power'" (*Composition and Resistance* 150–51). Here, we finally get a glimpse of the "tricky business" of liberatory teaching, of defining means and ends.

It is interesting to see, then, how slippery discussions of the means and ends of democratic education become when we turn to some of the more noted critiques of critical pedagogy. In "Considerations of American Freireistas," for instance, Victor Villanueva argues that while he shares the Freireans' revolutionary goals, he thinks their strategy of turning the classroom into a "political arena" is precisely the wrong means for the end. Villanueva reports on an ethnographic study of Floyd, a Freirean-trained teacher working in a Writer's Project for low-income, primarily black youths. By Freirean standards, Floyd seems perfect for the job: he's a talented black teacher and poet who grew up in the neighborhood where the project is located. He's overtly political, has participated in literacy campaigns in Nicaragua and Grenada (where he even met Freire). He taught the Writing Project students about black history and culture, about ideology and oppression. He encouraged them to become radical intellectuals: they wrote; they participated in antiracism demonstrations. And yet, in the end, although Floyd inspired some of his students, Villanueva claims that Floyd's political message reached only those already predisposed to accept his revolutionary agenda. Why would such a talented teacher fail? Because in America, Villanueva says, "counterhegemony cannot be easily sold" ✓ (251):

> Floyd's students . . . were in school to fulfill a dream, a longtime American dream of success through education. They were not in school to have their dreams destroyed. They would naturally resist any such attempt. Floyd's students could reason that no matter how slight their chances of getting into col-

lege or the middle class, they did have chances, maybe better than most. . . .
Floyd had himself made it through college, was a teacher, a published poet, a
world traveler to pan-African conferences. In the students' eyes, Floyd made
a better model of the bootstrap mentality than he made a model of the revolution. (256)

A more successful strategy, Villanueva claims, is based on the dialectic between
hegemony and counterhegemony, between tradition and change. Arguing that
students need to understand tradition in order to desire change, Villanueva designed a course in which students read one canonical and one noncanonical
text and discuss ways their own lived experience connects to the two. As a result, students develop an understanding of the dialectical relationship between
individuals and their environment—an understanding that, according to Villanueva, underlies students' willingness and ability to change both themselves
and their world.

Gregory Jay and Gerald Graff also propose an avowedly leftist political
pedagogy in "A Critique of Critical Pedagogy," but their complaint is not so
much that the means of critical pedagogy are ineffective but that they are un-
ethical—that is, undemocratic. Jay and Graff argue that although, in theory,
critical pedagogy speaks of dialogue and students' authority to initiate and
freely pursue critical analyses, in practice such a pedagogy merely reaffirms
the authority of the teacher who has the "political clarity" (the term is Freire's)
students lack. "How real can the Freirean dialogue be," Jay and Graff ask, when
"the proper outcome of critical pedagogy is already predetermined. . . . Who
the oppressors and the oppressed are is conceived not as an open question that
teachers and students might disagree about, but as a *given* of Freirean pedagogy" (203). By contrast, Graff's familiar "teach the conflicts" curriculum
would, they argue, explicitly foreground politics in the classroom without imposing any particular political agenda on students: "it would look to turn the
campus into a *polis*, a community where empowered citizens argue together
about the future of their society, and in so doing help students become active
participants in that argument rather than passive spectators" (213). The force
of Jay and Graff's argument about democratic means (and, indeed, their implicit claim that theirs is an argument only about means and not about ends)
rests on their assertion that critical pedagogy amounts to coercion and on the
perhaps dubious assumption that exposing students to counterhegemonic academic arguments is enough to more broadly or permanently shift students'
critical habits and to heighten their sense of political agency.[7]

One of the more conservative attacks on critical pedagogy, Maxine Hairston's "Diversity, Ideology, and Teaching Writing," is also presented, at least
partly, as an attack on educational means rather than ends. In this polemic
against radical teachers who put "dogma before diversity, politics before craft"
(180), Hairston identifies goals that she and other compositionists share with
radicals: the desire for social reform, for freedom of expression, and for "diversity and a genuine multicultural environment" (189). Indeed, according to
Hairston, it is the existence of these common goals that has enabled composi-

tionists to be so easily "co-opted by the radical left, coerced into acquiescing to methods that we abhor because, in the abstract, we have some mutual goals" (187). But, in addition to attacking the methods of radical teachers, Hairston also clearly defines different goals—for instance, her insistence that writing instructors "stay within [their] area of professional expertise" (186). Hairston argues that if compositionists try to teach students about complex socioeconomic or racial issues, they will all get into a terrible muddle. In doing so, Hairston ignores the fact that citizens in a democracy constantly need to make decisions about just such complex issues. In the final analysis, Hairston's argument seems as much about her desire to guard the independence of composition studies from critical theorists and "political zealots" as her goal to meet the needs of students living in an increasingly diverse society (192).

Oddly enough, it's the argument that seems to distance itself farthest from critical pedagogy—that criticizes both its means and its ends—that I find to be the most compelling challenge. Although not targeted specifically at critical pedagogy, Jeff Smith's essay, "Students' Goals, Gatekeeping, and Some Ques-✗ tions of Ethics," argues that radical teachers often willfully confuse means and ends, most obviously by their refusal to acknowledge that they function primarily as means to students' ends. If writing teachers are serious about being democratic, if they are serious about letting students set the agenda for their own education, then they should honor students' professed desires to get the credentials needed to secure professional-managerial jobs. "To do otherwise," Smith claims, "is undemocratic at best, if not infantilizing and frankly oppressive" (317). "We *are* ethically bound by students' own aims," he continues, "even if those aims seem uncomfortably close to elite values. Our distrust of such values does not permit us to tell students what they 'really' want, or should want" (317).

Hence, Smith accepts the obligation to be useful to students, teaching the grammar and generic conventions they will need to succeed. My sympathies for Smith's argument stem, in part, from a similar uneasiness with some of what I read in critical pedagogy texts. Hurlbert and Blitz, for instance, celebrate a student who "resisted composure" by ignoring the conventions of an assigned research paper and turning in, instead, a series of quotations followed by a series of reflective paragraphs. The authors suggest that one thing composition teachers can do to subvert dominant ideology is "to stop teaching students to underwrite the university, to stop demanding written material which can be easily *gathered* and *assessed*" (*Composition and Resistance* 7). Now I am not a great fan of wrapped-in-a-tidy-package-with-a-bow papers, but such proclamations make me nervous, for while students benefit from having both the impulse and the rhetorical wherewithal to "resist composure," there is work in the world (quite often the kind that pays the rent but also various forms of political activism) that requires them to be proficiently, even eloquently composed.

What interests me about Smith's position is that in some ways it is much closer to Freire's or Shor's than readers might initially imagine. First of all, allowing students to direct their own education, as Smith says instructors should, is a cornerstone of critical pedagogy. In addition, Freirean teachers believe, as does Smith, in providing students with useful education, for although Freire argues in *A Pedagogy for Liberation* that he's not doing his duty if he doesn't try to move students beyond purely vocational goals, the idea of not training them well for their chosen careers is, he says, "an absurdity. . . . What is impossible is to be an *incompetent* educator because I am a revolutionary" (Shor and Freire 69). According to Freire, the liberatory teacher will, thus, train students yet simultaneously problematize that training—will, for instance, teach standard English and correct usage while also problematizing their status as inherently superior to other dialects or grammars. Finally, although Smith says a teacher's role is to provide means, not to have ends, Smith, like critical teachers, has his own ends for students and for the larger society—ends that constitute part, if not all, of what critical pedagogy seeks: "I want the world that I and those I care about are going to live in to have capable people doing the kinds of jobs students say they're looking to do. . . . I want what I teach to be good not just for people, not even just for citizens, but for future doctors and lawyers and organic chemistry majors" (318–19).

The difference, then, between Smith and practitioners of critical pedagogy is not a simple one of opposing means and ends, for Smith says the instructor is the means expert, and Smith presumably would approve of any means that produce "capable people." Rather, the essential differences may stem from Smith's insistence that means can be separated from ends—"good things are learned even by less than ideal means" (310)—and that students have sole responsibility for setting the goals of their education without any input from instructors. Nevertheless, Smith, the critic who seems least interested in Freirean pedagogy, sometimes, through his ethical commitment to equality, democratic education, and students' needs, comes closer to Freire's position than some avowedly leftist instructors. Shor is right; this *is* a tricky business.

✧ "WHO IS TO BE LIBERATED FROM WHAT?"

When Gregory Jay and Gerald Graff complain that Freire's pedagogy closes off disagreement over key issues such as the identity of the oppressed and of their oppressors, Freire is impatient with what he sees as Graff's "misguided relativism" (Freire and Macedo, "A Dialogue" 386); especially in Brazil, but even in the United States, Freire argues, it is easy to identify the poor, the hungry, the homeless. Nevertheless, when American writing teachers step into the classroom—or look into the mirror, for that matter—identifying the oppressed and the oppressors can become a task fraught with difficulties. Hence, in *Critical Teaching and the Idea of Literacy*, Knoblauch and Brannon wonder whether the traditional goal of liberatory pedagogy to empower "outsiders" fits the complexities of American society, leaving all sorts of bewildering questions:

> Who is to be liberated from what? Who gets to do the liberating? Is the U.S. government an oppressor in the same sense that the South African government is? Are middle-class black persons as "outside" as underclass Hispanic? Is Eliz-

abeth Dole an outsider? Where exactly is the inside? Is the goal to make the outsider into an insider? Is it to transform one inside into another? Is it to abolish capitalism? Does the moral commitment, and the political authority, of the critical teacher properly mandate a change in the consciousness of arguably disenfranchised students regardless of their own wishes, their own sense of what they might gain or lose from accommodating themselves to the dominant culture? (60)

And for the large number of writing instructors like me who walk into classrooms filled almost entirely with white, middle-class students who will likely fare very well in the system, it can be pretty hard to see their work as liberating oppressed students. In fact, radical American teachers often seem to assume just the opposite—that students belong to the oppressor group. What can liberatory pedagogy possibly mean under these circumstances? Knoblauch wonders, for instance, if liberatory teaching is even plausible, given the self-interest that stands in the way of students' critical examination of their status: "Is critical teaching anything more than an intellectual game in such circumstances? . . . What do my students have to gain from a scrutiny of values and conditions that work to ensure their privilege?" (60, 64).

Linda Finlay and Valerie Faith offer an answer in their essay "Illiteracy and Alienation in American Colleges: Is Paulo Freire's Pedagogy Relevant?," which reports on their work with upper-middle-class university students in remedial writing courses. Using keywords to uncover their students' generative themes, Finlay and Faith found that their students felt a gulf between their public (institutionally controlled, inauthentic) and private (emotionally satisfying, free, "real") lives, a gulf that caused them to feel oppressed despite their acknowledged economic privilege. Their students believed, Finlay and Faith explain, that their education was nothing more than a means to funnel them into appropriate middle-class jobs; it would not enable them to either enlarge the private realm or challenge the public. Finlay and Faith also learned that their students' resistance to writing—part of their public life—was linked to this sense of domination; once students connected language use to their private lives, their writing improved dramatically. Students' literacy, then, is intimately connected to what Freire has called "the world"; furthermore, students occupy multiple and often contradictory positions in relation to dominant culture:

> [they] fear and distrust the culture that runs the schools, a culture that they perceive as subordinating individual activity to the needs of a consumer economy. Since our students are not children, however, their education is complicated by their awareness that they have become accomplices in maintaining this culture and its values. They want those consumer goods, they want the college degree for earning power, political power, social power of many kinds. We and our students had to face the contradiction between the values of the consumer society—the products of which they enjoy—and their "childlike" instinct for personal determination. (82)

If students present untold complexities for critical teachers to sort out, teachers need to examine their own positions no less critically. Knoblauch and Brannon ask:

> What is the meaning of "radical teacher" for faculty in . . . privileged institutions—paid by the capitalist state, protected from many of the obligations as well as the consequences of social action by the speculativeness of academic commitment, engaged in a seemingly trivial dramatization of utopian thought that the university itself blandly sponsors as satisfying testimony to its own open-mindedness? (60)

Questions such as these cause Stephen North ("Rhetoric, Responsibility, and the 'Language of the Left'") to refuse to adopt the language of critical pedagogy although he admires many of its advocates. One sticking point for North is what he sees as a mismatch between the revolutionary pedagogy he'd advocate inside the classroom and the hours he spends outside the classroom "in or on a life that I would characterize as a system-supporting, system-supported, pro-capitalist, American mainstream life" (132). If he were truly to commit himself to radical teaching, North argues, he'd feel compelled to change his lifestyle.

It's a point that should perhaps worry more radical teachers than it does. Freire quips about this inconsistency, noting how many American Marxists "have never drunk coffee in the house of a worker!" The distance between our academic lives as compositionists and our everyday, concrete experience, between what Freire calls the word and the world, "makes us more able to *play* with theories" (Shor and Freire 136). Freire describes the particularly American dilemma of teachers who come to critical pedagogy not because of their experience of injustice but because of something they have read in a book (and I recognize myself in this description): "What happens? He or she comes to the classroom with a new conviction, but this new teacher was already shaped into the dichotomy between text and context. Then, it is hard to overcome the old dichotomy and integrate words and worlds" (Shor and Freire 136). Some radical teachers go to great lengths to integrate words and worlds; Kozol and Shor, for instance, both spent a number of years living in the neighborhoods of the students they taught. Few of us, I'm afraid, have that kind of commitment. Then what? Do we just give up so as not to make a mockery of radical pedagogy? Maybe. You see, my fears of "bamboozlement" persist. But I'm also wary of setting up radicalness requirements, and I suspect that there's a place in critical pedagogy for the not-yet-radical among us, although it's a place that remains unimagined in the scholarship.

⤴ FREEDOM AND AUTHORITY

As teachers concerned with social justice, we seem unfailingly attracted to the notion of an egalitarian space. We look for it in cyberspace; we look in liberatory classrooms. In Shor's first book, for instance, he talks about the teacher "withering away" (*Critical Teaching* 98).[8] Similarly, Shor defines dialogue as "democratic, directed, and critical discourse" which "challenges power relations in the classroom and in society" (*Empowering Education* 87), and, in what can only be a utopian vision, Giroux describes a classroom in which "all voices in their differences become unified both in their efforts to identify and recall moments of human suffering and in their attempts to overcome the conditions that perpetuate such suffering" ("Literacy" 21).

But at numerous points in their arguments, critical educators have backpedaled from this too-easy equation of dialogue and democracy. Hence, Freire insists, "The dialogical relationship does not have the power to create such an impossible equality" between teachers and students (Shor and Freire 92). In fact, he says that it's the difference in students and teachers that make the liberatory project possible—"no one liberates himself by his own efforts" (*Pedagogy of the Oppressed* 53); in other words, transformation depends on different and, often, unequal voices interacting, and the primary source of that superior voice, Shor suggests, is the more knowledgeable, more analytical, more politically committed teacher. Also, because dialogue is a means toward an end (it is not, Freire and Macedo and Shor insist, just talk, not aimless blah-blah-blah, not a rap or gripe session), it is directed activity. Freire says, "Dialogue does not exist in a political vacuum. It is not a 'free space' where you may do what you want. Dialogue takes place inside some kind of program and context. . . . Dialogue means a permanent tension in the relation between authority and liberty" (Shor and Freire 102).

Authority in the radical, democratic classroom? Freire says there's no getting around it: "without authority it is very difficult for the liberties of the students to be shaped. Freedom needs authority to become free. It is a paradox but it is true" (Shor and Freire 91). A teacher, by definition, has authority; for a teacher to deny that authority, Freire claims, results in license, not liberty. For Freire, it's important to distinguish between authority, which teachers must have, and authoritarianism, which is the abuse of power—a distinction that's easy enough to understand if not always to apply. Sometimes, however, radical educators work so hard to explain away teachers' obvious authority that their language could set off a doublespeak alarm. Giroux and McLaren, for instance, coin the term "emancipatory authority" (225), a little piece of bamboozlement that roughly translates "it's okay to use authority if you do it in the name of social justice." Shor and Freire run into similar difficulties trying to reconcile their notion of democratic dialogue with the fact that teachers often know more than their students: they admit that when teachers plan courses and select texts, they understand the object of study better than students, but they claim—as if to reinforce the teacher's role as just another student—"the teacher *re-learns* the objects through studying them with the students" (100). Shor and Freire seem to want to insist that the classroom is egalitarian even when common sense would say that it isn't—indeed, even when they themselves have argued that it isn't.[9]

Much more useful and interesting, then, are examples of how critical teachers actually do decenter their classrooms, and Shor is the best place to look for these. His power-sharing moves include authorizing students to negotiate grading contracts right down to the attendance policies, to help develop the syllabus by bringing in readings and voting on unit themes, and to write bylaws for classroom behavior. In *When Students Have Power*, Shor also talks at length about the after-class group: he and a small group of students met to evaluate the day's session and to plan future classes and projects. Shor's students offered up a tremendous amount of feedback including some scathing criticisms of his choice of texts and time management; the result was a remarkable redistribution of power, knowledge, and responsibility. Shor's power and knowledge had not been erased; instead, another avenue of power had been explicitly constructed—it was now, as Shor says, a two-way street: "I found myself *immediately and continually accountable to students*" (125). Perhaps more than any other aspect of Shor's pedagogy, the after-class group undercuts complaints that critical pedagogy is all about teacher's imposing themselves on students, for within this space, students can take responsibility for the means and ends of the course. My own experience with an after-class group has convinced me that it can provide invaluable information for writing instructors, critical or otherwise, about students' interests and needs, about what's getting through and what isn't; more important, though, an after-class group can create a sense of enlarged possibilities for students and instructors as they tackle together the difficulties inherent in classrooms. My group was less brutal and less assertive than Shor's—they still tended to see their feedback as serving me rather than serving themselves—but they clearly wanted interesting, challenging work, and they pushed me and the other students to raise the level of discussion and to expand their options for writing and learning.

Behind Shor's power-sharing practices lies his realization that "*both teachers and students start out at less than zero and more than zero simultaneously. . . . Both bring resources and obstacles to class*" (*Empowering Education* 201). Students' absorption in mass culture hinders their critical study, but, Shor argues, teachers' culture of schooling equally hinders learning—and that's assuming teachers aren't also caught up in mass culture (don't we faithfully watch *ER* or *The X-Files*?). I find Shor's more-than- and less-than-zero approach to classroom status particularly productive, for then teachers are not the standard against which students' knowledge or power (or lack thereof) is measured. In addition, to the extent that Shor's line of thinking encourages teachers to recognize their own (and not just their students') multiple and contradictory positions in relation to dominant culture, it may open up a place in critical pedagogy for not-yet-radical teachers like me. That is, the lack of "political clarity" or radical commitment that might seem like a minus may actually be a plus in the critical classroom because it means one less barrier between teacher and student—simultaneous criticism of and entanglement in dominant culture can become one more problem that instructor and students sort through together.

How to think about and deal with barriers between students and teachers—with student resistance to leftist politics—is an especially vexed question for critical teachers. Freire asks, "What kind of educator would I be if I did not feel moved by a powerful impulse to seek, without lying, convincing arguments in defense of the dreams for which I struggle?" (*Pedagogy of Hope* 83), but with his next breath, he insists that a critical teacher must never impose topics or politics on students. Except, of course, we *do* impose, after-class groups notwithstanding, especially when students enroll in a required writing course only to find a liberatory teacher greeting them from a back-row seat. Shor says that he never forces critical pedagogy on a class; when enough students voice discomfort with the instruction, he reverts to the role of traditional teacher for that course. But even he admits to asking several oppositional students every semester to leave the class. Berlin quips that when his students resisted a course in cultural critique, he finally "decided that was a victory because it would have been easy for them to play along with me" (Hurlbert and Blitz 9); however, Knoblauch puts such student resistance in a different light: "Well, you know 'resistance' may characterize in one way or another our relationship with some social reality, but I wonder what words characterize our implicating of our students in our resistances. You know, they're not resisting, except maybe us" (Hurlbert and Blitz 9).

☙ CONCLUSION: TEACHING WITH/IN PARADOX

Patricia Bizzell's *Academic Discourse and Critical Consciousness* (1992) traces her search for means by which writing teachers might foster democratic discourse and social justice. It is a book I admire tremendously. It's not just that I like what Bizzell has to say (I do). I admire the persistence of her search, her willingness to abandon old positions and allies (Freire is one such), admire the fact that she keeps growing. Writers on all sides of the critical pedagogy debate often seem just a little too sure of themselves; Bizzell can reach a position, argue for it passionately, and still admit doubt.

In the book, Bizzell describes her early attempts to promote social equality by teaching academic discourse. She did so believing that "the critical detachment academic discourse affords" would "more or less automatically" produce both "insight into social injustices and the will to correct them" (20). But even as she worked to substantiate this claim, she began to doubt that any analytical method, in and of itself, would lead to the enlightened political commitment she hoped for. The need for such commitment is not self-evident; arguments have to be made for it, and Freire, she realized, did not make those arguments. Thus, Bizzell turned to rhetoric, determined "to figure out how to persuade [students] to identify with social justice as the common good. [She had] to figure out how we can all use rhetorical power to effect democratic political change" (30).

As I've noted, Hairston attacks Bizzell's decision to use her power, rhetorical or otherwise, to argue political issues in composition classes. "By the logic of the cultural left," Hairston reasons, "any teacher should be free to use his or her classroom to promote any ideology. Why not facism [sic]? Racial superiority? Religious fundamentalism? Anti-abortion beliefs? Can't any professor claim the right to indoctrinate students simply because he or she is right?" (188). But Bizzell's argument and practice are not so much about her *personal* agenda (although Bizzell is quite clear about her personal and passionate commitment to it) as they are about what Dennis Lynch calls "the political values and agendas we share by virtue of living in a democracy" (353)—those values that Hairston, herself, says "all of us" share: respect for difference, fairness, a forum for the free exchange of ideas. Disavowing any foundational grounds for establishing her authority as a speaker, the central question for Bizzell becomes, "What is the legitimate authority of teachers, or any other orators?" (273). (That equation may give readers pause.) Her answer, following Isocrates, is that her authority "would be established rhetorically" (283). That is, making arguments in the classroom (or anywhere else) is not simply a matter of a teacher imposing her beliefs on students; rather, she can persuade only insofar as she builds her case on the values her students already hold. For example, Bizzell might argue against sexism by appealing to the American desire for equality, a value embedded in our founding documents as well as our current communal discourse.

That having been said, however, Bizzell still worries that her practice may violate the very democratic values she is trying to instill. Her hedges against this are, first, to help students develop their own rhetorical authority to persuade others in the class, including her, and second, to highlight through her course materials the commonalities among Americans, not by glossing over difference but by emphasizing that Americans are "united by a common experiment in negotiating difference" (293). These materials, collected in the textbook she and Bruce Herzberg produced called *Negotiating Difference*, are designed to enable students to investigate historical instances when groups negotiated differences in the search for social justice, to discover interests they share with other groups, and to learn that some past movements toward greater equality have, indeed, been successful.

Given the difficulties Bizzell faces in imagining and enacting her practice as well as the controversy her work has provoked, two points suggest themselves by way of closure. The first is the difficulty of generalizing about or judging the overall project of critical pedagogy. It seems certain that some radical teachers do abuse their authority, attempting simply to indoctrinate students. But, as in all aspects of education, so much depends on the instructor, the students, the physical classroom space and available resources, the curriculum, the school, the community (and the list goes on) that it strikes me as foolhardy to pronounce as, for instance, Jay and Graff do, that "it is just such notions of respect, trust, and faith that critical and oppositional pedagogies reject" (208), as if "critical pedagogy" were a monolith, as if it were "pedagogies" and not individual teachers and students together in a classroom who create or reject respect and trust.

Second, if critical pedagogy is plagued by bamboozlement or ambiguity, I'd suggest that this is not simply due to the inadequacies of its theory and methods. Rather some complications result from the inevitable presence of paradoxes, from having to live and teach with the knowledge that "human action can move in several directions at once, that something can contain itself and its opposite also" (Shor and Freire 69). So, we train and problematize; we create freedom with authority; we teach resistance and hope for cooperation. These paradoxes are neither solvable nor necessarily debilitating. They keep teachers honest and inventive and, well, critical of their work. In an interview with Gary Olson, Freire notes the complicated position of the radical writing instructor who stands with one foot in the system, the present, today's reality, and the other foot outside the system, in the future, in utopia: "This is why it's so difficult . . . for us to walk: we have to walk like this. [With a playful smile, Freire begins to waddle across the room.] Life is like this. This is reality and history" (163).

Notes

1. For ease of reference, I use the term *critical pedagogy* to denote this whole group of teaching praxes, but it's important to note that although these pedagogies share assumptions about dominant culture as well as egalitarian goals, they often have distinct emphases. For instance, bell hooks sees her engaged pedagogy as more demanding than critical pedagogy: she insists that teachers can emancipate students only by themselves actively pursuing "self-actualization," a well-being springing from the union of mind, body, and soul (15). hooks's praxis thus emphasizes the role of the body, of pleasure and desire in learning.

2. Freire began his eighteen-year exile working in Chile as a UNESCO consultant on adult education for the Agrarian Reform Training and Research Institute; in 1969, he received an appointment to Harvard University's Center for the Study of Development and Social Change, and the following year, he accepted a position in Geneva as a consultant to the Office of Education of the World Council of Churches, where he developed literacy programs for Tanzania and Guinea-Bissau (an account of which is recorded in *Pedagogy in Process: Letters to Guinea-Bissau*). In 1981, he returned to Brazil, teaching at universities in Sao Paulo until his death in 1997.

3. Freire's later texts avoid this sexist language, a topic he addresses in his final book, *A Pedagogy of Hope*. Freire has been criticized, even rejected, by some feminist scholars who find his language problematic. bell hooks writes in *Teaching to Transgress* that she once publicly confronted Freire about his sexist language, but she nonetheless defends his work as vital to the project of radical education.

4. Freire stresses the need for teachers to conduct extensive ethnographic research about their students' lives rather than guessing what might be important to the class. For Freire, this involved lengthy, multilayered study: an investigative team, which included prospective students, conducted extensive discussions with and observations of people in the community where a literacy program was to be set up. These data were then further developed by a larger team of educators, disciplinary experts, and sociologists who, in consultation with community members, generated a set of themes to " 're-present' . . . to the people from whom [they] first received it" (*Pedagogy of the Oppressed* 101). For a more detailed account of this process, see chapter 3 of *Pedagogy of the Oppressed*.

5. Interested readers can find provocative analyses of the 1980s debate over the crisis in education in Aronowitz and Giroux, Shor (*Freire for the Classroom* and *Culture Wars*), Donaldo Macedo, and Knoblauch and Brannon.

6. The parallels between Dewey and Freire are sometimes astonishing. For instance, Freire's critique of the banking model of education in which students are seen as receptacles waiting to be filled echoes Dewey's criticisms of "teaching by pouring in, learning by passive absorption." Dewey continues, "Education is not an affair of 'telling' and being told, but an active and constructive process" (*Democracy and Education* 46). In addition, when explaining the centrality of dialogue for critical pedagogy, Freire asserts that "only dialogue, which requires critical thinking, is also capable of generating critical thinking. Without dialogue there is no communication, and without communication there can be no true education" (*Pedagogy of the Oppressed* 81). Similarly, Dewey establishes the necessity for dialogue in education and communal life, claiming that "society not only continues to exist *by* transmission, *by* communication, but it may fairly be said to exist *in* transmission, *in* communication. . . . Not only is social life identical with communication, but all communication . . . is educative," both for listeners who gain an "enlarged and changed experience" and for speakers whose understanding of an experience necessarily changes as they formulate it to share with others (*Democracy and Education* 5–6). Dewey expands on the connection between literacy, art, and democracy in *The Public and Its Problems* (1927).

7. For the record, it's not clear that Jay and Graff have ever participated in or even observed a Freirean classroom, nor (and this is true of many arguments against critical pedagogy—a point not lost on Freire) do they cite any of Freire's texts besides *The Pedagogy of the Oppressed* which, by the time of their writing, was twenty-five years old and which had been further developed and qualified. It is also ironic that although Jay and Graff advocate helping students become "active participants" rather than "passive spectators," the example of democratic pedagogy they present involved a faculty symposium in which Graff and two other instructors debated revisions of Chicago's general education humanities course before a two-hundred-member student audience.

8. It's hard not to see parallels between this early version of Shor's pedagogy and Peter Elbow's "writing without teachers." Indeed, Knoblauch and Brannon argue that despite radicals' attacks on expressivism as "solipsistic" and "politically disengaged," expressivist pedagogies should be recognized as the "precursors" of critical pedagogy (126). Expressivist and critical pedagogies, they claim, share the goal of empowering students working within a narrow, authoritarian system; furthermore, Knoblauch and Brannon point out that, methodologically, "arguments for critical teaching have tended largely to reiterate the tactics of whole language and writing process classrooms"—decentered classrooms and emphasis on dialogue; use of small, collaborative groups; and attention to nonanalytic forms of expression such as narrative (129).

9. Elizabeth Ellsworth's article, "Why Doesn't This Feel Empowering? Working Through the Repressive Myths of Critical Pedagogy," discusses her experience trying to work with and through this sometimes idealistic or befuddled language in a graduate education course she taught called "Media and Anti-Racist Pedagogies." Ellsworth's course attracted an ethnically and religiously diverse group of men and women from the United States as well as international students, all of whom were committed to combating campus racism. Despite their apparently common goal, however, the group soon fractured into smaller "affinity groups," each with its own agenda and methods. Additionally, Ellsworth claims that the vision of the classroom as safe space emphasized in critical pedagogy scholarship made her and her students reluctant to jettison the dialogic method even though it was proving counterpro-

ductive: her students did not feel safe to speak nor did members of minority groups want to *dialogue* about their oppression; they wanted to talk back or present monologues. Further, she felt that her position as a white, middle-class professional woman left her with little authority, emancipated or otherwise, to help liberate her often marginalized students. Ellsworth argues, in short, that notions of dialogue, solidarity, and authority in critical pedagogy theory were inadequate for dealing with the power dynamics of the class; hers is one of the most extensive critiques to come from within the ranks of radical teachers.

Bibliography

Aronowitz, Stanley and Henry Giroux. *Education Under Seige: The Conservative, Liberal, and Radical Debate over Schooling.* South Hadley, MA: Bergin & Garvey, 1985.

Berlin, James. "Freirean Pedagogy in the U.S.: A Response." *(Inter)views: Cross-Disciplinary Perspectives on Rhetoric and Literacy.* Ed. Gary A. Olson and Irene Gales. Carbondale: Southern Illinois UP, 1991. 169–76.

Bizzell, Patricia. *Academic Discourse and Critical Consciousness.* Pittsburgh: U of Pittsburgh P, 1992.

Bizzell, Patricia, and Bruce Herzberg. *Negotiating Difference: Cultural Case Studies for Composition.* Boston: Bedford Books, 1996.

Dewey, John. *Democracy and Education: An Introduction to the Philosophy of Education.* New York: Macmillan Co., 1916.

———. *The Public and Its Problems.* New York: H. Holt & Co., 1927.

Elbow, Peter. *Embracing Contraries: Explorations in Learning and Teaching.* New York: Oxford UP, 1986.

Ellsworth, Elizabeth. "Why Doesn't This Feel Empowering?: Working Through the Repressive Myths of Critical Pedagogy." *Harvard Educational Review* 59 (1989): 297–324.

Finlay, Linda Shaw and Valerie Faith. "Illiteracy and Alienation in American Colleges: Is Paulo Freire's Pedagogy Relevant?" Shor, *Freire for the Classroom* 63–86.

Freire, Paulo. *Pedagogy in Process: Letters to Guinea-Bissau.* New York: Seabury, 1978.

———. *Pedagogy of Hope: Reliving Pedagogy of the Oppressed.* New York: Continuum, 1994.

———. *Pedagogy of the Oppressed.* New York: Seabury, 1970.

Freire, Paulo, and Donaldo Macedo. "A Dialogue: Culture, Language, and Race." *Harvard Educational Review* 65 (1995): 377–402.

Giroux, Henry. "Liberal Arts Education and the Struggle for Public Life: Dreaming About Democracy." *South Atlantic Quarterly* 89 (1990): 113–38.

———. "Literacy and the Pedagogy of Political Empowerment." Introduction. *Literacy: Reading the Word and the World.* Paulo Freire and Donaldo Macedo. South Hadley, MA: Bergin & Garvey, 1987. 1–27.

———. *Schooling and the Struggle for Public Life: Critical Pedagogy in the Modern Age.* Minneapolis: U of Minnesota P, 1988.

———. *Theory and Resistance in Education: A Pedagogy for the Opposition.* Westport, CT: Greenwood, Bergin-Garvey, 1983.

Giroux, Henry, and Peter McLaren. "Teacher Education and the Politics of Engagement: The Case for Democratic Schooling." *Harvard Educational Review* 56 (1986): 213–38.

Hairston, Maxine. "Diversity, Ideology, and Teaching Writing." *CCC* 43 (1992): 179–93.

hooks, bell. *Teaching to Transgress: Education as the Practice of Freedom.* New York: Routledge, 1994.

Hurlbert, Mark, and Michael Blitz, eds. *Composition and Resistance*. Portsmouth, NH: Boynton/Cook, 1991.

Jay, Gregory, and Gerald Graff. "A Critique of Critical Pedagogy." *Higher Education Under Fire: Politics, Economics, and the Crisis of the Humanities*. Ed. Michael Bérubé and Cary Nelson. New York: Routledge, 1995.

Knoblauch, C. H., and Lil Brannon. *Critical Teaching and the Idea of Literacy*. Portsmouth, NH: Boynton/Cook, 1993.

Kozol, Jonathan. *Illiterate America*. New York: Anchor/Doubleday, 1985.

Lynch, Dennis A. "Teaching Rhetorical Values and the Question of Student Autonomy." *Rhetoric Review* 13 (1995): 350–70.

Macedo, Donaldo. *Literacies of Power: What Americans Are Not Allowed to Know*. Boulder, CO: Westview P, 1994.

McLaren, Peter. *Life in Schools: An Introduction to Critical Pedagogy in the Foundations of Education*. New York: Longman, 1989.

McLeod, Alex. "Critical Literacy: Taking Control of Our Own Lives." *Language Arts* 63 (1986): 37–50.

North, Stephen M. "Rhetoric, Responsibility, and the 'Language of the Left.'" Hurlbert and Blitz 127–36.

Olson, Gary A., and Irene Gale, eds. *(Inter)views: Cross-disciplinary Perspectives on Rhetoric and Literacy*. Carbondale: Southern Illinois UP, 1991.

Rose, Mike. *Lives on the Boundary*. New York: Penguin, 1989.

Shor, Ira. *Critical Teaching and Everyday Life*. 1980. Chicago: U of Chicago P, 1987.

———. *Culture Wars: School and Society in the Conservative Restoration, 1969–1984*. New York: Routledge and Kegan Paul/Methuen, 1986.

———. *Empowering Education: Critical Teaching for Social Change*. Chicago: U of Chicago P, 1992.

———. *Freire for the Classroom: A Sourcebook for Liberatory Teaching*. Portsmouth, NH: Heinemann, 1987.

———. *When Students Have Power: Negotiating Authority in a Critical Pedagogy*. Chicago: U of Chicago P, 1996.

Shor, Ira, and Paulo Freire. *A Pedagogy for Liberation: Dialogues on Transformative Education*. Westport, CT: Greenwood, Bergin-Garvey, 1987.

Simon, Roger. "Empowerment as a Pedagogy of Possibility." *Language Arts* 64 (1987): 370–82.

Smith, Jeff. "Students' Goals, Gatekeeping, and Some Questions of Ethics." *College English* 59 (1997): 299–320.

Villaneuva, Victor, Jr. "Considerations of American Freireistas." *The Politics of Writing Instruction: Postsecondary*. Ed. Richard Bullock and John Trimbur. Portsmouth, NH: Boynton/Cook, 1991.

Feminist Pedagogy

S U S A N   C .   J A R R A T T

Feminist pedagogy in composition emerged out of the women's movement of the 1970s, which itself grew out of the civil rights and antiwar movements beginning in the 1960s. Groups such as Students for a Democratic Society, the Southern Christian Leadership Conference, the Black Panthers, and others connected with the New Left involved men and women who based their activism on an analysis of class and race oppression. Women in these groups began to apply the same analysis to sex difference, recognizing the unequal treatment of women worldwide as a parallel phenomenon (Morgan). They observed that we live in a patriarchy—meaning literally "rule of fathers" but more analogically that men lead and thus essentially control the most important functions of our society—legislatures and courts, businesses, schools, and families—and often that control is not benevolent: that is, it is accompanied by the physical, cultural, and spiritual subordination of women as a group and the closing off of opportunities for full humanity to them. Rejecting the old rationale of separate spheres, women began to explore these new revelations in consciousness-raising (cr) groups, sitting in someone's living room, talking about their experiences as women—at home, at work, in bed, in the doctor's office—that they had never before shared. They were giving words to what Betty Friedan called "the problem that has no name." One of the most influential books of this early period was a doctoral dissertation by a literature student, Kate Millett. *Sexual Politics* offered a bold analysis of sexism in canonical male-authored literature. Alice Echols' *Daring to Be Bad* offers a detailed historical review of the beginnings of the women's movement, including sometimes gossipy interviews with many of the women involved in radical groups.

This movement was called the "second wave" of feminism, in reference to the first wave of nineteenth-century women's activism, which brought together black and white women in political groups working for the abolition of slavery and for women's suffrage. Angela Y. Davis' brilliant and very readable *Women, Race, and Class* tells stories of the inspiring but sometimes painful struggles of that time, including references to women's education, writing, and public speaking. This book provides excellent background, works very well with undergraduate students, and integrates analyses of gender, race, and class like almost no other I know.

This history is a necessary context for understanding the twentieth-century women's movement and is particularly important for those of us in composition studies who are interested in the rhetorical and institutional roots of our contemporary feminist practice. Women had fewer opportunities for higher education in the nineteenth century and were supposedly forbidden from speaking in public. But some women did make it into universities (Solomon), and a passionate few—both university trained and not—defied the conventions barring women from public speaking. They have left a legacy of educational innovation, writing, and rhetorical performance documented in books like Shirley Wilson Logan's *With Pen and Voice*, chapters in Andrea Lunsford's collection *Reclaiming Rhetorica*, and Catherine Hobbes' *Nineteenth-Century Women Learn to Write* (see also Campbell; Royster). Familiarity with this rhetorical and political history can deeply enrich a contemporary practice of feminist composition pedagogy.

By the 1960s, women were attending universities in equal numbers with men, and the student protests of that era gave rise to open admissions policies at major universities like CUNY, allowing working-class students and students of color access to universities in unprecedented numbers. This set of circumstances contributed to the emergence of the new field of composition studies, which appeared slightly in advance of the feminist movement but was driven by similar egalitarian political forces. The work of Mina Shaughnessy in analyzing the errors of her new students at CUNY, the institution-challenging ideas about writing introduced by Peter Elbow, and the new process writing theories began to establish "composition" as an alternative institutional site—one responsive to student needs and working against the grain of an elitist literary culture that had dominated English departments. These innovations would seem in retrospect to have created a welcoming situation for a feminist practice, but, aside from a couple of early essays (Bolker; Howe), it wasn't until the 1980s that feminists began to make contributions to composition pedagogy with broad impact. The reason for this delay may lie in the cultural status of women as educators and in the (related) demographics of the teaching of writing, subjects that have become fruitful areas for feminist composition scholarship.

Sue Ellen Holbrook and Susan Miller ("Feminization"[1]) have offered documentation and insightful analyses of the status of women as composition teachers. Both show that women have indeed been very involved in the teaching of writing for decades but most often as part-time and temporary employees—what Eileen Schell, in her excellent recent study of women in composition, calls "contingent workers." Miller describes the field as one "that collects, like bugs in a web, women whose persistently marginalized status demands political action" (39).[2] Women's accounts of their experiences in composition have given specificity to the statistics (Fontaine and Hunter; Phelps and Emig). The few women advancing early on to higher academic levels in composition encountered sexist barriers, like women in other academic fields (Bloom; Crowley), but they were doubly disenfranchised within traditional departments of English, as women and as compositionists. It was then both understandable and ironic that literary studies—given Miller's discussion of its "masculinized" nature—was the place where feminist work in English really took fire in the 1970s: understandable because women scholars from this more prestigious side of the aisle in English departments had more power with which to challenge the androcentric (male-centered) tradition. Courses and publications on women writers in British and American literature (e.g., Gilbert and Gubar; Moers; Showalter) and in feminist theory and criticism from scholars in the United States and France (Cixous; Irigaray[3]; Kolodny) opened up space for women and feminism in English departments. Some of the earliest publications on feminist pedagogy in composition come from compositionists who had worked with women's published writing from a literary perspective and then began to apply those lenses and questions to their writing classes (e.g., Flynn). Since these rather late beginnings, feminist composition pedagogy has grown into a substantial field with a recognized body of scholarship.

⬦ DEFINITIONS

What makes a composition pedagogy "feminist"? In my view, engaging in feminist pedagogy does not necessarily entail an overt discussion of feminism as a politics or movement, although some teachers do include such discussions in their classes. At the end of the essay, I'll return to this subject. In lieu of a direct advocacy approach, then, feminist pedagogy can be described as a practice. But defining this practice is vexing because of feminists' desire not to reinscribe an orthodoxy, disciplining those who fail to subscribe. Feminist linguist Paula Treichler puts the dilemma in dramatic terms, and in the process, outlines some common practices of feminist pedagogy:

> I am not sure that there is or that there should be such a thing as "feminist pedagogy" as constituted by a set of practices: chairs in a circle, first names, collaborative agenda setting, and (as much of the literature puts it) collective revisioning of the production of knowledge. Many women, many feminists, are not comfortable with these practices, particularly when they are sometimes seen to be as expected and institutionally dictated as the most classically delivered "masculine" lecture by a pipe-smoking gentleman scholar in tweeds. (88)

Accepting Treichler's reservations, we can still note that these basic practices of feminist pedagogy are ones it shares with the pedagogical innovations of the process revolution in writing instruction: the decentering or sharing of authority, the recognition of students as sources of knowledge, a focus on processes (of writing and teaching) over products. But what makes feminist pedagogy distinctive is its investment in a view of contemporary society as sexist and patriarchal, and of the complicity of reading, writing, and teaching in those conditions. Those who define their professional activities in ways that include efforts to transform that world are feminist pedagogues. Questions guiding this pedagogy ask of composition: Who created the knowledge and practices of this field? In whose interests do they operate? Are there realms of experience left out in the traditions of this body of knowledge? Who gets to teach this material? Who gets to learn it? Are there ways of teaching and learning that seem more suitable for one gender or another? Any compositionists who apply these questions to their teaching (whether or not they employ the strategies named above) could be said to practice feminist pedagogy.

One of the recurring anxieties about feminist pedagogy concerns inclusion: Who can do it and whom does it benefit? Can only female teachers claim to be feminist pedagogues? Does this pedagogy work well only for female students? While some male scholars in composition and rhetoric suggest that feminism operates in exclusive ways (Connors; Vitanza), many others have found places within it to explore gender issues (see references below to Bleich, Kraemer, Schilb, and Tobin). Anyone interested in social justice, as so many of us who choose composition as a field are, has a stake in moving society toward more equitable arrangements on every front. Just as many women in the feminist movement are deeply committed to antiracism, and straight people work toward the eradication of homophobia and raising consciousness about discrimination toward gay and lesbian people, men have a deep stake in the goals of feminism. In fact, the male teacher who adopts feminist pedagogical strategies can sometimes be more effective than a female teacher because his students won't be as tempted to read his pedagogy as a self-interested choice based on membership in a "special interest" group. Likewise, male students have much to gain from feminist pedagogy. We're all shaped by gender processes of our culture—messages telling us very powerfully how to talk, walk, play, work, and love. When the rich variety of all those ways of being is divided up into two columns, with one virtually off limits to the other group, everyone loses. Teaching students how this system works—and, perhaps even more important, learning from their experiences how it works now and in many different ways— is centrally connected with the teaching of writing—not a digressive special interest affair.

To bring this argument closer to the home of composition, looking at the ways gender structures language and other symbol systems enables the kind of close attention to words and their effects that any composition teacher should strive for. In its interest in the social contexts for writing, the belief that language does things, and the concern with the operations of power, feminist pedagogy has strong links with rhetorical, cultural, and critical pedagogies (see chapters herein by William Covino, Diana George and John Trimbur, and Ann George; see also hooks, *Teaching*). Another way that feminist pedagogy refutes the "only-for-women" position comes out of the transformations of U.S. feminism in the 1980s, when women of color and lesbians began speaking out and developing frameworks for analyzing the intersections of multiple social differences, including race/ethnicity, class, sexual orientation, ability, and others (Lorde). The most significant of these works are deeply concerned with writing: e.g., hooks' *Talking Back;* Gloria Anzaldúa's *Borderlands/La Frontera* and her edited collection, *Hacienda Caras;* and Cherríe Moraga and Anzaldúa's collection *This Bridge Called My Back.* In the words of hooks, the "liberatory feminist movement aims to transform society by eradicating patriarchy, by ending sexism and sexist oppression, by challenging the politics of domination *on all fronts*" (*Talking Back* 50, emphasis added).[4]

Of course there are differences within "feminism," and some of the essays recommended here write about women as though they were an undifferentiated group; some fail to make connections with other forms of social difference. Indeed, there are some feminists who still cling to a politics of separatism, who would disagree with me that feminism is for men as well as women. Women who hold such views have sometimes been labeled "essentialists," either because of their explicitly stated belief that men are biologically and thus essentially different from women (see, for example, Phelps and Emig; Daly), or through assumptions implicit in their writing about "women" as an undifferentiated group. An alternative position reads differences between men and women as widely variable outcomes of social processes of gendering. Debates over this issue constitute one of the major theoretical questions in feminism since its reemergence and have deep significance for research and teaching in composition. Philosopher Linda Alcoff outlines these differences in terms of different "schools" of feminism. For current discussions of the ways essentialism has entered into feminist composition, see essays by Laura Brady and Joy Ritchie, as well as Elizabeth Flynn's recent review (see also Fuss; Looser). All these scholars eschew easy categories and the potentially damaging practice of labeling others' work and recommend instead rhetorical approaches to identity categories such as "woman." In the present essay, you'll find references to important work on feminist pedagogy from both orientations. Feminist pedagogy needs both to talk about women as a group—women teachers, women students—but also to notice differences within gendered categories, especially when it comes to student writing and reading practices. Only a few scholars today confidently write about women's or men's writing and speaking as though they were fixed quantities. It seems that most feminist compositionists today focus on gender construction rather than sex difference, but the ethics of feminist politics and argument suggest that, in our ongoing collective project, we not dismiss the work of those who hold other positions nor see those positions as outdated and superseded. Lynn Worsham's "After Words" to Susan Jarratt and Worsham's *Feminism and Composition Studies* makes a strong case for connection across generations in feminisms. One of the strengths of feminist pedagogy is its relentless capacity for dialogue and self-critique, and its ability to read and listen rhetorically. Most feminists see differences as productive signs of a dynamic movement, just as differences in composition pedagogies included in this volume index a strong and open field of academic work.

What difference does gender make? This is the question feminist pedagogy applies to the scene of composition—to teachers and students and the practices in which they engage: exercising (or renouncing) teacherly authority, talking (in class discussion, collaborative groups, and on e-mail), writing (in genres like journal, narrative, and argument), reading, and assessment. Discussions about practices make reference to frameworks of ideas undergirding them, sometimes called "epistemology" (how we know what we know) or "theory" (first principles or assumptions). Those who engage in feminist pedagogy accept that some version of the social dilemma laid out in the beginning of this essay still obtains in the United States in 1998 (as I'm writing), but few of us enter into our pedagogical practice believing that we already know exactly how gender difference operates in the lives of our students or exactly how the gender dynamics of any particular class will work in advance. Feminist writing teachers bring historical and political knowledge of the feminist movement, sexism, and patriarchal structures, along with tools of gender analysis, into the classroom. Then we work in dialogic ways with our students, enabling them to share with us their knowledge and experience through language within these frameworks. Feminist pedagogy, to my mind, is *not* about forcing all the students to subscribe to a particular political position but rather engaging with students on the terrain of language in the gendered world we all currently inhabit.

✎ GENDERED TEACHERS AND POWER

One of the central tasks of feminist pedagogy has been reflecting on what it means to be a woman teaching writing. Miller's brilliant analysis of composition as a "feminized" profession links the demographics outlined by Holbrook with an analysis of the roots of nineteenth-century "English studies" in a vernacular literature that needed to assert "symbolic, manly associations with religious and nationalistic ideals" in order to compete with the classics and science in the university ("Feminization" 44). The teaching of writing, then, becomes the "distaff partner" to a masculine enterprise (literary criticism)—a domain for women and children, "the counterpart, the handmaiden, and low-order basement attached to vernacular literary study" (40–42). A crucial aspect of this "feminization" is the association of the composition teacher with a mythologized mother, endowed with qualities of "self-sacrifice, dedication, caring and enormous capacities for untheorized attention to detail" but also symbolizing "authority, precision, and . . . taste," prompting expectations of censure and disapproval (46). The mother/composition teacher attends to the rudimentary needs of students who are more like children than adults. In a similar analysis, Margo Culley and colleagues explain the double bind for women in the academy in terms of the psychological dynamics of the family. As women academics, "our maternal power is feared, our paternal authority is mistrusted" (14). On the other hand, some feminists buy into an unambiguously positive feminized identity for composition, building a feminist pedagogy on a maternal basis that emphasizes caring and nurturing (Däumer and Runzo; Grumet; Ruddick). Indeed, a teacher's attitude of caring and nurturing seems very compatible with process writing practices, within which the teacher shifts from the older role of making assignments, waiting for a product, then judging its value, to the position of encouraging, supportive guide. This compatibility surely constitutes one of the pleasurable foundations of feminist pedagogy. But when women step into this role, we reinforce gendered stereotypes dividing intellect from emotion, authority from caring, the public from the personal.

Susan Stanford Friedman's short essay in an early (and unfortunately out-of-print) but still extremely useful collection edited by Margo Culley and Catherine Portuges offers an exemplary feminist response to the dilemma posed by a choice between adopting masculine authority and thus reproducing the existing hierarchies of educational institutions versus opting for a feminine "facilitator" role, and in so doing, reproducing the "patriarchal denial of the mind to women" (207). Enacting one of feminism's most useful *topoi*—substituting for the binary choice of "either/or" the multiple perspectives allowed by "both/and"—Friedman rejects a kind of authority that oppresses students and adopts instead one that recognizes the teacher's knowledge and experience (208). Such feminist authority would celebrate women's intellect without setting aside the emotional and relational richness of the pedagogical site. Likewise, Miller's institutional history/cultural analysis does not recommend setting aside composition's feminized "call to identity" in favor of a masculinized (and thus more powerful) alternative but rather invites a femin*ist* reclamation of the "low" site of composition through political/institutional activism in areas of, for example, employment, placement, and assessment.

A number of feminist scholars clearly recommend that women teachers adopt positions of power in their classrooms. In Kathleen Weiler's *Women Teaching for Change*, feminist teachers present themselves "as gendered subjects with a personal perspective on issues of gender and race. They are overtly political in their presentation and both will use personal anecdotes and will challenge and engage students on these topics" (131). hooks, likewise, eschews the nurturing posture for one of engagement: "Unlike the stereotypical feminist model that suggests women best come to voice in an atmosphere of safety (one in which we are all going to be kind and nurturing), I encourage students to work at coming to voice in an atmosphere where they may be afraid or see themselves at risk" (*Talking Back* 53). She sees the feminist classroom as one marked by struggle. (See also Bauer and Jarratt; Jarratt, "Feminism"). Gail Stygall advocates feminist authority in collaborative group writing contexts. Her analysis of some published collaborative group discussions reveals that the equity claimed for these composition practices often ignores the way male students gain advantages from the gender inequities built into everyday conversational practice. The teacher should use feminist critical authority to intervene in that process. In related studies, John Schilb takes up the question of the male teacher in a feminist classroom, and essays in the collection edited by Gabriel and Smithson foreground issues of power. The collaborative group of Jill Eichhorn and colleagues offers reflections on the ways graduate student status can exacerbate the power issues for a female feminist in the composition class.

There are several ways for students and teachers to attend to the gendering of power and authority in the classroom, asking students to notice their responses to male and female teachers, and leading teachers to examine their

students' responses to them. Cheryl Johnson's reflective essay on the body of
the teacher models a kind of case study exploration of situations arising from
a setting in which the teacher does not fit into the neutral, assumed social categories: white, male, straight, able-bodied, etc. Asking students to write infor-
mally about their expectations of a college teacher, as Karen Hayes did, is one
way to do this (Eichhorn et al.) Another way to address this subject might invite students to think about the gendered ways teachers are represented in the
media: e.g., the creative, exciting (male) poetry teacher in *Dead Poet's Society*
versus supposedly unattractive and sex-starved (female) teacher in *The Mirror
Has Two Faces* (see Bauer, "Proposals"). Feminist pedagogy doesn't dictate one
particular stance for the teacher in relation to these issues, nor does it guarantee that students will respond in any particular way (i.e., all male students will
resist the authority of any female teacher). It simply invites reflection on them—
brings them out of invisibility so that their sources and effects in the context
of a sexist culture can be examined.

✧ THE POLITICS OF SPEAKING

The fact that women are now students in U.S. colleges and universities in numbers equal to or greater than men constitutes one of the gains of the "longest
revolution" (Mitchell). But studies such as Bernice Sandler's "chilly climate"
project reveal that their experiences "are often unsatisfactory in ways that are
not recognized by most university teachers" (Kramarae and Treichler 41).
Among the reasons is the gendered structure of classroom interaction. Taking
women students seriously, borrowing the title of an important early essay by
Adrienne Rich,[5] means for feminist pedagogy in composition listening to the
ways women speak (or remain silent) in class. In the 1980s, feminist sociolin-
guists such as Dale Spender, Robin Lakoff, Pamela Fishman, and others conducted empirical research on women's speech, using techniques of discourse
analysis such as measuring time-on-turn and counting interruptions, tags (the
uncertain raising of the pitch of the voice at the end of a statement, turning it
into a question), and topic shifts.[6] Paula Treichler's convenient summary of a
representative study on language and gender highlights cross-sex communication differences with implications for conversation in the writing classroom:

> (1) women see questions as part of conversational maintenance while men see
> them as requests for information; (2) women explicitly acknowledge previous
> utterances and try to connect with them while men have no such role and of-
> ten ignore previous comments; (3) women interpret aggression as personal,
> negative, and disruptive while men view it as simply another conventional,
> organizing structure for conversation; (4) men shift topics quickly while women
> develop them progressively and shift gradually; (5) women respond to prob-
> lems by sharing experiences, offering reassurances, and giving support; men
> hear problems as requests for solutions and respond by giving direction and
> advice, acting as experts or lecturing their audience. (78)

Since the early work in this area, scholars have begun to pay more attention to the ways class, region, and race differences in conversational patterns inflect findings related to gender. Deborah Tannen, for example, points out in her recent popular book *You Just Don't Understand* that membership in other social categories may override gender patterns. Her own urban, Jewish location puts her in a language group for whom interruption is not a form of domination but a way of connecting with the speech of others. In a later essay on speaking in feminist classrooms, Treichler narrates scenarios that suggest less hesitance on the part of black and working-class women to engage in conflict and challenging others in class discussion.

The best way to use this body of research is to let it make you and your students aware of the interplay of gender in classroom interaction and provide categories of discourse analysis but not to determine in advance the ways men and women will speak in your class. Students can be asked to become discourse analysts in "natural language" settings of their choosing. When they record and analyze speech in class, in dorm rooms, in social settings, and among family members, they can compare their own results with the findings of feminist scholars. Discourse analysis may be even more useful for the feminist pedagogue. To model discourse analysis for my own writing class, I made a series of audiotapes of our class discussions. Listening to the tapes revealed to me that, despite my awareness of the results of sociolinguistic research, I was still giving men more speaking time than women and was quicker to interrupt women than men in my composition classes. As teacher, I also took more speaking time than my self-serving memories of class interaction had recorded! Feminist pedagogues can use this research to make certain women are included in class discussions and to encourage women in ways of speaking that allow them to be heard. The feminist pedagogue, like any good teacher, will aim to create contexts for class discussion in which all students will have opportunities to express their ideas and to learn to listen attentively and respectfully to the ideas of others.

Some composition teachers have begun to incorporate another mode of verbal interaction into their classes in the form of e-mail exchanges and on-line "conversations." Despite utopian hopes that electronic communication would minimize inequitable power relations, early research on gender and electronic communication has shown that they manifest themselves in this medium just as they do in others, sometimes even more virulently (see Faigley, Wilson). As Shannon Wilson suggests, though, transcripts of e-mail exchange offer teachers and students the opportunity to review and reflect on their responses, gaining insight at a distance on the operations of gender and other differences in this medium that places people in a new set of temporal, spatial, and discursive relations to each other.

✧ WRITING (AND READING) . . . DIFFERENTLY?

The core of the composition class is, of course, writing, and perhaps the most interesting research on feminist pedagogy—and the most controversial—

concerns gender and writing. Do men and women write differently? If so, is this a good thing? A "natural" phenomenon? Are particular genres, styles, or voices feminine or masculine? How should teachers respond to gendered styles? Several important researchers work in, around, and against a binary division of gender and styles of writing into male/masculine/argumentative/ rational/linear/academic over against female/feminine/personal/emotional/ digressive. As usual, there are multiple feminist positions on this subject.

One line of research and pedagogical practice makes a positive identifica-tion of women with the personal and emotional, valuing women's storytelling, journal writing (Gannet), and autobiography (Hollis; Peterson). The androcen-tric knowledge generated by universities pretends to be objective and com-plete; women's accounts of their experiences in every area of life (e.g., of bodies, home, nature, pasts) challenge the completeness and value neutrality claimed for this one-sided knowledge (Lather). The feminist validation of personal ex-perience fits well with many composition theorists' focus on student experi-ence as a necessary starting point (Macrorie) or legitimate focus (Murray) for writing; both feminists and expressive compositionists are strongly committed to admitting the presence of the whole person into the educational scene. Har-riet Malinowitz's study of gay and lesbian writers in "gay-themed composi-tion classes" has made the case persuasively that students on the margins do better when they are given opportunities to write about their lives. Women of color and postcolonial feminists have made passionate articulations of their ex-periences in a dazzling variety of written forms—poetry and poetic prose (e.g., Trinh), mixed genre (Williams), and mixed language essays (Anzaldúa, *Bor-derlands*)—making the case in unconventional arguments that the borders defin-ing academic discourse are similar to the boundaries dividing genders, races, classes, and sexualities: limits that have more than symbolic significance (e.g., Gil-Gomez). Disrupting form is a disruption of the gendered rules keeping women (and other members of nondominant groups) out of places of power and influence (see also Bleich).

This critique of academic discourse has led a number of feminists to sug-gest that argument is a particularly masculine genre and as such either is ag-onistic, even violent, and thus shouldn't be used by feminists, or, because it is based in a masculine tradition of logic and linear reasoning, does not allow for the expression of women's experiences and ways of making sense of the world. Two examples of this strand of feminist pedagogy are Jane Tompkins' "Me and My Shadow," a personal reflection on alienating ways academics criticize oth-ers, and Olivia Frey's argument against "Literary Darwinism," the constant struggle to put others down in literary critical practice so as to survive in the academy. Catherine Lamb, in a similar vein, offers feminist/Rogerian media-tion as a substitute for agonistic argument. Another form this research has taken derives from French feminists Luce Irigaray and Hélène Cixous, who (despite distinct differences between them) both recommend and practice a radically unconventional writing style. This *écriture féminine*—women's writing—is shaped in response to philosophical and psychoanalytic theories that under-stand language as a symbolic system associated deeply with masculinity. Some scholars have proposed to teach a form of "women's writing" in composition classes (Junker), while Lynn Worsham ("Writing") argues that to turn this practice into a pedagogy runs against the grain of its radical disruption of just such systems of institutionalization. Lillian Bridwell-Bowles offers sensible advice about ways of incorporating diverse styles into writing classes.

Another take on the issue of writing and sexual difference appears in Elizabeth Flynn's "Composing as a Woman," an influential early essay that actually brought feminism into the light of day for most compositionists. Her study highlights personal narratives written by male and female students: the women's stories feature interaction and connection; the men's, achievement, frustrated achievement, or separation. Flynn chooses to discuss these narratives because they are suggestive of differences in psychological, epistemological, and moral orientations of men and women as they have been explored in feminist research of Nancy Chodorow, Mary Belenky and colleagues, and Carol Gilligan. Flynn doesn't claim to find essential differences in male and female writing but something more like predictable choices of masculine and feminine topics. In her pedagogical suggestions, Flynn advises constructing courses that foreground gender in readings and writing. Another early essay, by Pamela Annas, "Style as Politics," connects the analysis of style in women's published writings, such as Virginia Woolf's *A Room of One's Own*, and the writing of women students.[7] Annas makes an interesting link between feminism and composition by focusing on subjectivity and objectivity in writing and research. Attuned to the fact that women are frequently accused of being subjective (emotional, even irrational) in their thinking and writing, she found women in her class writing at two stylistic extremes: adopting either a smooth, distanced, objectifying style—one that obscures the speaker—or a diffuse, subjective style often too coded to communicate well. Annas believes that feminist teachers should help student writers mediate between the two modes, but she believes it's particularly important to encourage women to write political essays because of the ways they have historically been "channeled toward private forms and denied access to more public forms" (369).

Peterson works strictly with autobiography in an empirical study seeking to discover whether men or women are more comfortable with such personal essays. Her results, like Flynn's, indicate that women write more often about relational topics and men about topics that focus on the self. She draws numerous thoughtful implications for teaching and suggestions for students from her study, including the observation that evaluation can (but should not) privilege certain gender-specific modes of self-representation. She also speaks personally of her negative response to male-authored stories of adventure— " 'wild canoe trips down raging rivers . . . like one of those Miller beer commercials,' " as one of her students put it (175), admonishing herself to examine critically her own gender-linked preferences in assigning and evaluating student essays. In a related essay, Lad Tobin dives deeper into most writing teachers' (male as well as female) resistance to the male-authored adventure narrative in his essay "Car Wrecks, Baseball Caps, and Man-to-Man Defense." Tobin argues that, in our resistance, we may be less able to see discontinuities and potential in the writing of young male students—that we will be less able to follow their work "beneath the surface," a reading strategy used to help students move toward more complexity and depth in their writing. Tobin supports a gender-based feminist pedagogy when he claims that, "[by] studying the ways that masculinity is constructed for me in the larger culture, we could begin to understand the ways that male students struggle to construct themselves in our classrooms" (167). For more discussions of gender and teachers' response to writing, see Duane Roen, Donnalee Rubin, and Stygall and colleagues.

Despite the fact that some research shows female students' affinity for personal writing, some feminist compositionists have voiced warnings about the misuses of the personal. Min-Zhan Lu describes a pedagogical situation in which students' written responses to readings came from personal experience but had the effect of blocking their understanding of differences other than gender. "The task facing a teacher," she writes, "is to help students rethink ways of using personal experience so that readings through the personal will not be at the expense of other stories and selves" (42). See also Gesa Kirsch and Joy Ritchie on this subject. bell hooks advises that, while we respect students' experiences and recognize their need to speak about them in classroom settings, we must also "explore ways individuals acquire knowledge about an experience they have not lived, asking ourselves what moral questions are raised when they speak for or about a reality that they do not know experientially" (*Teaching* 88–89). The research in this area suggests that again a specifically feminist dynamic is at work in reflections on "personal/narrative" writing and "public/academic" argument. Rather than privilege one over the other, many feminist compositionists reject a strict division between the two poles, teaching students how to develop reflective positions within their narratives and to find and understand the experiential roots of their public arguments.

Two practices that have become standard within composition are especially useful for advancing these feminist goals: collaboration and revision. As Lisa Ede and Andrea Lunsford explain in *Singular Texts/Plural Authors*, writing collaboratively challenges the notion of an isolated and autonomous self—a masculinist model—and replaces it with a multivocal, relational writing process. Revision, as well, has radical feminist potential as yet little recognized. Rich, in two beautifully reflective pieces about the movement of her own opinions and ways of writing, demonstrates how textual revision can index deeply considered challenges to social structures and ways of being ("Awaken"; "Notes"). In the next few years, we should be seeing exciting new work in feminist composition pedagogy in these areas of reflective writing, collaboration, and revision.

↝ FEMINISM AS A TOPIC IN
THE COMPOSITION CLASSROOM

As you can tell by the summaries of this work, little is settled in the area of feminist pedagogy, which is better represented as a set of questions than a list of practices. Despite differences in practice, feminist teachers report similar experiences when "feminism" is considered a topic in the composition class. We have learned some lessons in recent years about how best to approach this subject. Because of the current, widely shared negative attitudes about feminism in the United States, it's good to have some advance notice about what to expect from students and to develop strategies for encountering the resistance so many offer even to the very word itself.

If many students resist the exercise of power by a female teacher, even more react against the feminist teacher. Dale Bauer's essay "The Other 'F' Word" examines student evaluations, showing how feminism becomes a frightening specter for some students, especially in an era of what Susan Faludi terms "backlash." In her extensive and very readable study, Faludi demonstrates persuasively that patriarchal culture recoiled at many levels from the feminist gains of the 1970s—i.e., the entry of more women into higher level jobs, the increase of women's salaries, and the struggles to make domestic arrangements more equitable. In popular culture, the politics of the new right, the work place, and elsewhere, this "undeclared war against women" has undermined feminist gains and deeply influenced public opinion.

Students often echo backlash attitudes. The most common response my students make when the issue of feminism comes up is that all the inequities of the past were remedied sometime earlier and that anyone still talking about feminism is an embittered, power-hungry woman who wants to "bash" men. The violence invested in this symbolic representation of angry feminists is captured powerfully in Rush Limbaugh's ubiquitous coinage, "feminazi." These commonplaces themselves lead to focused work with language. What does it mean to "bash" men? What's the difference between "whining" and making a legitimate argument or giving an account of real human pain? In what ways are participants in the U.S. women's movement like Nazis? Asking students to examine closely the language they use in discussing social issues makes them more attentive to language in general and gives them practice in analyzing cultural stereotypes and clichés.

Another opportunity to examine language arises with the use of gendered pronouns. Reading and discussing the nonsexist language statement in the textbook you're using or one developed by your composition program puts the intersection of language and gender on the agenda in a useful (if usually contentious) way. For a book-length study of this subject, see Francine Frank and Treichler, or contact NCTE for a copy of their nonsexist language statement. The section of Dale Spender's *Man Made Language* titled *"He/man* language" makes a provocative reading assignment; it debunks the claim for inclusiveness of group nouns "man" and "mankind" by tracing the historical arguments by male grammarians for their use and reviewing empirical studies of the contemporary effects of exclusive language on male and female students (147–62). Other readings can help to fill in information and provide a range of perspectives. For excellent definitional essays on the terms *sexism* and *oppression*, see Marilyn Frye. Several irreverent new collections by twenty-something feminists (Findlen; Walker) provide perspectives and experiences closer to those of traditional 18- to 22-year-old students than the now-classic second-wave feminist texts. Many readers have sections devoted to gender, and there are some focused solely on gender issues (e.g., Costello). Newspapers, news magazines, and popular media are all excellent resources for raising gender issues. Techniques for analyzing gender in popular media discussed in the essay in this volume on cultural studies (see D. George and Trimbur) are useful for feminist pedagogical aims as well.

Feminist teachers take a lot of heat, but for me and the feminist teachers I know, there's really no choice about whether or not to do feminist pedagogy, only how to go about it. As one of my colleagues says, anyone who's paying attention today is a feminist. Students, institutions, regional politics, and teachers themselves differ so much; this pedagogy must be shaped to fit the circumstances and possibilities under which you work. Form a pedagogy group at your institution, so you can get moral support and share ideas and approaches. The payoff comes in recognizing that as we teach our students how to shape their words, we're working together to reshape our world.

Notes

1. Another version of this material appears in Miller's *Textual Carnivals*; see chapter 4, "The Sad Woman in the Basement: Images of Composition Teaching" (121–41).

2. It might help you and your students to get a local picture of this phenomenon by charting the demographics of your institution and department: finding out numbers of faculty by gender at the various levels in the areas of literature and composition.

3. Many U.S. academics gained access to the work of French feminism through the anthology of translated excerpts edited by Elaine Marks and Isabelle Courtivron.

4. For an extended discussion of feminism and composition, see my essay "As We Were Saying . . . ," the introduction to *Feminism and Composition Studies: In Other Words*.

5. This preeminent feminist poet and essayist has much to offer compositionists interested in feminism. Her collections of essays *On Lies, Secrets, and Silence* and *Bread, Blood, and Poetry* especially contain much useful material about women, language, and writing.

6. The bibliography in this area is vast. For a recent summary of central positions and sources in woman and language research, see Stygall (252–58).

7. Virginia Woolf deserves special mention in any work concerning women, gender, and writing. See Krista Ratcliffe's rhetorical analysis of Woolf's feminist prose and Barrett's collection of her writings about women and feminism.

Bibliography

Alcoff, Linda. "Cultural Feminism Versus Post-Structuralism: The Identity Crisis in Feminist Theory." *Signs* 13.3 (1988): 405–36.

Annas, Pamela. "Style as Politics: A Feminist Approach to the Teaching of Writing." *College English* 47 (1985): 360–71.

Anzaldúa, Gloria. *Borderlands/La Frontera: The New Mestiza*. San Francisco: Spinsters/ Aunt Lute, 1987.

Anzaldúa, Gloria, ed. *Hacienda Caras. Making Face, Making Soul: Creative and Critical Perspectives by Women of Color*. San Francisco: Aunt Lute Foundation Books, 1990.

Barrett, Michèle, ed. *Virginia Woolf: Women and Writing*. London: The Women's Press, 1979.

Bauer, Dale M. "Indecent Proposals: Teachers in the Movies." *College English* 60 (1998): 303–17.

———. "The Other 'F' Word: The Feminist in the Classroom." *College English* 52 (1990): 385–96.

Bauer, Dale M., and Susan C. Jarratt. "Feminist Sophistics: Teaching with an Attitude." Downing 149–65.

Belenky, Mary, et al. *Women's Ways of Knowing: The Development of Self, Voice, and Mind*. New York: Basic Books, 1986.

Bleich, David. "Genders of Writing." *Journal of Advanced Composition* 9 (1989): 10–25.

Bloom, Lynn Z. "Hearing Our Own Voices: Life-Saving Stories." Fontaine and Hunter 89–102.

Bolker, Joan. "Teaching Griselda to Write." *College English* 40 (1979): 906–08.

Brady, Laura. "The Reproduction of Othering." Jarratt and Worsham 21–44.

Bridwell-Bowles, Lillian. "Discourse and Diversity: Experimental Writing Within the Academy." *College Composition and Communication* 43 (1992): 349–68.

Campbell, Karlyn K. *Man Cannot Speak for Her*. 2 vols. New York: Praeger, 1989.

Chodorow, Nancy. *The Reproduction of Mothering: Psychoanalysis and the Sociology of Gender*. Berkeley: U of California P, 1978.

Cixous, Hélène. "The Laugh of the Medusa." Marks and de Courtivron 245–64.

Connors, Robert J. "Teaching and Learning as a Man." *College English* 58 (1996): 137–57.

Costello, Karin Bergstrom. *Gendered Voices: Readings from the American Experience*. Fort Worth: Harcourt Brace, 1996.

Crowley, Sharon. "Three Heroines: An Oral History." *Pre/Text* (Fall/Winter 1988): 202–06.

Culley, Margo, and Catherine Portuges, eds. *Gendered Subjects: The Dynamics of Feminist Teaching*. New York: Routledge, 1985.

Culley, Margo, et al. "The Politics of Nurturance." Culley and Portuges 11–20.

Daly, Mary. *Beyond God the Father: Toward a Philosophy of Women's Liberation*. Boston: Beacon Press, 1973.

Däumer, Elisabeth, and Sandra Runzo. "Transforming the Composition Classroom." *Teaching Writing: Pedagogy, Gender, and Equity*. Ed. Cynthia L. Caywood and Gillian R. Overing. Albany: SUNY P, 1987. 45–62.

Davis, Angela Y. *Women, Race, and Class*. New York: Vintage Books, 1983.

Downing, David B., ed. *Changing Classroom Practices: Resources for Literary and Cultural Studies*. Urbana, IL: NCTE, 1994.

Echols, Alice. *Daring to Be Bad: Radical Feminism in America. 1967–1975*. Minneapolis: U of Minnesota P, 1989.

Ede, Lisa, and Andrea Lunsford. *Singular Texts/Plural Authors*. Carbondale: Southern Illinois UP, 1990.

Eichhorn, Jill, et al. "A Symposium on Feminist Experience in the Composition Classroom." *College Composition and Communication* 43 (1992): 297–322.

Elbow, Peter. *Writing Without Teachers*. New York: Oxford UP, 1973.

Faigley, Lester. *Fragments of Rationality. Postmodernity and the Subject of Composition*. Pittsburgh: U of Pittsburgh P, 1992.

Faludi, Susan. *Backlash: The Undeclared War Against American Women*. New York: Crown, 1991.

Findlen, Barbara, ed. *Listen Up: Voices from the Next Feminist Generation*. Seattle: Seal P, 1995.

Fishman, Pamela. "Interaction: The Work Women Do." *Social Problems* 25 (1977): 397–406.

Flynn, Elizabeth A. "Composing as a Woman." *College Composition and Communication* 39 (1988): 423–35. [Rpt. in Gabriel and Smithson 112–26.]

———. "Review: Feminist Theories/Feminist Composition." *College English* 57 (1995): 201–12.

Fontaine, Sheryl L., and Susan Hunter, eds. *Writing Ourselves into the Story: Unheard Voices from Composition Studies*. Carbondale: Southern Illinois UP, 1993.

Frank, Francine Wattman, and Paula Treichler. *Language, Gender, and Professional Writing: Theoretical Approaches and Guidelines for Nonsexist Usage*. New York: MLA, 1989.

Frey, Olivia. "Beyond Literary Darwinism: Women's Voices and Critical Discourse." *College English* 52 (1990): 507–26.

Friedan, Betty. *The Feminine Mystique*. New York: Dell, 1963.

Friedman, Susan Stanford. "Authority in the Feminist Classroom: A Contradiction in Terms." Culley and Portuges 203–08.

Frye, Marilyn. *The Politics of Reality*. Freedom, CA: Crossing P, 1983.

Fuss, Diana. *Essentially Speaking: Feminism, Nature, and Difference*. New York: Routledge, 1989.

Gabriel, Susan L., and Isaiah Smithson, eds. *Gender in the Classroom: Power and Pedagogy*. Urbana: U of Illinois P, 1990.

Gannet, Cinthia. *Gender and the Journal*. Albany: SUNY P, 1992.

Gilbert, Sandra M., and Susan Gubar. *The Madwoman in the Attic: The Woman Writer and the Nineteenth-Century Literary Imagination*. New Haven, CT: Yale UP, 1979.

Gil-Gomez, Ellen M. "The Practice of Piece-Making: Subject Positions in the Classroom." Jarratt and Worsham 198–205.

Gilligan, Carol. *In a Different Voice*. Cambridge, MA: Harvard UP, 1982.

Grumet, Madeline R. *Bitter Milk: Women and Teaching*. Amherst: U of Massachusetts P, 1988.

Harkin, Patricia, and John Schilb, eds. *Contending with Words: Composition and Rhetoric in a Postmodern Age*. New York: MLA, 1991.

Hobbes, Catherine. *Nineteenth-Century Women Learn to Write*. Charlottesville: U of Virginia P, 1995.

Holbrook, Sue Ellen. "Women's Work: The Feminizing of Composition." *Rhetoric Review* 9 (1991): 201–29.

Hollis, Karyn. "Liberating Voices: Autobiographical Writing at the Bryn Mawr Summer School for Women Workers, 1921–1938." *College Composition and Communication* 45 (1994): 31–60.

hooks, bell. *Talking Back: Thinking Feminist, Thinking Black*. Boston: South End, 1989.

———. *Teaching to Transgress: Education as the Practice of Freedom*. New York: Routledge, 1994.

Howe, Florence. "Identity and Expression: A Writing Course for Women." *College English* 32 (1971): 863–71.

Irigaray, Luce. "This Sex Which Is Not One." *This Sex Which Is Not One*. Trans. Catherine Porter. Ithaca, NY: Cornell UP, 1985. 23–33.

Jarratt, Susan C. "As We Were Saying. . . ." Jarratt and Worsham 1–18.

———. "Feminism and Composition: The Case for Conflict." Harkin and Schilb 105–23.

Jarratt, Susan C., and Lynn Worsham, eds. *Feminism and Composition Studies: In Other Words*. New York: MLA, 1998.

Johnson, Cheryl. "Participatory Rhetoric and the Teacher as Racial/Gendered Subject." *College English* 36 (1994): 409–19.

Junker, Clara. "Writing (with) Cixous." *College English* 50 (1988): 424–36.

Kirsch, Gesa E., and Joy S. Ritchie. "Beyond the Personal: Theorizing a Politics of Location in Composition Research." *College Composition and Communication* 46 (1995): 7–29.

Kolodny, Annette. "Dancing Through the Minefield: Some Observations on the Theory, Practice and Politics of a Feminist Literary Criticism." *Feminist Studies* 6 (1980): 1–25.

Kraemer, Don J., Jr. "Gender and the Autobiographical Essay: A Critical Extension of the Research." *College Composition and Communication* 43 (1992): 323–39.

Kramarae, Cheris, and Paula A. Treichler. "Power Relationships in the Classroom." Gabriel and Smithson 41–59.

Lakoff, Robin. *Language and Woman's Place.* New York: Harper, 1975.

Lamb, Catherine E. "Beyond Argument in Feminist Composition." *College Composition and Communication* 42 (1991): 11–24.

Lather, Patti. *Getting Smart: Feminist Research and Pedagogy with/in the Postmodern.* New York: Routledge, 1991.

Logan, Shirley Wilson, ed. *With Pen and Voice: A Critical Anthology of Nineteenth-Century African-American Women.* Carbondale: Southern Illinois UP, 1995.

Looser, Devoney. "Composing as an 'Essentialist'?: New Directions for Feminist Composition Theories." *Rhetoric Review* 12 (1993): 54–69.

Lorde, Audre. "Age, Race, Class, and Sex: Women Redefining Difference." *Race, Class, and Gender in the United States: An Integrated Study.* Ed. Paula S. Rothenberg. New York: St. Martin's, 1995. 445–51.

Lu, Min-Zhan. "Reading and Writing Differences: The Problematic of Experience." Jarratt and Worsham 239–51.

Lunsford, Andrea A., ed. *Reclaiming Rhetorica: Women in the Rhetorical Tradition.* Pittsburgh: U of Pittsburgh P, 1995.

Macrorie, Ken. *Searching Writing.* Portsmouth, NH: Boynton/Cook, 1988.

Malinowitz, Harriet. *Textual Orientations: Lesbian and Gay Students and the Making of Discourse Communities.* Portsmouth, NH: Boynton/Cook, 1995.

Marks, Elaine, and Isabelle de Courtivron, eds. *New French Feminisms.* New York: Schocken. 1981.

Miller, Susan. "The Feminization of Composition." *The Politics of Writing Instruction: Postsecondary.* Ed. Richard Bullock and John Trimbur. Portsmouth, NH: Boynton/Cook, 1996. 39–53.

———. *Textual Carnivals: The Politics of Composition.* Carbondale: Southern Illinois UP, 1991.

Millett, Kate. *Sexual Politics.* Garden City, NY: Doubleday, 1970.

Mitchell, Juliet. "Women: The Longest Revolution." *Women, Class, and the Feminist Imagination: A Socialist-Feminist Reader.* Ed. Karen V. Hansen and Ilene J. Philipson. Philadelphia: Temple UP, 1990. 43–73.

Moers, Ellen. *Literary Women: The Great Writers.* New York: Doubleday, 1976.

Moraga, Cherríe, and Gloria Anzaldúa, eds. *This Bridge Called My Back: Writings by Radical Women of Color.* Watertown, MA: Persephone, 1981; New York: Kitchen Table/Women of Color, 1983.

Morgan, Robin, ed. *Sisterhood Is Powerful.* New York: Random House, 1970.

Murray, Donald. *Write to Learn.* 2nd ed. New York: Holt, Reinhart, and Winston, 1987.

Peterson, Linda H. "Gender and the Autobiographical Essay: Research Perspectives, Pedagogical Practices." *College Composition and Communication* 42 (1991): 70–83.

Phelps, Louise Wetherbee, and Janet Emig, eds. *Feminine Principles and Women's Experience.* Pittsburgh: U of Pittsburgh P, 1995.

Ratcliffe, Krista. *Anglo-American Feminist Challenges to the Rhetorical Traditions: Virginia Woolf, Mary Daly, and Adrienne Rich*. Carbondale: Southern Illinois UP, 1996.

Rich, Adrienne. "Notes Toward a Politics of Location." *Blood, Bread, and Poetry: Selected Prose 1979–1985*. New York: Norton, 1986. 210–31.

———. "Taking Women Students Seriously." *On Lies, Secrets, and Silence. Selected Prose 1966–1978*. New York: Norton, 1978. 237–45.

———. "When We Dead Awaken: Writing as Revision." *On Lies, Secrets, and Silence. Selected Prose 1966–1978*. New York: Norton, 1978. 33–49.

Ritchie, Joy. "Confronting the 'Essential' Problem: Reconnecting Feminist Theory and Pedagogy." *Journal of Advanced Composition* 10 (1990): 249–71.

Roen, Duane H. "Gender and Teacher Response to Student Writing." *Gender Issues in the Teaching of English*. Ed. Nancy Mellin McCracken and Bruce C. Appleby. Portsmouth, NH: Boynton/Cook-Heinemann, 1992. 126–41.

Royster, Jacqueline Jones. *Southern Horrors and Other Writings. The Anti-Lynching Campaign of Ida B. Wells, 1892–1900*. Boston: Bedford, 1997.

Rubin, Donnalee. *Gender Influences: Reading Student Texts*. Carbondale: Southern Illinois UP, 1993.

Ruddick, Sara. "Maternal Thinking." *Feminist Studies* 6 (1980): 70–96.

Sandler, Bernice Resnick, Lisa A. Silverberg, and Roberta M. Hall. *The Chilly Classroom Climate: A Guide to Improve the Education of Women*. Washington, DC: National Association for Women in Education, 1996.

Schell, Eileen E. "The Costs of Caring: 'Femininism' and Contingent Women Workers in Composition Studies." Jarratt and Worsham 74–93.

Schilb, John. "Pedagogy of the Oppressors?" Culley and Portuges 253–64.

Shaughnessy, Mina P. *Errors and Expectations: A Guide for the Teacher of Basic Writing*. New York: Oxford UP, 1977.

Showalter, Elaine. *A Literature of Their Own: British Women Novelists from Brontë to Lessing*. Princeton, NJ: Princeton UP. 1977.

Solomon, Barbara Miller. *In the Company of Educated Women*. New Haven, CT: Yale UP, 1985.

Spender, Dale. *Man Made Language*. 2nd ed. London: Pandora, 1990.

Stygall, Gail. "Women and Language in the Collaborative Writing Classroom." Jarratt and Worsham 252–75.

Stygall, Gail, et al. "Gendered Textuality: Assigning Gender to Portfolios." *New Directions in Portfolio Assessment: Reflective Practice, Critical Theory, and Large Scale Scoring*. Ed. Laurel Black, et al. Portsmouth, NH: Boynton/Cook, Heinemann, 1994. 248–62.

Tannen, Deborah. *You Just Don't Understand: Women and Men in Conversation*. New York: Ballantine, 1990.

Tobin, Lad. "Car Wrecks, Baseball Caps, and Man-to-Man Defense: The Personal Narratives of Adolescent Males." *College English* 58 (1996): 158–75.

Tompkins, Jane. "Me and My Shadow." *New Literary History* 19:1 (1987): 169–78.

Treichler, Paula A. "A Room of Whose Own?: Lessons from Feminist Classroom Narratives." Downing 75–103.

Trinh, T. Minh-ha. *Woman, Native, Other: Writing, Postcoloniality and Feminism*. Indianapolis: Indiana UP, 1989.

Vitanza, Victor. *Negation, Subjectivity, and the History of Rhetoric*. Albany: SUNY P, 1997.

Walker, Rebecca. *To Be Real: Telling the Truth and Changing the Face of Feminism*. New York: Anchor, 1995.

Weiler, Kathleen. *Women Teaching for Change: Gender, Class, and Power*. New York: Bergin and Garvey, 1988.

Williams, Patricia J. *The Alchemy of Race and Rights*. Cambridge, MA: Harvard UP, 1991.

Wilson, Shannon. "Recursive Discussions of Difference: The Possibilities and Pitfalls of On-Line Exchange." Presentation. *Conference on College Composition and Communication*. Milwaukee, 1996.

Woolf, Virginia. *A Room of One's Own*. New York: Harcourt, Brace, & World, 1929.

Worsham, Lynn. "After Words: A Choice of Words Remains." Jarratt and Worsham 329–56.

———. "Writing Against Writing: The Predicament of *Écriture Féminine* in Composition Studies." Harkin and Schilb 82–104.

Community-Service Pedagogy

L A U R A   J U L I E R

A colleague and I were standing in the hall, catching up after his semester on leave, talking about where we were each investing our energies, what projects we were envisioning for ourselves. My colleague had just received a grant from the Michigan Campus Compact[1] for a couple of pilot sections of one of the required, first-year writing courses taught by our department. Although all of our department's courses vary slightly in their focus on a particular aspect of American cultural history, all share goals for first-year writing instruction. The grant would support him in designing a new course, maintaining the same core goals but using a service learning pedagogy. In this new course he envisioned, while students read, critically analyzed, and responded in class to issues raised by American literary and historical texts, they would simultaneously work with various community nonprofit and social service agencies on projects that would engage them in what my colleague called "real world writing." As an untenured faculty member, I had been feeling fragmented, doubting whether I could sustain the multidisciplinary research and teaching agenda that I had brought with me to this department, and whether "the profession"—and the colleagues who would soon pass judgment on my tenure—would conclude that I had managed to sustain it fruitfully, successfully, and with integrity.

As we talked in the hall and he listened to my ambivalence about being able to do the kind of teaching and research to which I was committed and to balance those with my community activist commitments, he made a very generous offer to include me in the pilot project. The possibilities were immediately compelling to me. I began to see how in teaching my course, which focused on women in America, I might engage students in first-hand experiences with local agencies and organizations that dealt directly with the issues about which we would be reading, writing, and researching. I intuitively sensed that such first-hand experience would at best subvert and at the very least complicate the often-pat constructions and commonplaces upon which so many first-year college students relied as they composed writing for the academy. What my colleague informed me was known as service learning seemed a way to integrate on many levels my teaching and research, my commitments to social change and social justice, to active learning and women's studies and to the teaching of writing. I was hooked. I have now come to see, however, that like some of the turns many of us make at one point or another in our lives, I had jumped without really knowing what it was I was jumping into.

✦ SERVICE LEARNING

The literature of the service learning movement ranges widely in theoretical assumptions and philosophical foundations. There are a number of attempts to trace the roots of service learning, to give it a pedigree. In her first chapter to *Service-Learning in Higher Education*, Barbara Jacoby situates it in the context of calls, such as those by Derek Bok and Ernest Boyer, for the reform of higher education, for universities "to become actively engaged in responding to" (3) the problems of contemporary society. Like many who write about the ways in which the practices and goals of service learning meet a deep need in American culture today, she cites Harvard psychiatrist Robert Coles' work with and research on the moral and spiritual activities and commitments of young people over the course of thirty years. Her overview of the history, purposes, key concepts, and ways of institutionalizing service learning is also shaped by looking back to the late 1950s and 1960s Civil Rights movement and the varied initiatives for national service that yielded the Peace Corps and VISTA.

Alan S. Waterman begins the first chapter of his *Service-Learning: Applications from the Research* by claiming that "We have been doing 'service-learning' in our society for far longer than we have applied the label to this approach to experiential education" (1), and in this way grounds his discussion in another conversation. He traces two strands of a lineage for service learning. One looks back to "the American tradition of service to the community" (2) voiced by Thomas Jefferson and William James, a tradition developing into such community-service programs as the Civilian Conservation Corps, the Peace Corps, and the National and Community Service Act of 1990. The other strand Waterman locates in the educational philosophies of John Dewey, who "viewed community as an integral part of educational experiences, because what is learned in the school must be taken and utilized beyond its bounds, both for the advancement of the student and the betterment of future societies" (2). From the rich field of experiential education inspired by Dewey, the work of David Kolb (particularly his experiential learning cycle) and of Donald Schön is crucial for those thinking about service learning.

In seeking the roots of major threads of contemporary American educational philosophies, Waterman is not alone in focusing on the pre-World War II struggle over the means and ends of liberal education, a struggle represented on the one hand by Robert Maynard Hutchins and Mortimer J. Adler of the University of Chicago, who argued for a model of education based on the Great Books tradition, and on the other by John Dewey, who argued for the application of the fruits of intellectual study to the problems of contemporary experience. As Thomas Ehrlich asserts in the foreword to Jacoby's book, "The premise of service-learning [is] that Dewey was right and Hutchins was wrong" (xi). Ira Harkevy and Lee Benson also see service learning as "a pedagogy derived from a theory of democratic education and schooling developed by John Dewey to replace Plato's aristocratic theory of education and society" (11). And casting back from Dewey for the "anti-Platonic precursors of service learning" (12), they take up Cicero, Bacon, and Benjamin Franklin. Dewey, indeed, is a touchstone in the literature of service learning pedagogy, most notably in articles by John Saltmarsh, by Dwight Giles and Janet Eyler, and by David Cooper.[2]

Others see in service learning the appropriate pedagogical complement to educating for civic virtue and democratic citizenship. It is a conversation that takes up work in American studies, in values education, in civic literacy, and in communitarianism and democratic processes and frequently cites, among others, Benjamin Barber, Barber and Richard Battistoni, Sandra Stotsky, Harry Boyte, Amitai Etzioni, and Robert Bellah and his colleagues. As C. David Lisman argues in his new book, *Toward a Civil Society: Civic Literacy and Service Learning*, a focus on investigating and creating commitments to community seems, to those concerned with moral and civic literacy, the most appropriate grounding for service learning. Civic literacy is at the heart of Stotsky's argument that "independent and moral thinking are fundamental to scholarship and the meaning of citizenship in a republican form of government" (129). She further asserts that the teaching of writing, which has ignored its ethical concerns and moral obligations other than in issues of plagiarism or discussions of logical fallacies, is integral to preparing students adequately for their roles as citizens.

For Jeffrey P. F. Howard, service learning stands as a "counternormative pedagogy," not merely "a panacea for the perceived shortcomings of the information-dissemination model that prevails in higher education" (21), but a means to "reconceptualiz[e] the teaching-learning process" (25). Service learning is taken up by those, like Howard, who look for models of such reform to alternative and liberatory pedagogies such as that of Paulo Freire, whose emphasis on praxis, the movement back and forth between action and reflection, is a key component of service learning pedagogy. As Edward Zlotkowski observes, "In its baggage, service learning packs a whole wardrobe of theoretical and epistemological challenges to the status quo" ("A Service Learning Approach" 82).

Service learning is not national service, community service, or volunteer service or voluntarism, nor is it the same as an academic internship or field placement. As Waterman explains, "[i]n the case of service-learning, the projects are designed, enacted, supervised, and evaluated with the educational benefits of the experiences as one of the consciously held goals" (3). Thomas Jeavons defines service learning as "a form of active pedagogy that involves students in activities that both provide service to a community and engage students in an experience where they acquire knowledge, skills, or perspectives that broaden and deepen their understanding of a particular concept or subject matter" (135). The Wingspread Report's "Principles of Good Practice for Combining Service and Learning" were developed (under the aegis of the National Society for Internships and Experiential Education, a group representing dozens of organizations interested in service learning) to make clear that the connections between service and "reflective learning" must be integral, not secondary, to any service learning program (Honnet and Poulsen). And as Jacoby suggests, although their varied traditions and missions lead colleges and universities that have "embraced" service learning to take up some of the key components of service learning pedagogy in particular ways,[3] nonetheless certain core concepts and practices stand out. The theory and philosophy shaping any program or course, for instance, must in some way engage questions about the meaning of service, about how students will be engaged in something other than voluntarism or community service. There must be some way to seek reciprocity and balance between those serving and those served, an effort to avoid the tendency toward condescension, patronizing, or self-serving tenor that so often accompanies "charity" work. And finally, students and faculty must self-consciously reflect upon that reciprocity.

Those who write about service learning pedagogy have at times used the terms *community-service learning* (Deans; Watters and Ford), or *community-service writing* (Bacon; Flower), or *academic service learning* (Rhoads and Howard), among others. Ed Zlotkowski argues for keeping the terminology consistent with the broader service learning literature: "Given the fact that one of the most serious misconceptions service-learning advocates have to deal with is the academic public's tendency to conflate service-learning with community service, it is remarkable how effortlessly most have adopted the hybrid 'community-service learning'" ("Does Service-Learning Have a Future?" 131). Each has, I have come to see, different emphases, connotations, and politics, and the differences are worth attending to. Because I locate the history and some of the philosophical grounding of service learning in literature that uses that term, I use it far more often than I use community-service pedagogy.

↪ SERVICE LEARNING IN THE DISCIPLINES

Yet in spite of these rather impressive pedigrees and theoretical or philosophical lineages, in some ways service learning has been "relatively untheorized" (Adler-Kassner, Crooks, and Watters 14). In researchers Giles and Eyler's words, it is questionable "whether [service learning] is a field or a social movement" in part because it "suffers from the lack of a well articulated conceptual framework" (77). Rationales for the use of service learning are often assumed to be self-evident, its good a given—perhaps, ironically, because it is taken up by so many different intellectual communities and has a foot in so many varied conversations. And perhaps because it is untheorized, it is sometimes criticized as feel-good pedagogy, not rigorous, not academic enough. Many faculty do not see any intellectual or professional warrant for adopting such a complex rethinking and reconceiving of their teaching. Failure to take service learning seriously may indeed result from the fact that it does not locate itself in a discipline, the coin of the academic realm. In thinking about English departments as a "home" for service learning, Aaron Schutz and Anne Ruggles Gere note that service learning has been '[u]nencumbered by a disciplinary identity," and "has for a number of years, moved freely within the academy, sometimes attaching itself to sociology or psychology, sometimes to education or social work" (129). Indeed, much of the conversation about service learning speaks about intellectual goals that make much more immediate sense to teacher-scholars in those fields than, for example, to those in the humanities. "Until recently," according to Zlotkowski, "the service-learning movement has more often seen 'moral and civic values' as the horse pulling the cart of 'enhanced learning' rather than vice versa" ("Does Service-Learning Have a Future?" 126). As editor for the American Association of Higher Education's Series on Service-Learning in the Disciplines, Zlotkowski has been the leading voice in calling for those involved in service learning to begin to address the specific ways in which a service learning pedagogy enhances the learning in particular disciplines or enriches its content:

> What is needed now is a broad-based adjustment that invests far more intellectual energy in specifically academic concerns. Only by paying careful attention to the needs of individual disciplines and by allying itself with other academic interest groups will the service-learning movement succeed in becoming an established feature of American higher education. ("Does Service-Learning Have a Future?" 123)

It is no small irony that what took shape as a multivocal, multidisciplined conversation is now being urged to find its place within disciplinary contexts. But like many other moves to transform educational practice that blur or cross disciplinary boundaries, service learning seems to have arrived at a seemingly inevitable point. To gain institutional legitimacy—that is, for teaching and curricular innovations and research projects to be valued and rewarded in hiring criteria, funding priorities, merit raise considerations, and tenure and promotion decisions—advocates and practitioners of service learning pedagogy are being asked to take it up as a subject of research and scholarship within disciplinary contexts. Tom Deans looks to David Russell's assertions about the history of writing across the curriculum and finds a lesson for service learning advocates: that the very character of universities, divided into self-interested departments that compete for resources and reward research above teaching, dooms any cross-curricular initiative. Like writing across the curriculum (WAC), service learning is often seen as a pedagogical reform more than a curricular one, a "mode of learning" (Deans 35) more than an area of research, and like WAC, such initiatives tend to remain institutionally adrift if they insist on their multidisciplinary and cross-disciplinary roots.

But as Zlotkowski argues in "Does Service Learning Have a Future?," seeking institutional legitimation should not "be misconstrued as a 'selling out' of the service-learning vision—as a pursuit of academic acceptance at any price" (129). He at least is not arguing for turning "service-learning into still another academic specialty" (129). Instead, he sees in service learning a means to effect "a transformation of contemporary academic culture: the transformation of a set of elitist, self-referential academic assumptions into . . . 'the engaged campus'" (130). Zlotkowski's call pushes service learning advocates to examine both the practices and the content in their courses, to problematize concepts such as community and democracy and to engage them as subjects of intellectual inquiry. In so doing, he suggests that while the site of theory and research may be in the disciplines, the goal of such work is a transformation of the entire postsecondary culture and mission.

↔ SERVICE LEARNING PEDAGOGY IN THE TEACHING OF COMPOSITION

Why take up a community-service pedagogy to enhance the teaching of writing? Service learning pedagogy can seem—as it did to me and as it often sounds in published articles and conference presentations—like a panacea, a gospel to be spread, a silver bullet that will energize and invigorate teachers, motivate students, connect academic activities with "real world" learning, and effect social change. Many of the reasons for excitement about service learning offered in those articles and conference sessions skim tired old surfaces even if with the enthusiasm of the newly converted. Passing comments about how service learning in the writing class motivated students, eliminated the empty assignment syndrome, gave students "real" audiences to write for and "real" purposes for their writing seem a throwback to our discipline's conversations of twenty-five and thirty years ago. Because much recent scholarship in composition studies has demonstrated and explored the complexities of these issues, one would expect the statement of the problem to have changed, not to be made so uncritically. Likewise there is often too little attention paid to questioning or problematizing the service activities and the writing requirements, inquiring into and reconstituting, for instance, the idea of service, or what is meant by community and whose community, or how course assignments construct students and academic purposes in relationship to communities.

There are those, however, who make the case that service to community groups is precisely the place for students to study the complexities of writing and discourse. Explaining the rationale for the service learning experience in his writing class at Bentley College, for example, Bruce Herzberg writes:

> The effort to reach into the composition class with a curriculum aimed at democracy and social justice is an attempt to make schools function . . . as radically democratic institutions, with the goal not only of making individual students more successful, but also of making better citizens, citizens in the strongest sense of those who take responsibility for communal welfare. These efforts belong in the composition class because of the rhetorical as well as the practical nature of citizenship and social transformation. ("Community Service and Critical Teaching" 317)

Nora Bacon argues that engaging students in writing in community settings "demonstrates [to students] the enormous variety in written discourse and the degree to which the forms, processes, and purposes of writing are embedded in particular contexts," and consequently "points us toward a curriculum of textual studies based on inquiry into variation in discourse" ("Community Service Writing" 53). Certain configurations of what she calls community-based writing courses can be a means to problematize the idea of audience and purpose, to "denaturalize academic writing, . . . introducing self-consciousness about the business of writing for a teacher" ("Community Service Writing" 43). For Bacon, not only are service learning writing courses appropriate sites for inquiry by students, but also sites for faculty inquiry and theorizing of the field itself:

> As they investigate questions such as these, students may develop an understanding of rhetorical variation that prepares them to navigate in multiple discourse communities. As we participate in the investigation, we may extend and refine the theories of writing that inform our work. We may remember why rhetoric was for so many years the cornerstone of higher education. ("Community Service Writing" 53)

Although she does not take up service learning explicitly as a pedagogy in "The Rhetorician as Agent of Social Change," Ellen Cushman argues even more powerfully than Bacon that the study of rhetoric move beyond academic boundaries: "Given the role rhetoricians have historically played in the politics of their communities, I believe modern rhetoric and composition scholars can be agents of social change outside the university" (7). Schutz and Gere, on the other hand, point to the effect of theoretical changes in the field on institutional identities to find a rationale for English studies taking up service learning pedagogy: "English departments have begun to emphasize the social processes of consuming and producing texts. . . . Both theoretically and practically, service learning fits particularly well in English departments that foreground the ways people read and write, attend to cultural studies, and entertain questions about public policy" (130).

⟿ THEORETICAL AND CURRICULAR COMMITMENTS

Describing the community-service writing program at Stanford University—"launched . . . just after composition theory took its 'social turn,' shifting its focus from the cognitive processes of individual writers to the relationship between texts and their social contexts" ("Community Service Writing" 39)—Bacon explains that it was only as the program expanded that she "learned how it blended—or collided—with the theories of writing that informed our teaching practices" ("Community Service Writing" 39). This is, I have come to believe, a common story.

The pilot program in which my colleague had invited me to share was modeled, I learned, on the well-established and respected one at Stanford. Our students worked in small groups with different community agencies and organizations on writing projects that the agencies needed or requested. They wrote public announcements for the Girl Scouts, trying to counter recent negative publicity; revised a job application manual for unemployed teens; wrote articles for newsletters for a senior care facility and a homeless shelter; and created informational brochures for a public health clinic. Although the projects varied in form, scope, and length, what characterized them was that students needed to learn about the audience for whom they wrote as well as the agency on whose behalf they were writing. They had to research the information (from sources as varied as oral interviews, library searching, and public opinion surveys), write collaboratively, and work through multiple drafts. At the same time, our students read from American literary and historical texts,[4] analyzing and discussing them in class, writing in response to them, and engaging in a process of recursively returning to consider key concepts and ideas—such as the idea of the common good and of community, and the changing history and meanings of service—in order to develop an increasingly complex understanding of them. We also used their own writing early in the semester to raise issues about the processes of composing and the production of texts, and to begin to think about and engage in discourse analysis. The concepts raised by the texts we read often challenged students with distant language and abstractions, while their work with agencies in their communities gave them a new site from which to think and talk about those abstractions more concretely.

As I taught and learned through the semester of the pilot program, I was indeed excited and energized by the many possibilities and new configurations for teaching writing. Issues of rhetorical strategies and effects that in a previous incarnation of this course might never have been discussed in the whole class had immediacy as student writers—working to meet deadlines that were not teacher imposed—needed answers. Reasons for choices of phrasing and organization were not mine, not chosen because "that's what she wants," but because student writers had figured them out for themselves in light of what they understood to be the audience's needs or the agency's purposes. Lots of good things were happening in the development of students' writing, and the kind of talk I overheard or facilitated in small groups over the course of the semester was the kind for which teachers of writing aim. It was generative, it was detailed, it was collaborative as well as contentious. But it rarely involved, I later realized, any conversation about ways their work with discourses outside the academy might lead them to a critical engagement with academic discourses, or about the ways their work might be socially transformative in the community. Those failures, I came to realize, were mine, because I did not anticipate the ways in which a service learning pedagogy would challenge me with its logistics and its possibilities.

My experience with this particular model for how collaboration with the needs of community agencies and organizations might mutually benefit both the students and the community raised a number of theoretical and philosophical questions for me. Some of those questions and issues are at the center of the discussion and scholarship on service learning in composition as well as in other disciplinary and interdisciplinary contexts; some of them resonate with and are shaped by the particular history and theories of teaching writing in this country. In·seeking to link service learning pedagogy with the teaching of writing, that is, I found myself thrown back upon some of the basic questions with which all teachers of writing must come to terms. In essence, mine was the "prior question" that Erika Lindemann claims we as a profession have not sufficiently addressed: what is the purpose of a writing course? What goals in the development of writing do my theoretical commitments lead me to establish for my teaching? It was the need to articulate clearly the pedagogical goals of one's course of instruction, the philosophical and theoretical understandings about language and writing development, and the curricular place of composition courses in particular institutions that my experiments with service learning pedagogy impressed upon me anew.

Competing claims for the purposes and focus of postsecondary writing courses characterize composition studies' professional and scholarly conversations. Attempts to organize these theories and assumptions have been useful in helping teachers and researchers find ways to think through such questions, even as they have at times been used to impose rigid distinctions rather than to encourage generative pluralism in the field. Some of the more frequently cited include Lester Faigley's taxonomy of expressive, cognitive, and social theories of composing and James Berlin's theories of composition pedagogies as shaped by the ideologies of cognitive, expressionist, and social-epistemic rhetorics. David Bartholomae and Peter Elbow, in ongoing discussions at the CCCC and in the pages of College English, debate the value or appropriateness of academic discourse as the focus of instruction. Others, most recently, for instance, Schutz and Gere, prefer a frame that distinguishes between public and private sites and purposes of writing instruction. Richard L. Larson, in the foreword to Stotsky's Connecting Civic Education and Language Education, sees those competing claims in terms of the following opposition, and argues for the latter: on one hand is instruction that "elicit[s] autobiographic and introspective pieces, . . . instruct[s] students in composing 'processes' and rhetorical techniques," and focuses on "only one, most often private, purpose for writing" (ix); on the other hand is writing instruction which would help students to achieve "a public purpose (e.g., moving readers to an informed judgment, encouraging wise action)" (x) and to develop "the qualities of character and mind and the powers of language needed for public discourse" (xi).

In another ongoing conversation in College English on the use of literature in first-year composition courses, Erika Lindemann considers the ways in which regarding "writing primarily as a product, a process, or a system of social actions" (289) leads individual instructors to value pedagogical strategies and make pedagogical choices in certain ways. Although it might seem at first that teachers of writing courses who make use of a service learning pedagogy or a community-service component are among those who view writing as a system of social actions, in fact there are service learning programs, courses, and teachers whose curricular and pedagogical choices replicate these varied and competing theoretical positions.[5]

Nora Bacon first began to distinguish between types of service learning writing courses in a brief note in the *National Society for Experiential Education Quarterly*, describing courses in which students write about service experiences and courses in which students' writing is the service. In the first of these, such as the program at UCLA, service in the community provides material for writing and for research, a site for testing claims and concepts from readings. Service placements expose students firsthand to social issues about which they are studying, and from which, presumably, they have been previously sheltered. Instructors find the community-service experience "encourages critical thinking" (Bacon, "Community Service and Writing Instruction" 14). Bacon cites the director of the UCLA project, Randal Woodland, who claims that "By using their own experiences as part of the paper, students join the academic conversation from a position of authority" ("Community Service and Writing Instruction" 14), an authority that Rosemary L. Arca, among others, argues is especially crucial for basic writers.

Ilona McGuiness, for example, began to include community-service placements in her writing class at Loyola College in Baltimore in response to Jane Peterson's call to heed "a new urgency" to develop "students' ability to appreciate cultural diversity and multiple ways of reading and writing" (315). Students elect from among a variety of community-service opportunities such as spending a Saturday morning helping at a soup kitchen or Habitat for Humanity building site. In the classroom, they read about issues of social justice, economic disparity, or social identity. McGuiness sees the community service as helping students "accept the responsibility of building a knowledge base" about "people who live in circumstances far different from their own" (3) before they can enter into reasonable public discussions about a variety of issues such as questions of social justice. They write reflectively about their service experiences, but also use those experiences as subjects through which to engage the readings.[6]

Service placements help McGuiness' students to "achieve the kind of 'distance and objectivity toward their experience'" (4) that, quoting Christopher Burnham, she says is necessary before "college writers [can] use a wide range of cognitive skills . . . systematically and rigorously" (5). "Even the best [instructional materials]," she claims, "still keep students removed from the realities" (4) of the issues about which they are engaged in formulating positions. Service learning experiences give students ways to confront and find language for both the differences among people and the common ground that enables them to work together. Thus, in McGuiness' course, while much of the writing connected to their service work is aimed at helping students to "articulate their personal values" (5), she intends that the struggle be not only emotional but intellectual: much of the rest of the work, she writes, "help focus that struggle in ways that complement the academic goals of the writing course" (5).

Reflection on service experiences is almost universally understood as essential to service learning (see Jacoby et al. 6–7; Waterman 7–10; de Acosta; Greco; but especially Anson; and Cooper). Although reflection may take place in any number of contexts, journals—variously constituted—seem to be the most common site for reflection. While Herzberg articulates important cautions about the use of journals for reflection on service experiences, others—notably Anson and Cooper—describe and elaborate on using journals to teach critical reflection. Asking students to write reflectively, in journals or other contexts, can, however, end up having the opposite effect on goals such as McGuiness'. Because such writing usually privileges individual experience, as Herzberg notes, students may also come to "regard social problems as chiefly or only personal, [and] they will not search beyond the personal for a systemic explanation" ("Community Service" 58).

Without thoughtful consideration about the meaning, the mutuality, or the purposes of service, service learning writing courses may also, as Rosemary Arca, Herzberg, Linda Adler-Kassner, and others argue, raise issues of class distinctions and replicate divisions between service provider and service recipient with which some students—such as many underprepared writers or nontraditional or community college students—have had too much personal experience. The rhetoric of sending students "out" into "the" community may, in some settings and course designs, confirm for students an insider-outsider understanding of academic purposes, and replicate condescending models of charity and missionary work that do more to undermine than to advance the goals of multicultural education and social transformation. Issues of social class, race, and gender play out variously when we ask students to engage in service of any kind to communities; in the literature of service learning, only class issues have begun to be considered, and not widely. Those issues can also suggest differing goals and configurations for service learning writing courses. Adler-Kassner, in responding to Herzberg, raises the question, "Should issues about social structures, ideology, and social justice be focuses for community-service course [sic] for underprepared students?" (554), and answers, "The primary difference between Herzberg's course and [mine] is that the primary emphasis in my courses was not on raising critical consciousness, but in helping students articulate whatever consciousness they had in a way that was acceptable in the academy" (555).

Neither an example of Adler-Kassner's "pragmatic" (555) course nor Herzberg's focus on ideology, the pilot course that my colleague and I taught required students to produce documents and engage in writing projects to be used by the community agency to which they were assigned. Students' writing furthered the cause of the organization and was itself service to the community. In this sort of course, students immerse themselves in a specific discourse community, write for purposes that are the agency's, and speak on behalf of the agency, as if their commitments were the agency's. Their writing accomplishes purposes primarily in and for the community, not only the teacher. Advocates of writing as service point to the authenticity of the "real world" writing situations as its pedagogical benefit, which some, like Paul Heilker, see as "more important work . . . than simply helping students master the conventions of academic discourse" (75). That writing for community audiences is more "real" than writing for academic readers is a claim Bacon compellingly disputes in "Community Service Writing." As her stories of some service learning "failures" demonstrate, it is possible for students to experience classrooms as more authentic rhetorical environments than community agencies with which they have had limited contact or investment. The agency and its clientele are a discourse community to which students are very often outsiders; producing the document requires immersing themselves in that community (or communities, depending on who the agency is and who its clients are) in order to determine the necessary background, technical and/or institutional vocabulary, purposes, and audience needs. Furthermore, writing for an agency's purposes may require students to take on positions and intentions that are not their own and to which they cannot subscribe, a situation that is merely another version of the academic artificiality of writing "what the teacher wants me to say." There is nothing, in other words, to guarantee that the student will find this situation any more "real" than the classroom.

Adopting a means to assess writing tasks that have been defined by the agency, not the instructor, that will be developed according to criteria established by the agency, the effectiveness of which will be determined by the agency and its clients, is both a humbling—as Bacon describes—and a crucial component of courses in which students write for community agencies. The instructor, more of a facilitator than primary audience of the writing, is nonetheless also in a significant sense part of the audience, since students are in an academic course for which a grade is still one of the end products.

At the same time that I saw the students in my course challenged in just these ways by the writing they were asked to do for the community agencies, there were also ways in which this type of service made me very uncomfortable. Students in this course, for instance, could write brochures about STDs for the public health clinic without ever setting foot inside the clinic or without ever having to talk to any of the clients. I was also to some degree troubled with how the focus of instruction and of students' attention could easily turn to forms and conventions, as when my students came to me needing to know how to create a brochure, which software application to use, what a "trifold" was, and whether brochures could use graphics. In the same way that some configurations of writing across the curriculum presume that an introductory course with readings from across disciplines can "give" students what they need to write a research proposal in physics without the in-depth, contextual knowledge of that particular discourse community and its social context, arrangements for students to write documents effectively for community agencies at which they were only temporary visitors required more insider information on my part, more advanced planning so that students might anticipate the challenges and the questions that would enable them to negotiate the often-complex writing contexts and tasks.

With the social turn in composition studies, many scholars and teachers have situated themselves within literacy instruction: looking to Dewey and Freire, they see literacy as enabling learners to become active, critical, responsible participants in democratic processes; with Henry Giroux and Peter McLaren, and Donald Macedo building on Freire's work, they also see literacy as critical reading of cultural texts and cultural practices. Literacy, then, has come to refer to practices that are not only text based and school based; literacy projects recognize a variety of discourses within and without the university, taking shape within diverse communities, and thus also recognize and urge the necessity of engaging and valuing multiple literacies and multiple discourses.[7] In programs such as the Dayton Literacy Project (see Conniff and Youngkin), Herzberg's course at Bentley, and the tutoring project at the Ellis School in Pittsburgh that Norma Greco describes, literacy itself is both the service and the subject of investigation. As students engage in literacy tutoring, they develop a new expertise: their experience becomes a position from which they are invited to recompose themselves and their knowledge. They reflect upon and investigate discursive practices to better understand how they shape the nature of social issues.

In "Community Service and Critical Teaching," Herzberg describes the evolution of community-service learning in the Bentley College curriculum, from courses in which students worked in soup kitchens and wrote about it, to courses in which students did audits and bookkeeping for nonprofit agencies. He describes a composition course in which students serve as literacy tutors at a downtown shelter; their writing engages them in inquiry into "the study of literacy and schooling, examin[ing] the ways that literacy is gained or not gained in the United States" (310). None of these configurations, Herzberg says, necessarily engaged students in critical analysis of the issues raised by community service. He agrees with Campus Compact director Susan Stroud that if service learning courses do not result in such analysis, "then we are not involved in education and social change—we are involved in charity" (309). But he also claims that the connection between composition instruction and the questions raised by community service about social structures and social justice "is by no means obvious" (309).

Carnegie Mellon's Community Literacy Project engages students in writing *with* the community—which Linda Flower has represented as a third alternative to Bacon's writing *as* and writing *about* (*Problem-Solving* 306)—and focuses on collaboration between community and university to address local social problems. In "Partners in Inquiry: A Logic for Community Outreach," one of the most comprehensive and incisive articles in the conversation on service learning in composition studies,[8] Flower distinguishes among kinds of community service (and kinds of community/university collaboration) by elaborating four "logics" that inform them: the logic of cultural mission, of technical expertise, of compassion and identity, and of prophetic pragmatism and problem solving. It is the fourth that informs the Community Literacy Project, the work of which is built around what Flower calls community problem-solving dialogues. She describes a community-service writing project that deals with issues of collaboration and mutuality, investigates discourse and literate practices, engages in intercultural inquiry and in social action by working with community members as they solve their own problems. It is a program that asks what counts as literacy, or whose literacy counts, as a way of studying and developing community literacies.

What characterizes these conversations on service learning in writing are, more than anything, the philosophical and ideological differences among instructors' commitments. The tensions—disruptive but also generative—arising from those differences have been at times confusing, at times comical or absurd, as when a couple of years ago the CCCC scheduled two special interest groups—one titled service learning, the other social justice writing—at the same time, with some participants running back and forth wondering what the difference was and which better represented their own interests, and others making a decision based on whichever recently published scholar had chosen a particular room. The tensions are also represented in postings to the several listservs[9] that have sprung up, postings that discuss "practical writing" in contrast to concerns for social justice, or alternatively, enthusiastically proclaim ways in which courses or programs gain funding or student praise for teaching "real world skills."

These differences, I would argue, emphasize how singularly apt the idea of service learning is to the teaching of writing: in it, we see possibilities and arguments about the theories that inform our thinking and our practices, our commitments and our visions. The challenges, opportunities, and questions that service learning forces composition studies back upon—because of the diversity of its roots and its ideologies, but especially as it interacts with other disciplines in configuring courses and programs shaped by service learning pedagogy—present possibilities for the kind of restructuring of composition about which Gere wrote in the introduction to *Into the Field*, when she imagined teachers and theorists "reconceptualizing the discipline, deconstructing received boundaries, and reconstructing relations between theory and application" (3).

Notes

1. Campus Compact is a national organization of college and university presidents, established in the mid-1980s to promote student public service. There are chapters of Campus Compact in every state.

2. Dewey's work, of course, also undergirds much composition theory, although as Stephen Fishman argues, that grounding is more often tacit than elaborated.

3. Another useful and telling map for distinguishing service-learning programs (not only service-learning writing courses) is Jacoby's. She lists "church-related colleges and universities [where] service learning is firmly grounded in the institution's spiritual mission and in the quest for social justice"; programs based "on the relationship of service to citizenship, civic responsibility, and participatory democracy"; programs at which "a center for service-learning links service to academic study"; and programs involving "community partnerships and public problem solving" (17).

4. For example, students that semester read selections from Alexis de Tocqueville, Martin Luther King, Jr., Hannah Arendt, Jane Addams, Ida B. Wells, Sojourner Truth, President Wm. J. Clinton, and Thomas Jefferson. For the complete syllabus for this course, see David Cooper and Laura Julier, *Writing in the Public Interest*, 37–47.

5. For detailed descriptions of courses—syllabi, assignments, examples of student service projects, etc.—see McGuiness; Flower, *Problem-Solving Strategies*; Wayne Peck,

Linda Flower, and Lorraine Higgins; Cooper and Julier; Watters and Ford; and Zlotkowski, *Successful Service-Learning Programs.*

6. The size and mission of Loyola, a small liberal arts Jesuit college, encourage and allow for college-wide symposia that take up themes such as economic justice or human rights over the course of an academic year and in different disciplinary and cross-disciplinary sites, thus integrating service learning into the entire curriculum as well as the writing course.

7. For an example of the ways in which this understanding of literacy is reshaping departments and programs—the institutionalization of this view of composition studies, that is—see Deborah Minter, Gere, and Deborah Keller-Cohen writing about the program at the University of Michigan, which also includes a service-learning component.

8. *Problem-Solving Strategies for Writing in College and Community* is Flower's textbook for a program or course such as Carnegie Mellon's. Chapter 14 is especially useful in thinking about reasons and ways to focus a service learning writing course. Peck, Flower, and Higgins' "Community Literacy" describes the Community Literacy Center in more detail.

9. The web site created in 1999 by the National Council of Teachers of English's Service-Learning Committee tries to maintain links to most of the useful sites on service learning and the teaching of writing, as well as to national organizations which support service learning. See http://www.ncte.org/service/.

Bibliography

Adler-Kassner, Linda. "Digging a Groundwork for Writing: Underprepared Students and Community Service Courses." *College Composition and Communication* 46.4 (Dec. 1995): 552–55.

Adler-Kassner, Linda, Robert Crooks, and Ann Watters. *Writing the Community.* Urbana, IL: AAHE/NCTE, 1997.

Anson, Chris M. "On Reflection: The Role of Logs and Journals in Service-Learning Courses." Adler-Kassner, Crooks, and Watters. 167–80.

Arca, Rosemary L. "Systems Thinking, Symbiosis, and Service: The Road to Authority for Basic Writers." Adler-Kassner, Crooks, and Watters. 133–41.

Bacon, Nora. "Community Service and Writing Instruction." *National Society for Experiential Education Quarterly,* Spring 1994:14, 27.

———. "Community Service Writing: Problems, Challenges, Questions." Adler-Kassner, Crooks, and Watters. 39–55.

Barber, Benjamin. *An Aristocracy of Everyone: The Politics of Education and the Future of America.* New York: Oxford UP, 1992.

Barber, Benjamin, and Richard M. Battistoni, eds. *Education for Democracy.* Dubuque, IA: Kendall/Hunt, 1993.

Bartholomae, David, and Peter Elbow. "Writing in Schools: A Dialogue on Academic Discourse." Conference of College Composition and Communication, Boston, 1991.

Bellah, Robert, et al. *Habits of the Heart: Individualism and Commitment in America Life.* Berkeley: U of California P, 1985.

Berlin, James. "Rhetoric and Ideology in the Writing Class." *College English* 50.5 (Sept. 1988): 477–94.

Bok, Derek. *Universities and the Future of America.* Durham, NC: Duke UP, 1990.

Boyer, Ernest L. "Creating the New American College." *Chronicle of Higher Education,* March 9, 1994: A48.

Boyte, Harry C. "Community Service and Civic Education." *Phi Delta Kappan* 72 (1991): 765+.

Coles, Robert. *The Call to Service: A Witness to Idealism.* Boston: Houghton Mifflin, 1993.

Conniff, Brian, and Betty Rogers Youngkin. "The Literacy Paradox: Service-Learning and the Traditional English Department." *Michigan Journal of Community Service Learning,* Fall 1995: 86–94.

Cooper, David D. "Reading, Writing, and Reflection." Rhoads and Howard. 47–56.

Cooper, David D., and Laura Julier. *Writing in the Public Interest: Service Learning and the Writing Classroom.* East Lansing: Michigan State, 1995.

Cushman, Ellen. "The Rhetorician as Agent of Social Change." *College Composition and Communication* 47.1 (Feb. 1996): 7–28.

de Acosta, Martha. "Journal Writing in Service-Learning: Lessons from a Mentoring Project." *Michigan Journal of Community Service Learning* (Fall 1995): 141–49.

Deans, Tom. "Writing Across the Curriculum and Community Service Learning: Correspondences, Cautions, and Futures." Adler-Kassner, Crooks, and Watters. 29–37.

Dewey, John. *Democracy and Education.* New York: Macmillan, 1916.

———. *Experience and Education.* New York: Macmillan, 1956.

Ehrlich, Thomas. Foreword. Jacoby and Associates. xi–xvi.

Elbow, Peter. "Being a Writer vs. Being an Academic: A Conflict in Goals." Conference on College Composition and Communication, Boston, 1991.

———. "Reflections on Academic Discourse: How It Relates to Freshmen and Colleagues." *College English* 53.2 (Feb. 1991): 135–55.

Etzioni, Amitai. *The Spirit of Community: Rights, Responsibilities and the Communitarian Agenda.* New York: Crown, 1993.

Faigley, Lester. "Competing Theories of Process: A Critique and a Proposal." *College English* 48.6 (Oct. 1986): 527–42.

Fishman, Stephen. "Explicating Our Tacit Tradition: John Dewey and Composition Studies." *College Composition and Communication* 44.3 (1993): 315–30.

Flower, Linda. "Partners in Inquiry: A Logic for Community Outreach." Adler-Kassner, Crooks, and Watters. 95–117.

———. *Problem-Solving Strategies for Writing in College and Community.* Fort Worth: Harcourt Brace, 1998.

Freire, Paulo, and Donald Macedo. *Literacy: Reading the Word and the World.* New York: Bergin, 1987.

Gere, Anne Ruggles, ed. *Into the Field: Sites of Composition Studies.* New York: MLA, 1993.

Giles, Dwight, and Janet Eyler. "The Theoretical Roots of Service-Learning in John Dewey." *Michigan Journal of Community Service Learning,* Fall 1994: 77–85.

Giroux, Henry A., and Peter McLaren. "Teacher Education and the Politics of Engagement: The Case for Democratic Schooling." *Harvard Educational Review* 56.3 (1986): 213–38.

Greco, Norma. "Critical Literacy and Community Service: Reading and Writing the World." *English Journal* 81.5 (1992): 83–84.

Harkevy, Ira, and Lee Benson. "De-Platonizing and Democratizing Education as the Bases of Service Learning." Rhoads and Howard. 11–20.

Heilker, Paul. "Rhetoric Made Real: Civic Discourse and Writing Beyond the Curriculum." Adler-Kassner, Crooks, and Watters. 71–7.

Herzberg, Bruce. "Community Service and Critical Teaching." *College Composition and*

Communication 45.3 (Oct. 1994): 307–19. Rpt. in Adler-Kassner, Crooks, and Watters. 57–69.

————. Response to Linda Adler-Kassner. *College Composition and Communication* 46.4 (December 1995): 555–6.

Honnet, Ellen Porter, and Susan J. Poulsen, eds. *Wingspread Special Report: Principles of Good Practice for Combining Service and Learning.* Racine, WI: The Johnson Foundation, 1989.

Howard, Jeffrey P. F. "Academic Service Learning: A Counternormative Pedagogy." Rhoads and Howard. 21–29.

Jacoby, Barbara, and Associates. *Service-Learning in Higher Education.* San Francisco: Jossey-Bass, 1996.

Jeavons, Thomas H. "Service-Learning and Liberal Learning: A Marriage of Convenience." *Michigan Journal of Community Service Learning* (Fall 1995): 134–40.

Kolb, David. *Experiential Learning: Experience as the Source of Learning and Development.* Englewood Cliffs, NJ: Prentice-Hall, 1984.

Larson, Richard L. Foreword. Stotsky. ix–xi.

Lindemann, Erika. "Three Views of English 101." *College English* 57.3 (Mar. 1995): 287–302.

Lisman, C. David. *Toward a Civil Society: Civic Literacy and Service Learning.* Westport, CT: Bergin & Garvey, 1998.

McGuiness, Ilona M. "Educating for Participation and Democracy: Service-Learning in the Writing Classroom." *The Scholarship of Teaching* 1.2 (1995): 3–12.

Minter, Deborah Williams, Anne Ruggles Gere, and Deborah Keller-Cohen. "Learning Literacies." *College English* 57.6 (Oct. 1995): 669–87.

Peck, Wayne, Linda Flower, and Lorraine Higgins. "Community Literacy." *College Composition and Communication* 46.2 (1995): 199–222.

Peterson, Jane. "Through the Looking-Glass: A Response." *College English* 57.3 (Mar. 1995): 310–18.

Rhoads, Robert A., and Jeffrey P. F. Howard, eds. *Academic Service Learning: A Pedagogy of Action and Reflection.* San Francisco: Jossey-Bass, 1998.

Saltmarsh, John. "Education for Critical Citizenship: John Dewey's Contribution to the Pedagogy of Community Service Learning," *Michigan Journal of Community Service Learning,* Fall 1996: 13–21.

Schön, Donald A. *The Reflective Practitioner.* New York: Basic Books, 1983.

Schutz, Aaron, and Anne Ruggles Gere. "Service Learning and English Studies: Rethinking 'Public' Service." *College English* 60.2 (1998): 129–49.

Stotsky, Sandra. "Teaching Academic Writing as Moral and Civic Thinking." *Connecting Civic Education and Language Education: The Contemporary Challenge.* Ed. Sandra Stotsky. New York: Teachers College P, 1991. 129–66.

Waterman, Alan S., ed. *Service-Learning: Applications from the Research.* Mahwah, NJ: Lawrence Erlbaum, 1997.

Watters, Ann, and Marjorie Ford. *A Guide for Change: Resources for Implementing Community Service Writing.* New York: McGraw-Hill, 1995.

Zlotkowski, Edward. "Does Service-Learning Have a Future?" *Michigan Journal of Community Service Learning,* Fall 1995: 123–33.

————. "A Service Learning Approach to Faculty Development." Rhoads and Howard. 81–88.

————. *Successful Service-Learning Programs: New Models of Excellence in Higher Education.* Jaffrey, NH: Anker, 1998.

The Pedagogy of Writing Across the Curriculum

S U S A N   M c L E O D

❧ ORIGINS OF WAC

Chances are good that if you are in the field of rhetoric and composition, you have heard of writing across the curriculum. As an educational reform movement, it has been around more than twenty-five years—about as long as the National Writing Project,[1] its counterpart in elementary and secondary schools. It was born in the 1970s during a time of curricular and demographic change in higher education, when college teachers found themselves with students who struggled with college writing tasks. The widespread use of the "objective" multiple-choice/true-false test in public education meant that many students had little practice with extended writing tasks by the time they got to college; at the same time, the rapid growth of higher education coupled with open admissions at some institutions brought a new population of first-generation college students to the institution. Faced with what looked like declining skills, faculty felt the need to do something, anything, about the state of student writing. The first WAC faculty seminar came about in 1969–70 at Central College in Pella, Iowa (Russell, *Writing* 283), when Barbara Walvoord's Chaucer seminar didn't make; to fill the void she organized a regular meeting of faculty to discuss issues of student writing. She went on to write the first book on teaching writing that was aimed at faculty in the disciplines, *Helping Students Write Well: A Guide for Teachers in All Disciplines*, first published in 1982. This book, now in its second edition, is still the standard reference for teachers in fields outside of English who need a guidebook to help them understand how to assign and respond to student writing. True to its title, the book is for those who want to help students learn to write well, as most faculty do.

All of us who have been involved in WAC since its beginnings have a story to tell about how we got started facilitating faculty seminars. The story usually involves faculty colleagues like Barbara's who were at their collective wits' end trying to deal with the student writing problems they were encountering.

Here's mine. One day I was cornered just outside my office by a friend who taught history, who was furious with me and with (it appeared) not only the English Department but the entire discipline of English. "Why can't you people teach these students how to write?" he thundered. I was defensive—of course I was teaching them how to write. I had stacks of papers waiting to be graded to prove it. After we had both finished harumphing and started to listen to each other, I asked to see the papers he was so distressed about. Among them was a paper from a former student of mine, one who had done reasonably well in my freshman comp class the previous semester. He was right; it was abysmal. He had asked for analysis and discussion of historical data, and she had responded with vague generalities and personal opinion. Like all progressive writing teachers at that time, I was trying to help my students find their authentic voices. But my history colleague was not interested in this student's authentic voice; he wanted her to try to think and write like a historian. My class, based as it was on literary notions of what good writing was, had not helped her figure out how to do that. Out of cross-disciplinary faculty conversations like this one, out of seminars like the one Walvoord started, the WAC movement was born.

❧ WHAT IS WAC?

Like the term *general education, writing across the curriculum* has come to have an aura that is vaguely positive, something that is good for students. Like general education programs, WAC programs are defined in part by their intended outcomes—helping students to become critical thinkers and problem-solvers as well as developing their communications skills. But unlike general education, WAC is uniquely defined by its pedagogy. Indeed, one might say that WAC has been, more than any other recent educational reform movement, one aimed at transforming pedagogy at the college level, at moving away from the lecture mode of teaching (the "delivery of information" model) to a model of active student engagement with the material and with the genres of the discipline through writing, not just in English classes but in all classes across the university. WAC draws on many pedagogical techniques used in general composition classes, but unlike those classes (for example, freshman composition) it focuses around a particular body of information. Where freshman composition might focus on teaching the general features of what we term "academic discourse," WAC focuses not on writing skills per se, but on teaching both the content of the discipline and the particular discourse features used in writing about that content.

When we speak of WAC pedagogy, we are talking about two somewhat different approaches: we may think of these under the headings of "writing to learn" and "writing to communicate."[2] The former is the pedagogy most identified with WAC programs, one that caught on quickly in the form of one of its most popular assignments, the journal. Based on the theories of language and learning articulated by James Britton and by Janet Emig in her article "Writing as a Mode of Learning," this pedagogy encourages teachers to use ungraded writing (writing to the self as audience) in order to have students think on paper, to objectify their knowledge and therefore to help them discover both what they know and what they need to learn. The latter approach, writing to communicate, is pedagogically more complex. It is based on theories of the social construction of knowledge, best summarized in Kenneth Bruffee's article "Collaborative Learning and the 'Conversation of Mankind.' " The most obvious pedagogical manifestation of this approach is the use of peer groups in the classroom and approaches to teaching that take into account analysis of the discourse of the disciplines and genre theory. The rest of this essay will be devoted to these two pedagogical approaches for classrooms—writing to learn and writing to communicate—and will in addition consider the appropriate pedagogy for one of the most important elements of a WAC program, the faculty workshop.

Before reviewing these approaches, however, I feel it necessary to warn readers away from a view of writing to learn and writing to communicate somehow in conflict with each other. There are two articles in the WAC literature that present such a view: C. A. Knoblauch and Lil Brannon's "Writing as Learning Through the Curriculum," and more recently, Daniel Mahala's "Writing Utopias: Writing Across the Curriculum and the Promise of Reform." The former article appeared in *College English* before it became a refereed journal; it presents a vision of then-existing WAC programs as being largely "grammar across the curriculum," a claim that is not backed by any proof and certainly not borne out by the results of national WAC surveys that I have now twice conducted (McLeod; Miraglia and McLeod). The authors' discussion of the textbook *Writing in the Arts and Sciences* by Elaine Maimon and her colleagues (mentioned below) is a good example of what I see as a false dichotomy, characterizing that text as an introduction to mere forms and formats and opposing it to "writing to learn." The same approach is taken by Mahala, who sets up a dichotomy between "American formalism" and "British expressivism," again misrepresenting the approach of Maimon and colleagues by quoting out of context from their work in order to argue his case. Neither of these articles is taken seriously by the WAC discourse community at large. On the contrary, most of us who have been involved in WAC programs from the beginning see "writing to learn" and "writing to communicate" as two complementary, even synergistic, approaches to writing across the curriculum.

↬ WRITING TO LEARN

Writing to learn pedagogy encourages teachers to use writing as a tool for learning as well as a test for learning, or as James Moffett would say at workshops, ✗ "writing to *know* as well as to *show*." This branch of WAC has its roots in the language across the curriculum movement in British secondary schools, sparked by James Britton and his colleagues and associated in the United States with Toby Fulwiler and his colleagues at Michigan Technological University.

In *Language and Learning*, Britton argued that language is central to learning because it is through language that we organize our representations of the world (214). His research called for the use of more "expressive" writing in the curriculum—writing that will help students explore and assimilate new ideas, create links between the unfamiliar and the familiar, mull over possibilities, explain things to the self before explaining them to others. The analog for this kind of student writing is the expert's notebook—the scientist's lab book, the engineer's notebook, the artist's and architect's sketchbook (the journals of Thomas Edison and of Leonardo da Vinci are prototypical examples). It is not polished work intended for an outside audience; sometimes it is comprehensible only to the writer.

For such writing to be useful in the classroom as a tool for learning, it must be ungraded. The teacher does respond, but as a facilitator and coach rather than as a judge. As I mentioned earlier, the most popular writing to learn assignment, one that caught on very quickly across the curriculum, is the journal. In *The Journal Book*, Toby Fulwiler has gathered together more than forty accounts from teachers across the disciplines who use journals in their classrooms. The actual assignments vary. Ann Berthoff describes the dialectical notebook—a double-entry notebook, with summaries of readings or passages copied out on one side and the student's responses (or metacomments) on the facing page (11–18). Jana Staton discusses the dialogue journal, in which elementary school students comment and the teacher responds, creating a private conversation between teacher and student about course content (47–63). French teacher Karen Wiley Sandler describes the use of the journal in the foreign language class as a place to experiment and make mistakes (as we all do when learning a language) without fear of penalty; the journal becomes a place to approximate, to play with the new language (312–20). Catherine Larson and Margaret Merrion describe the music journal, used to help students understand and describe the aesthetic experience of listening to music (254–60). Stephen BeMiller describes the mathematics notebook, in which students do their practice work—explorations of possible solutions to problems, discussions of the course challenges, questions, outlines of concepts, and self-tests of comprehension (359–66). All the descriptions have one thing in common: student use of informal, speculative, personal writing to make sense of the course material with the teacher acting as prompter and guide.

Of course, the journal is not the only assignment teachers have integrated into their pedagogical repertoire. Another way to facilitate writing as a mode of learning is the "quick write" or "focused freewrite" that has become popularized by Thomas Angelo and K. Patricia Cross in *Classroom Assessment Techniques*[3] as the "minute paper" (148–58). Where the journal is more suitable for smaller classes in which the teacher can collect and respond to student writing periodically, the minute paper has been used successfully in classes of all sizes, including large lecture classes. The technique is simple: at some point in the class, the students write for one minute answering a question that asks them to evaluate their learning in some way. For example, at the end of a lecture, students might be asked to jot down the two or three most important points of the lecture, and also what puzzled them about the material. These jottings, usually no more than half a page, give the teacher instant feedback as to the success of the lecture and show her what issues may need clarification. Angelo and Cross give this example: a history teacher might ask students two questions: "What is the single most significant reason that Italy became a center of the Renaissance?" and "What one question puzzles you about Italy's role in the Renaissance?" Because they are writing anonymously, students are free to express their genuine puzzlement, and the teacher can see immediately how to address their confusion about cause and effect in the next lecture. The minute paper is not only a mode of learning for the students, it is also for the teacher a window into their learning, a method of establishing communication between teacher and student in large classes.

There are many other ways to use writing to learn assignments. John Bean, in *Engaging Ideas: The Professor's Guide to Integrating Writing, Critical Thinking, and Active Learning in the Classroom*, devotes chapter 6 to twenty-five varieties of what he calls "exploratory writing." These include versions of the journal and the minute paper as well as creative approaches (having students write an imaginary dialogue between historical figures) and practice pieces for what will eventually be graded writing (for example, dry run essay exams). Bean also answers the common objections teachers have to using this kind of writing (it will take too much time; students will regard it as busy work; if it's not corrected it will promote bad writing habits), and provides useful suggestions for responding to the assignments and managing the paper load.

Two major characteristics of WAC write-to-learn pedagogy should be clear by now. First, such pedagogy is student centered. College faculty who focus on and are concerned about their students' learning are those who pick up WAC techniques and use them successfully; they are quick to see the value of assignments like those described above that promote active learning and critical thinking. Second, it is reflective. These exploratory writing assignments are all ones that provide a feedback loop to the teacher as to the progress of student learning, allowing her or him to adjust the teaching accordingly. It also takes the teacher out of the role of judge for awhile, allowing her to play the role of coach. As the now-famous active learning mantra goes, the teacher moves from being the sage on the stage to the guide on the side.

✧ WRITING TO COMMUNICATE — DISCIPLINARY

Writing to communicate is the other branch of WAC. It is closely related and interconnected with writing to learn, but has these important differences: it focuses on writing to an audience outside the self in order to inform that audience, and the writing therefore is revised, crafted, and polished. Writing to communicate is reader based rather than writer based, and uses the formal language of a particular discourse community to communicate information. This branch of WAC is sometimes called WID, writing in the disciplines. It is most closely identified with Elaine Maimon's WAC program at Beaver College, which started about the same time as Toby Fulwiler's program at Michigan Tech. Maimon's program, like Walvoord's and Fulwiler's, also grew out of a close collaboration of faculty colleagues, faculty talking to each other in a series of workshops about how to help students with their writing. Out of that program grew a textbook, *Writing in the Arts and Sciences*, now out of print.[4] In that text, Maimon (who invited Kenneth Bruffee, among others, to help lead the faculty workshops at her institution) articulates not only writing-to-learn principles, but also what has become known as the "social turn" in teaching writing: "Writing in every discipline is a form of social behavior in that discipline" (xii).

The notion of discourse communities is a commonplace now in the field of rhetoric and composition, but was not so obvious to composition teachers in the 1980s. In my own experience, at least, conversations with faculty in other disciplines helped me understand the nature of the differences in disciplinary discourses. Permit me another story. I was working with a group of graduate students in our American Studies program at my institution, students who shuttled back and forth between seminars in English and in history. Some of them were having mysterious difficulties with their papers for those classes; both history and English professors were circling their verbs and writing "tense" in the margins. The students were stumped. They had never had such problems as undergraduate history or English majors. I sat down with a history colleague, and together we discovered what should have been obvious. In English, we use the present tense to quote the words of authors long dead: "As Shakespeare says. . . . " For us, these authors live on in their texts; they are not of an age but for all time. But in history dates are very important, and one must mark the tense accordingly to indicate which authors are current and which are historical (e.g., dead). A historian would never write, "Gibbon says." The question was not just one of verb tense, but of epistemology.

WAC as writing to communicate, as differentiated from writing to learn, puts the teacher in a somewhat different but related pedagogical situation. The teacher is still a guide, but is focusing now on helping students learn the discourse of the discipline; the relationship is that of seasoned professional to apprentice, or in anthropological terms, of tribal elder to initiate. The person who knows best how to initiate the newcomer is not the composition teacher, but the teacher who is already grounded in the content of the field and who is fluent in the disciplinary discourse—the history teacher, the biology teacher, the math teacher.

This is not to say that we as writing teachers can't make students aware that there are different discourse communities and teach them some strategies for asking the right questions about discourse expectations in their other classes. Patricia Linton and her associates, in an excellent (and too little known) article on the role of the general composition course in WAC, describe how such a class might be set up: teaching students to observe disciplinary patterns in the way discourse is structured, helping them understand the various rhetorical moves that are accepted within particular discourse communities, explaining conventions of reference and of language. Composition teachers, the authors argue, are no strangers to teaching discourse analysis; we just need to enlarge our notions of what discourse we should be helping students analyze. Linton and her associates, this time with Madigan as the lead author,[5] demonstrate in another article how one might go about analyzing the language of psychology; in this article they suggest something far more complex than teaching students how to cite sources in APA as well as MLA style in first-year composition. Instead, they demonstrate convincingly that APA style is the embodiment of social science epistemology; the style reflects the values of the discipline. I think of a student I had recently, a theater major named Ginger, who was given to large dramatic gestures in class and double exclamation points in her prose. One day she brought in a draft of a paper she was writing in her introductory psychology class. She was researching child abuse in the United States, and had written "the statistics are horrifying." The teacher had circled the last word and written in the margin "diction." In a conference with the teacher Ginger had been told she couldn't use such a word in APA style. She came to me to vent: Why couldn't she???? What was wrong with saying that, since it was true???? After she had calmed down somewhat, we discussed some of the values of psychology, in particular the detached, objective tone. Although she wasn't happy about it, Ginger saw the point and changed "horrifying" to "cause for concern."

Having said that composition teachers can make students aware of disciplinary differences, of the fact that "good writing" (in academe as elsewhere) is a relative term, I must go on to state that such a course is only a first step toward helping students write to communicate in their own disciplines. The person who has the disciplinary knowledge base and writes the discourse as a mother tongue is the person who can best serve as mentor in this professional-apprentice relationship.[6]

The fact that academics are so grounded in their own disciplinary discourse conventions presents an immediate challenge, however, precisely because the conventions seem so natural to those fluent in them that it is difficult for them to see why students struggle as they learn them, or why writing in other disciplines has different but equally valid conventions. The psychology teacher is so used to the passive voice as a signal of objectivity in social science writing that she thinks of it as the norm, and of writing in the humanities as "flowery." I will say something in the final section about how WAC directors might approach this issue of disciplinary ethnocentrism in a WAC workshop; for now let us assume that faculty in the disciplines are aware of these differences and wish to demystify their own disciplinary discourse for students, helping them learn appropriate ways to write to those in their field as well as to audiences outside their field. How might they go about it?

There are various resources for teachers in the disciplines, many of them written by colleagues in those disciplines. I will mention just a few here. *Mathematical Writing*, edited by Donald Knuth and his associates and published by the Mathematical Association of America, is a book by and for mathematicians. It consists of lecture transcripts and handouts from a course of the same name offered at Stanford University in 1987. The course involved various star guest lecturers, and it focused on writing in computer science as well as in mathematics.[7] Robert Day's *How to Write and Publish a Scientific Paper* is a readable and lively book which at first glance seems to deal only with forms and formats, but in fact deals with the way knowledge is created in scientific fields; the chapter entitled "How to List the Authors," for example, deals with the thorny issue of who is really an "author" when a team of scientists has contributed to the findings. Perhaps the ultimate disciplinary discourse may be found in the foreign language curriculum, where the discourse to be learned is indeed an entirely different language. Claire Gaudiani's *Teaching Composition in the Foreign Language Curriculum* focuses on the issue of developing fluency in prose written in the target language, focusing on how learning to write in a foreign language differs considerably from learning to write in one's native language. Finally, there are a number of sites rapidly developing on the World Wide Web for teachers in the disciplines to consult. The most useful of these from my point of view is the WAC Clearinghouse at http://aw.colostate. edu/resource_list.htm. The site has answers to questions frequently asked about WAC and provides links to other WAC sites on the Web.

These and other resources like them for faculty in the disciplines may be thought of in light of genre theory. As Carol Berkenkotter and Thomas Huckin say in their book *Genre Knowledge in Disciplinary Communication*, "[g]enres are the media through which scholars and scientists communicate with their peers. Genres are intimately linked to a discipline's methodology, and they package information in ways that conform to a discipline's norms, values, and ideology" (1). Teaching the genres of the discourse community is therefore inseparable from teaching the disciplinary knowledge of the discipline. The pedagogy connected with such teaching is not one of forms and formats; it involves setting up various practice sessions for students to model the writing behaviors and practices they will need as members of particular discourse communities. This means doing away with the usual kinds of school assignments, writing only for the teacher as examiner, and having students try out as much as possible writing to real audiences for real professional purposes.

Teachers have known for some time that there is something wrong with the "school" writing assignment; in 1965, W. Earl Britton had this to say:

> I believe that in all too many instances, at least in college, the student writes the wrong thing, for the wrong reason, to the wrong person, who evaluates it on the wrong basis. That is, he writes about a subject he is not thoroughly informed upon, in order to exhibit his knowledge rather than explain something the reader does not understand, and he writes to a professor who already knows more than he does about the matter and who evaluates the paper, not in terms of what he has derived, but in terms of what he thinks the writer knows. In every respect, this is the converse of what happens in professional life, where the writer is the authority; he writes to transmit new or unfamiliar knowledge to someone who does not know but needs to, and who evaluates the paper in terms of what he derives and understands. (116)

The pedagogy of WAC as writing to communicate invites teachers to think about how they might place students in rhetorical situations that approximate those they will encounter as professionals in their fields and learn to use the appropriate genres and discourse conventions. For example, the College of Engineering at my institution has a capstone course in which students form teams that become consulting firms; they must go out into the community, find a client, and work up a project for that client, who then has a say in their final grade for the class. Business schools pioneered the use of the case method for situated learning, giving students a narrative describing a realistic scenario in which they might find themselves in their work and asking them to provide possible solutions to the problem described; this method has been used successfully by teachers in other disciplines to create writing assignments like the ones students will encounter in their professions.[8] Teachers in fields that are not charged with preparing students for such specific professions (for example, the liberal arts) are nevertheless able to create writing assignments that have audiences other than the teacher as examiner and have some purpose other than testing student knowledge and comprehension.

Genre theory also brings with it the promise of a pedagogical approach aimed at helping linguistically marginalized groups in academe—those whose home language is not standard English. Using a functional linguistics approach developed by M. A. K. Halliday at the University of Sydney (and promulgated by Gunther Kress in the United Kingdom), researchers in Australia have developed an "explicit pedagogy for inclusion and access" (Cope and Kalantzis 63), one that focuses explicitly on the teaching of genre as a way of teaching academic literacy. According to Bill Cope and Mary Kalantzis, this approach has been very successful with aboriginal children in Australia. Such a pedagogy is not without its critics, however; Berkenkotter and Huckin provide a useful examination of the issues in chapter 8 of *Genre Knowledge in Disciplinary Communication* (a chapter they title "Suffer the Little Children"). Their most telling critique is this: "It may be that a genre approach to the teaching of writing does not fit many language arts and composition teachers' conception of their role, given their training, ideological loyalties, and professional allegiances. If this is the case, rethinking the training of language arts and composition teachers as well as the current curricula in language arts and university writing courses may be what is called for" (163). Russell's article "Rethinking Genre in School and Society: An Activity Theory Analysis" also provides a useful overview of the issues involved in explicit teaching of genres.

Writing in the disciplines involves more than just learning genres and discourse conventions, however. It also involves learning the processes by which experts in the field develop and disseminate knowledge. Russell, in a 1993 article, argues the matter thus: "[Since writing is] a matter of learning to participate in some historically situated human activity that requires some kind(s) of writing, it cannot be learned apart from the problems, the habits, the activities—the subject matter—of some group that found the need to write in that way to solve a problem or carry on its activities" ("Vygotsky" 194).

What are some of the "habits and activities" Russell refers to that might be translated into pedagogical practice? One obvious answer is collaborative learning techniques, which are based on assumptions about the social nature of learning as well as of the collaborative construction of disciplinary knowledge. Donald Finkel and G. Stephen Monk's "Teachers and Learning Groups: Dissolution of the Atlas Complex" was an early resource for teachers in the disciplines. This piece encourages teachers to view their classrooms as social systems, and offers suggestions about how to get out of the two-person model of interaction (teacher-student) and encourage interaction among students that models the mode of debate and intellectual exchange among colleagues in the discipline. Finkel and Monk do not advocate exclusive use of group work, but differentiate among teaching functions (lecture, Socratic questioning, guided group work) and encourage teachers to think about which particular function suits each part of the course. Once teachers in the disciplines begin to see the teacher/student relationship as one of professional/apprentice, and once they also begin to view their classrooms as social systems that model the methods and the discourse of their particular discipline, it is not a large step for them to see that it makes sense for apprentices to follow the same process that the experts do when writing papers. If the experts draft papers and revise according to readers' and editors' comments, students should become familiar with this process. One of the most interesting quiet revolutions that has taken place on college campuses as a result of successful WAC programs is the use by many teachers in the disciplines of what we have come to think of as the "process approach" in teaching writing—not only allowing revision of student work, but requiring it, often using peer groups in the classroom to respond to drafts.

The increased use of peers for responding to student writing is most obvious in that now-familiar unit on campus, the writing center. It is not coincidental that WAC and writing centers have grown up together during the past twenty-five years, since they are natural partners and in many institutions mutually dependent on one another. One early (1984) article by Bruffee, "Peer Tutoring and the 'Conversation of Mankind,'" ties the theory of peer tutoring to the notion of the disciplinary conversation, showing how tutoring from a knowledgeable peer can help model the "habits and activities" (to use Russell's term again) of the knowledge-constructing processes in the disciplines. Ray Wallace's "The Writing Center's Role in the Writing Across the Curriculum Program: Theory and Practice" discusses not only theory but also gives some practical guidelines for tying the writing center firmly to a WAC program—including a helpful outline of a WAC tutor-training course.

⇿ SHOWING, NOT TELLING, AT A WRITING WORKSHOP

I have borrowed the heading for the final section of this essay from Toby Fulwiler's early article on how a WAC faculty workshop should be run because it summarizes the main point to be made about all such workshops: they must model the pedagogy they are promulgating. Faculty don't like being told what to do in their own classrooms, and rightly so—not every technique is workable in every class. Faculty need to try out various techniques and decide for themselves how to adapt them to their own teaching and achieve their own pedagogical ends. Would-be facilitators of WAC faculty workshops should think carefully about how to use the pedagogical techniques they are suggesting in order to demonstrate their power. There are two rules of thumb: faculty should themselves write, and faculty should have opportunities to talk to each other about writing. Both writing-to-learn and writing-to-communicate pedagogies should be integral parts of every WAC faculty workshop. I said at the beginning that WAC programs grew out of cross-disciplinary faculty conversations, and that faculty workshops are at the heart of any WAC program. The reason for this is rather simple: faculty tend to teach as they were taught. The lecture mode is still one of the most common modes of instruction at research institutions, where faculty get their degrees. The faculty workshop is a place for faculty to learn other modes of instruction by experiencing these modes themselves and understanding from the inside out, as it were, how something other than a lecture-quiz approach to learning might work.

If you wish to set up and facilitate a faculty workshop, there are two sorts of resources available to you: those of the "how to" variety, which are of most use to the workshop facilitator, and those that can be used in the workshop as texts or resources for the workshop faculty. Fulwiler's article, mentioned earlier, is of the first sort, explaining how various types of workshops may be set up and managed. Anne Herrington's "Writing to Learn: Writing Across the Disciplines" also lays out some of the issues one needs to think about in planning a faculty workshop. For example, workshops often ask faculty to write out their course objectives and expected learning outcomes for one of their classes to bring to the workshop, so that they can design writing assignments connected to those course objectives. Often college faculty, most of whom have had no formal pedagogical training, find this small exercise one of the most useful parts of the workshop, since they have thought about course objectives and expected outcomes only tacitly. Joyce Magnotto and Barbara Stout have written the most direct and comprehensive piece on how to run a faculty workshop; it is full of advice on all aspects of such an event, and includes a sample syllabus. Some books that can be very helpful to the would-be WAC workshop leader are now available from commercial presses. The most useful of these is *The Harcourt Brace Guide to Writing Across the Curriculum* by Christopher Thaiss. Thaiss deals not only with conducting a workshop but also with how to launch a WAC program, WAC options for the curriculum, assessment, and research. It is the most compact, comprehensive book on WAC to date; this is not surprising, given the fact that Thaiss is the head of the Board of Consultants of the National Network of Writing Across the Curriculum Programs. The Board meets once a year as a Special Interest Group at the Conference on College Composition and Communication and consists of seasoned WAC directors who can be brought to campus as consultants.[9] If you are asked to start a WAC program on your campus, the outside consultant is a time-honored way of getting faculty involved. I should also mention here the book that I co-edited with Margot Soven, *Writing Across the Curriculum: A Guide to Developing Programs*; this book, with chapters from some of the members of the Board of Consultants of the National Network of WAC programs, gives advice on starting and sustaining WAC programs and is intended for administrators as well as faculty.

There are several books that may be used as texts for a workshop and resources for teachers in the disciplines, books that have been written by experienced workshop facilitators and based in large part on their own versions of the WAC workshop. The earliest of these, *Improving Student Writing: A Guidebook for Faculty in All Disciplines* by Andrew Moss and Carol Holder, is short, affordable, and full of practical tips for teachers; its virtue is that parts of it (for example, the chapter on designing writing assignments) may be used as a basis for a segment of a seminar, but it is also a useful reference book for teachers after the seminar. True to its title, it really is a guidebook. More recently, Margot Soven has published a similar short guide, *Write to Learn: A Guide to Writing Across the Curriculum*. Soven's book provides instructions and models for academic assignments that are sequenced from journal writing to more formal academic assignments. (Bean's useful book, mentioned earlier, is a good resource for a faculty seminar, but probably too expensive to order copies for all participants.) Fulwiler's *Teaching with Writing* grew out of the many workshops Fulwiler has facilitated and may be used either as a text for a workshop or as a sort of workbook to be used by an individual teacher interested in learning more about using writing as a pedagogical tool.

As I said above, WAC workshop pedagogy should model both write-to-learn and write-to-communicate pedagogies. Let me give just two examples. I always begin a WAC faculty workshop with an exercise I saw modeled long ago at a WAC conference. First, I ask participants to write for a few minutes about the student writing problems they encounter; there is no lack of interest in this topic, and participants write busily. We then discuss what they have written and try to come to a consensus about the most important writing problems (the discussion invariably focuses on conceptual problems as being more important than the grammatical issues). I then give them a truly dreadful student paper and ask them to mark it as if it were a paper for one of their classes; then I ask them to tally up the sorts of marks they have made. Even though we have just discussed the fact that conceptual issues are more important than grammatical ones, they find that most of their marks are for spelling and punctuation errors. I then ask them to write for a few moments about how they might establish a hierarchy of problems to respond to in student writing, and we discuss possible grading rubrics. Finally, I ask them to step back and think about the way we used writing in this particular segment of the workshop—to begin the discussion, to think through the issue of responding to student papers, and we talk about possible applications to their own classes. We discuss writing to learn only after they have used it as a technique for their own thinking and learning.

To get at the issue of disciplinary discourse and get participants out of their disciplinary ethnocentrism a bit, I hand out a one-page student paper and ask

faculty to grade it, using whatever criteria they wish—but they have to articulate their criteria for the rest of us. Invariably, teachers from the humanities
grade it low, saying "lack of development" is the problem. Teachers from the
sciences and from business grade it high, saying it is "concise." This always
leads into a lively discussion of discourse values and of articulating those values for students. One of the more interesting discussions I have heard among
faculty on this issue had to do with the use of headings: the engineering faculty member said he graded a paper down if it didn't have headings, since
these were important signposts for the reader of technical material. Technical
reports are not read front to back, but readers skip around to find the most important and relevant information. The history teacher said he graded papers
down if they *did* have headings; history involves writing a careful, analytical
narrative. Clearly, a student who relied on headings for this narrative hadn't
yet learned how to use transitions gracefully. Hearing discussions like these
helps teachers understand why students can be confused about disciplinary
discourse conventions.

✣ FINAL THOUGHTS: THE FUTURE OF WAC

A recent thread on the Writing Program Administration listserv was titled "Is
WAC dead?" A lively discussion ensued in cyberspace, with those of us who
have been involved in WAC most of our professional lives saying "Of course
not!" and pointing to the record attendance at the last (1997) national WAC
conference.[10] But on reflection, I can see why the question was asked. In the
early days of WAC, funding was readily available for programs; outside funding for WAC programs is now rare. Book publishers are no longer slapping a
WAC subtitle on their more popular composition textbooks, hoping to push
their sales higher. WAC is no longer the new initiative that deans want to claim
on their CVs as they climb up the administrative ladder toward a position as
provost.

But the interesting thing about the WAC reform movement is that over the
decades it has been able to tie into and become part of whatever new initiative
was thrust upon higher education. For example, the 1980s may be thought of
as the decade of assessment and accountability in higher education. Institutions of higher learning were being pressured by legislators and by the tax-
paying public to show that they were really doing what they claimed to do.
Many of us involved in WAC programs had already developed extensive assessment tools to examine student writing; WAC and the assessment movement became allies in many universities. At my own institution, for example,
we were called upon to present baseline data for freshmen writing skills, mid-
point data, and end-of-program assessment data. Because our WAC program
already involved a placement test for freshmen and a rising junior writing portfolio, we were able not only to provide the data but to track students longitu-
dinally and show improvement in their writing between entry and mid-point
assessment. I mentioned the book by Angelo and Cross earlier; that book is a

good example of WAC techniques that are cast as assessment techniques—not necessarily in the sense of testing student knowledge but of assessing where students are, how well the instruction as well as the learning is progressing.

If the decade of the 1980s was one of assessment, that of the 1990s has been the decade of technology. Legislators and administrators alike are backing technology initiatives not only in the classroom but beyond; many institutions (my own included) are investing heavily in distance learning technologies, creating virtual classrooms and interacting with students on-line as well as (or often instead of) in person. WAC is part of this movement, although that fact may not be apparent. The most interesting recent WAC book doesn't even have the word "writing" in the title: it is called *Electronic Communication Across the Curriculum* (Reiss, Selfe, and Young). WAC has become ECAC.

What is the future of WAC? I am confident that it will continue as it has for the last twenty-five years, as an educational movement aimed at transforming college pedagogy and encouraging active learning as students understand and become part of the construction of knowledge in the disciplines. In the next twenty-five years, the term *writing across the curriculum* itself may disappear. Who cares? As long as there are teachers focusing on writing to learn and writing to communicate in the disciplines, WAC will continue to be part of the landscape of higher education.

Notes

1. The educational reform movement now known as the National Writing Project began in 1974 as the Bay Area Writing Project; by 1976 it was a model for statewide staff development, and by 1979 it had become the National Writing Project. See Russell, *Writing* 280–82.

2. James Britton and his associates called these "expressive" and "transactional" in his influential book *The Development of Writing Abilities* (11–18).

3. Although their book does not have WAC in its title, Angelo and Cross describe many pedagogical techniques and assignments that are drawn from WAC pedagogy.

4. The book is available in some university libraries. Maimon is coauthoring a new text (with Janice Peritz), *College Research and Writing: A Guide and Handbook for Students*, that she says will be a second-generation *Writing in the Arts and Sciences*. It will be available in 2000 or 2001.

5. Madigan is the psychologist of this interdisciplinary team; putting his name first is an example of the very style the authors are discussing, in which the lead author is put first to ensure that he or she will get the citation.

6. Here I would be remiss if I did not mention my own mentors as I attempted to enter the discourse community of writing across the curriculum. When I set up my first WAC workshop, Carol Holder of California Polytechnic University, Pomona, was extremely generous with her time and materials, even coming down to run one session for me. Later, an administrator sent me to one of the meetings on WAC held at the University of Chicago to meet Elaine Maimon, who was a speaker at the meeting. In spite of her busy schedule, she met with me and gave me invaluable advice. Both Carol and Elaine urged me to call Toby Fulwiler, who likewise helped gener-

ously, coming out to my present institution when I started a WAC program here. I continue to be grateful to these three early leaders in WAC for their help and encouragement as I was learning my way in the field.

7. Videotapes of the class sessions are in the Mathematical and Computer Sciences Library at Stanford.

8. For further information about the case method, see Hutchings, *Using Cases to Improve College Teaching.*

9. Thaiss may be contacted at the Department of English, George Mason University. Those interested in being involved in on-line conversations about WAC might want to join the WAC listserv. To subscribe, send a message to listserv@postoffice.cso. uiuc.edu. In the body of the message type: subscribe WAC-L ⟨your name⟩.

10. The WPA list is archived on the Web at http://gcinfo.gc.maricopa.edu/~wpa/ The national WAC conferences (held every two years) are organized through Cornell University. For information about the next conference, contact Jonathan Monroe (jbm3@cornell.edu) or Katherine Gottschalk (kkg1@cornell.edu).

Bibliography

Angelo, Thomas A., and K. Patricia Cross. *Classroom Assessment Techniques: A Handbook for College Teachers.* 2nd ed. San Francisco: Jossey-Bass, 1993.

Bean, John. *Engaging Ideas: The Professor's Guide to Integrating Writing, Critical Thinking, and Active Learning in the Classroom.* San Francisco: Jossey-Bass, 1996.

Berkenkotter, Carol, and Thomas N. Huckin. *Genre Knowledge in Disciplinary Communication: Cognition/Culture/Power.* Hillsdale, NJ: Erlbaum, 1995.

Britton, James. *Language and Learning.* London: Penguin, 1970.

Britton, James, et al. *The Development of Writing Abilities (11–18).* London: Macmillan, 1975.

Britton, W. Earl. "What Is Technical Writing?" *College Composition and Communication* 16 (1965): 113–16.

Bruffee, Kenneth A. "Collaborative Learning and the 'Conversation of Mankind.'" *College English* 46 (1984): 635–52.

——. "Peer Tutoring and the 'Conversation of Mankind.'" *Writing Centers: Theory and Administration.* Ed. Gary Olson. Urbana, IL: NCTE, 1984. 3–15.

Cope, Bill, and Mary Kalantzis. "The Power of Literacy and the Literacy of Power." *The Powers of Literacy: A Genre Approach to Teaching Writing.* Ed. Bill Cope and Mary Kalantzis. Pittsburgh: U of Pittsburgh P, 1993. 63–89.

Day, Robert. *How to Write and Publish a Scientific Paper.* Phoenix: Oryx, 1994.

Emig, Janet. "Writing as a Mode of Learning." *College Composition and Communication* 28 (1977): 122–28.

Finkel, Donald L., and G. Stephen Monk. "Teachers and Learning Groups: Dissolution of the Atlas Complex." *Learning in Groups.* Ed. Clark Bouton and Russell Y. Garth. New Directions for Teaching and Learning 14. San Francisco: Jossey-Bass, 1983. 83–97.

Fulwiler, Toby. *The Journal Book.* Portsmouth, NH: Boynton/Cook-Heinemann, 1987.

——. "Showing, Not Telling, at a Writing Workshop." *College English* 43 (1981): 55–63.

——. *Teaching with Writing.* Upper Montclair, NJ: Boynton/Cook, 1987.

Gaudiani, Claire. *Teaching Composition in the Foreign Language Curriculum.* Washington, DC: Center for Applied Linguistics, 1981.

Herrington, Anne J. "Writing to Learn: Writing Across the Disciplines." *College English* 43 (1984): 379–87.

Hutchings, Pat. *Using Cases to Improve College Teaching: A Guide to More Reflective Practice.* Washington, DC: American Association of Higher Education, 1993.

Knoblauch, C.A., and Lil Brannon. "Writing as Learning Through the Curriculum." *College English* 45 (1983): 465–74.

Knuth, Donald E., Tracy Larrabee, and Paul M. Roberts. *Mathematical Writing.* MAA Notes 14. Mathematical Association of America, 1989.

Linton, Patricia, Robert Madigan, and Susan Johnson. "Introducing Students to Disciplinary Genres: The Role of the General Composition Course." *Language and Learning Across the Disciplines* 1 (1994): 63–78.

Madigan, Robert, Susan Johnson, and Patricia Linton. "The Language of Psychology: APA Style as Epistemology." *American Psychologist* 50 (1995): 428–36.

Magnotto, Joyce Neff, and Barbara R. Stout. "Faculty Workshops." *Writing Across the Curriculum: A Guide to Developing Programs.* Ed. Susan H. McLeod and Margot Soven. Newbury Park, CA: Sage, 1992.

Mahala, Daniel. "Writing Utopias: Writing Across the Curriculum and the Promise of Reform." *College English* 53 (1991): 773–89.

Maimon, Elaine, et al. *Writing in the Arts and Sciences.* Cambridge, MA: Winthrop, 1981.

McLeod, Susan H. "Writing Across the Curriculum: The Second Stage, and Beyond." *College Composition and Communication* 40 (1989): 337–43. Rpt. in *Landmarks in Writing Across the Curriculum.* Ed. David R. Russell and Charles Bazerman. Davis, CA: Hermagoras, 1994. 79–86.

McLeod, Susan H., and Margot Soven, eds. *Writing Across the Curriculum: A Guide to Developing Programs.* Newbury Park, CA: Sage, 1992.

Miraglia, Eric, and Susan H. McLeod. "Whither WAC?: Interpreting the Stories/Histories of Mature WAC Programs." *WPA: Writing Program Administration* (1997): 46–65.

Moss, Andrew, and Carol Holder. *Improving Student Writing: A Guidebook for Faculty in All Disciplines.* Dubuque, IA: Kendall Hunt, 1988.

Reiss, Donna, Dickie Selfe, and Art Young, eds. *Electronic Communication Across the Curriculum.* Urbana, IL: NCTE, 1998.

Russell, David R. "Rethinking Genre in School and Society: An Activity Theory Analysis." *Written Communication* 14 (1997): 504–54.

———. "Vygotsky, Dewey, and Externalism: Beyond the Student/Discipline Dichotomy." *Journal of Advanced Composition* 13 (1993): 173–97.

———. *Writing in the Academic Disciplines, 1870–1990.* Carbondale: Southern Illinois UP, 1991.

Soven, Margot K. *Write to Learn: A Guide to Writing Across the Curriculum.* Cincinnati: South-Western, 1996.

Thaiss, Christopher. *The Harcourt Brace Guide to Writing Across the Curriculum.* Fort Worth: Harcourt, 1998.

Wallace, Ray. "The Writing Center's Role in the Writing Across the Curriculum Program: Theory and Practice." *The Writing Center Journal* 8.2 (1988): 43–48. Rpt. in *Landmark Essays on Writing Centers.* Ed. Christina Murphy and Joe Law. Davis, CA: Hermagoras, 1995. 191–5.

Walvoord, Barbara Fassler. *Helping Students Write Well: A Guide for Teachers in All Disciplines.* New York: MLA, 1982. 2nd ed. 1986.

Writing Center Pedagogy[1]

ERIC H. HOBSON

Since the early 1970s the growth rate of writing centers on primary, middle, secondary, postsecondary, and graduate campuses has been remarkable. Wallace and Simpson state in *The Writing Center: New Directions* (1991) that "nearly 90% of the institutions of higher education in the United States have developed writing centers or learning centers where writing is taught" (ix). Although that projection was probably optimistic in 1991, a decade later the writing center community's continued growth justifies those numbers. Membership in the National Writing Centers Association (NWCA) is at a record level, as is participation in NWCA affiliate organizations and conferences. In addition, demand for NWCA Press publications is strong (particularly the *Writing Center Resource Manual*, edited by Bobbie Silk) and the conversation on the e-mail discussion group Wcenter ⟨wcenter@ttacs6.ttu.edu⟩ is lively.[2] These indicators suggest that writing centers have become fixtures in North American education and, to a lesser extent, education worldwide.[3]

Their pervasiveness underscores the important role that writing centers play in instructing and supporting writers across the educational spectrum. The opportunities for continued instruction that one-on-one and small group tutorials offer writers at all skill levels are important to students' educational and rhetorical development. Writing centers, like the writing across the curriculum (WAC) and writing in the disciplines (WID) programs with which they frequently collaborate, offer writers an environment and activity that can differ significantly from that found in many writing classes.

The differences between current writing pedagogy as found in composition, WAC, and WID classes and that practiced in the writing center are not as great as they once were. The writing center literature documents many instances of writing centers during the "process revolution" of the late 1970s and early 1980s that were limited by direct mandate or other institutional and programmatic pressures to an exclusively drill-and-workbook remediative practice; ironically, many of these same writing centers often served process-based writing courses. The relationship was not pedagogically pretty: writing courses dealt with *writing* (e.g., invention, drafting, revision, development of authors' voices, etc.) while writing center staff were allocated the demanding and ethically questionable task of "cleaning up" writers' editing skills, of eradicating minority dialects and "nonstandard" grammars, and of "dealing with" non-native writers. Despite such restrictions, writing centers typically worked with writers to develop all parts of their writing process, albeit often covertly. By the mid-1980s, however, writing centers had moved their longstanding process-based brand of one-to-one writing instruction to the forefront of their public persona, billing themselves as legitimate sites of writing instruction serving all areas of the curriculum. This process of focusing attention on the full range of writing center educational activity is most deftly recounted and critiqued by Peter Carino in "Early Writing Centers: Toward a History." As he shows, over the past decade or so, differences in pedagogy between most writing courses and the writing center have become largely differences of focus and degree.

In "The Idea of a Writing Center"—the most frequently cited article in the writing center community's literature—Stephen North explains what writing center personnel strive to achieve in writing center tutorials and why this activity is academically legitimate. "[I]n a writing center," he writes, "the object is to make sure that writers, and not necessarily their texts, are what get changed by instruction. In axiom form it goes like this: Our job is to produce better writers, not better writing" (438). Writing center tutors are educated, interested readers/writers who play the role of an engaged and supportive, yet simultaneously critical audience for texts in development. They provide tailored, one-to-one guidance to authors learning how to change their writing process with regard to specific rhetorical and/or mechanical issues.[4] Without the onus of having to grade writers' efforts in specific texts, writing center practitioners have long argued that the writing center tutorial is a unique pedagogical space.

✷ THE LOOK OF A WRITING CENTER TUTORIAL

Discussing writing center tutorials in specific, yet inclusive, terms is made easier by establishing a frame of common reference. Doing so, however, is not simple. Writing centers are highly idiosyncratic spaces; their physical location and organization, their institutional location and allegiances, their consulting routines, staffing choices, and even administrative makeup are all determined as much by local contexts as by any disciplinary norm. This eclectic diversity is the thesis that links the thirteen chapters in Joyce A. Kinkead and Jeannette Harris' edited collection, *Writing Centers in Context: Twelve Case Studies* (1993). Each chapter in this important resource provides an extensive description of the writing center profiled, revealing each program's unique contours while attesting to common parentage. In "A Multiservice Writing Lab in a Multiversity: The Purdue University Writing Lab," Muriel Harris describes a busy day in the writing center that most experienced writing center staff and administrators would call typical:

If there were a magic device to freeze frame a moment during one of the busier times of the day, we would see the following. Near the entrance are several students leaning over the sign-in table, filling out record forms in preparation to see a tutor. At the reception desk is a small knot of people: one asking for a handout, another wondering if she could see a tutor soon, another [wanting] to use one of the computers, and yet another student who is twenty minutes late for his appointment and wonders if his tutor is waiting for him. . . . Meanwhile, sitting on the couches are a few students, waiting to see tutors. One, a freshman composition student, looks around anxiously. He hasn't been here before and isn't sure what to expect. A senior, anxious to finish her resume, is adding some handwritten corrections to the draft of the application letter she wants to review with a writing consultant.

In addition, two ESL students, each waiting for a different tutor, are sitting on another sofa, talking quietly in their native language. An education major, about to make another attempt at passing the writing proficiency exam in the office next door, is tapping her pencil angrily on a history text she reads while waiting for her tutor. . . . At one of the tutoring tables, an older student sits with a tutor, sheaves of paper spread around the table. . . . At another table is a student in freshman composition, explaining his assignment to the tutor so that they can begin some planning. Another tutor on the far side of the room is winding up her tutorial with a student she has been working with for several weeks. (Comfortable with each other, they have figured out what needs to be done before the next tutorial and are spending a moment rehashing the disastrous campus football game played last weekend.) At the telephone is a lab instructor who has agreed to interrupt a tutorial to answer a grammar hotline call . . . and who is thumbing furiously through dictionaries in the reference bookcase near the telephone to see if, as the caller has asked, there really is a word such as *bodacious*.

While all this is going on up front, in the back room several peer tutors are chatting at the reception desk, waiting for students from the developmental course to come in. Sitting with them is one of the students in the peer-tutor training course. He has been listening to tutoring "war stories" and wants to hear more, hoping to become experienced simply by soaking in all these tales. (7–8)

Although Harris' description creates an image of frenetic activity, it is representative. Irene Clark states in "The Writing Center at the University of Southern California: Couches, Carrels, Computers, and Conversation" that capturing the rhythm of a typical day in the writing center at the University of Southern California is hard because "so many activities occur simultaneously, a bit like a three-ring circus" (106).

Julie Neff's chapter provides a more specific description of writing center pedagogy in action. Focusing on what could easily be the tutorial involving the anxious first-year student mentioned in the previous excerpt, Neff invites the reader to peer into a tutor-client interaction that, although choreographed to meet the immediate situation, is typical enough to serve as a model writing center tutorial:

> Maria picks up an empty pop can and throws it into the recycling bin under a table, files the comment sheets left from the day before, and checks the appointment book for her first appointment of the day. Andrew, a timid freshman, approaches the desk, "Is this the Center for Writing Across the Curriculum?" he asks.
>
> "Yes it is," Maria says with a smile. "Come on in and have a seat." Maria pulls a white 8½" × 11" conference form from the drawer and records the student's name, date, major, and address, all the time chatting with the student to put him at ease. As she finishes, she looks up, smoothly making the transition to the conference, "What brings you to the center this morning?"
>
> The student pulls out a handwritten draft of a Humanities 102 paper, apologizing for it being "so messy." Maria smiles and says, "Don't give it a thought. We don't care if it's messy; after all, it's still a draft." . . .
>
> Maria finishes reading the student paper, makes several positive comments about the topic and the examples the student has chosen, and then moves on to respond to the paper's focus or lack of it. . . .
>
> With a "thank you" and "I'll be back," the humanities student loads his backpack and leaves for class. Maria writes a one-paragraph evaluation of the appointment, which includes the kind of paper, its strengths and weaknesses, what suggestions she made to the student, and what the student intended to do with the paper after the conference; she then pulls the file on her next appointment—a freshman she has worked with before. (131–32)

While the circumstances surrounding each writing center tutorial differ, their texture is usually consistent. The session starts with tutor and client establishing session goals appropriate to the project's current state of development. Thomas Reigstad and Donald McAndrew's writing conference planning strategy of sorting and prioritizing the many valid goals that writer and tutor bring to the tutorial into "higher-order" global issues, and "lower-order" surface issues is widely endorsed. Following this planning stage, tutors often use such active listening techniques as reflective listening and guided response to help the writer (1) assess the project's current status and (2) plan and begin further action—research, drafting, revision, and so on—to strengthen the project to meet the writer's goals. Finally, tutors summarize the session (often copied on a coordinating conference summary form) to see if both participants agree as to the ends reached and encourage the writer to use the center in the future.

❖ FOUNDATIONS OF WRITING CENTER PEDAGOGY

The variety of programs and practices operating under the rubric of "writing center" is one aspect of the writing center community that catches newcomers to composition studies off guard. No two writing centers are alike; each program has a distinct personality; each center is defined as much by its local context as by any overarching definition of "writing center." Thomas Nash states matter of factly that "we espouse many theories and owe devotion to many creeds" (32), and this variety has been a longstanding hallmark of the writing center community. North summarizes the situation in 1984 thus: "if there is one thing the ten or so years of often helter-skelter growth of the writing center movement have *not* done, it is to create uniformity" ("Writing Center Research" 27). Quite possibly, given the differences witnessed across the writing center community, it is a sense of community itself that binds writing centers more persuasively than names, philosophy, or methods. To think about writing center pedagogy as a monolith ignores the cultural situatedness of particular centers, the extent to which each center is defined by local context (institutional, philosophical, educational, physical, communal).

To those trying to make sense of a newly encountered area of teaching activity—be it the writing center, WAC programs, computer-assisted instruction—across-the-board consistency is comforting, providing a stable frame of reference. Vast variety can suggest chaos and a make-it-up-as-you-go attitude. While such an assumption might hold true elsewhere, applied to the complex calculus of writing center practice that assumption does not hold. As Angela Petit argues, building on the work of Carino ("What Do We Talk About"), Ede, Hemmeter, and Hobson ("Maintaining Our Balance," "Writing Center Practice"), "situating writing centers within . . . separable categories brings with it the danger that we will perceive centers, as . . . 'purified spaces' " (111). Instead, any comprehensive audit of writing centers' educational foundations reveals enough underlying theoretical and methodological unity to provide a desired community adhesive. With care, unifying principles can be parsed out of the writing center community's theoretical and methodological commitment to individualized instruction and collaborative learning.

✤ INDIVIDUALIZED INSTRUCTION

Writing centers are often billed as sites within largely impersonal educational structures where students can receive individual attention, instruction that reacts to each student's particular needs as a developing writer. In "Talking to the Boss: A Preface," Diana George echoes a dominant sentiment held by writing-center-based educators:

> Writing centers work with individuals. They provide the one place on campus where instruction is flexible and non-evaluative. . . . [T]he writing center can do things that the classroom simply cannot: One-to-one instruction can be varied with the learning style of the student. Some students are more visual, some are more verbal, some more introspective or more extroverted. Some need encouragement; others need to be left alone. (3–4)

Such a system is useful, even necessary. In the modern university, for example, the large number of students makes across-the-board individual instruction impractical (and certainly not cost effective). And yet, students benefit from one-to-one tutoring. Individualized instruction makes possible a somewhat more equitable system of higher education for students who have not had the benefit of the best secondary educations. As such critics of education as Henry Giroux, James Berlin, and Ira Shor (among others) have noted, funding inequities, class discrimination, racial discrimination, and countless other factors restrict many students from access to positions of power within the dominant culture. Writing centers play a role in realizing the democratic ideal of equal access to education for all students by providing support that helps many students stay in school in the face of the many obstacles placed before them.

This commitment to working with individuals is reflected in the official descriptions of the foundations on which writing centers should be built. The most strongly asserted point in Jeanne Simpson's NWCA-endorsed "What Lies Ahead for Writing Centers: Position Statement on Professional Concerns of Writing Center Directors" states, "Regardless of its organization and design, a writing center should be based on the idea of individualized instruction" (38). Individualized instruction as the community's *modus operandi* is echoed by North:

> [A]ll writing centers—or places that can be designated writing centers—rest on this single theoretical assumption: that the ideal situation for teaching and learning writing is the tutorial, the one-to-one, face-to-face interaction between a writer and a trained, experienced tutor; and that the object of this interaction is to intervene in and ultimately alter the composing process of the writer. ("Writing Center Research" 28)

Set against the dominant large-group-based backdrop of American education, the writing center's individualized instruction is a nontraditional, atypical learning situation. As Muriel Harris notes, "what writing centers are about is the antithesis of generic, mass instruction." She drives her point home by adding, "We are committed to individualized instruction, to taking the student out of the group and to looking at her as an individual, as a person in all her uniqueness" ("What's Up" 19).

⋄ COLLABORATIVE LEARNING

While individualized instruction provides writing centers a pragmatic base, collaborative learning gives the writing center community a more idealized base as well. Although many writers have argued eloquently about the collaborative nature of writing center tutorials, Kenneth Bruffee's work is considered seminal. Particularly in "Peer Tutoring and the 'Conversation of Mankind,'" Bruffee synthesized the work of such thinkers as Michael Oakeshott, Thomas Kuhn, Richard Rorty, and Lev Vygotsky to argue that the "conversation" that occurs in the writing center tutorial is analogous to the cultural conversation and negotiation from which knowledge emerges.[5] Working from this constructivist premise, Muriel Harris argues in "Talking in the Middle: Why Writers Need Writing Tutors" that writing center tutorials are best seen not as extensions of classroom instruction, but as distinct sites of knowledge making.

As presented most often in the writing center community's literature and discussions, collaborative learning is an educational philosophy that builds on people's tendency to learn from each other when they desire to grasp difficult concepts or to overcome common obstacles. Such activity has always been part of student cultures (e.g., rap sessions and study groups). Collaborative learning

> formalizes and builds upon the unofficial study group, the self-help circles that students have always formed. . . . Tutors and tutees work collaboratively to arrive at a shared language. Collaborative learning is the process of reaching consensus on the language needed to solve problems, to deal with the task at hand. . . . Peers not only learn together. Just as important, the language they generate helps them to know that they are learning—a critical step in turning information into knowledge. (Trimbur, "Benefits of Collaborative Learning" 2)

Collaborative learning provides writing centers with an educational philosophy that dovetails with the "liberal concept of developing students' potentials and facilitating their intellectual growth" that writing centers embody (Murphy, "Writing Centers in Context" 277). By encouraging collaboration between tutors and clients, writing centers help students succeed within a context that often works actively against them (Harris, "What's Up" 16).

Peer tutoring is the means through which collaborative learning has played its most prominent role in shaping writing center theory and practice. Peer tutoring as a form of collaborative learning assumes that helping other writers to learn to handle concepts and skills more effectively creates an education system built around a community of learners instead of single authority figures.[6] Collaborative learning thus provides an educational environment in which students can engage in self-motivated learning.

Harvey Kail and John Trimbur offer the common justification for peer tutoring as collaborative learning in "The Politics of Peer Tutoring." "[P]eer tutoring based on collaborative learning," they write, "offers an alternative to the dominant hierarchical code of teaching and learning, an alternative based on voluntary social interaction among students. It replaces the metaphor of the generation and transmission of knowledge with that of a conversation" (9). The conversational focus underlying most discussions of collaborative learning assumes knowledge is socially constructed, culturally and historically located, dependent on individuals reaching consensus. Knowledge is the product of like-minded communities, and writing centers offer students a place to meet to share in this process and its products.

✎ TECHNOLOGY

Technological developments within the past decade have made it necessary for the writing center community to adapt its dominant pedagogy to meet shifting writer demographics (more writers writing on disk and online) and to address the influence of powerful cultural expectations (students must have as much computer experience as possible).[7] The advent of networked computers and the Internet has compelled writing centers to explore, test, and implement (although rarely reject) more and more computer-based activities. Given their commitment to collaborative learning, writing center personnel have been particularly interested in such claims as those that state that having students write using networked computers and electronic communications technologies places them in uniquely collaborative learning situations.[8] Such claims have prompted explorations into how to use networked computers, the Internet, and the World Wide Web (WWW) to help writers develop the communicative proficiency they need to succeed in academic, vocational, and nonacademic settings. Increasing numbers of students are offered computer-mediated writing center services ranging from handouts and workshops located on WWW pages to synchronous and asynchronous online tutoring.

The personal computer has affected writing center pedagogy in ways that are just beginning to be understood, appreciated, and questioned.[9] On-line writing centers (OWLs), in particular, have attracted much attention as many people have written about the OWLs they have built and others work to replicate these efforts. Stuart Blythe's "Networked Computers + Writing Centers = ? Thinking About Networked Computers in Writing Center Practice"; David Coogan's "E-mail Tutoring: A New Way to Do New Work"; Katherine Grubbs' "Some Questions About the Politics of Online Tutoring in Electronic Writing Centers" typify the best of ongoing discussions of innovations attempted and the attendant pedagogical, managerial, and political implications. Such articles provide the foundation for *Wiring the Writing Center* (1998), edited by Eric Hobson, the first book-length discussion of computers in writing center pedagogy. This collection's overriding sense is one of guarded optimism, a desire to bring a level of careful critique to the often unchecked enthusiasm, even naiveté, found in many early articles about technology in the writing center. *Wiring the Writing Center* is a recommended introduction to the community's efforts to integrate computers meaningfully into writing center pedagogy.[10]

Writing center staff have traditionally been in the vanguard of writing teachers exploring, implementing, and adapting technology for sound pedagogical use. Ray Wallace (1998) believes his more than fifteen years spent grappling with the roles that technology can and should play in teaching writing includes experiences common among writing center administrators. He writes in "Random Memories of the Wired Writing Center: The Modes-to-Nodes Problem," that while they might not have received the press they deserved for their contribution to teasing out pedagogically sound uses for computers in writing instruction, writing center staff involvement in that process makes historical and practical sense:

First, writing center directors generally kept current on technological innovation in the field. They read the main pedagogic journals and, more than others perhaps, read the ancillary journals related to educational technology to see how others were using this technology to improve education in their respective fields. Hence, when a particular technological innovation came to the fore, the use of the personal computer to teach writing for example, writing center directors were usually more aware of what had been tried and what were the possibilities for future growth, than, say, their colleagues in more traditional literary fields. Second, writing centers themselves were generally small spaces requiring relatively little economic investment in order to ensure effective pedagogy. (163)

This claim for the writing center as ground zero for computers in writing instruction is supported by Ellen Mohr's account of the extent to which her position as writing center director at Johnson County Community College in Kansas City, Missouri, demanded that she learn as much as she could about computers, writing instruction, network technologies, the Internet, and the World Wide Web. While she shows more bruises from her journey than Wallace and other authors in *Wiring the Writing Center*, her chronicle, "The Community College Mission and the Electronic Writing Center" is valuable reading. Mohr offers an honest, less-than-smooth history, replete with the concomitant repercussions, of technology use within writing center—real and virtual. Nancy Grimm presents a caution to embracing electronic tutoring in "Computer Centers and Writing Centers: An Argument for Ballast."

The single best discussion of the writing center community's long involvement with educational technology, excluding personal computers, is Neal Lerner's, "Drill Pads, Teaching Machines, and Programmed Texts: Origins of Instructional Technology in Writing Centers." Beginning with debates in *College English* in the 1920s and 1930s, Lerner's essay provides an unparalleled account of how writing centers have used, abandoned, and appropriated various educational "technologies" to serve their students and institutions; this essay is itself a short course in the major influences on American educational administration and pedagogy in the past century. Particularly important is Lerner's tracing of the powerful influence that mechanistic and behaviorist models of learning have had on dominant approaches to teaching throughout the twentieth century, resulting in the mass adoption of drill-based workbooks, "programmed" learning designed to ensure "mastery" of conventions of usage and forms of expression.

Equally important is Peter Carino's "Computers in the Writing Center: A Cautionary History," a careful critique of why and how writing centers have integrated computers into their work. Paying particular attention to the fact that computers and technology have become cultural ciphers for "progress," "valuable," and "good," he examines how writing centers are adapting their pedagogy to fit the contours offered by electronic avenues for communication and instruction. What he finds, while stimulating, gives him pause and brings to the fore important questions about how suited writing center pedagogy is to these emerging environments. Carino's conclusion is cautiously optimistic:

> If OWLs are going to carry us into flight rather than eat us like rodents, if MOOs are going to produce more milk than dung, if we are going to cruise the information superhighway without becoming roadkill, our vigilance will need to equal our enthusiasm. I think this history shows that generally it has, though not always in the best proportions, and will continue to do so. The question will be whether we can remain vigilant in the inertia of our enthusiasm. (193)

As with all areas of writing center pedagogy, such critical reflection and vigilance is not only warranted, it is essential to the community's continued contributions to individual student's development as writers, to educational institutions' abilities to provide a comprehensive educational experience to their constituents, and to composition as a discipline.

✥ THE WRITING CENTER'S MANY PRACTICE SETTINGS

Writing centers have expanded their services to meet needs in specific contexts. Programs created to work with writers within specific discourse communities are no longer anomalies, with writing centers located within such professional programs as law, medicine, nursing, pharmacy, and business.[11] Likewise, recognizing graduate students' needs as writers, a number of graduate schools have established writing centers to support their students and faculty. Satellite centers have even opened in such unlikely locations as prisons in recognition of the roles that unique contexts (incarceration certainly rates as a unique educational context) play in defining the ways that writing centers can meet the educational needs of atypical groups of writers.[12]

An often overlooked area of writing center pedagogy is the increasingly important role these programs play in developing future educators: writing centers serve as preservice training sites for primary and secondary school teachers, as sites for on-going educational research, and as sites for initial and advanced training for college and university graduate teaching assistants. This training allows new teachers opportunities to develop a coherent and consistent practice base before entering their first classrooms. The issue of how writing center experience helps preservice teachers to develop the knowledge, skills, and attitudes needed to make a smooth and educationally effective transition to the classroom has been addressed in a number of articles over the past two decades. Particularly useful are the following: In "Preparing Future Composition Teachers in the Writing Center," Irene Clark recounts the benefits for teachers-in-training from their work as writing center tutors. Robert Child's article, "Tutor-Teachers: An Examination of How Writing Center and Classroom Environments Inform Each Other," supports Clark's claims via a comparison of the classroom effectiveness of new college composition teachers who were and were not first trained as writing center tutors.[13] Brad Wilcox and Norma Decker Collins show in "Formative Assessment as Educational and Administrative Adhesive: Establishing an Elementary School Writing Center" that the value of writing center experience during teacher training extends to elementary education pre-service teachers as well.

This description of writing centers, however glowing, is one-dimensional; its microlevel focus lacks depth, lauding the most commonly recognized effects that writing centers can have on individual students. A richer description must also note the macrolevel effects that writing centers have on their home institutions. Two chapters in *The Writing Center Resource Manual* (Jeanne Simpson's "Assessing Needs, Identifying an Institutional Home, and Developing a Proposal," and Neal Lerner's "Research in the Writing Center") show that the collegial, collaborative, and mentoring relationships that are encouraged by writing centers affect many critical areas of institutional life, including retention efforts, institutional assessment, student satisfaction, even institutional fund raising.[15]

✎ WRITING CENTER THEORY-PRACTICE

As Peter Carino ("Early Writing Centers"), among others, notes, it is popular to trace the writing center community's development using a progressive model, one that represents that development as evolutionary, moving from less-legitimate current-traditional to more-legitimate social-constructionist theoretical and pedagogical allegiances and practices. Two seminal articles are Lisa Ede's "Writing as a Social Process: A Theoretical Foundation for Writing Centers?," which linked the goals of one-to-one tutorials to a social understanding of meaning making, and Alice Gillam's "Writing Center Ecology: A Bakhtinian Perspective," which introduced Bahktinian semiotics to discussions of the writing tutorial. Following Ede and Gillam, Andrea Lunsford, in "Collaboration, Control, and the Idea of the Writing Center," did much to codify a progressive history of writing center development from current-traditional "storehouses" to expressivist "garrets" to social constructivist "Burkean parlors."

The best single introduction to the tension that exists between writing center theory—and, by extension, the history called upon to substantiate and to justify theoretical claims—and writing center practice is *Intersections: Theory-Practice in the Writing Center* (1994), edited by Joan Mullin and Ray Wallace. Echoing the unifying theme of the collection's chapters, Alice Gillam argues, in "Collaborative Learning Theory and Peer Tutoring Practice," that "the writing center offers a fertile site for engaging in reflective practice and for generating paradoxical, contingent knowledge" (51). Working specifically with the "problem" of the paradoxical nature of the writing center theory-practice nexus, Eric Hobson, in "Writing Center Practice Often Counters Its Theory. So What?," reviews writing center history as commonly articulated in order to note the many disjunctions that occur between the community's statements of its theoretical foundations and the pedagogy used to enact these tenets. His critique of the gaps found between theory and practice does not lessen the value of

writing center practices that lack one-to-one correspondences to guiding theoretical principles. Rather, he writes, "the unique circumstances of every instance
of application require a unique appropriation and implementation of theory
into practice. . . . [N]o single theory can dictate writing center instruction.
Instead, we must reshape theory to fit our particular needs in the particular
historically located situations in which writing center practitioners find themselves" (8).

Christina Murphy's chapter, "The Writing Center and Social Constructionist Theory," highlights the extent to which the social constructionist version of knowledge as communal consensus fails to account for the individual
as an individuated ego, a somewhat autonomous agent unaccounted for in the
abstract architecture of constructionist social theory. In "Writing Centers in Context: Responding to Current Educational Theory," a chapter in Wallace and
Simpson's *The Writing Center: New Directions* (1991), Murphy carefully demonstrates that the writing center community's adherence to Lunsford's historical
narrative sterilizes, oversimplifies, and decontextualizes writing center practice.

Closely attuned to arguments presented in *Intersections*, Hobson, in "Maintaining Our Balance: Walking the Tightrope of Competing Epistemologies,"
demonstrates that commonly held writing center practice holds simultaneous
loyalties to epistemologies often discussed as mutually exclusive. Rather than
striving for a single, pristine writing center theory and resulting practice, he
argues, writing center personnel should see "contradiction" between their idealized theories and their site-specific practice not as signs of weakness but as
opportunities to further explore the theory-practice nexus. In "Theorizing Writing Centers: An Uneasy Task," Peter Carino follows Hobson's argument and
explains the difficulties encountered in crafting a representative writing center
theory-practice and shows how such a theoretical framework might be constructed by enlarging the community's knowledge of its history and its
social/political position within composition studies.

Admittedly, writing center personnel have often fostered and employed
the rhetorical tactic of stressing a significant distance between "traditional"
composition classes (with "traditional" defined as instruction grounded in the
positivist assumptions underlying current-traditional rhetoric, and applied
rather indiscriminately to composition classes at large) and writing center
pedagogy. On one level, doing so was politically motivated; such a move po-
sitioned writing center activity as legitimate pedagogy in opposition to pedagogically bankrupt "other." On another, more productive level, this perceived
polarity has provided a useful framework and a discrete discursive space
within which to chronicle the common misunderstandings, even active marginalization, that writing center personnel encountered as they created and nur-
tured their centers. A glance through many of the annotations found in *Writing
Centers: An Annotated Bibliography* (Murphy, Law and Sherwood) reveals how
prevalent is this narrative thread.

Distancing writing center activity from the writing classroom is a tactic that
is overstated, overused, and arguably less accurate than it once was. Writing
centers have contributed markedly to developing classroom pedagogies used
currently in general, advanced, and discipline-specific writing classes. Writing

centers provided a place uniquely suited for working out the kinks between the often idealized initial descriptions of such commonly accepted pedagogies as one-to-one, student-teacher writing conferences, and peer writing/editing workshops, and the more work-a-day, pragmatic ways in which they are typically employed in writing classes across the curriculum. Donald Murray's "The Listening Eye" provided an engaging, even seductive, picture of the writing conference as a model of instruction that made intuitive sense. In many ways, however, it took writing center-based educators such as Muriel Harris to investigate and to state forthrightly the amount of work necessary to achieve the seamless, everyone-wins vision of writers' development that such teacher-writers as Murray hinted at. Harris' *Teaching One-to-One: The Writing Conference* (1986) remains one of the most important guides to learning how to work effectively and efficiently with writers in the context of individualized instruction. Equally useful is Irene Clark's *Writing in the Center: Teaching in a Writing Center Setting*. Like all of Harris' and Clark's work, the lessons presented, while not always originating in the writing center, were developed, refined, and formalized there.[16]

A kernel of usefulness remains, however, in this perceived polarity between writing center activity and composition instruction as practiced in many classrooms. Because writing centers most often are not linked exclusively to composition sequences, their staff have opportunities to maintain longer relationships with students and thus engage in more longitudinal writing instruction that is, ideally, more extensive and of a higher order than most instructors can offer within the framework of writing courses that are limited to one, two, or three terms of ten or fifteen weeks. The potential for ongoing engagement between a tutor and client makes it likely that they will work together to decipher a broad range of assignments, discuss ways to accommodate many readers, and strive to understand and to manipulate many available document formats. These activities reflect progress toward educational end points common to composition classes and writing centers, including the development of a large repertoire of audience analysis and accommodation. Yet, because writing centers most often employ teaching methods that focus on ongoing formative assessment—few programs assign grades for writing center-based activity—a writer's performance on specific writing tasks is always understood and discussed within the context of the writer's individual development and goals.

∿ CONCLUSION

The writing center community has actively contributed to knowledge-making in composition studies. The literature recording the development of writing centers, writing center pedagogy, and the (inter)relationships with composition studies is both broad and challenging—for instance, *Writing Centers: An Annotated Bibliography*, annotates 1,447 books, articles, and resource items directly related to writing centers. However, the writing center community's contribution to composition studies is easy to overlook if one attempts to monitor the writing center's impact via its presence in the discipline's most prestigious journals. While articles dealing with writing center topics do appear in such journals as *College English* and *College Composition and Communication*, they do so with less frequency than other topics. That absence, however, ignores a large literature, one that extends from the early decades of the twentieth century to the present.

The writing center's increased visibility in American education within the past two to three decades suggests that anyone studying writing instruction's history and dominant pedagogies will have heard of and, hopefully, made use of writing centers and their services. More to the point, it suggests that anyone intending to teach writing, to conduct research, and to critique writing instruction should know the work that the writing center community is engaged in. Because of its centeredness within most academic institutions, the writing center provides academic and intellectual homes to an eclectic mix of personalities, epistemologies, philosophies, pedagogies, and methodologies. In doing so, it makes what many theorists see as irreconcilable polarities coexist, or even collaborate, to create powerful educational environments. The ability to bridge gaps in hierarchical educational structures, unequal power relationships, faculty and student culture(s), and institutionally and individually determined educational goals attests to the writing center's centrality in North American education.

Notes

1. This chapter owes its strength to the thorough and challenging response provided by Dr. Carla McDonough (Eastern Illinois University). Thanks as well to my Albany College of Pharmacy writing center colleagues, Laura Rogers and Carolyn Statler, for workshopping an earlier draft.

2. To join the discussion group Wcenter, send to ⟨listproc@listserv.ttu.edu⟩ the following message in the body of the e-mail: subscribe wcenter ⟨your name⟩.

3. In 1998, NWCA added a twelfth affiliate organization, the European Writing Centers Association. For fairly recent discussions about writing centers in educational institutions outside of North America, see articles by Kathy Howard; Christina Kock and Lotte Rienecker; Peter McMillan; and Vivian Chase.

4. The best introduction to the many goals that can be achieved during the one-to-one writing conference remains Muriel Harris' *Teaching One-to-One: The Writing Conference*.

5. Bruffee published a version of this argument prefaced by a slightly different introduction as "Collaborative Learning and the 'Conversation of Mankind.'" While his book *Collaborative Learning: Higher Education, Interdependence, and the Authority of Knowledge* expands his discussion of collaborative learning as a site of social constructed knowledge, his basic argument remains unchanged.

6. The idea that writing center peer tutors are in reality "power equal" has been challenged. Trimbur provides a compelling deconstruction and critique of claims for shared status between tutor and client within the collaborative writing conference ("Peer Tutoring: A Contradiction in Terms").

7. Dickie Selfe refers to this pressure as "the massive and often blind 'will to technologize'" in this culture.

8. As it has in composition studies at large, so too has it become common to hear the following claims about the benefits of computers in writing center instruction: Computers in the tutorial setting allow for more equitable and convenient access to center resources and services (Gardner; Kinkead); computers and computer networks encourage collaboration among writers (Farrell; Jordan-Henley and Maid "Tutoring in Cyberspace"); computers decenter authority and enhance tutor training (Chappell; Johanek and Rickly); virtual tutoring represents the future (Coogan; Crump); computers in writing center tutorials help to create writing environments and collaborative relationships that are more natural than the artificial ones found in typical face-to-face tutorials (Chappell; Crump; Jordan-Henley and Maid "MOOving").

9. For an accessible introduction to these issues and a synthesis of the literature, see Hobson, "Straddling the Virtual Fence."

10. The issue of *Computers and Composition* 12 (1995) dedicated to writing centers can serve as a useful prelude to many of the topics addressed in *Wiring the Writing Center*. Although this volume is undoubtedly considered the baseline against which subsequent discussions of electronic writing center instruction is measured, because of the speed of technological-based change, many of these articles have aged quickly. This fate is particularly true in the case of the material presented in *The Writing Center Journal* 8.1 (1987), an issue dedicated to the topic of the computer's role in writing centers.

11. North (1994) speaks of the need to focus writing center activity on the needs of specific discourse communities, arguing implicitly for satellite, specialized writing centers instead of a central "do it all" center.

12. To read more about writing centers located in correctional institutions, see Maeck.

13. Recent articles along this line are by Van Dyke, by Broder, and by Magnuson.

14. Trimmer offers a narrative history similar to Lunsford's. As with Lunsford's model, Trimmer's version of writing center history is particularly neat, unproblematic, and upbeat.

15. For more on writing center rolls in retention and institutional research, see Poziwilko.

16. Another popular text about teaching writing through writing conferences—student-teacher or peer tutoring conferences—is *The Practical Tutor* (1987) by Meyer and Smith. Although this, the Harris, and the Clark books are, on average, a dozen years old, they still constitute "essential" reading in areas of the composition studies community beyond the writing center community. For texts dealing exclusively with the training of peer tutors, to work in one-to-one and small-group tutorial settings, see also, *The St. Martin's Sourcebook for Writing Tutors* (1995) by Murphy and Sherwood and *The Bedford Guide for Writing Tutors* (1998) by Ryan.

Bibliography

Berlin, James A. *Rhetoric and Reality*. Carbondale, IL: Southern Illinois UP, 1987.
Blythe, Stuart. "Networked Computers + Writing Centers = ?: Thinking About Networked Computers in Writing Center Practice." *The Writing Center Journal* 17.2 (1997): 89–110.

Broder, Peggy F. "Writing Centers and Teacher Training." *WPA: Writing Program Administration* 13.3 (1990): 37–45.

Bruffee, Kenneth A. "Collaborative Learning and the 'Conversation of Mankind.'" *College English* 46 (1984): 635–52.

———. *Collaborative Learning: Higher Education, Interdependence, and the Authority of Knowledge.* Baltimore: Johns Hopkins UP, 1993.

———. "Peer Tutoring and the 'Conversation of Mankind.'" Olson 77–84.

Carino, Peter. "Computers in the Writing Center: A Cautionary History." Hobson 171–93.

———. "Early Writing Centers: Toward a History." *The Writing Center Journal* 15.2 (1995): 103–15.

———. "Open Admissions and the Construction of Writing Center History: A Tale of Three Models." *The Writing Center Journal* 17.1 (1996): 30–48.

———. "Theorizing Writing Centers: An Uneasy Task." *Dialogue: A Journal for Writing Specialists* 2.1 (1995): 23–37.

———. "What Do We Talk About When We Talk About Our Metaphors: A Cultural Critique of Clinic, Lab, and Center." *The Writing Center Journal* 13.1 (1992): 31–42.

Chappell, Virginia. "Theorizing in Practice: Tutor Training 'Live, from the VAX Lab.'" *Computers and Composition* 12 (1995): 227–36.

Chase, Vivian. "Starting Up a Writing Center in an International Setting." *Writing Lab Newsletter* 21.8 (1997): 14–16.

Child, Robert. "Tutor-Teachers: An Examination of How Writing Center and Classroom Environments Inform Each Other." Wallace and Simpson 169–83.

Clark, Irene L. "Preparing Future Composition Teachers in the Writing Center." *College Composition and Communication* 39.3 (1988): 347–50.

———. "The Writing Center at the University of Southern California: Couches, Carrels, Computers, and Conversation." Kinkead and Harris 97–113.

———. *Writing in the Center: Teaching in a Writing Center Setting.* 2nd ed. Dubuque, IA: Kendall/Hunt, 1992.

Coogan, David. "E-mail Tutoring: A New Way to Do New Work." *Computers and Composition* 12 (1995): 171–81.

Crump, Eric. "A Dialogue on OWLing in the Writing Lab: Some Thoughts on Michael Spooner's Thoughts." *The Writing Lab Newsletter* 18.6 (1994): 6–8.

Ede, Lisa. "Writing as a Social Process: A Theoretical Foundation for Writing Centers?" *The Writing Center Journal* 9.2 (1989): 3–13.

Farrell, Pamela B. "Writer, Peer Tutor, and Computer: A Unique Relationship." *The Writing Center Journal* 8.1 (1987): 29–34.

Gardner, Clinton. "Have You Visited Your Online Writing Center Today?: Learning, Writing, and Teaching Online at a Community College." Hobson 75–84.

George, Diana. "Talking to the Boss: A Preface." *The Writing Center Journal* 9.1 (1988): 37–44.

Gillam, Alice. "Collaborative Learning Theory and Peer Tutoring Practice." Mullin and Wallace 39–53.

———. "Writing Center Ecology: A Bakhtinian Perspective." *The Writing Center Journal* 11.2 (1991): 3–12.

Giroux, Henry A. *Teachers as Intellectuals.* Granby, MA: Bergin and Garvey, 1988.

Grimm, Nancy. "Computer Centers and Writing Centers: An Argument for Ballast." *Computers and Composition* 12 (1995): 171–81.

Grubbs, Katherine. "Some Questions About the Politics of Online Tutoring in Electronic Writing Centers." *Writing Lab Newsletter* 19.2 (1994): 7, 12.

Harris, Murial. "A Multiservice Writing Lab in a Multiversity: The Purdue University Writing Lab." Kinkead and Harris 1–27.

———. "Talking in the Middle: Why Writers Need Writing Tutors." *College English* 57 (1995): 27–42.

———. *Teaching One-to-One: The Writing Conference.* Urbana, IL: NCTE, 1986.

———. "What's Up and What's In: Trends and Traditions in Writing Centers." *The Writing Center Journal* 11.1 (1990): 15–25.

Hemmeter. Thomas, "The 'Smack of Difference': The Language of Writing Center Discourse." *The Writing Center Journal* 11.1 (1990): 35–48.

Hobson, Eric H. "Maintaining Our Balance: Walking the Tightrope of Competing Epistemologies." *The Writing Center Journal* 13.1 (1992): 65–75.

———. "Straddling the Virtual Fence." Hobson ix–xxvi.

———. "Writing Center Practice Often Counters Its Theory. So What?" Mullin and Wallace 1–10.

Hobson, Eric H., ed. *Wiring the Writing Center.* Logan: Utah State UP, 1998.

Howard, Kathy. "Writing Centers: The Hong Kong Experience." *Writing Lab Newsletter* 18.8 (1994): 10–11.

Johanek, Cindy, and Rebecca Rickly. "Online Tutor Training: Synchronous Conferencing in a Professional Community." *Computers and Composition* 12 (1995): 237–46.

Jordan-Henley, Jennifer, and Barry Maid. "MOOving Along the Information Superhighway: Writing Centers in Cyberspace." *The Writing Lab Newsletter* 19.5 (1995): 1–6.

———. "Tutoring in Cyberspace: Student Impact and College/University Collaboration." *Computers and Composition* 12 (1995): 211–18.

Kail, Harvey, and John Trimbur. "The Politics of Peer Tutoring." *WPA: Writing Program Administration* 11.1–2 (1987): 5–12.

Kinkead, Joyce A. "The Electronic Writing Tutor." *The Writing Lab Newsletter* 12.4 (1988): 4–5.

Kinkead, Joyce A., and Jeanette G. Harris, eds. *Writing Centers in Context: Twelve Case Studies.* Urbana, IL: NCTE, 1993.

Kock, Christina, and Lotte Rienecker. "A Writing Lab in Copenhagen, Denmark." *Writing Lab Newsletter* 20.9 (1996): 4–6.

Lerner, Neal. "Drill Pads, Teaching Machines, and Programmed Texts: Origins of Instructional Technology in Writing Centers." Hobson 119–136.

———. "Research in the Writing Center." *Silk* IV.6.1–IV.6.11.

Lunsford, Andrea. "Collaboration, Control, and the Idea of the Writing Center." *The Writing Center Journal* 12.1 (1991): 3–10.

Maeck, Alexandra. "Report from a Correctional Institution: I Need Help." *Writing Lab Newsletter* 19.7 (1995): 13–14.

Magnuson, Robin. "Preventing Writing Wrecks: The Role of the Writing Lab in Teacher Preparation." *The Writing Lab Newsletter* 10.8 (1986): 11–14.

McMillan, Peter. "Tadpoles and Topic Sentences: A Writing Center in Asia." *Writing Lab Newsletter* 11.3 (1986): 1–3.

Meyer, Emily, and Louise Z. Smith. *The Practical Tutor.* New York: Oxford UP, 1987.

Mohr, Ellen. "The Community College Mission and the Electronic Writing Center." Hobson 151–62.

Mullin, Joan, and Ray Wallace, eds. *Intersections: Theory-Practice in the Writing Center.* Urbana, IL: NCTE, 1994.

Murphy, Christina, Joe Law, and Steve Sherwood, eds. *Writing Centers: An Annotated Bibliography.* Westport, CT: Greenwood, 1996.

Murphy, Christina, and Steve Sherwood. *The St. Martin's Sourcebook for Writing Tutors.* New York: St. Martin's, 1995.

————. "The Writing Center and Social Constructionist Theory." Wallace and Simpson 276–88.

————. "Writing Centers in Context: Responding to Current Educational Theory." Mullin and Wallace 25–38.

Murray, Donald. *Learning by Teaching*. Montclair, NJ: Boynton/Cook, 1982.

Nash, Thomas, "The Writing Center: Life on the Frontier." *Journal of Developmental and Remedial Education* 7.1 (1983): 3–5, 31–2.

Neff, Julie. "The Writing Center at the University of Puget Sound: The Center of Academic Life." Kinkead and Harris 127–144.

North, Stephen M. "The Idea of a Writing Center." *College English* 46.5 (1984): 433–46.

————. "Revisiting the Idea of a Writing Center." *The Writing Center Journal* 15.1 (1994): 7–19.

————. "Writing Center Research: Testing Our Assumptions." Olson 24–35.

Olson, Gary A., ed. *Writing Centers: Theory and Administration*. Urbana, IL: NCTE, 1984.

Petit, Angela. "The Writing Center as 'Purified Space': Competing Discourses and the Dangers of Definition." *The Writing Center Journal* 17.2 (1997): 111–22.

Poziwilko, Linda. "Writing Centers, Retention, and the Institution: A Fortuitous Nexus." *Writing Lab Newsletter* 22.2 (1997): 1–4.

Reigstad, Thomas J., and Donald A. McAndrew. *Training Tutors for Writing Conferences*. NCTE Theory and Research into Practice Series. Urbana, IL: ERIC/NCTE, 1984.

Ryan, Leigh. *The Bedford Guide for Writing Tutors*. 2nd ed. Boston: Bedford, 1998.

Selfe, Dickie. "Surfing the Tsunami: Electronic Environments in the Writing Center." *Computers and Composition* 12 (1995): 311–22.

Shor, Ira. *Culture Wars*. New York: Routledge, Kegan Paul, 1986.

Silk, Bobbie Bayliss, ed. *The Writing Center Resource Manual*. Emmitsburg, MD: NWCA, 1998.

Simpson, Jeanne. "Assessing Needs, Identifying an Institutional Home, and Developing a Proposal." *Silk* II.2.1–II.2.16.

————. "What Lies Ahead for Writing Centers: Position Statement on Professional Concerns." *Writing Center Journal* 5.2/6.1 (1985): 35–39.

Trimbur, John. "Peer Tutoring: A Contradiction in Terms." *The Writing Center Journal* 7.2 (1987): 21–8.

————. "Peer Tutoring and the Benefits of Collaborative Learning." *Writing Lab Newsletter* 7.9 (1983): 1–3.

Trimmer, Joseph. "Story Time: All About Writing Centers." *Focuses* 1.2 (1988): 27–35.

Van Dyke, Christina. "From Tutor to TA: Transferring Pedagogy from the Writing Center to the Classroom." *The Writing Lab Newsletter* 21.8 (1997): 1–3, 10.

Wallace, Ray. "Random Memories of the Wired Writing Center: The Modes-to-Nodes Problem." Hobson 163–70.

Wallace, Ray, and Jeanne Simpson, eds. *The Writing Center: New Directions*. New York: Garland, 1991.

Wilcox, Brad, and Norma D. Collins. "Formative Assessment as Educational and Administrative Adhesive: Establishing an Elementary School Writing Center." *The Clearing House* 71 (2): 109–12.

On the Academic Margins:
Basic Writing Pedagogy

DEBORAH MUTNICK

The story of basic writing from its inception in the late 1960s and early 1970s to its present precarious position in colleges and universities can be read as a parable for our times.[1] From the radical sixties to the conservative eighties and the "new world order" of the nineties, basic writing reflects both this country's promise and its deepening contradictions. It signifies struggles for inclusion, diversity, and equal opportunity; debates over standards and linguistic hegemony; the exploitation of faculty and staff on the academic margins; and the policies that opened and now threaten to close higher education's doors to masses of people. It has played a key role not only in providing opportunities for research on adult literacy but also in illuminating the politics of writing in terms of race, class, ethnicity, and other social structures that would have remained invisible in the mostly white, middle-class classrooms that have traditionally constituted the "mainstream."

As of this writing, in the summer of 1998, the City University of New York (CUNY) is on the verge of eliminating the courses that put basic writing on the national map. This reversal of Open Admissions reverberates with numerous calls by composition experts, at least since 1992, to abolish basic writing. Members of the composition community, suspicious of institutional motives, have been careful to place such proposals in the context of the students' best interests. But in this period of educational downsizing, the fate of CUNY students and others nationwide who place into basic writing appears to be in jeopardy. The national mania for standards and assessment as well as popular accounts of the failure of mass education like James Traub's *City on a Hill* complicate our internal debates. How the future of basic writing instruction unfolds will depend, to some extent, on how well we understand the history, theories, and debates that have shaped what Mina Shaughnessy once called the "pedagogical West."

ON THE "FRONTIER": MINA SHAUGHNESSY'S LEGACY

My own involvement in basic writing started in 1986 when I was hired as an adjunct instructor to teach composition at the Brooklyn campus of Long Island University. Although I had majored in English and gone on to get an MFA in writing, I had never taken a composition course, much less taught one. Nor was I prepared for the gritty, urban working-class scene I encountered, despite having grown up in a progressive household in which I routinely heard critiques of capitalism at the dinner table. I remember sitting that winter at a small kitchen table in my walk-up tenement apartment in the East Village laboriously marking student papers, perplexed not only by how poorly written they were—some incomprehensible, others just vapid—but also by my own feelings of incompetence as a teacher. What could I possibly say to these students or write in the margins of their papers that would help them?

It is this archetypal image of the writing teacher poring anxiously over compositions that Shaughnessy recalls in the opening pages of *Errors and Expectations*, in which she describes "sitting alone in the worn urban classroom" reading the "stunningly unskilled" papers of CUNY Open Admissions students. As I read Jane Maher's recent biography of Shaughnessy and reread Shaughnessy's articles[2] and book several years after completing my own research on basic writing, I found myself paraphrasing Mark Twain's famous quip about his father: Shaughnessy seems to have learned a great deal since I carefully worded my critique in *Writing in an Alien World* of what I saw then as her essentialist depiction of the basic writer. Certainly she was not a revolutionary in the sense of having a penetrating analysis of social problems or supporting radical socioeconomic change; but she understood that the literacy crisis of her day was in response to "the declining literacy of the affluent" rather than the plight of the "traditionally illiterate" and that our failure to address the needs of the latter would "continue to cultivate advanced literacy as a privilege rather than an entitlement" ("The English Professor's Malady" 297).

Despite concern that her almost mythical status in the field has detracted attention from other important scholars and created an inaccurate record of remedial writing instruction (see, e.g., Horner, "Discoursing Basic Writing"),[3] it seems to me not only that much of her work remains relevant for us today but that she herself is the figure with whom most basic writing scholars and researchers still contend. The other major influence on basic writing instruction and research is David Bartholomae, who acknowledges his debt to Shaughnessy at the same time he advocates for a significantly different kind of pedagogy. While Bartholomae by no means ignores the problem of error, he and his colleagues at the University of Pittsburgh helped shift the emphasis of instruction from grammatical to rhetorical concerns—from surface error to semantic and critical content—transforming the traditional skills-drills course into a theoretically driven seminar with challenging reading and writing assignments.

The Pittsburgh basic reading and writing program described by Bartholomae and Anthony Petrosky in *Facts, Artifacts, and Counterfacts* also reflects the influence of postmodern theories of discourse on composition scholars. In particular, the Pittsburgh courses were designed to initiate students into an academic discourse community, similar in some respects to Shaughnessy's approach but framed by a more theoretically sophisticated perspective than had permeated academia when she wrote *Errors and Expectations*. Other Pittsburgh exponents like Nicholas Coles, Susan V. Wall, Mariolina Salvatori, and Min-Zhan Lu have also made important contributions to the field of basic writing. But although they have modified the theory and method set forth in *Facts, Artifacts, and Counterfacts*, they have adhered fairly closely to its central tenets.

More than the scholars who followed in her footsteps, Shaughnessy consistently shifted the focus of her research and writing on the problems of Open Admissions from the students to teachers, administrators, and society in general. She believed that basic writing would alter not only the students who enrolled in courses but also the institutions that offered them. As she maintains in "Open Admissions and the Disadvantaged Teacher,"

> Open Admissions began as a remedial wing to a few departments on traditional college campuses, but it is now transforming the colleges themselves, exposing far more than the deficiencies of the new students. By probing into the nature of those deficiencies and resisting those who have tried to isolate the phenomenon of disadvantage from the society that caused it, Open Admissions is forcing the real question—not how many people society is willing to salvage, but how much this society is willing to pay to salvage itself. (254)

Similarly, in "Diving In: An Introduction to Basic Writing," Shaughnessy applies a developmental scale, usually reserved for students, to teachers. Describing stages ranging from a traditional defense of Western values to missionary zeal and critical inquiry, Shaughnessy ultimately calls on the teacher to "remediate himself, to become a student of new disciplines and of his students . . . " (262). Throughout her career, she spoke out courageously about the sociohistorical and political causes of the students' unpreparedness; the institution's responsibility for undertaking their education; and the larger democratic values at stake in Open Admission's success or failure. Regardless of her personal politics, she articulated a radical position on Open Admissions, at the heart of which was her conviction that basic writers are indeed educable.

Thus it was with sadness and frustration that she lamented the budget cuts of the 1970s, which, only a few short years after Open Admissions began, heralded its slow demise. More than twenty years ago, forecasting our plight today, Shaughnessy speculated that the cutbacks occurred because " . . . the times have shifted and allowed the society to settle back into its comfortable notions about merit, notions which have produced a meritocratic scheme that perpetuates the various brands of race and class prejudice that have pervaded this society since its creation" ("Miserable" 264). It was in the face of these obstacles that Shaughnessy pioneered what she referred to as a frontier, "unmapped

except for a scattering of impressionistic articles and a few blazed trails . . . "
(4). This pedagogical frontier now contains an impressive amount of research
and scholarship as well as innovative methods and theories of instruction. Yet
almost by definition basic writing remains a frontier, a border crossing, hope-
ful, desperate, unsettled. And one of its most troubling markers, so central to
Shaughnessy's work, is the issue of error.

⊷ THEORIES OF ERROR: SHAUGHNESSY AND BEYOND

Shaughnessy adamantly believed that although error should never become the
sole focus of teaching writing, it was crucial for both political and academic
reasons to see it as a linchpin of instruction for the new generation of Open
Admissions students whom she called basic writers. As she put it:

> The absence of errors, it is true, does not automatically guarantee good writ-
> ing, yet the pile-up of errors that characterizes basic writing papers reflects
> more difficulty with written English than the term "error" is likely to imply.
> . . . [E]rror is more than a mishap; it is a barrier that keeps [the student] not
> only from writing something in formal English but from having something to
> write. ("Speaking" 274–75)

In *Errors and Expectations*, anticipating composition's use of methods of literary criticism to read student writing, Shaughnessy analyzes thousands of
CUNY placement exams, categorized under the chapter headings "Handwrit-
ing and Punctuation," "Syntax," "Common Errors," "Spelling," and "Vocabulary." On the basis of her experience at CUNY, she believed that the kinds of
errors made by basic writers are a key to their development as writers. Aware
of new pressures in the 1970s on teachers sympathetic to students to eschew
error out of respect for linguistic variation, Shaughnessy cogently argues that
basic writing errors are produced by a mixture of "[v]ariant and standard forms
. . . as if students had half-learned two inflectional systems," indicating not dialect interference or vernacular speech but hybrid codes created by the writer's
attempt to appear literate.

Thus error, as indicated by the title of her book,[4] is central to the instructional methods she encouraged. Her central, brilliant premise is that errors
represent the writer's attempt to systematize language, to approximate the standard written code in the absence of adequate instruction and practice. The
teacher's responsibility, therefore, is to understand the logic of the writer's errors in order to untangle the syntactic and grammatical knots made in the effort to write correctly. Shaughnessy's approach revealed error to be logical, a
sign of intention and intelligence as the writer groped for conventional forms.
Along with suggesting a method of instruction that could help basic writers
become more literate, her research refuted assumptions based on developmental models that basic writers are cognitively deficient or immature.

Shaughnessy's focus on error sparked both criticism and further research. One of her early critics, John Rouse, argues in his essay "The Politics of Composition" that Shaughnessy's program trains basic writing students "to follow authority, however willful or arbitrary," thus perpetuating their marginal status (4). Using Basil Bernstein's theory of restricted and elaborated speech codes to characterize lower-class students, he maintains that Shaughnessy's focus on error reinforces the restricted speech code that had limited basic writers in the first place rather than enabling them to learn "an elaborated speech code and the habits of mind that go with it" (4). In "Putting Error in Its Place," Isabella Halsted anticipates a dominant trend in basic writing instruction to deemphasize error. Published in 1975, two years before *Errors and Expectations*, Halsted concludes that the focus of a writing course should be communication and that teachers should foster dialogue, functioning as "interested, skeptical and close readers who want to know what our students have to say" (81).

Alice Horning, on the other hand, praises *Errors and Expectations* as "a starting point for major research" but maintains it did not provide a "cohesive, testable theory of language acquisition" (1). To that end, in *Teaching Writing as a Second Language*, she proposes that basic writers develop writing skills in the same way that other adults develop second language skills. In "The Study of Error," Bartholomae also views the appropriation of academic discourse in light of second language acquisition. Rather than learn language per se, basic writers have to learn written academic discourse. The sentences basic writers compose do not signify immaturity or "arrested cognitive development"; instead, they represent "a variety of writing," an "interlanguage," an "occasion to learn." Bartholomae suggests that error analysis, a linguistic technique developed in research on second language acquisition, provides basic writing teachers with both a means of analyzing errors and a theory of error. He recommends its use both as a diagnostic tool and as a method of instruction for teaching students how to edit, an easier task than teaching correctness at the point of composing.

Also of interest in research on basic writing errors is Mary Epes' 1985 article in which she traces the errors of adult basic writers to encoding processes. Epes distinguishes between "encoding" the visual symbols of written language and "composing" meaning through writing. In her case studies of thirteen standard dialect speakers and thirteen nonstandard dialect speakers, she finds that "the overwhelming problem for error-prone writers [is] the inability to perceive errors on the page" (30). Like Bartholomae, she argues that basic writing teachers should separate "encoding" from "composing" activities in the classroom and concludes that instruction "designed to develop perceptual skills in transcribing and editing are of paramount importance to basic writers" (30).

For several decades following Shaughnessy's ground-breaking research on error, the prevailing view, based on study after study, was that formal grammar instruction in the writing class was at best ineffective and could be harmful to student writers if it detracted from more rhetorical aspects of learning to write. A useful article on the limits of grammar instruction is Patrick Hartwell's "Grammar, Grammars, and the Teaching of Grammar." Hartwell reminds us that repeated calls for a renewed emphasis on grammar instruction are nothing new. He explains the limits of experimental research, which tends to be supported or refuted on the basis of prior assumptions rather than objective results, and goes on to ask the "right questions" about perceptions, definitions, and theories of grammar. The key conclusion he draws is that error is not a linguistic problem but a "problem of metacognition and metalinguistic awareness" (364). In other words, written language functions as both statement and linguistic artifact, demanding of the reader an "awareness of language as language" (365).

More recently, as Hartwell would predict, there have been further attempts to rethink grammar instruction, including Rei R. Noguchi's *Grammar and the Teaching of Writing*; Susan Hunter and Ray Wallace's *The Place of Grammar in Writing Instruction*; and Constance Weaver's *Teaching Grammar in Context*. Many of these reconsidered views on grammar seek a middle ground, establishing which rules are teachable and how and when to teach them. In practice, at least in my department, the debate on error and grammar instruction continues unabated. By the late 1970s, however, theoretical interest in a process approach to teaching writing had pushed researchers to focus on acts of composing rather than written products.

✒ PROCESS AND COGNITIVE THEORIES: FROM PRODUCT TO PROCESS AND PERSON

Sondra Perl's 1979 study of unskilled college writers showed how overattention to editing undermined their ability to compose fluently, while their recursive style of writing proved them to be writers whose " . . . lack of proficiency may be attributable to the way in which premature and rigid attempts to correct and edit their work truncate the flow of composing without substantially improving the form of what they have written" (328). Nancy Sommers' 1980 comparison of the revision strategies of student writers and experienced adult writers found that students' strategies for revision were limited to lexical rather than conceptual or semantic changes, and that they lacked "procedures or heuristics" to imagine an audience or question their own purposes. As she puts it in a later essay, "Responding to Student Writing," "We need to show our students how to seek, in the possibility of revision, the dissonances of discovery . . . and thus to show them the potential for development implicit in their own writing" (156).

Along with the shift in focus from product to process, several basic writing researchers in the late 1970s and early 1980s were influenced by cognitive theory. In "What We Know—and Don't Know—About Remedial Writing," Andrea Lunsford reports on a study at Ohio State University in the late 1970s. Inspired by Shaughnessy's calls for research on basic writing, she designed a study of ninety-two students who scored 10 or below on the ACT English test. On the basis of data collected from the pilot program, Lunsford describes the students as poor readers whose writing was marked by syntactic immaturity, abundant error, and ineffective writing strategies. In light of the study's findings, she draws several implications for remedial writing instruction: language skills are related and need to be integrated into the college curriculum; the level of reading difficulty should not be diluted for basic writers; sentence-combining exercises should be redesigned to foster abstract thinking; and teachers need to be better trained.

Several of Lunsford's suggestions have become standard practice for many basic writing teachers, particularly her insistence on the curricular integration of language skills and the use of challenging reading materials. But she goes on in 1979 to argue even more adamantly that basic writers are cognitively deficient. Briefly summarizing the theoretical perspectives on cognitive development of Vygotsky, Piaget, and Chomsky, Britton, and Polanyi, she concludes that "basic writing students are most often characterized by the inability to analyze and synthesize" ("Cognitive" 452).

By the mid-1980s and the rise of what James Berlin calls "social-epistemic" rhetoric[5] in writing pedagogy, many composition scholars had begun to reject theories of cognitive deficiency. Patricia Bizzell argues in her 1986 article, "What Happens When Basic Writers Come to College," that the tendency to see the problems of basic writers as rooted in either dialect, discourse conventions, or cognitive functioning has led to "an excessively narrow focus" of their experience (296). Mike Rose also challenges the view of basic writers as cognitively deficient, noting that to see such students as "locked . . . at the Piagetian level of concrete (vs. formal) operations" is to misinterpret Piaget, who assumed that normal functioning adults are by definition capable of analyzing and generalizing ("Remedial" 336). Similarly, on the basis of her case studies of three students at Medgar Evers College, Brenda M. Greene refutes descriptions of basic writers as "egocentric," a trait often attributed to basic writers by cognitivists, and concludes that they are aware of problems of audience related to cohesiveness, coherence, development, and clarity but not of larger rhetorical problems related to argument and structure.[6]

✧ RHETORICAL THEORIES: THE "SOCIAL TURN" AND BASIC WRITING

The "social turn" in composition studies in the 1980s highlighted research on cultural difference as well as persistent tensions between dominant and subordinate discourses as increasing numbers of nontraditional students entered university classrooms. According to Bizzell, in order to develop the deliberative stance intrinsic to academic writing, students need to acquire a "new world view," resulting in a sort of "biculturalism." It is this biculturalism, she argues, not linguistic or cognitive differences, that makes academic discourse difficult for basic writers. To be successful in college, Bizzell suggests, basic writers must eventually choose academic culture and its more socially powerful discourse over their own cultural beliefs despite having "more to lose in modifying their earlier world views" (301) than their mainstream academic counterparts.

In "Teacher Background and Student Needs," Peter Rondinone, now a professor at CUNY, describes his experience there in the early 1970s as an Open Admissions student. Rather than giving him a sense of loss, his academic achievement constituted an escape from the negative influences of his home culture. On the basis of his own experience and the results of classroom exercises he uses to explore attitudes toward language and problems with writing, Rondinone concludes that students may have to resist or even abandon friends and family in order to acquire literacy skills. This belief is contested by critics of monoculturalism like Keith Gilyard, whose book *Voices of the Self*[7] documents the development of his own linguistic competence in both standard and Black English. Gilyard insists that biculturalism and bidialectalism are not only possible but preferable to abandoning one's culture and language of origin.

The issue of students' right to their own language, the subject of a heated debate in the NCTE in the 1970s leading to the publication of "Students' Right to Their Own Language" (Butler), might seem moot in light of current conservative trends such as the English Only movement and the discourse on national standards. But it still affects our perceptions of our students and the curricular choices we make. In 1987, Geneva Smitherman proposed a national public policy on language that would mandate tripartite instruction in the "language of wider communication"—in the United States, standard English, the mother tongue, and one or more foreign languages. Given the abstruseness of much academic discourse, one might wonder whether it counts as a "language of wider communication." Nevertheless, the acquisition or appropriation of academic writing has been viewed as a key task for college students, particularly basic writers.

In his widely read essay, "Inventing the University," David Bartholomae investigates the discursive conventions by which students appropriate academic language, arguing that successful writers must "see themselves within a privileged discourse" (277). Rather than invention and discovery, the process of becoming a writer, according to Bartholomae, involves imitation or parody. To write, then, writers must locate themselves within particular discourse communities. For the basic writer, this relocation means moving from the outside—the margins—to the inside, a process Bartholomae characterizes in "Writing on the Margins" as true of "most of us" whose "lives as students were marked initially by a struggle to enter into those habits of mind . . . that define the center of English Studies" (67).

This valorization of academic discourse is problematic for several reasons. For one, Bartholomae compares the undergraduate experience of English faculty to that of basic writers. While some college professors like Rondinone may have passed through basic or remedial writing classes, most are middle class and relatively privileged. Moreover, Bartholomae's theory of the margins accounts for privilege in terms of knowledge rather than race, class, gender, or other social structures that overlap the academic margin and construct the category of basic writing. He implies that exclusion from higher education is caused by the individual's failure to appropriate the knowledge and the discursive conventions of the academy, rather than by the failure of political or social structures to accommodate the individual. Thus, for Bartholomae, writers must see themselves as "insiders" in order to write academic discourse.

The "inside" of Bartholomae's academy requires "counterfactuality," a term connoting potential and translatable—as opposed to factual—meanings that he and Anthony Petrosky borrow from George Steiner and adopt for the title of *Facts, Artifacts, and Counterfacts*. In their account of the basic reading and writing program they helped develop at the University of Pittsburgh, Bartholomae and Petrosky argue that basic writing students not only must move toward the center but also " . . . have learned (and perhaps in a way that their 'mainstream' counterparts cannot) that successful readers and writers actively seek out the margins and aggressively poise themselves in a hesitant and tenuous relationship to the language and methods of the university" (41). This theory of reading and writing formed the basis of the Pittsburgh model, not a laboratory for grammar drill but a thematic course designed as a graduate seminar in which basic writing students read whole books and become "experts" who theorize and debate intellectual problems pertaining to themes such as adolescence or work.

At LIU, we developed an East Coast, urban version of the Pittsburgh model to accommodate a larger, more nontraditional population of basic writers—typically, more than sixty percent of entering students—including, among others, working parents, older or returning students, and recent graduates of decrepit inner-city high schools. In our courses, like those at Pittsburgh, we integrate reading and writing; invite students to appropriate the language of the university through fully engaging in reading, writing, discussion, and analysis; and view acts of reading and writing as meaningful, purposeful, not fragmented, skills-driven exercises in correctness.

⤴ THE POLITICS OF BASIC WRITING: SOCIAL REPRODUCTION, SOCIAL LOCATION

Despite the Pittsburgh program's theoretical advances, Bartholomae and Petrosky continued to elide the political basis for excluding social groups from cultural institutions like universities; their narrative of basic writing omits the race, class, and gender inequities that pervade higher education. This perspective overlooks the sociohistorical structures that determine the inside and the outside, leaving those on the margins with the unenviable task of inventing themselves in the image of those who have dominated the center—generally speaking, white, middle-class males. Needless to say, many basic writers are social outsiders, many of whom would like nothing better than to get "inside" the system. But Bartholomae and Petrosky assume the academy is an ideologically neutral zone that fosters critical thinking and self-criticism, rather than a key site for the reproduction of the dominant culture, and that literacy is indeed a ticket to upward social mobility.

In "Standards and Access," Tom Fox astutely challenges the relationship between language mastery and academic or economic access. Citing Raymond

Williams' *Keywords,* Fox shows how "standards," used as a singular plural syn-
onymous with "quality," operates powerfully to build consensual agreement.
Consequently, he argues, Shaughnessy's pedagogy and the initiation theories
of Bartholomae, Bizzell, Rose, and Bruffee support neoconservatives' belief in
a universal standard of literacy upon which academic or economic success is
contingent. Carol Severino makes a different point about language mastery in
her critique of Bartholomae and other scholars, who she believes view literacy
acquisition as a form of "club membership" or a "road" or "bridge" to the
promised land of reading and writing. According to Severino, both metaphors
of insidership and transportation overemphasize the distance between home
and academic languages and cultures. She maintains, conversely, that U.S. urban culture is porous and permeable and that journalistic and leisure activities
provide a better common ground for "extending the practice of rhetoric" (13)
than do traditional definitions of academic discourse. Learning is a "two way
rhetorical street"; instead of "trying to 'transport' students to academic culture," teachers can foster a common ground through collaboration and cultural
change.

In a similar vein, Coles and Wall observe that basic writers are "people
who live 'between two worlds,'" moving back and forth, transforming both
worlds. Rather than insist on "critical detachment" as the proper stance for academic study, they propose that a more enabling pedagogy would support readers' "intensified engagement and even partisanship" with texts. This strategy
of "identification" helps foster an ability "to imagine oneself in another's
place," a necessary component of academic work, but also one that enables
"connection" and "commitment" (307), rather than the separation from and
abandonment of one's own history. For to become an "insider," as Bartholomae suggests basic writers need to do, one must assume the existence of outsiders and accept a system of exclusion, a proposition that subjects basic writers
to a kind of cultural schizophrenia. Rather than undergo a "split" between one's
culture of origin and the culture of the university, Coles and Wall argue, it is
possible to enrich both realms through a process of mutual recognition. Otherwise, they observe, "[t]he focus of metaphors such as 'initiation' and 'assimilation' is on what must change in our students, how they must become other
than they are in order to accommodate our discourse" (299).

This expectation is closely examined in "Remediation as Social Construct,"
by Glynda Hull and colleagues. In their analysis of the classroom discourse involving one student in a remedial writing class, the authors explore ways that
"we, as teachers, can inadvertently participate in the social construction of attitudes and beliefs about remediation which may limit the learning that takes
place in our classroom" (300). They find that the student, a young woman who
placed into basic writing and enjoyed writing, was viewed by the teacher as a
"scattered thinker" on the basis of what appeared to be a "relatively minor dis-
junction between teacher expectation and student behavior" (311), which in
turn undermined the teacher's sense of authority. The authors go on to examine the implications of labeling students as "low achievers" and locating school
problems within the individual, viewed as cognitively defective or culturally
deprived, rather than in social structures and institutions. Underlying these as-

sumptions, the authors argue, are "unexamined cultural biases," including "our legacy of racism and class bias" (316).

In "Conflict and Struggle," Lu argues that education is a process of transformation through conflict and struggle. Continuing the critique of Shaughnessy's essentialist view of language she began in "Redefining the Legacy of Mina Shaughnessy," Lu argues that students on the social margins inevitably undergo change as they become educated. Like Bizzell, she believes that the clash of values and ideas they experience between the academic world and their culture of origin forces them to make choices and resituate themselves. But Lu differentiates between two versions of loss that are often collapsed together: a pedagogy of acculturation rooted in an essentialist view of language in which Western culture is assumed to be superior; and a pedagogy of accommodation rooted in a utopian view of discourse communities in which cultural conflict does not exist.

Lu, on the other hand, understands education as repositioning. She defines the educator's role in terms of enabling students to make conscious, possibly painful choices in this process of inevitable change, rather than initiating them into the dominant culture or falsely leading them to believe that their cultural identity can remain intact when they enter the world of academic discourse. From her postmodern perspective, Lu suggests we reread basic writing pioneers like Shaughnessy in light of current theoretical debates on language and "border" writers like Gloria Anzaldua whose "mestiza consciousness" enables her to sustain and profit from contradiction. For Lu, language itself is contradictory, fluid, heterogeneous, and learning a new discourse necessarily results in changed consciousness, a new awareness that the learner can direct both toward inner and social change.

One problem, however, with this view of education is that people are often resistant to change. In "On the Subjects of Class and Gender in the 'Literacy Letters,'" Linda Brodkey describes the ideologically driven responses of teachers to basic writers with whom they corresponded as part of a graduate class project. She found that both teachers and students told "class-based narratives," which for the teachers revolved around busy professional lives and for the students centered on external threats to themselves, their families, or their neighbors. In these exchanges, according to Brodkey, "we see that the teacher's desire to be preserved as the unified subject of an educational discursive practice that transcends class overrides the student's desire to narrate herself as a subject unified in relation to the violence that visited her working-class neighborhood" (105). Brodkey concludes that "To *teach* is to authorize the subjects of educational discourse" (111, emphasis added).

For Gail Stygall, to *write* is to authorize the subjects of educational discourse, particularly in English departments. Using Brodkey's project as a model, Stygall assigned graduate students in her composition class at Miami University to correspond with basic writers, hoping their familiarity with Brodkey's article would enable them to resist the discursive codes revealed in her study. Rather than class as a unifying principle, Stygall found that her graduate students were driven by their relationship to the profession of English. Citing Foucault's notion of the "author function,"[8] Stygall argues that "the

teaching of basic writing is formulated around the educational discursive practices necessary to keep the author function dominant" (321). The graduate students' need to identify themselves as authors and scholars prevented them from
critically scrutinizing their representations of the basic writers. But, interestingly, Stygall reports that, as teachers, they were less invested in replicating institutional practices, enabling them to resist privilege and rethink the identity
politics of labeling writers.

Reproduction theory also has implications for basic writing as an institution. In his analysis of the discourse of basic writing, Bruce Horner argues that
Shaughnessy's book and her elevated status have eclipsed the history of remedial instruction and depoliticized the lessons learned from Open Admissions. The legitimization of basic writing, according to Horner, left intact harsh
realities confronting basic writing programs. He astutely points out that participants in the debate on basic writing and Open Admissions on both the left
and the right have viewed academic excellence in opposition not only to academic underpreparedness but also to minority students and political activism.
Instead of inverting this assumption and asserting that institutional integrity
depends on the admission of the Open Admissions students, proponents as well
as opponents of Open Admissions considered the policy to be a threat to academic excellence.

For basic writing advocates like Shaughnessy, Horner argues, the political
debate was resolved by accommodating all points of view—that is, support for
basic writers and a defense of academic standards. Horner maintains that this
accommodation capitulated to the belief that educability was a cognitive rather
than a political issue. Ultimately, the process of legitimization and the erasure
of the history of remedial instruction have reinforced administrative and leg-
islative views of basic writing as a temporary, marginal, expendable skills course.
As I have argued elsewhere, this denigration of basic writing as a skills course,
designed to "clean up" students' error-ridden writing and promote a univocal
standard language "reinforced linguistic prejudices and masked the underlying
problems of racism, class discrimination, and other forms of social inequality
that had necessitated Open Admissions in the first place" (Mutnick 9).

Critiques of Shaughnessy, going back to Rouse, have in turn inspired passionate defenses of her research and her work at CUNY. For example, Paul
Hunter criticizes Lu's essay on the politics of linguistic innocence, arguing that
we should view "Shaughnessy's work not as 'innocent,' but as a politics of experience forged in a revolutionary struggle to open the doors of our acade-
mies" (926). He points out that Lu's critique reflects a revisionist history of basic
writing evident as early as 1980 in an issue of the *Journal of Basic Writing* in
which reprinted speeches from a commemoration of Shaughnessy cast her as
an Arnoldian figure. Rather than an Open Admissions pioneer who fought for
a more democratic educational system, she is depicted in a speech by E. D.
Hirsch as a defender of conservative cultural values. Although Hunter's analysis is astute, his defense of Shaughnessy's radical values underscores how contested her legacy has become. A more recent example of a conservative
appropriation of Shaughnessy's work is James Traub's account of Open Admissions in *City on a Hill*. At the same time that he extols her "radical attack

on conventional pedagogy," Traub describes her as "the high-minded progressive and the radical populist" whose favorite authors, Milton and Bacon, redeemed her from the low-status "remedial-underworld" (115).

Patricia Laurence, a colleague of Shaughnessy's, also criticizes retrospective accounts like Lu's that she believes reduce composition "to one text, one voice, belying the 'dialogical' nature of educational movements . . . " (19). She, too, refutes Lu's view of basic writing and Shaughnessy's *Errors and Expectations* as a politics of linguistic innocence, arguing that Lu fails to address the complexities of the Open Admissions movement and that the basic writing pedagogy developed by Shaughnessy and others, herself included, was a response to "a given time in a given society" (20).[9] Underscoring the ferocity of the opposition to Open Admissions and the volatility of the CUNY campuses at which the struggle for mass education was taking place, Laurence praises Shaughnessy's political acumen and restraint. Absent from Lu's portrait of the era, she protests, are the real social tensions that drove the Open Admissions movement, resulting—she quotes T. S. Eliot—in a "dissociation of sensibility" and "an increasing refinement of language and theory" that leads to a "separation of thought and feeling" (21).

One problem with the current generation of theoretically driven basic writing critics is a revisionist tendency to see motives and behavior anachronistically. Horner, for example, asserts that Shaughnessy's emphasis on basic writers' educability "'naturalized' them both in a cognitive developmental and a civic sense" and portrayed them as eager "to join with rather than disrupt mainstream American society" (208). Although he observes that the linkage between Open Admissions students and political activists, particularly Puerto Ricans and Blacks, is misleading given the much larger number of conservative white ethnic students who enrolled at CUNY, he takes issue with Shaughnessy's belief that the new students were in college to improve their lives rather than "disrupt" society.

The half-truths in his argument are confusing: by most accounts Black and Latino/a students did lead the struggle for Open Admissions; and yet, then as now, the desire for upward social mobility and the belief that a college education enables self-improvement are widespread among all ethnic groups and, however mythical, understandable. For educated, mostly middle-class academics to dismiss such yearnings as a form of social reproduction or false consciousness is precisely what Lisa Delpit has warned against in her critique of process theory and progressive educators.

☙ THE FOURTH NATIONAL BASIC WRITING CONFERENCE AND NEW DIRECTIONS IN BASIC WRITING[10]

The tension between a more traditional view of writing instruction as an avenue to academic and professional success and poststructural theories of social reproduction continues to shape the debate on basic writing. A turning point in this debate occurred at the Fourth National Basic Writing Conference in 1992, much of the proceedings of which were published in the *Journal of Basic Writing* (1993). Of particular interest is the Special Issue devoted to the plenaries, featuring Bartholomae's keynote speech "The Tidy House." It is in this speech that Bartholomae opts to read against the grain of basic writing as "a grand narrative of liberal sympathy and liberal reform" and suggests that we have begun to think of it as "something naturally, inevitably, transparently there in the curriculum" (8).

Though once a site of struggle and contestation, Bartholomae argues, basic writing has become institutionalized, "reproducing the hierarchies we had meant to question and overthrow, way back then in the 1970s" (18). Alternatively, he uses Mary Louise Pratt's notion of a cultural "contact zone" to envision an introductory composition course for diverse students. This reenvisioned freshman writing course would use autobiography—autoethnography, in Pratt's terms—to reveal the history of social practices and help "history, class, and culture become manifest in the classroom," along the lines described by Carolyn Steedman in her study of working-class British girls in *The Tidy House*.

Although the conference generally reflected Bartholomae's newfound skepticism about the institution of basic writing, Karen Greenberg voiced strong objections to his views. In "The Politics of Basic Writing," she argues that resistance on the part of teachers to effective assessment procedures creates a vacuum that will be or has already been filled by university administrators, state legislators, and accrediting agencies. If compositionists do not assume responsibility for assessment, she warns, programs will be decimated or eliminated, a prediction that, despite her and her colleagues' efforts, has now come true at Hunter College, the CUNY senior college at which she ran the basic skills courses. Directly responding to a question Bartholomae posed at the conference about the usefulness of basic writing, Greenberg argued that although too much basic writing instruction is still based on a remedial model, Hunter courses were "useful and thoughtful" (66), and that the college's skills testing and developmental writing courses embody a "right-to-succeed" policy as opposed to a "right-to-fail" theory often associated with Open Admissions education (70).

Like many of the conference participants, Peter Dow Adams questioned the benefit of homogeneous classes and speculated that the message sent to basic writers is "We don't expect you to be able to write well" (23). Pointing out that basic writing is essentially a form of tracking on the college level, he reminds us that tracking has long been seen as a problem on the secondary level because it segregates students according to race and class rather than ability. Adams also observes that research findings over the last twenty years—from the conclusion that drills are ineffective to recommendations to address error in context—have persuaded many of us to design similar courses for students at different levels of development, obviating the need for a special basic writing course. He calls on the profession to collect systematic data on basic writing programs, to rethink how freshman composition can respond to a wider range of students, and to pilot mainstreaming programs on a volunteer basis.

✦ RECENT TRENDS: STUDIOS, MAINSTREAMING, AND THE "YOGURT" MODEL

Although basic writing experts have debated the problems of basic writing instruction in the larger context of the politics of higher education and concern for the students' best interests, the institutional ax has already begun to fall. In "Repositioning Remediation," Rhonda Grego and Nancy Thompson describe the alternative to the University of South Carolina's remedial instruction devised when the state's Commission on Higher Education decided to eliminate college credit from their basic writing course. The fact that no teachers were consulted in the decision-making process drove home to faculty that the everyday work of teaching is shaped by institutional and political forces rather than by student needs. In response to the state's mandate, Grego and Thompson and their colleagues created an alternative form of writing assessment and instruction in which all first-year students enroll in freshman composition. In the first week of class, students produce writing histories that, along with required portfolios of previous work, become the basis for referrals to the Writing Studio. The Studio—a small group of students and an experienced teacher—meets once a week to work on the students' composition assignments. Based on "interactional inquiry" the Writing Studios use small-group dynamics and a cycle of action and reflection to foster "interpersonal agency" and give voice to the "emotional" component of knowledge-making silenced by traditional educational frameworks.

A somewhat different approach to mainstreaming is described by Mary Soliday in her reflections on the Enrichment Approach at City College, funded by a three-year Fund for the Improvement of Post-Secondary Education (FIPSE) grant. Explaining that Barbara Gleason's and her project emerged in the context of the CUNY struggle around Open Admissions and remedial courses, Soliday acknowledges that historically "remedial programs create sheltered educational pockets for academically marginal writers" (85). The Enrichment Approach represents "a progressive version of mainstreaming" in which all students place into freshman composition, bypassing test scores. Instead of a separate studio, Soliday and her colleagues reconceived instruction for multilingual urban students, designing a two-semester course worth six credits and a curriculum that focused in the first semester on language diversity and in the second on sociocultural difference. The goal is to "encourage students to use the unfamiliar language of the academy to describe and analyze familiar aspects of everyday language use and cultural experience" (87). Among their resources and tools are: undergraduate peer tutors, a public reading hour with another class, portfolio assessment, small group and workshop approaches, conferencing, and teacher portfolios documenting the experimental course.

Peter Elbow lent support to mainstreaming in his address in 1993 at the Conference on Composition in the Twenty-first Century: Crisis and Change. Arguing that his utopian vision of the writing class of the future "builds on crucial pedagogical consensus . . . that instruction in composition does not de-

pend on everyone having the same knowledge or skill and that the same instruction should go on in basic classrooms as goes on in regular ones" (89), Elbow suggests what he calls "the yogurt model." In this "Burkean parlor" or
"writing studio," students would work as long as they needed to produce a
passing portfolio, at which point they would receive three credits and complete
the course. Another aspect of this "competence-based" model that departs from
traditional educational structures is that the class would constantly change as
students trickled in and out, completing the writing requirements faster or
slower, perhaps taking much longer than the standard fourteen-week semester, depending on their skills, abilities, and effort.

We are in the midst of a vital pedagogical debate about whether to place students into basic writing courses, mainstream them into new versions of freshman composition, or, as Daniel J. Royer and Roger Gilles suggest in a recent
issue of *College Composition and Communication*, develop methods of "directed
self-placement." But as we debate the theory and method of writing placement
and instruction, we should beware the politics of higher education at this junc-
ture of history. The outcome of legal and administrative proceedings at CUNY
that will determine the fate of remedial courses in the senior colleges has yet
to be decided. If these courses are restricted to the community colleges, the
Open Admissions era will, in effect, have come to an end. Those of us who
teach, administer, and research basic writing will need, as Horner argues, to
know the history of remedial instruction if we are to deal with the larger implications of current trends in higher education, not only the elimination of remedial courses but also attacks on affirmative action and other equal
opportunity programs designed to give masses of people access to higher education. We will need to understand linguistic theories of error, the relationship between language and meaning, and approaches to teaching and learning
in diverse cultural contexts. And we will need to continue to research literacy
acquisition and the writing process of adult writers, a project that, as numerous scholars have suggested, illuminates the complexities of written language
for us all. But we will also, I believe, have to become more savvy, more politically astute and active, if we are to be the ones to decide which courses best
serve the students we teach.

Notes

1. The limits of space prohibit me from including more than a few references outside
   the field of basic writing. While the following is a very partial list of theorists and
   pedagogies that have been important to me, I recommend them and urge anyone
   interested in teaching basic writing to read across the disciplines. Among key theorists relevant to basic writing are: Mikhail Bakhtin, Lev Vygotsky, Paulo Freire, and
   Stanley Aronowitz and Henry Giroux. Also of special significance for basic writing
   teachers are the discussions in this volume and elsewhere of feminist and critical
   pedagogies. Finally, within the field of basic writing, two invaluable resources to

which I refer frequently but want to give special emphasis are the *Journal of Basic Writing* and *A Sourcebook for Basic Writing Teachers.*

2. Maher's biography includes a valuable set of appendixes of Shaughnessy's published and unpublished articles and other writing, to which I refer throughout this essay.

3. The terms *basic writing, remedial,* and *developmental* tend to be used interchangeably. Both "remedial" and "developmental" have pejorative connotations, implying a condition that needs to be cured in the first case and a cognitive problem in the second. The term "basic writing" represents, in part, an attempt to avoid such connotations; it also refers historically to the Open Admissions era in which it was first used, as opposed to "remedial," which dates back in English instruction at least to the 1920s (see, e.g., Rose, "The Language of Exclusion"). The semantic battles may distract us from the underlying social problems that perpetuate educational inequities, a dilemma underscored by more recent questions about the stereotypical implications of the term "basic writing." Ultimately, I believe, it is not the terms we use so much as it is the category we attempt to name—and the sociohistorical conditions that gave rise to it—that are so problematic.

4. Maher points out very interestingly in her biography that the title of Shaughnessy's book, which draws so much attention to the issue of error, was suggested by her editor at Oxford, John Wright.

5. Berlin defines this rhetoric as follows: " . . . the real is located in a relationship that involves the dialectical interaction of the observer, the discourse community (social group) in which the observer is functioning, and the material conditions of existence" (488).

6. Other important research calling into question cognitive theories of language development includes Sylvia Scribner and Michael Cole's 1988 study of multiliteracy among the Vai people of northwestern Liberia; Shirley Brice Heath's classic study of the language development of children in three different North Carolina communities in *Ways With Words*; and William Labov's linguistic studies of nonstandard English speakers that challenge the assumption that school language is preferable to other cultural languages.

7. Along with Gilyard's literacy autobiography, Mike Rose's *Lives on the Boundary* and Victor Villanueva's *Bootstraps* deal with basic writing issues from personal and pedagogical perspectives. All three books are useful resources both for teacher training and undergraduate writing instruction.

8. According to Stygall, Foucault's term *author function* means "how the concept of the author constitutes and regulates French academic and literary discourse" (321), a term she argues is equally applicable to Anglo-American academic and literary discourse.

9. Among Shaughnessy's contemporaries, Adrienne Rich gives an especially useful and vibrant account in "Teaching Language in Open Admissions" of the social era of the late 1960s and early 1970s, which reflects both her deep respect for Shaughnessy and her own more politicized and poetic response to the times.

10. Several conference participants addressed working conditions, a key issue for basic writing teachers that bears directly on pedagogy. In the conference proceedings published in the *Journal of Basic Writing,* see Jeanne Gunner's "The Status of Basic Writing Teachers" and Mary Jo Berger's "Funding and Support for Basic Writing."

Also see Mary Cupiec Cayton's interesting account in "Writing as Outsiders" of how her marginal position as a temporary instructor in the academy created conditions similar to those of basic writers.

Bibliography

Adams, Peter Dow. "Basic Writing Reconsidered." *Journal of Basic Writing* 12.1 (1993): 22–36.

Aronowitz, Stanley, and Henry Giroux. *Education Under Siege.* South Hadley, MA: Bergin & Garvey, 1985.

Bakhtin, Mikhail. *The Dialogic Imagination.* Ed. Michael Holquist. Trans. Caryl Emerson. Austin: U of Texas P, 1981.

Bartholomae, David. "Inventing the University." *Perspectives on Literacy.* Ed. Eugene R. Kintgen, Barry M. Kroll, and Mike Rose. Carbondale: Southern Illinois UP, 1988. 273–85.

———. "The Study of Error." *The Writing Teacher's Sourcebook.* Ed. Gary Tate and Edward P. J. Corbett. 2nd ed. New York: Oxford UP, 1988. 303–17.

———. "The Tidy House: Basic Writing in the American Curriculum." *Journal of Basic Writing* 12.1 (1993): 4–21.

———. "Writing on the Margins: The Concept of Literacy in Higher Education." *A Sourcebook for Basic Writing Teachers.* Ed. Theresa Enos. New York: Random House, 1987. 66–83.

Bartholomae, David, and Anthony Petrosky. *Facts, Artifacts, and Counterfacts: Theory and Method for a Reading and Writing Course.* Portsmouth, NH: Boynton/Cook, 1986.

Berger, Mary Jo. "Funding and Support for Basic Writing: Why Is There So Little?" *Journal of Basic Writing* 12.1 (1993): 81–89.

Berlin, James. "Rhetoric and Ideology in the Writing Class." *College English* 50 (Sept. 1988): 477–94.

Bizzell, Patricia. "What Happens When Basic Writers Come to College." *College Composition and Communication* 37 (Oct. 1986): 294–301.

Brodkey, Linda. "On the Subjects of Class and Gender in the 'Literacy Letters.'" *Becoming Political: Readings and Writings in the Politics of Literacy Education.* Ed. Patrick Shannon. Portsmouth, NH: Heinemann, 1992.

Butler, Melvin A., and Members of the Committee on CCCC Language Statement. "Students' Right to Their Own Language." Urbana, IL: NCTE, 1974.

Cayton, Mary Kupiec. "Writing as Outsiders: Academic Discourse and Marginalized Faculty." *College English* 53 (Oct. 1991): 647–60.

Coles, Nicholas, and Susan V. Wall. "Conflict and Power in the Reader-Responses of Adult Basic Writers." *College English* 49 (Mar. 1987): 298–314.

Delpit, Lisa. "The Silenced Dialogue: Power and Pedagogy in Educating Other People's Children." *Harvard Educational Review* 58 (Aug. 1988): 280–98.

Elbow, Peter. "Writing Assessment in the 21st Century: A Utopian View." *Composition in the Twenty-first Century: Crisis and Change.* Ed. Lynn Z. Bloom, Donald A. Daiker, and Edward M. White. Carbondale: Southern Illinois UP, 1996. 83–100.

Epes, Mary. "Tracing Errors to Their Sources: A Study of the Encoding Processes of Adult Basic Writers." *Journal of Basic Writing* 4.1 (1985): 4–33.

Fox, Tom. "Standards and Access." *Journal of Basic Writing* 12.1 (1993): 37–45.

Freire, Paulo. *Pedagogy of the Oppressed.* Trans. Myra Bergman Ramos. New York: Continuum, 1988.

Gilyard, Keith. *Voices of the Self: A Study of Language Competence.* Detroit: Wayne State UP, 1991.

Greenberg, Karen. "The Politics of Basic Writing." *Journal of Basic Writing* 12.1 (1993): 64–71.

Greene, Brenda M. "Empowerment and the Problem Identification and Resolution Strategies of Basic Writers." *Journal of Basic Writing* 11.2 (1992): 4–27.

Grego, Rhonda, and Nancy Thompson. "Repositioning Remediation: Renegotiating Composition's Work in the Academy." *College Composition and Communication* 47 (Feb. 1996): 62–84.

Gunner, Jeanne. "The Status of Basic Writing Teachers: Do We Need a 'Maryland Resolution'?" *Journal of Basic Writing* 12.1 (1993): 57–63.

Halsted, Isabel. "Putting Error in Its Place." *Journal of Basic Writing* 1.1 (1975): 72–86.

Hartwell, Patrick. "Grammar, Grammars, and the Teaching of Grammar." *A Sourcebook for Basic Writing Teachers.* Ed. Theresa Enos. New York: Random House, 1987. 348–72.

Heath, Shirley Brice. *Ways with Words: Language, Life, and Work in Communities and Classrooms.* Cambridge: Cambridge UP, 1983.

Horner, Bruce. "Discoursing Basic Writing." *College Composition and Communication* 47 (May 1996): 199–222.

Horning, Alice S. *Teaching Writing as a Second Language.* Carbondale: Southern Illinois UP, 1987.

Hull, Glenda, et al. "Remediation as Social Construct: Perspectives from an Analysis of Classroom Discourse." *College Composition and Communication* 42 (Oct. 1991): 299–329.

Hunter, Paul. "'Waiting for Aristotle' in the Basic Writing Movement." *College English* 54 (Dec. 1992): 914–27.

Hunter, Susan, and Ray Wallace. *The Place of Grammar in Writing Instruction: Past, Present, Future.* Portsmouth, NH: Boynton/Cook, 1993.

Labov, William. *Language in the Inner City: Studies in the Black English Vernacular.* Philadelphia: U of Pennsylvania P, 1972.

Laurence, Patricia. "The Vanishing Site of Mina Shaughnessy's *Errors and Expectations.*" *Journal of Basic Writing* 12.2 (1993): 18–27.

Lu, Min-Zhan. "Conflict and Struggle: The Enemies or Preconditions of Basic Writing." *College English* 54 (Dec. 1992): 887–913.

———. "Redefining the Legacy of Mina Shaughnessy: A Critique of the Politics of Linguistic Innocence." *Journal of Basic Writing* 10.1 (Spring 1991): 26–40.

Lunsford, Andrea. "Cognitive Development and the Basic Writer." 1979. *A Sourcebook for Basic Writing Teachers.* Ed. Theresa Enos. New York: Random House, 1987. 449–59.

———. "What We Know—and Don't Know—About Remedial Writing." *College Composition and Communication* 29 (Feb. 1978): 47–52.

Maher, Jane. *Mina P. Shaughnessy: Her Life and Work.* Urbana, IL: NCTE, 1997.

Mutnick, Deborah. *Writing in an Alien World: Basic Writing and the Struggle for Equality in Higher Education.* Portsmouth, NH: Boynton/Cook, 1996.

Noguchi, Rei R. *Grammar and the Teaching of Writing: Limits and Possibilities.* Urbana, IL: NCTE, 1991.

Perl, Sondra. "The Composing Processes of Unskilled College Writers." *Research in the Teaching of English* 13 (1979): 317–36.

Rich, Adrienne. "Teaching Language in Open Admissions." *On Lies, Secrets, and Silence: Selected Prose 1966–1978.* New York: W.W. Norton, 1979.

Rondinone, Peter. "Teacher Background and Student Needs." *Journal of Basic Writing* 10.1 (1991): 41–53.

Rose, Mike. "The Language of Exclusion: Writing Instruction at the University." *College English* 47 (April 1985): 341–59.

———. *Lives on the Boundary.* New York: Penguin, 1989.

———. "Remedial Writing Courses: A Critique and a Proposal." *The Writing Teacher's Sourcebook.* 2nd ed. Ed. Gary Tate and Edward P. J. Corbett. New York: Oxford UP, 1988. 318–36.

Rouse, John. "The Politics of Composition." *College English* 41 (Sept. 1979): 1–12.

Royer, Daniel J., and Roger Gilles. "Directed Self-Placement: An Attitude of Orientation." *College Composition and Communication* 50 (Sept. 1998): 54–70.

Scribner, Sylvia, and Michael Cole. "Unpackaging Literacy." *Perspectives on Literacy.* Ed. Eugene R. Kintgen, Barry M. Kroll, and Mike Rose. Carbondale: Southern Illinois UP, 1988. 57–70.

Severino, Carol. "Where the Cultures of Basic Writers and Academia Intersect: Cultivating the Common Ground." *Journal of Basic Writing* 11.1 (1992): 4–15.

Shaughnessy, Mina. "Diving In: An Introduction to Basic Writing." *Mina P. Shaughnessy: Her Life and Work.* Jane Maher. Urbana, IL: NCTE, 1997. 255–62.

———. "The English Professor's Malady." *Mina P. Shaughnessy: Her Life and Work.* Jane Maher. Urbana, IL: NCTE, 1997. 291–98.

———. *Errors and Expectations: A Guide for the Teacher of Basic Writing.* New York: Oxford UP, 1977.

———. "The Miserable Truth." *Mina P. Shaughnessy: Her Life and Work.* Jane Maher. Urbana, IL: NCTE, 1997. 263–69.

———. "Open Admissions and the Disadvantaged Teacher." *Mina P. Shaughnessy: Her Life and Work.* Jane Maher. Urbana, IL: NCTE, 1997. 249–54.

———. "Speaking and Doublespeaking About Standards." *Mina P. Shaughnessy: Her Life and Work.* Jane Maher. Urbana, IL: NCTE, 1997. 270–78.

Smitherman, Geneva. "Toward a National Public Policy on Language." *College English* 49 (Jan. 1987): 29–36.

Soliday, Mary. "From the Margins to the Mainstream: Reconceiving Remediation." *College Composition and Communication* 47 (Feb. 1996): 85–100.

Sommers, Nancy. "Responding to Student Writing." *College Composition and Communication* 33 (May 1982): 148–56.

———. "Revision Strategies of Student Writers and Experienced Adult Writers." *College Composition and Communication* 31 (1980): 378–88.

Steedman, Carolyn. *The Tidy House.* London: Virago, 1982.

Stygall, Gail. "Resisting Privilege: Basic Writing and Foucault's Author Function." *College Composition and Communication* 45 (Oct. 1994): 320–41.

Traub, James. *City on a Hill: Testing the American Dream at City College.* Reading, PA: Addison-Wesley, 1994.

Villanueva, Victor. *Bootstraps: From an American Academic of Color.* Urbana, IL: NCTE, 1993.

Vygotsky, Lev. *Mind in Society: The Development of Higher Psychological Processes.* Ed. Michael Cole, et al. Cambridge, MA: Harvard UP, 1978.

Weaver, Constance. *Teaching Grammar in Context.* Portsmouth, NH: Boynton/Cook, 1996.

Technology and the Teaching of Writing

CHARLES MORAN

As computer technology has evolved over the past two decades, writing teachers have found that they could adapt this emerging technology to radically different pedagogies. In the early 1980s, the "age of the microcomputer," technology seemed to support invention, writing, and revising, activities that defined process-based pedagogies. At the same time, however, this same technology supported microcomputer-based skill-and-drill exercises, which grew from the print-based workbooks that were a staple of the current-traditional curriculum. In the early 1990s, when local area networks and the Internet began to become more readily available, these new manifestations of computer-based technology supported a social, constructivist pedagogy. Today, as the Web captures our imaginations, we find that composing in hypermedia and adding graphics and sound to our writing seem increasingly appropriate activities in our writing courses, and as our students gain access to the Web, the research paper returns to the center of our consciousness, though perhaps in new forms.

Even though there is not a specific pedagogy associated with emerging technologies, writing teachers need to know about these technologies so that they may incorporate their use, or not, as they deem appropriate, into their classroom practice, and so that they may advise and teach those of their students who have access to these technologies and who are using them in their writing. I don't mean to suggest that we should all uncritically "dive in" to the new technology. As Cynthia L. Selfe pointed out in her Chair's address at the 1998 annual meeting of the Conference on College Composition and Communication, parents, taxpayers, and legislators seem to be willing to invest in educational technology even as they are disinvesting in public K–12 education. There is pressure on colleges and universities, too, to keep up with technology. If one does not, as the saying goes, one is roadkill on the information highway. This pressure on educators to use technology exists despite the fact that, as Todd Oppenheimer has noted, there is no proof yet that technology improves students' learning. In my own situation at the University of Massachusetts, we cheerfully spend money on computer-equipped classrooms, money that, if it were spent instead on direct instruction (teachers), would reduce our average class size significantly. Is spending our resources on technology cost effective? It depends on the calculus we use.

Whether we choose to dive in, or resist, or merely float along with the current, technology is affecting our work as writing teachers. Indeed, computers have entered the mainstream. No longer is computer talk the province of enthusiast publications like *Wired* or *Byte*. *The New York Times* now has a full section headed "Circuits" that it runs every Thursday, with, on August 13, 1998, articles on the ways in which computer vocabulary has moved into the lexicon of daily speech and writing, on new Web search engines, on an online textbook store for students, and on a present danger: the transmission of viruses through e-mail. A popular magazine on things scientific, *Discover*, now runs a "personal tech" column. Even *Consumer Reports* does what it can to review computers, modems, and software, and it now runs a regular section titled "Living with Technology," with, in its August 1998 issue, advice about finding and joining newsgroups and about dealing with problems you might be having with your Web browser. Computers invisibly schedule our air travel, conduct our financial transactions, and, as we drive our automobiles, control the engine's valve timing, spark advance, and fuel injection systems. In our field, our students will increasingly use computers to mediate their reading and writing; and as teachers we will increasingly use computers to mediate and support our students' learning.

At the moment, the "home computer" is the unit of currency, a large, clunky piece of machinery, obtrusively the staple of our computer-equipped writing classrooms. As liquid-crystal display (LCD) screens evolve and as computers continue to become smaller and more powerful, we will be teaching, and our students learning, assisted by technology that works for us unobtrusively, invisibly, as now is the case in our automobiles. It is my belief that technology will gradually infuse the work we writing teachers do, eventually becoming, in Mark Weiser's phrase, "ubiquitous computing," or, in the phrase adopted by the Carnegie-Mellon Institute for Complex Engineered Systems, "wearable computing" (Jannot). Whether this future is seen as "good" or "bad" depends on one's perspective. There are prophets of doom like Sven Birkirts, who see in the advent of screen text the end of civilization as we know it; there are prophet evangelists like Michael Joyce, who see the new text as inherently democratic, a medium that will release creativity and empower the individual. In this chapter, and in my own teaching, I take the pragmatic view: computers have altered our landscape. They have changed the medium in which some fraction of our students read and write. Therefore we, as writing teachers, need to pay attention to what is happening. On the basis of this knowledge, we will be able to make informed decisions about our use of technology in our teaching.

To make our subject manageable, I will begin with an overview of general bibliographic resources in our field. I will then move into the several applications of computer technology that writing teachers have included in their classroom practice: word processing, electronic mail, online chat programs, and the

Web/hypertext/hypermedia. I make these divisions, knowing as I do that computer applications in our field are steadily converging: e-mail and the Web are
now interrelated, and we can compose Web pages on word processors. But the
taxonomy I have chosen, though not "true," will be useful, because it maps
easily onto the activities that seem likely to continue to be the staples of our
writing classrooms: writing, revising, and editing; class discussion; responding
to writing; and research. In each of these sections I will summarize what we
think we know about the implications of the application for our teaching practice. After these "applications" sections, I will describe a number of issues that
confront us as we work with emerging technologies: the ways in which gender, race, and social class may affect our students as online writers; the implications of the new technology for writers who are second-language learners;
and what we think and know about the ways in which the new technology affects basic writers. I will conclude with a section on an issue that includes and
sharpens the others: our students' differential access to technology.

✎ AN OVERVIEW OF SOURCES IN THE FIELD: HISTORIES, BIBLIOGRAPHIES, ONLINE RESOURCES

A great deal has been written in the past twenty-five years about the integration of computers into our work as writing teachers. For a review and history
of much of this writing, I refer you to Gail Hawisher and colleagues' *Computers and the Teaching of Writing in American Higher Education, 1979–1994: A History* (1996). This book, the first in the Ablex series titled New Directions in
Computers and Composition Studies, approaches its subject chronologically:
chapter 1 is headed "1979–1982: The Profession's Early Experience with Modern Technology"; chapter 2 "1983–1985: Growth and Enthusiasm"; chapter 3
"1986–1988: Emerging Research, Theory, and Professionalism"; chapter 4
"1989–1991: Coming of Age: The Rise of Cross-Disciplinary Perspectives and a
Consideration of Difference"; and chapter 5 "1992–1994: Looking Forward."
The final section is an edited transcript of an online discussion by young
teacher/scholars then just entering the profession. Each of the five chapters
opens with its period's scholarly and pedagogical context, then presents the
technological context, then reviews the work of writing teachers and scholars
who were using technology during this time, and concludes with an interview
of a teacher/scholar who was particularly central to that period. The book is
useful to the teacher who believes that the past may have value to those who
will chart the future. It does not tell the whole story, as reviewers have pointed
out: the book does not include the work that has been done in teaching writing to second-language learners; and it does not attempt to include a history
of computer-assisted instruction (CAI).

For an update, one could turn to *Transitions: Teaching Writing in Computer-
Supported and Traditional Classrooms* (1998), by Mike Palmquist and co-workers.
This book includes as an appendix a fourteen-page "List of Related Readings"
that is nicely divided into sections of selected titles under headings such as

"Computers and Collaboration," "Human Factors Issues," "Computer Classroom Design," and "Software Selection, Evaluation, and Development." The list carries titles as recent as 1996. The book is addressed to teachers teaching in computer-supported classrooms, a topic that five years ago would have rated its own major heading, but today seems too specialized and potentially dated. The PC-filled room, though it may be with us in some places for some time, is a stage in our evolution as writing teachers. When and if most of our students have access to computers in dormitory room or home settings, the computer-equipped classroom will seem much less necessary than it now does to writing programs. Yet a number of us do teach writing in computer-supported facilities, and there is therefore a substantial literature on this subject. For the teacher who is contemplating a semester in a computer-supported writing classroom, *Transitions* is the best single source. The book draws on and summarizes previous research carried out in computer-equipped classrooms, and it adds to and updates earlier research through its authors' own research study. As is the case with all books and even most print articles on technology, the Web was an infant when the research was done, so the book is extremely light on Web-related pedagogy.

Both *Transitions* and *Computers and the Teaching of Writing in American Higher Education* are the work of a community of teachers/scholars that has grown up around a journal, *Computers and Composition*, that has been regularly published since November 1983, co-edited first by Cynthia L. Selfe and Kathleen E. Kiefer, and since 1988 (vol. 5, no. 3) by Selfe and Gail E. Hawisher. This group had its origins in the Conference on College Composition and Communication (CCCC) and in particular one of this conference's special interest groups, "The Fifth C." The group continues to meet at its own annual Computers and Writing Conference, a good place to meet fellow teachers/scholars and to hear papers that specifically address issues in this field. *Computers and Composition* is now a substantial journal, published triquarterly by Ablex. It is carried by major libraries, but if you have difficulty finding print copy, the journal, as of this writing, maintains a Web site, http://www.cwrl.utexas.edu/~ccjrnl, where you can find archived text from back issues, going back to volume 1, number 1. This Web site is accessible as well through the NCTE Web site, which may be a more permanent and reliable address: http://www.ncte.org. As of this writing, in October 1998, full texts of articles are online through volume 10 (1993), and abstracts are available through the current issue. The editors are adding full texts of articles, though it is not clear at this writing whether the print journal's publisher will smile on the project of publishing online issues that are still subject to copyright.

For other bibliographical sources, I'd suggest CCC Online, a Web site with a searchable archive (abstracts only) of articles and reviews in *College Composition and Communication* going back to 1991. The Council is in the process of deciding whether to move full texts online. You can reach CCC Online through the above-mentioned NCTE Web site. The "Annotated Bibliography of Research in the Teaching of English," published annually in the May issue of *Research in the Teaching of English,* is worth looking at, too. Its scope includes K–12 as well as postsecondary education. I do not suggest what might seem an obvious print source, the CCCC *Bibliography of Composition and Rhetoric*, because this bibliography, notoriously difficult to access by subject, has stalled at 1994, at least for the short term. At this writing, plans are afoot to update the bibliography and put it online. If and when this happens, it will be found through the NCTE Web site, most likely located at a revised CCC Online site. For the ways in which technology has changed the field of technical and professional writing, the best entry point is Patricia Sullivan and Jennie Dauterman's *Electronic Literacies in the Workplace*. The chapters in this 1996 anthology look at corporate e-mail, classroom use of work-place simulation, online editing, and work-place writing with electronic tools. A further resource is the *IEEE Transactions on Professional Communication*, a journal sponsored by the Institute of Electrical and Electronics Engineers. Articles in this journal are abstracted in the IEEE Bibliographies Online, at http://www.ieee.org, though one has to be a member to use this resource.

✧ APPLICATIONS OF COMPUTER TECHNOLOGIES FOR WRITERS AND TEACHERS

Word Processing

Depending on our situation, some, many, or all of our students will have access to word processing. These students may be composing differently on screen than they would on paper, though the evidence for this difference is not at all clear, and differences, where they exist, are likely to be determined by context more than they are by essential differences between screen and paper. Early research on online writers attempted to discover essential, global differences between writers who worked online and offline. In 1991 Elizabeth Klem and I summarized the best research in the field up to that time in a chapter titled "Computers and Instructional Strategies in the Teaching of Writing." In this summary we found that students might (Sudol) or might not (Daiute) be revising more online than they had on paper; that writers might be having difficulty seeing their text whole (Haas "Seeing"), might be spending less time planning before they wrote (Haas "Planning"), and might be helped (Kiefer and Smith) or hindered (Dobrin) by spell checkers and grammar checkers.

In retrospect it seems clear that looking for essential differences between screen text and print text is a dead end, because writers write differently, and even a given writer will write differently on different occasions. Yet these early studies alert us to the different ways in which writers may react to a move, forced or voluntary, from print to screen. And although these early studies focus on word processing, which is practically a transparent technology these days, until there is universal access technology—not a likely scenario—we will always be teaching students for whom writing online is a new or strange experience. So to a degree, as teachers of writing, we are teachers of word processing—not teachers of computer literacy, for that is not our job, but teachers who have read the relevant research and who, as online writers ourselves, have discovered helpful procedures. It may be, for example, that a particular student writer includes large swatches of unedited freewriting in her final draft. She will do this on line, let us say, because cutting and pasting is so easy. She does her freewriting and then, without opening a new file, starts her essay by writing an introductory paragraph before the freewriting, which she includes whole and unedited in her final draft. She will need to be coached in a particular way: helped to preserve the generative power of her freewriting, while editing it toward the needs of a reader. Another student writer may revise by adding new material to the end of his piece. His editors suggest that he should include X in his piece, so he does—in a section tacked on to the end of his earlier draft. This student writer will need to be helped to plan, to outline, online, before writing or during. Yet another writer who is being intimidated by a grammar checker may need to be helped to understand that computers can't read and that most of the advice he is getting is not useful to him. This writer's desk partner, however, may be one whose sentences are habitually lengthy and complex and may be able to make good use of the information that the grammar checker can supply.

All student writers will need to be helped to understand that they can to a degree control their writing environment by manipulating the word processing program they are writing with. If auto-correct functions irritate, distract, or mislead, they can be turned off. If, as Haas suggests ("Seeing"), writers online have difficulty extrapolating the whole text from the segment that is on screen, then writers can be taught one or more of the word processing functions that help a writer navigate the digitized text: bookmarks, the search function, the keystrokes that move one swiftly to the beginning and end of the document, and Windows functions that make it possible to "see" more than one section of the text on the same screen. If it is the case for writers that the liveliest and most prestigious part of the screen is the menu bars and scroll bars that surround the text, as Stephen Bernhardt suggests, then they can be shown how to optimize their screens for writing by taking control of the screen through the "view" function on the toolbar. Some handbooks have sections titled "Working on a Word Processor," which give advice that is inevitably generic and qualified. Much better than generic handbook advice is the context-sensitive advice given by a teacher who knows the research in the field, has written online, and has reflected on that practice.

The best recent articles on the subject of computer-mediated writing are Bernhardt's "The Shape of Text to Come: The Texture of Print on Screens" and Carolyn Dowling's "Word Processing and the Ongoing Difficulty of Writing." Bernhardt gives us "nine dimensions of variation that help map the differences between paper and on-screen text" (151): relative to print on paper, online text tends to be more "situationally embedded," "interactive," "functionally mapped," "modular," "navigable," "hierarchically embedded," "spacious," "graphically rich," and "customizable and publishable" (151–52). This taxonomy of difference will be helpful to teachers and students as they themselves move between paper and screen. In "Word Processing and the Ongoing Difficulty of Writing" Dowling begins with the premise that writing is, simply, hard work, and that those who believe that the computer will somehow make this work easier are in for an unpleasant surprise. Indeed, if computers do seem to make writing easier, perhaps it is because some important writer work is being bypassed. Dowling notes that some writers report feeling "alienated" from their screen text; that others feel that when they write online they lose all sense of audience other than themselves; and that others find it difficult to come to closure when composing with text that can so easily be changed. Dowling's conclusion is extremely explicit, and, in my view, as close to the last word as we will find in this area: "The fact that writing continues to be perceived as a difficult activity . . . suggests the possibility that benefits of word processing might be counterbalanced . . . by aspects of the computing environment that render the activity, for some individuals, as fraught with problems in this medium as in others" (234).

Electronic Mail

Electronic mail (e-mail) makes it possible for teachers and students to communicate with one another during the intervals between their classes. E-mail is often included in the larger category of computer-mediated communication, or CMC, particularly in the field of distance learning, where students and teacher meet seldom, if at all, face to face. Writing teachers in campus settings may find that e-mail is a useful adjunct to their course, particularly if their class meets once each week and/or if students commute from a distance. Through e-mail, a teacher can construct a listserv for discussions; through e-mail a teacher can respond to student writing. The best present introduction to e-mail, for the writing teacher or for the student, is *English Online*, by Nick Carbone and Eric Crump. This handbook leads the reader gently through such e-mail-related topics as online conventions ("Netiquette"), e-mail acronyms and emoticons, signature files, mailing lists, telnet, and file transfer protocols (ftp).

If a writing teacher decides to use e-mail in a course, she or he needs to think about some of the characteristics of this medium. First, the language of e-mail bears a problematic relationship to American Standard English, a dialect that most of us believe we are privileging in our writing classes. Gail Hawisher and I summarized much of the research on the languages of e-mail in "The Rhetorics and Languages of Electronic Mail," a chapter in Ilana Snyder's *Page to Screen: Taking Literacy into the Electronic Era*. In this chapter we noted that the language of e-mail has been seen since its beginnings as related both to the written and spoken languages. We summarized recent studies of electronic language in Susan Herring's *Computer-mediated Communication: Linguistic, Social, and Cross-cultural Perspectives*: Collot and Belmore's analysis of the language used on bulletin board systems; Yates' analysis of the language of online conferences on the British conferencing network, CoSy; and Werry's analysis of the language used on what he terms Internet Relay Chat, something like real-time e-mail. All three studies found that in these rather different applications of e-mail, the language used has significant differences from both the written and spoken languages. Whether these differences signify a separate language or dialect is a matter of definition. What is clear is that writing in this medium is different from writing in print. The significance of this finding for teachers of writing is that we will find it difficult to insist that our students' e-mail writing conform to the standards we will apply to their formal essay writing.

Second, and certainly a contributor to the differences in language, is that the e-mail encounter is characteristically informal. Though I have received exquisitely formal e-mail from lawyers and from the occasional friend new to the medium, e-mail in the academic world tends to be chatty, invoking a relationship between correspondents that is casual and, in its ease and informality, potentially at odds with the conventional teacher-student relationship. Unlike the draft-by-draft revising that we encourage in our classes, e-mail is characteristically rapidly composed, uncensored, a species of freewriting. This is most true if the author composes online; with more advanced e-mail systems like Eudora, one can compose offline, at leisure, and then upload the message to the host computer. Yet even with Eudora correspondents, e-mail seems spontaneous, quick, and therefore open to dialogues that generate and exacerbate conflict.

Third, e-mail as a medium evokes intimacy, up to and including virtual, online sex. This sense of intimacy is a paradox because, unlike postal mail, e-mail has no envelope. E-mail is recorded and can, theoretically, be read by the system operator and anyone with system operator privileges. E-mail can also be copied and printed; it can be forwarded to other individuals without the author's knowledge; and it can be posted to lists. Most of us have been embarrassed at least once by a colleague who mistakenly posted to an entire department a message intended for one person's eyes only. This illusion of intimacy poses a problem for a teacher: How do we maintain appropriate authority online? As Gail Hawisher and I noted in 1997,

> In the conventional classroom, the teacher can draw on the students' previous experience—perhaps we should call it training?—of K–12 schooling. In the conventional classroom, this training has been associated with an array of visual cues that the teacher can use to signal expected behavior . . . the teacher's desk, the clock, the lectern, the gradebook, perhaps even the American flag! On-line, we usually have, for now, written language alone. In the new medium, the teacher and student together will have to establish what is, and what is not, appropriate behavior. (118)

Teachers who are considering online responding to students' writing should read what I consider the best recent book on the larger subject of responding to student writing generally: *Writing to Learn: Strategies for Assigning and Responding to Writing Across the Disciplines*, edited by Mary Deane Sorcinelli and Peter Elbow. This book includes, among others, chapters by Toby Fulwiler on the letter as response, by Art Young on response as "academic conversation," by Anne Herrington on "Developing and Responding to Major Writing Projects," and by Peter Elbow on high-stakes and low-stakes writing. For our particular subject, the Hawisher/Moran chapter titled "Responding to Writing On-Line" is directly pertinent, in that it brings together what we know about e-mail correspondence and applies it to the business of responding to student writing. The authors of this chapter argue that as a medium e-mail is so different from handwritten comments-in-the-margins that as we begin to respond online, we may be forced to rethink our assumptions about responding to student writing.

The teacher who incorporates e-mail in her pedagogy needs to remember that the digital "language" of e-mail is ASCII, the American Standard Code for Information Exchange. As Cynthia L. Selfe and Richard J. Selfe, Jr. have noted, ASCII is an ancient code that can handle only ninety-five characters. It can therefore cope only with lowercase and uppercase letters, numerals, and marks of punctuation: no diacritics or non-English characters. In our chapter on the rhetorics and languages of e-mail, Gail Hawisher and I build on the Selfes' work, noting that "to e-mail our friends Martín or Björn, we are obliged to 'english' their names, omitting the accents on the 'i' of Martín and the 'o' of Björn, leaving both somewhat Ellis-islanded, Americanised" (97). On e-mail, and in ASCII, all names are not considered equal. As teachers, we need to remember this. We can't change it, but we can make our students aware of the situation, and make it clear that as we use e-mail in our classes, we are unwittingly supporting the "English-only" movement that is today gaining ground in our country.

Finally, the teacher who considers using e-mail in her class needs to consider the extent to which her work load may increase as a result of this new practice. The great boon, and the great evil, of computer-mediated communication is that it makes it possible for us to be available twenty-four hours a day, seven days a week, in effect putting in unpaid hours for our employers. Offline, we have evolved strategies for limiting our availability: we post office hours when students can meet with us, and we have some way of screening our incoming telephone calls—either a secretary/receptionist or a voice-mail system. Online, until and unless we develop conventions that will protect us— such as telling our students that we don't read our e-mail on weekends—we can be reached at all hours, Monday through Sunday.

Online Discussion

Online, synchronous discussions are possible inside and outside computer-equipped classrooms: through distance-learning networks such as CoSy, through LAN-based software such as Daedalus *Interchange*, and through Web-based courseware like *Web-CT*. When LAN-based chat programs first appeared, they were hailed by writing teachers as an unalloyed good. Class discussions, it was argued, were now written, not oral, and therefore furthered our goals as writing teachers by increasing the amount of writing our students were doing. A number of researchers believed that these online discussions were more democratic than offline discussions: online, the argument was made, people who were marginalized in face-to-face group dynamics could and did move from the margins into the center (e.g., Faigley "Subverting the Electronic Work-book," *Fragments of Rationality*). Women in particular, it was widely believed, gained voice in the online forum. Later research, however, has discovered that we carry our culture with us as we move online. Two good sources on this topic are Susan Romano's "The Egalitarianism Narrative: Whose Story? Which Yard-stick?" and Selfe and Paul Meyer's "Testing Claims for On-Line Conferences."

The issue of authority arises in online discussions, and in very much the same form as it did in our consideration of e-mail. Reduced to its simplest ex-pression, the issue is this: Will students behave when they move online? A num-ber of teachers have reported online discussions that moved rapidly off topic; others have reported that in the online discussion students are more likely to "flame" one another or to use language that is hurtful to others in the discus-sion. Why this happens is in doubt. Most researchers have adopted the "re-duced social cues" hypothesis, arguing that because online we can't see or hear our correspondent, we are freed from social constraints that govern face-to-face communication and become asocial or antisocial in our behavior (e.g., Sproull and Kiesler). Others argue that in the absence of social cues we fall back on the cultural stereotypes that we have available to us, becoming, for example, the "aggressive male fraternity jock" (Spears and Lea). In this view, we are not freed from constraint, but are driven to accept narrowly defined and often in-appropriate models of behavior. In either case the phenomenon is the same: online discourse can and does get out of hand, apparently more rapidly than face-to-face discourse. The teacher, therefore, needs to decide what kind of mod-erator she will be. Andrew Feenberg, in a useful chapter titled "The Written World: On the Theory and Practice of Computer Conferencing," argues for a "strong" moderator (33), one who both contextualizes the individual messages in the discussion and acts as a monitor. In my own practice, admittedly con-servative, I follow Feenberg's advice, making as certain as I can that the online discussion has direction: a problem that the group must solve, a brainstorm session to generate material, or a chance for individual writers to update oth-ers on their progress on a particular assignment.

A full account of a class that fully utilized the online discussion capability of its computer-supported classroom is "Visible Conversation and Academic Inquiry" by Gregory G. Colomb and Joyce A. Simutis. This account carefully documents students' learning as they participate in extended Interchange ses-sions. As they report on their study, Columb and Simutis squarely face the ped-agogical, sociological, and psychological issues that I have outlined above, and they do so in a way that will be extremely helpful to the teacher who is con-sidering adding online discussion to the curriculum.

The Web/Hypertext/Hypermedia

In what now seem the "old times," which is to say the early 1990s, it would have been possible to treat the Web, hypertext, and hypermedia separately. In-deed, there was in the early 1990s a powerful literature that defined *hypertext* as a new field. George Landow and others at Brown University reported on huge hypertexts that were developed in connection with literature courses (Delany and Landow). Michael Joyce, Stuart Moulthrop, and others developed and reported on *Storyspace*, a program for composing in hypertext designed for computer-supported classrooms. While *hypertext* was being used in English and in composition studies, in the larger world the defining term was *hypermedia*, as graphics, sound, and video were linked to text, and vice versa, in online help manuals and in CD-ROM encyclopedias and other reference works. Today the development of the Web browser and the consequent evolution of the Web have, for our purposes, subsumed the earlier technologies. At the moment I write this, hypertext seems a somewhat antique and limited conception, and hypermedia the very warp and woof of the Web.

For the writing teacher in today's classroom, knowing about these media is essential. A quick way in is Nicholas C. Burbules' chapter, "The Rhetorics of the Web." Burbules argues that reading on the Web is not the same as reading a book, despite the fact that the Web uses the page as its founding metaphor. When we read in a book, we will "link" what we read with previous reading or other experience. The links we make as we read print are our own links. One could argue, of course, that these links have been "made" by our prior experience: that we have already been written, linked. But still, if we grant the reader any agency at all, connections made in print are more the reader's than those discovered on the Web. When we read on the Web we click on links that have been made by others. Burbules argues therefore that we need to be teaching "critical hyperreading" (118): readers should

> know what goes into selecting material for a page, making links, organizing a cluster of separate pages into a hyperlinked Web site. . . . The more that one is aware of *how* this is done, the more one can be aware *that* it was done and that it *could* have been done otherwise. This discloses the apparent "naturalness" or invisibility of such designer/author choices, and grants the hyperreader the opportunity to stand outside them—to question, criticize, and imagine alternatives. (118–19)

Burbules notes as well that hypertextual reading habits include "surfing," which, if assumed as a reading practice, drives the need for the quick "hook," a dance on the surface, as opposed to a long read in which attention is sustained. He looks at links through "tropes" or "tools" of rhetoric: the link as metaphor, metonymy, antistasis—the link as a rhetorical device that is persuasive, not neutral.

The Web is not only a place where readers read; it is a place where student writers can, and if they can they will, do research. Unlike a college or university library, however, on the Web there is no librarian or print editor watching over the materials that are included in the collection. On the Web a search may turn up the home page of *The New York Times* and the home page of a 10-year-old preteen. Both will be presented by the screen as they are, with no indication that one is more authoritative than the other. So students and teachers will need to wrestle with the question of the authority of the writers' sources—not a new question, certainly, but one that we now have to ask more steadily. College/university librarians will be on top of this problem and are the teacher's first and best resource, though they may be unduly suspicious of the Web and its contents. Many libraries maintain "Internet toolboxes" on their Web sites, filled with links to search engines and advice about using and citing online sources. Both the MLA and APA lay out their conventions for online citation on their Web sites, and Diana Hacker's "Bedford Booklet," *Research and Documentation in the Electronic Age*, includes not only major library resources—indexes, encyclopedias, dictionaries, companions—but also major Web sites in the subdisciplines of the humanities, social sciences, and sciences, as well as advice on search engines, Internet search strategies, and ways of evaluating Internet sources.

Will the results of online research be fundamentally different from results of print research? The jury is out on this question. In "'Pulling Down' Books vs. 'Pulling Up' Files," Karen Ruhleder looks at what has happened to research in the field of classics since the widespread use of the *Thesaurus Linguae Grecae*, a CD-ROM-based, searchable database that contains the texts of classic Greek literature. She finds that in Classics "the textual landscape has become broader, but it has also become flatter" (187), as researchers trade the breadth of reference made possible by the searchable database for the depth that Ruhleder sees in scholarship that was the result of having spent years working with a single text. On the other hand, journalists tend to see the Web as a necessity for reporters and their writing, because its breadth and speed suit their work exactly.

An online resource for teachers who want to connect the Web with their pedagogies and with their classroom practice is *Kairos*, an electronic journal described by its editor, Greg Siering, as "designed to serve as a peer reviewed resource for teachers, researchers, and tutors of writing at the college and university level, including Technical Writing, Business Writing, Professional Communication, Creative Writing, Composition, and Literature." The editorial board describes their focus in these terms: "Our goal at *Kairos* is to offer a progressive and innovative online forum for the exploration of writing, learning, and teaching in hypertextual environments like the World Wide Web." Though Web sites come and go, I'm guessing that *Kairos* will persist. Kairos' Web address is http://english.ttu.edu/kairos.

↪ ISSUES

Computers and "Difference"

In the previous sections we have looked at applications of computer technology without substantially considering how these applications might be used differently by, and have different effects on, different populations of students. It should be obvious that this technology is not neutral: as Selfe and Selfe have clearly demonstrated, computer interfaces, with their desktops, files, telephones, and faxes, reflect the values of the white collar professions; and as I noted above in the section on e-mail, the language of our computers is English, relegating all other languages and their cultures to second-class status. It should be intuitively obvious to us as well, however, that our students differ from one another: each brings to writing and reading, and to working with emerging technologies, a distinct history that helps determine how they will connect with the activity that we are trying to help them learn. If our intuition in this matter should need some support, it can be found in the work of Shirley Brice Heath, Lisa Delpit, and others who have studied the ways in which literacy functions in different cultures. But how can these differences be best described? Predicted? Understood? Clearly teachers who are planning to teach in computer classrooms need to know the best of what we now know about possible differences in the ways in which our students are connecting with technology. These differences can be seen along the axes of race, gender, and social class, and they can be seen in terms of the overlapping categories current in our field: the teaching of underprepared writers (basic writing) and the teaching of second-language learners (ESL instruction). In the paragraphs that follow, I will lay out what seems to me to be the best advice we can find as we begin to foreground the fact that technology is not neutral and that it may affect different people differently.

There has been a great deal of research on the ways in which women and men connect with computers. A good entry point to this subject is Emily Jessup's "Feminism and Computers in Composition Instruction." This 1991 study summarizes then-extant research on the gender gap in school computer use, where the computer is seen as a "boy's toy" (339). It gives statistics on computer camp attendance, subscriptions to computer magazines, and studies of computer user's confidence, all of which show a distinct gender gap. For the reader who wants to go further in the work of this time, the Fall 1990 issue of *Signs* is a rich lode. In this issue Ruth Perry and Lisa Greber look at the historical relationship between women and technology, argue that computers are bad for women in that they fragment work, isolate, and constitute a health hazard, and conclude that "as feminists we must decipher how and to what extent technologies reflect or reinforce the patriarchal order" (76). In "The Army and the Microworld," Paul N. Edwards reminds us of the close and continuing connection between computing and the military, still visible in the "abort-retry-fail" language that can surface even today when our computers "crash" or our applications and files are "killed." And in "Epistemological Pluralism: Styles and Voices Within the Computer Culture," Sherry Turkle and Seymour Papert report on their research into men's and women's programming styles. They see men generally using a "hard" programming style, what they call a "black box" formal approach: beginning with the big picture, planning. They see women programmers as at odds with this privileged mode, and wanting to program in a "soft" style: what Turkle and Papert, borrowing from Levi-Strauss, call "bricolage"—starting with bits and pieces and building up the program gradually (134–35).

For a more recent look at gender and computing, I suggest Gail Hawisher and Patricia Sullivan's "Women on the Networks," a chapter in *Feminism and Composition Studies*. Hawisher and Sullivan summarize the early research that claimed that online spaces were inherently egalitarian, and point to contemporary studies that see women as victims online, as they are, more often than men, offline. The authors summarize, too, the research that shows that even in apparently egalitarian online conferences, "women make fewer and shorter contributions than men and that both men and women respond more frequently to men's postings than to women's" (176). They turn from this summary, however, to document a "small group of academic women who persist." (176).

Though there is a great deal written about gender and technology, there is very little research explicitly on the ways in which race may make a difference in how students write and learn online. What we have suggests that race, by itself, is not a useful set of categories to work with. In "Race on the Superhighway: How E-mail Affects African American Student Writers," Teresa Redd and Victoria Massey find that African American students do not find enfranchisement online and that they "used fewer features of the African American oral tradition than we expected, fewer AAE grammatical forms and fewer 'styling' devices" (262). I can only speculate here, but it seems to me that the students studied knew that they were in school, under the watchful gaze of the teacher, and that they were writing to that audience, one that has traditionally disapproved of students' African American English in a classroom context. They were therefore, even on e-mail, on their best "school" behavior, perhaps experiencing what Keith Gilyard has called "a kind of enforced educational schizophrenia" (163) which he argues is a common element in the experience of African American students in America's schools. And Todd Taylor, in "The Persistence of Difference in Networked Classrooms," gives us a short case study of three African Americans in his technical writing class. Taylor finds practically no common ground among these students as online writers. From this study he concludes that we need to look beyond or through any stereotypes we might be moved to create, and consider our students as "individuals who defy tight demographic or cultural grouping" (177).

Research on computers in basic writing and ESL classrooms can be seen to be implicitly about race and social class, given the demographics of these courses in American postsecondary education, so this is another important thread for the writing teacher to follow. A good entry point for research on computers and basic writing students is Lisa Gerrard's ancient-but-still-useful chapter, "Computers and Basic Writers." Gerrard finds that basic writers who write on computers "enjoy using the computer, spend more time revising, feel more confident and in control of their writing, and socialize more with their classmates" (96). She argues that "these changes in attitude and practice provide conditions that foster learning," though she notes that the technology "seems to have had a more discernible impact on writers than on their prose" (97). A more recent study, Susan Stan and Terence G. Collins' "Basic Writing: Curricular Interactions with the New Technology," is not so careful in its claims. The authors give us a substantial overview of the field of basic writing: its history, its growth, its relation to the field of composition studies, and the ways in which technology has been brought into the work of teaching basic writing students. They survey teachers of basic writing to find the applications these teachers are making of emerging technologies. They summarize teacher reports and small-scale studies that report that basic writers' attitudes toward writing are more positive after a semester's work in computer-supported classrooms, that computers seem to help their revising practices, and that computers improve the appearance and content of student papers. It is hard not to share the authors' enthusiasm here, but I finally do not trust what seems to be their deepest argument, one that surfaces in their last paragraph but is implicit throughout: that if basic writing programs could only get access to enough technology, their students' transitions into the academic world would be easier and faster.

A good introduction to the use of computers in ESL classrooms is "The Wired World of Second-Language Education," by Michele Knobel and colleagues. The authors of this chapter are refreshingly aware of the extent to which "educators and learners alike face massive hype and pressure from commercial and political sources to 'technologise' teaching and learning" (21). They usefully describe the various applications of the new technology in ESL classrooms, and then zoom in on what they term "asynchronous communications": e-mail and discussion lists. They summarize the claims that have been made for the value of this particular application and then examine the studies that have tested these claims. They conclude that "the sketchy 'evidence' available from studies and projects we have investigated suggests that proponents of e-mail are longer on 'process' than they are on 'outcomes,' and tend to emphasise attitudes and feelings over downright competence in language use" (47). A short recent account is George Braine's "Beyond Word Processing: Networked Computers in ESL Writing Classes." Braine summarizes past studies of ESL writers on chat programs housed in local area networks in computer-supported classrooms, studies that have found that writing on chat programs has a positive effect on ESL writers' attitudes but not always on their writing. He reports as well on his own study, which compared the first draft and finished writing of students who peer edited and discussed their writing online with that of students who peer edited and discussed offline. Braine's study finds that the first drafts and final drafts written in the networked classroom were of higher quality than those written in a standard classroom, but that the improvement between drafts was marginally higher in the standard classroom.

Access

An important difference among our writing students is the degree to which they have access to emerging technologies. If we believe that word processing, e-mail, or the Web are in any way useful to writers, then our students' equitable access to computers becomes an important issue. In my first-year writing class in spring 1997, a few students had their own enormously powerful computer workstations in their dormitory rooms; several had their own modest Macs or IBM clones; but more than half had to borrow computer time from roommates or friends or seek out the very few public access terminals that the university provides. The students with the expensive computers produced papers with Web research and graphics downloaded from the Web. Some students without their own computers submitted drafts written in ink. I have learned not to require "typewritten" drafts, because there are, of course, no typewriters to be found. "Typed" today means composed on, or typed into, a computer and printed out on a laser printer. I have worked with the faculty at a local community college, where students have essentially no access to computers, at home or at the college. However, at the expensive private colleges in our area, students have practically unlimited access to computers. Access here is a function of wealth: not gender, not race, but wealth. Certainly these are overlapping categories: in America you are more likely to be poor if you are a person of color; you are most likely to be poor, and your children as well, if you are a single mother. Yet women at Smith College, just ten miles west of us, have more access to technology than do most men at the University of Massachusetts. As Americans, we are reluctant to admit that we are a nation divided by wealth and social class. But we are, and this wealth gap produces a technology gap, just as it produces a health care gap, or an access-to-legal-services gap, or a gap in access to all goods and services that can be bought and paid for.

Technology has made this wealth gap, always present in our writing classes, more dramatically visible. When I began teaching, I would always bring in extra pencils and paper, so that a student who did not have access to the then current writing technology would not be at a disadvantage in my class. It was my way of leveling the playing field. Because pencil and paper were cheap, my tactic did not cost me a great deal. Today, an up-to-date PC and printer cost $1,500 at the least. Web and e-mail access are additional costs, as are backup hardware, surge suppressers, software, maintenance, and depreciation. In a recent article in *Scientific American*, W. Wayt Gibbs estimates that it costs a corporation $13,000 per year to own a PC. It is hard to imagine that it costs an institution, or an individual, substantially less.

So how can I today level the playing field for my students? A typical answer in our profession is "By creating more public access terminals" (e.g., Palmquist et al., 191). To this, I respond by drawing a distinction between what I will call "home access" and "institutional access." Home access is when you have your computer at "home," perhaps a home office or a dormitory room. On this computer is your software, with your settings. The Web browser has your bookmarks, the word processor has your screen and page settings, and the cursor travels at a speed that you have chosen. On your computer's hard drive are your files: course notes, earlier papers written for this and other courses. On your e-mail program is your personal address list. Your CD collection is nearby, your coffeemaker at hand. You have constructed a work environment that is productive for you.

Institutional access, on the other hand, is traveling across campus to a computer, bringing with you your floppy disk with your files. Maybe it is February, and, in New England, after 4:30 p.m. it is dark. Has the trip been dangerous?

Is the campus safe? Once you are at the lab, perhaps you have to wait for a computer, or perhaps not: this depends upon the hour and the academic calendar. If this is the week when papers are due in all courses, you will certainly have to wait. A sign on the wall reads "User time one hour. Be considerate!" Another sign reads "No Food or Drink in This Lab!" When you log on to the institution's terminal, you work with the institution's programs set in the way that the institution has determined. Perhaps in this lab the word processor's grammar-checker is on. If this disturbs you, you have to sort through "options" and "customize" menus to find out how to turn the program off. I'm painting a worst case scenario here, but it is not an unusual scenario. Some labs do allow food, some even allow or provide music. But the labs are still labs, not "home." And this is a great difference. Students with home access have a substantial advantage over students with institutional access.

What makes this access problem even more pressing for us than it may appear is that the wealth gap in America is increasing, and has been doing so for the past twenty years. This is a seemingly unstoppable trend: the rich get richer, the poor poorer. This topic does not get much press, despite the fact that a given issue of practically any national newspaper will contain articles about the "booming economy" and the "plight of the poor in America," often found in unintentionally ironic juxtaposition. A typical AP piece in our local newspaper, the *Daily Hampshire Gazette*, of May 12, 1998, begins, "Some 62,000 Massachusetts children younger than 12 go hungry during the year, despite the booming economy, according to the Physician Task Force on Child Hunger in Massachusetts" (10). A memorable issue of the Boston Sunday *Globe* of October 19, 1997, juxtaposed on its front page lead articles with these headlines: "Outgoing NU head tops in '96 Pay; Financial package for Curry near $1m," and "Rise seen in young homeless; Former wards of state swell ranks in shelters." The best book on the history, development, and causes of the American wealth gap is Paul Krugman's *Peddling Prosperity: Economic Sense and Nonsense in the Age of Diminished Expectations*. In the book he offers us this picture of what has been happening:

> Imagine two villages, each composed of one hundred families representing the percentiles of the family income distribution in a given year—in particular, a 1977 village and a 1989 village. According to CBO numbers, the total income of the 1989 village is about 10 percent higher than that of the 1977 village; but it is not true that the whole distribution is shifted up by 10 percent. Instead, the richest family in the 1989 village has twice the income of its counterpart in the 1977 village, while the bottom forty 1989 families actually have lower incomes than their 1977 counterparts. (138)

I wish that our field had written more on the question of access, but it has not. The best piece on the topic of access to computers is an early one, C. Paul Olson's chapter, "Who Computes?" in David Livingstone and colleagues' 1987 anthology, *Critical Pedagogy and Cultural Power*. In his chapter Olson considers the likely effect of computers on schooling, and argues that information technologies are likely to increase the wealth and power gap between rich and poor. In a chapter in the Hawisher and Selfe 1991 anthology titled *Evolving Perspectives on Computers and Composition Studies*, Mary Louise Gomez has argued for what she terms "equitable teaching" (320) with computers. She notes that even where there is sufficient software and hardware, "access and instruction are varied according to students' race, social class, and gender" (322). Other writers and researchers in our field either avoid this issue or give it a quick side glance and proceed. As I have said elsewhere, if as writing teachers we believe that writers are in any sense advantaged by technology, then access is the issue that drives all others before it.

Envoi

If you are a writing teacher, or a writing-teacher-in-training, you need to know the medium that most of your writing students will be working with. To the extent that these writers have access to technology, they will be using it. They will need, therefore, your best advice on moving between screen text and paper text as they compose and revise. If you are considering the use of e-mail or an online discussion as part of your course, or if you have students who will, whether you want them to or not, do their research on the Web, then you need to know about these scenes for writing. If you will be teaching in a computer-equipped classroom, then you need to think through your goals for your students' learning and consider the ways in which the available technology may help you and your students achieve these goals. Because your students are individuals, with different histories of experience, they will connect with the technology in different ways. To help them in their learning, you will need to know as much as you can about their access to, and attitudes toward, the technology that you will be asking them to use. Many of us early in our semesters have our students write their autobiographies as writers. In this way we hope to learn as much as we can about our students as writers, and we hope to help our students see themselves as writers. It is time now to add to this autobiography a new dimension: a question about the writing technologies your students use and their experience with, and attitudes toward, these technologies. In this way we will learn important information about our student writers, and we will help them become, as we are ourselves just now beginning to become, reflective and critical users of emerging technologies.

Bibliography

Bernhardt, Stephen A. "The Shape of Text to Come: The Texture of Print on Screens." *College Composition and Communication* 44 (1993): 151–75.

Birkirts, Sven. *The Gutenberg Elegies: The Fate of Reading in an Electronic Age*. New York: Ballantine, 1994.

Braine, George. "Beyond Word Processing: Networked Computers in ESL Writing Classes." *Computers and Composition* 14 (1997): 45–58.

Burbules, Nicholas C. "Rhetorics of the Web: Hyperreading and Critical Literacy." Snyder 102–22.

Carbone, Nick, and Eric Crump. *English Online*. Boston: Houghton Mifflin, 1997.

Colomb, Gregory G., and Joyce A. Simutis. "Visible Conversation and Academic Inquiry: CMC in a Culturally Diverse Classroom." Herring 201–22.

Daiute, Colette A. "Physical and Cognitive Factors in Revising: Insights from Studies with Computers." *Research in the Teaching of English* 20 (1986): 141–59.

Delany, Paul, and George P. Landow. *Hypermedia and Literary Studies*. Cambridge, MA: MIT P, 1990.

Delpit, Lisa. *Other People's Children*. New York: New Press, 1995.

Dobrin, David. "Style Analyzers Once More." *Computers and Composition* 3.3 (1986): 22–32.

Dowling, Carolyn. "Word Processing and the Ongoing Difficulty of Writing." *Computers and Composition* 11 (1994): 227–35.

Edwards, Paul N. "The Army and the Microworld: Computers and the Politics of Gender Identity." *Signs* 16.1 (1990): 102–27.

Faigley, Lester. *Fragments of Rationality*. Pittsburgh: U of Pittsburgh P, 1992.

———. "Subverting the Electronic Workbook: Teaching Writing Using Networked Computers." *The Writing Teacher as Researcher: Essays in the Theory and Practice of Classbased Research*. Ed. Donald A. Daiker and Max Morenberg. Portsmouth, NH: Boynton/Cook, 1990. 290–311.

Feenberg, Andrew. "The Written World: On the Theory and Practice of Computer Conferencing." *Mindweave*. Ed. Robin Mason and Anthony Kaye. Oxford: Pergamon, 1989. 22–39.

Gerrard, Lisa. "Computers and Basic Writers." Hawisher and Selfe, *Critical Perspectives* 94–108.

Gibbs, W. Wayt. "Taking Computers to Task." *Scientific American* 276.2 (1997): 82–89.

Gilyard, Keith. *Voices of the Self: A Study of Language Competence*. Detroit: Wayne State UP, 1991.

Gomez, Mary Louise. "The Equitable Teaching of Composition with Computers: A Case for Change." Hawisher and Selfe, *Evolving Perspectives* 318–35.

Haas, Christina. "How the Writing Medium Shapes the Writing Process: Effects of Word Processing on Planning." *Research in the Teaching of English* 23 (1989): 181–207.

———. "'Seeing It on the Screen Isn't Really Seeing It': Computer Writers' Reading Problems." Hawisher and Selfe, *Critical Perspectives* 16–29.

Hacker, Diana. *Research and Documentation in the Electronic Age*. Boston: St. Martin's P, 1998.

Hawisher, Gail E., Paul LeBlanc, Charles Moran, and Cynthia L Selfe. *Computers and the Teaching of Writing in American Higher Education, 1979–1994: A History*. Norwood, NJ: Ablex, 1996.

Hawisher, Gail E., and Charles Moran. "Responding to Writing On-Line." *Writing to Learn: Strategies for Assigning and Responding to Writing Across the Disciplines*. Ed. Mary Deane Sorcinelli and Peter Elbow. San Francisco: Jossey-Bass, 1997. 115–26.

Hawisher, Gail E., and Cynthia L. Selfe, eds. *Critical Perspectives on Computers and Composition Instruction*. New York: Teachers College P, 1989.

———. *Evolving Perspectives on Computers and Composition Studies: Questions for the 1990's*. Urbana, IL: NCTE, 1991.

Hawisher, Gail E., and Patricia Sullivan. "Women on the Networks: Searching for E-Spaces of Their Own." *Feminism and Composition Studies*. Ed. Susan C. Jarratt and Lynn Worsham. New York: MLA, 1998. 172–97.

Heath, Shirley Brice. *Ways with Words: Language, Life, and Work in Communities and Classrooms*. New York: Cambridge UP, 1983.

Herring, Susan C. *Computer-mediated Communication: Linguistic, Social and Cross-cultural Perspectives*. Amsterdam: Benjamins, 1996.

Jannot, Mark. "Future Ink." *Discover* 19.9 (1998): 44.

Jessup, Emily. "Feminism and Computers in Composition Instruction." In Hawisher and Selfe, *Evolving Perspectives* 336–55.

Joyce, Michael. *Of Two Minds: Hypertext, Pedagogy, and Poetics*. Ann Arbor: U of Michigan P, 1995.

Kiefer, Kathleen E., and Charles R. Smith. "Textual Analysis with Computers: Tests of Bell Laboratories' Computer Software." *Research in the Teaching of English* 17 (1983): 201–14.

Klem, Elizabeth, and Charles Moran. "Computers and Instructional Strategies in the Teaching of Writing." Hawisher and Selfe, *Evolving Perspectives*, 132–49.

Knobel, Michele, et al. "The Wired World of Second-Language Education." Snyder 20–50.

Krugman, Paul. *Peddling Prosperity: Economic Sense and Nonsense in the Age of Diminished Expectations*. New York: W.W. Norton, 1994.

Moran, Charles, and Gail E. Hawisher. "The Rhetorics and Languages of Electronic Mail." Snyder 80–101.

Olson, C. Paul. "Who Computes?" *Critical Pedagogy and Cultural Power*. Ed. David W. Livingstone, et al. South Hadley, MA: Bergin and Garvey, 1987. 179–204.

Oppenheimer, Todd. "The Computer Delusion." *The Atlantic Monthly* 280.1(1997): 45–62.

Palmquist, Mike, et al. *Transitions: Teaching Writing in Computer-supported and Traditional Classrooms*. Greenwich, CT: Ablex, 1998.

Perry, Ruth, and Lisa Greber. "Women and Computers: An Introduction." *Signs* 16.1 (1990): 74–101.

Redd, Teresa M., and Victoria W. Massey. "Race on the Superhighway: How E-mail Affects African American Student Writers." *Journal of Advanced Composition* 17.2 (1997): 245–66.

Romano, Susan. "The Egalitarianism Narrative: Whose Story? Which Yardstick?" *Computers and Composition* 10.3 (1993): 5–28.

Ruhleder, Karen. "'Pulling Down' Books vs. 'Pulling Up' Files: Textual Databanks and the Changing Culture of Classical Scholarship." The Cultures Star 181–195.

Selfe, Cynthia L., and Paul R. Meyer. "Testing Claims for On-Line Conferences." *Written Communication* 8.2 (1991): 163–92.

Selfe, Cynthia L., and Richard J. Selfe, Jr. "The Politics of the Interface." *College Composition and Communication* 45 (1994): 480–504.

Snyder, Ilana, ed. *Page to Screen: Taking Literacy into the Electronic Era*. Sydney: Allen and Unwin, 1997.

Spears, Russell, and Martin Lea. "Social Influence and the Influence of the Social in Computer-mediated Communication." *Contexts of Computer-mediated Communication*. Ed. Martin Lea. New York: Harvester/Wheatsheaf, 1992. 30–65.

Sorcinelli, Mary Deane, and Peter Elbow, eds. *Writing to Learn: Strategies for Assigning and Responding to Writing Across the Disciplines*. San Francisco: Jossey-Bass, 1997.

Sproull, Lee, and Sara Kiesler. *Connections: New Ways of Working in the Networked Organization*. Cambridge MA: MIT P, 1991.

Stan, Susan, and Terence G. Collins. "Basic Writing: Curricular Interactions with the New Technology." *Journal of Basic Writing* 17.1 (1998): 18–41.

Star, Susan Leigh, ed. *The Cultures of Computing*. Oxford: Blackwell, 1995.

Sudol, Ronald A. "Applied Word Processing: Notes on Authority, Responsibility, and Revision in a Workshop Model." *College Composition and Communication* 36 (1985): 331–35.

Sullivan, Patricia, and Jennie Dauterman, eds. *Electronic Literacies in the Workplace: Technologies of Writing.* Urbana, IL: NCTE, 1996.

Taylor, Todd. "The Persistence of Difference in Networked Classrooms: Non-Negotiable Difference and the African American Student Body." *Computers and Composition* 14 (1997): 169–78.

Turkle, Sherry, and Seymour Papert. "Epistemological Pluralism: Styles and Voices within the Computer Culture." *Signs* 16.1 (1990): 128–57.

Weiser, Mark. "The Computer for the 21st Century." *Scientific American* 265.3 (1991): 94–104.

Contributors

Christopher Burnham is Professor of English and Academic Department Head at New Mexico State University in Las Cruces. He has been on the faculty since 1981. He was Writing Program Director at NMSU from 1981 until 1997. His research and publications focus on expressivism, liberatory pedagogy, writing program development, and assessment.

William A. Covino is Professor and Chair of English at Florida Atlantic University. He is currently writing *Piety in the Sky: Magic, Rhetoric, and Desire in the New Millennium*, a study of contemporary rhetorical appeals to the desire for magic. Covino's research forces him to make regular visits to the primary U.S. site for the rhetoric of magic, Walt Disney World.

Ann George is an assistant professor at TCU. Her research and teaching interests include composition theory and pedagogy, and modern rhetorical theory. She is currently writing a book (coauthored with Jack Selzer) on the work of Kenneth Burke in the 1930s.

Diana George is at Michigan Technological University where she teaches composition theory and pedagogy, theories of visual representation, and British literature. She is coauthor, with John Trimbur, of *Reading Culture* (Longman), now in its third edition, and is editor of the upcoming Heinemann collection *Kitchen Cooks, Plate Twirlers, and Troubadours: Writing Program Administrators Tell Their Stories*. With Dennis Lynch and Marilyn Cooper, she won the 1998 CCCC Braddock Award for their article, "Moments of Argument: Agonistic Inquiry and Cooperative Confrontation," which appeared in the February 1997 issue of *College Composition and Communication*.

Eric H. Hobson, Associate Professor of Humanities at the Albany College of Pharmacy, directs the school's faculty development efforts. The 1998–99 president of the National Writing Centers Association, Eric is a national leader in developing writing centers and WAC programs in health care education. His books include *Wiring the Writing Center* (Utah State UP, 1998); *ARTiculating: Teaching Writing in a Visual World* with Pam Childers and Joan Mullin (Boynton/Cook, 1998); *Writing Center Perspectives* with Byron Stay and Christina Murphy (NWCA, 1995); and *Reading and Writing in High Schools* with R. Baird Shuman (NEA, 1990).

Rebecca Moore Howard is Associate Professor of Writing and Rhetoric at Syracuse University. She works in writing across the curriculum and writing program administration, but her scholarship focuses on print culture studies and stylistics. Her articles have appeared in the *Journal of Teaching Writing; WPA:*

Writing Program Administration; JAC: A Journal of Composition Theory; Computers and Composition; and *College English.* She is author of the forthcoming *Standing in the Shadow of Giants: Plagiarisms, Authorships, Collaborators* (Ablex) and coauthor of *The Bedford Guide to Teaching Writing in the Disciplines.*

Susan C. Jarratt earned her Ph.D. at the University of Texas in Austin in 1985. Since then she has taught history of rhetoric, composition, and women's studies at Miami University in Oxford, Ohio, where she has served as Director of College Composition and of the Women's Studies Program. She has also held the Lillian Radford Chair for Rhetoric and Composition at TCU (1993–94). Her 1991 book, *Rereading the Sophists: Classical Rhetoric Refigured,* won honorable mention for MLA's Mina Shaughnessy prize and has recently been rereleased in paperback. She co-edited *Feminism and Composition Studies: In Other Words* (1998) with Lynn Worsham, and is currently working on a book about rhetoric, critical theory, and public space with the assistance of an NEH Fellowship.

Laura Julier is Associate Professor of American Thought and Language at Michigan State University, where she teaches American literature, writing, and women's studies, and is also Associate Director of the Writing Center. She has been a faculty member in the MSU Service Learning Writing Project, and in 1995 was honored with the Michigan Campus Compact/Kellogg Foundation Community Service Learning Award as Outstanding Faculty. In addition to publications on service learning writing courses, she has published articles on the rhetoric of the Clothesline Project, and is writing a book on the rhetoric of representation in Indian captivity narratives.

Susan McLeod is Professor of English and Chair of the English Department at Washington State University, where she also directs the writing across the curriculum faculty seminars and teaches graduate and undergraduate courses. Her publications include *Strengthening Programs for Writing Across the Curriculum* (Jossey-Bass, 1988), *Writing Across the Curriculum: A Guide to Developing Programs* (Sage, 1991), a multicultural textbook for composition, *Writing About the World* (Harcourt, 1991, 2nd ed. 1995), and *Notes on the Heart: Affective Issues in the Writing Classroom* (Southern Illinois UP, 1997), as well as articles on writing across the curriculum and writing program administration. Her current project is a coedited collection tentatively entitled *WAC for the New Millennium.*

Charles Moran is coauthor, with Gail Hawisher, Paul LeBlanc, and Cynthia Selfe, of *Computers and the Teaching of Writing in American Higher Education, 1979–1994: A History;* he is co-editor with Anne Herrington of *Writing, Teaching, and Learning in the Disciplines;* he is co-director, with Diana Callahan, Patricia Hunter, and Bruce Penniman, of the Western Massachusetts Writing Project; and, with Kay Johnson Moran, is co-parent of Seth and Amy and, with Kay and Barbara Wells, cograndparent of Shannon.

Deborah Mutnick is Associate Professor of English and Director of Writing at Long Island University-Brooklyn. She is author of *Writing in an Alien World: Basic Writing and the Struggle for Equality in Higher Education,* and winner of the W. Ross Winterowd Award for the most outstanding book in composition theory in 1998. In addition to her work on basic writing, she has been doing research on autobiography and memoir, the role of the personal in composition studies, and the autobiographical writing of ordinary people, especially college students.

Lad Tobin directs the first-year writing program at Boston College where he also teaches courses on creative nonfiction, narrative, and pedagogy. His publications include *Writing Relationships* and *Taking Stock* (both from Boynton/Cook) and articles in journals such as *College English, College Composition and Communication, Reader,* and *Early American Literature.* His current research focuses on the relationship between critical theories and composition practices.

John Trimbur is Paris Fletcher Distinguished Professor of Humanities and Director of the Technical, Scientific, and Professional Communication program at Worcester Polytechnic Institute. He is coauthor, with Diana George, of the cultural studies reader *Reading Culture,* author of the rhetoric *The Call to Write,* and coeditor, with Richard Bullock and Charles Schuster, of the 1993 CCCC Outstanding Book Award-winning collection *The Politics of Writing Instruction.* Associate editor of *Pre/Text,* Trimbur has published numerous articles on writing theory, cultural studies of literacy, and collaborative learning.

Author Index

Title Index

Subject Index